BOOKS BY
Louise Hall Tharp

SAINT-GAUDENS
and the
GILDED ERA

SAINT-GAUDENS
and the
GILDED ERA

by

LOUISE HALL THARP

LITTLE, BROWN AND COMPANY • BOSTON • TORONTO

LIBRARY OF CONGRESS CATALOG CARD NO. 72–79372
FIRST EDITION

*Published simultaneously in Canada
by Little, Brown & Company (Canada) Limited*

PRINTED IN THE UNITED STATES OF AMERICA

To

Clara Bodman Hawks

Friendship is a sheltering tree
—Coleridge

Contents

List of Illustrations

SAINT-GAUDENS
and the
GILDED ERA

1

HORSE-DRAWN NEW YORK

A UGUSTUS SAINT-GAUDENS was born at the right time and
he grew up in the right place — the city of New York. Young
Saint-Gaudens was on the threshold of his career as a sculptor when
New York entered its gilded era — the beginning of America's brief
passion for the Renaissance in art. He knew both the tough dirty
streets, where his family could afford to live, and the pleasant residential areas of Washington Square and Gramercy Park, where he
went to deliver the shoes his father made.

Broome Street, Saint-Gaudens said, was so called because a broom
was never seen there.[1] This and other neighboring streets were his
playground, where play was rough, street gangs handy with rocks. Gus
was thin and often hungry, more courageous than prudent, but fast on
his feet when he had no recourse save to run. He not only survived this
life but determined to make a name for himself. After all, he felt that
his father, Bernard Paul Ernest Saint-Gaudens, was the best designer
of French boots and shoes for ladies, so why shouldn't Augustus Louis,
the oldest son, become the best sculptor in New York?

Horse-drawn New York was already a constantly changing city. By
the time Saint-Gaudens was looking for a commission for his first
public monument, men of modest beginnings were finding themselves
richer than princes of the Italian Renaissance. They had made their
fortunes in railroading, real estate, banking and manufacturing during
pre-income-tax years so that the money was theirs to spend as they
pleased. A few, like Peter Cooper, endowed education, having acquired riches with almost no schooling. Saint-Gaudens took free
modeling lessons at Cooper Union and eventually produced a heroic
statue of the founder. Other rich men were pleased to finance the
statues of national heroes whose efforts had helped to build an
economy in which a private individual could afford to buy a statue for

a public park. Some of his father's customers helped young Saint-Gaudens to get his much needed first commission – the *Admiral Farragut* for Madison Square. As a result of that mysterious quality called genius, Saint-Gaudens put just enough gilt on sword hilt and shoulder braid to please his public while creating a bronze of strength and dignity.

As the gilded era advanced, the architectural firm of McKim, Mead and White built brownstone Italian palaces for men's clubs and white marble French chateaux for the wives and daughters of American Renaissance princes. McKim and White were early and lifelong friends of Saint-Gaudens'. The Three Redheads, they called themselves, and they were comrades in play as well as work. McKim, the diplomat, arranged commissions for Saint-Gaudens, and White designed pedestals. It was Saint-Gaudens' golden *Diana* that swung in the wind on top of White's Madison Square Garden.

Portraits by John Singer Sargent were a badge of highest prestige during the gilded era. No other painter could do justice to pearls and yards of gleaming satin and if sometimes the face of the sitter revealed too much about a hard social climb, nobody dared to complain. It was also a badge of prestige to have a bust of the founder of the family to adorn the spacious hallway of a Fifth Avenue palace. Sargent and Saint-Gaudens were friends and it was Saint-Gaudens who was the man for portrait sculpture. To this he added an art of his own – that of medalist – with his portrait medallions of children being among his most charming work.

But not all of Saint-Gaudens' finest work was done for New York, of course. Boston's *Shaw Memorial,* a great bronze panel of marching men, stands in front of the Bulfinch Statehouse. It contains portraiture – the heads of Negro Americans who actually posed for Saint-Gaudens. There is a relentless motion in this unique work which speaks to the imagination of those brought up on the story of the young hero and his Negro regiment and to those who never heard of Robert Gould Shaw.

The mysterious figure, unnamed and without inscription but known as the *Adams Memorial,* in Rock Creek Cemetery in Washington, D.C., is often considered Saint-Gaudens' greatest work. It caused controversy and speculation, but Henry Adams, who commissioned it in memory of his wife, said that no Asiatic would need to ask its meaning.

In Chicago, it is the loneliness of the Saint-Gaudens *Lincoln* that sensitive people feel most. A woman stood looking at it one day and then, on impulse, she crossed the grass plot to stand beside it. "I wanted Lincoln to know I was on his side," she said.

Toward the end of his career Saint-Gaudens completed his equestrian *General Sherman,* his last statue for the city he loved. He was still in sympathy with his own gilded era when he laid three coats of solid gold leaf over the bronze. A hint of gold can be seen on the statue at the corner of Fifth Avenue and Central Park South — arresting the corrosive effect of city air pollution. Again, a sense of power and forward motion is something only Saint-Gaudens achieved at this particular time, when sculpture was becoming weak, overornamented and merely pretty.

Saint-Gaudens grew up thinking he was born in New York City, but he was not! And in Rome, when he was twenty-five, he still thought so. When a young American girl most imprudently fell in love with him at this time, she wrote to her parents in Boston, telling about the young man. "His father is a French shoe-maker in New York and poor, but Mr. Saint-Gaudens is a native-born American and except that he speaks French very fluently, there is nothing Frenchy about him."[2]

Augustus was certainly not "Frenchy." He insisted on an anglicized pronunciation of his name so that some of his fellow students at the École des Beaux-Arts in Paris humorously spelled it "Saint-Gawdens" to show that they had learned this barbarism of his. He supposed he had been born in New York like his two younger brothers, but as a matter of fact he was born in Dublin, Ireland, March 1, 1848. Six months later his mother, whose maiden name was Mary McGuiness, and his Gascon-French father embarked on the sailing ship *Desdemona,* Boston bound. Augustus may be excused for not remembering this — or perhaps choosing to overlook it.

Bernard Saint-Gaudens provided his children with some items of family fiction. The first Gaudens, he solemnly asserted, had been the architect of the Roman Colosseum. How did "Gaudens" get to be "Saint-Gaudens"? Well, this mythical architect was also the first Christian martyr in the Colosseum, so he became a saint and a town in the French Pyrenees was named for him. Augustus thought his father came to believe the story.

It was fact, not fiction, when Bernard Saint-Gaudens said he was born in the village of Aspet near the town of Saint-Gaudens. His mother sold eggs in the Aspet marketplace and in her old age she hoarded gold pieces under her bed. Bernard irreverently described his father as a soldier under Napoleon, who died at the age of thirty-five or forty after a glorious binge with comrades-in-arms who had come to visit him. The family moved from their hill town to the village of Salies-du-Salat on a plain a few miles away and the boys were apprenticed in trade, the oldest becoming the village shoemaker. The second son, Bertrand, left the mountains to establish a shoemaking shop in Carcassonne where he employed thirty or forty workers. He took his brother Bernard with him to learn the trade. François was educated for the church but went into the army. Augustus was to encounter him in Paris — by that time a contractor.

Bernard Saint-Gaudens was not the sort of man who could work for anyone but himself. As soon as he had completed his apprenticeship he took to the open road. There was a journeymen's guild called the Compagnons du Tour de France, pledged to help fellow members find work in far places, and Bernard became a member, proud of his sobriquet. Faithful in friendship, it meant, and so he always proved to be as he traveled across Europe, pausing here and there to make shoes. Over to London he went and to Ireland, his bag of tools upon his shoulder.

Dublin was not a city to attract the cheerful Gascon. There was infrequent sunshine, buildings were smoke-colored, the atmosphere gloomy. A stream in the center of town was so full of silt that it no longer flowed but merely rose and fell with the tide. It smelled abominably, for it was an open sewer.

Bernard gathered in some orders and set to work, making shoes which he sold to Dublin shops. At one shop he saw a young girl sewing bindings on slippers. She was the most beautiful girl in the world, he said then, and he continued to say it until the day of his death. Three months later Mary McGuiness and Bernard Saint-Gaudens were married. The year was 1841 and Bernard and his wife lived in Dublin for seven years.

They found rooms in an old Georgian brick house on Charlemount Street in the southeast part of the city. An ancient stone bridge arched a canal across the street; trees along the water shaded a grassy slope, making a pleasant place for a young woman to take her children. It was not necessarily healthy, however. George, the first child, died when he was six years old and Louis, the second child, lived only a few weeks.

There was famine in Ireland, so emigrants crowded aboard ships bound for America where there was food and also work. Bernard and Mary's third child was christened in Dublin — Augustus Louis Saint-Gaudens, the second name in memory of the infant they had lost. Perhaps this child would live to grow up in America, they hoped, as they took ship in August, 1848. It was a six weeks' voyage.

Bernard Saint-Gaudens immediately decided that Boston was no place for a French designer and maker of ladies' boots and shoes. Leaving his wife and baby with friends, he set out for New York. He found a considerable colony of Americans of French descent living there — some of them members of his ancient guild. There were also Masons, and in Ireland he had become an ardent Freemason, as was his father-in-law. He had a gift for friendship, in any case. French fashions were in style among fashionable New Yorkers and he soon had more work than he really cared to bother about. Within two months he had established himself sufficiently to warrant sending for his wife and child.

"French Ladies' Boots and Shoes," said the sign that Bernard Saint-Gaudens hung over his shop, but fortunately both French and American ladies became customers. He needed his wife to help him cope with them, and Mary's hand-sewn buttonholes were a work of art which ladies in high-buttoned boots appreciated.[3] Bernard first settled his family on Duane Street but soon found better quarters on Forsyth Street, near Houston.

Another boy, Andrew, was born on Houston Street on Halloween, but his older brother Augustus, now about three, could never remember whether the year was 1850 or 1851.[4] What Gus did remember was being carried in his father's arms aboard a train for Morrisania. The engine had red wheels. This now dismal area of lofts and junkyards was then a village where there were trees, fields and where white houses in the Dutch style had grass and flowers around them. Gus had never seen such a place before. On his return to New York he found that a baby brother had miraculously appeared in his mother's arms. His father gave Gus a toy train which he rather preferred to the new baby.[5]

Saint-Gaudens' own memories of Forsyth Street were vague save for the fact that there was an untended cemetery just over a high fence behind the house. Gus found a hole in the fence that he could squeeze through. There were wild flowers in the grass to pick in the twilight when no one would be apt to notice a small trespasser.

The next family move was to Broome Street — that place where a broom was never seen. To the little boy with the big nose, as Gus called himself, Broome Street had compensations, however. Over the front door of the house opposite was a carved and gilded eagle. Just down the street there was a sign; a brawny arm in high relief, all covered with gold! It did not take the future sculptor long to get acquainted with Jimmy Haddon, the boy whose father made gold leaf to gild carved eagles and owned the shop with the sign.

Four or five men with sinewy arms worked in that basement shop down the street. All day they swung their hammers, beating gold until it was so thin that a breath would blow it away. Sometimes Gus was allowed to stand very quietly in a corner of the cellar, holding his breath while he watched the gold-beaters at work.

Another memory of Broome Street lingered forever in the sculptor's mind. There was a German family who were always baking cake or stewing peaches. They lived in the same house as Saint-Gaudens, who never forgot the heavenly aroma that came from their kitchen. The neighbors never seemed to notice a thin little boy with hungry eyes who lingered near their door.

Gus remembered that his earliest crime was stealing bread, which he covered about an inch thick with butter and sugar. This crime took place in his mother's kitchen and he was properly spanked when caught. When he grew older and much bolder, he and his friends "hooked" sweet potatoes from street vendors, built fires in the street and roasted them. They tasted better than any others he ever ate, he said.

Death walked the streets of New York, as it had in Dublin, with children the favorite victims. Cholera infantum, they called it, when children died from infected milk or putrid meat. Mary Saint-Gaudens felt sure that bananas were especially dangerous, but somehow Gus acquired a penny with which he bought a banana from an old woman who sold them on the street corner. From whatever cause, he almost died.

Time passed during which the boy was delirious. Then he awoke one night to find his mother and a woman friend on their knees, praying beside his bed. There was a candle burning and by its light Gus saw that his mother was in tears. It had never occurred to him that she loved him so much.

Gus recovered slowly, so they sent him to Staten Island, which he remembered as beautiful and green. There was another illness, typhoid this time, and again Staten Island was the place to recuperate. He remembered that he lived with family friends in a house once occupied by General Garibaldi, in exile. Later he doubted this tale, but it was quite true that Garibaldi lived on Staten Island for several months during 1850.

Like most New Yorkers, the Saint-Gaudens family was always on the move. Their next address was 41 Lispenard Street. Formerly Lispenard's Swamp, the street ran from Broadway to Canal. Trees once bordered the old canal, but, like the river in Dublin, it was an open sewer. Now it was roofed over with masonry to become a source of civic pride, the widest and handsomest street crossing the Bowery.

Bernard Saint-Gaudens' shop was eight blocks uptown from Stewart's fashionable department store on Broadway. Above Stewart's, Broadway was lined with ice-cream "saloons," delightful places decorated with silver paper, gilded mirrors, and red velvet draperies, and "highly illuminated" by gaslight. Ladies stopped on their way from Stewart's to eat the new confection, along with tea and sandwiches. Gus had a passion for ice cream, rarely indulged until he grew up. From the ice-cream saloons it was an easy stroll to the French shoeshop on Lispenard Street where the shoes were so pretty, all arranged in a star shape on a big round table. The shoemaker's little boy Augustus arranged them that way, the customers noticed.

On Lispenard Street, Bernard Saint-Gaudens became a landlord by renting a whole building and subletting space to tenants of his own, most of them French refugees. Augustus remembered Dr. Martinach, a French physician and political refugee whose daughter Sylvia would one day marry the American sculptor Olin Warner.

Less distinguished was the tenant who kept a wineshop on the ground floor. He was an enormously fat Frenchman who caroused with his cronies at the shop. Cossidierre was his name and he too had left France, but his departure might have been better described as flight rather than exile.

On a higher plane, both literally and figuratively, was the Union Fraternelle Française for which Bernard provided a meeting hall on the top floor of his building. He himself had organized this club and he was devoted to it. Whether rent was paid or not, it was all in the good cause of friendship.

Seven years in Ireland had also provided Bernard with Irish friends, some of whom found their way to New York. The Gascon-French shoemaker loved to go to Irish festivities and make speeches in what he said was Gaelic. For these occasions he had a gloriously bright-colored costume, kelly-green tailcoat and stovepipe hat to match. It was an outfit intensely embarrassing to his boys, now beginning to grow up and longing ardently to be considered regular Americans.

There were three sons in the Saint-Gaudens family. On January 8, 1854, Louis was born — and his older brother Augustus dropped the middle name of Louis, his until now. This time, Gus was not taken to the country but woke up one morning to find a little boy in a cradle in the room. He had recently found a red dog in the street, which he had brought home. They made him give up the dog, so now he asked if he could keep the baby. They said yes.

Gus loved this younger brother's winning ways. Louis was exceedingly shy and Gus had a shy streak of his own but was ready to take on his brother's battles in life, if he could. "Augustus was more of a father to me than a brother," Louis said, looking back over their life together.

At home, Bernard Saint-Gaudens spoke French to his boys, English with a strong Irish brogue to his wife. The boys spoke French to their father, English to their mother — and she spoke Irish-English to all of them.

Bernard was full of proverbs, adapted from Ireland or from France and edited to suit himself. "You are about as handy with your hands as a pig with his tail," he would say scornfully to one of his workmen. Anything superfluous was "about as much use as a mustard plaster on a wooden leg," and to his son Augustus, "What you are saying and nothing at all is the same thing." Gus was not a fluent talker, so the comment was painful.

There had been a few school days for Augustus when he lived on Forsyth Street and was taken to the Chrystie Street school nearby. Then came the horror of being dragged to the North Moore Street school. It was run by "Pop" Beldon, whose pleasure was in punishment. Every afternoon he lined up fifteen or more boys in what he called his private classroom and armed himself with a brassbound ruler. The boys held out their hands for one or more blows, according to the extent of their crimes, and the boy who pulled back his hand before the blow came down got double punishment. All the boys tried to take the blows without a sound. Gus remembered nothing whatever about his studies at this time.

Lispenard Street was a rough playground. Gangs formed around rival fire-engine companies and street fights began with the enemies from West Broadway, who ran with Fire-Engine Company Number Sixteen, the "Gotham." The loyalty of Lispenard Street boys was pledged to Engine Number Forty, named Lady Washington's White Ghost, which "lay" in Elm Street. There were showers of stones hurled during heroic charges up and down Lispenard Street, bold forays into the enemy's ground.

More serious were the solitary encounters, for Gus was soon old enough to go on errands for his father. Sometimes a piece of shoe last or leather findings got lost in the fray or arrived at the shop in as battered a condition as Gus, who said he received "lickings galore" at home, at school and in the street.

If no street fight were in progress there was a milder form of entertainment. Tall stovepipe hats were worn by almost every male from clerk to alderman, and the game was to fasten a string to the top of a high wagon left on the side of the street, then climb the steps to some house opposite. At the right moment the string was stretched tight, a man walked under it and off came his top hat. This was very funny until the night when a policeman wearing his beehive-shaped helmet walked under the string. Augustus remembered the terror and flight to their homes as the boys disappeared. No one was caught, and he remembered their glee over the policeman's loss of dignity.[6]

Gus knew most of his father's customers, but it was the prettiest girl who came to the Lispenard Street shop that he remembered best. She was Theresa Bagiole, daughter of an Italian music teacher. At the age of seventeen she married Daniel Edgar Sickles,[7] a New York lawyer, and Bernard Saint-Gaudens made shoes for her trousseau. Four years later, in 1857, her husband was elected to Congress and she ordered many pairs of satin slippers to take with her to Washington. In Washington she met Philip Barton Key, son of Francis Scott Key, and her husband thought the young man was too much attracted to her. On February 27, 1859, Congressman Sickles shot and killed Philip Key on the street in Washington. The Saint-Gaudens family and their friends all knew little Theresa, and Gus never forgot how cruel the scandal was.

In May, 1860, Bernard Saint-Gaudens made one more move uptown. He rented a small brick house one door beyond the corner of Fourth Avenue and Twenty-third Street and put an elegant canopy over the entrance to his shop. His clientele, although not large, was socially prominent. There were the ladies in the family of Edward Denison Morgan, governor of New York, and those of another New York governor, Major General John Adams Dix. Augustus delivered shoes to these gentry, who later rather reluctantly helped him in his career as a sculptor. Eventually they were among the many who enjoyed reflected glory by claiming to be early patrons of the shoemaker's son.

The Saint-Gaudens family no longer lived in rooms over their own shop. They found an apartment over a grocery store on Twenty-first Street between Second and Third avenues.[8] Gramercy Park was between the apartment and the shoeshop, a block or so from each. Brick town houses bordered the park, some of them with lacelike wrought iron framing doors and verandas in the New Orleans manner. In front of one house were Mayor's Lamps in which the gas flames flickered all night, because James Harper, a founder of Harper and Brothers, publishers, who lived there, had also been mayor of New York. On Gramercy Park at one time or another lived Washington Irving, Bayard Taylor, the poetry-writing Carey sisters, and Horace Greeley. The Greeleys were customers of Bernard Saint-Gaudens'.

It was said that Horace Greeley disagreed with Saint-Gaudens as to how his daughters' shoes should be designed. Saint-Gaudens demonstrated his theory — that the foot be held firmly about two inches behind the toes, then that there should be room forward for the toes to spread. It would seem that he had contrived arch support with comfort at a time when women's shoes were pointed-toed instruments of torture. Horace Greeley would have none of it, however, and in the argument, Bernard Saint-Gaudens must have been eloquent in French, Dublin Irish and Gaelic. But the fiery editor won. The Greeley girls, Gabriella and Ida, wore shoes made by Saint-Gaudens but designed by their father!

Mary Saint-Gaudens still worked in her husband's shop from time to time.[9] When he was absent long enough, she could run it, and at a better profit. Children from Gramercy Park were brought to the Saint-Gaudens shop in autumn to have long leggings made to match their winter coats, so they could play in the snow. One of them always remembered how carefully Mrs. Saint-Gaudens measured for buttons and buttonholes and how beautifully she made the buttonholes by hand. Augustus walked along the street called Gramercy Park every day, but for him there was no playing in the snow — and in the park itself the gates were locked, with only residents having a key.

Drawing of Mary Saint-Gaudens by her son, done just before he left for Paris
(Courtesy of the Board of Trustees of Dartmouth College)

*Bust of Bernard Saint-Gaudens by his son, done just before he left for Paris
(Saint-Gaudens National Historic Site)*

Gus profited by the family's new address, just the same. He now went to the Twentieth Street school, taught by David B. Scott, who had written a textbook on American history. There was good discipline in this school, with very little need of punishment. Mr. Scott belonged to a generation that did not consider it naive to admire national heroes, or childish to honor a flag that men had died to defend. His teaching of history stressed action and brought scenes to life, some of which took place on the very ground his students walked on. Gus suddenly awoke to the drama of history and the magic of books. He really studied for the first time in his life.

In summer there were country excursions, even for city boys. On Sundays, Bernard Saint-Gaudens would give Augustus and Andrew five cents each. Four cents were to pay for the Canal Street ferry to New Jersey and return. On the Jersey side the boys walked to a place called the "Elysian Fields," where there were great trees to lie under — almost a forest. They had one penny each to spend. Perhaps it was Mr. Scott who discovered that Augustus loved the only semblance of a forest that he knew. In any case, someone put *Hiawatha* into his hands, and again his imagination took fire. For a while, Hiawatha became his hero, rather than George Washington, and all his dreams were of aborigines — as for that matter were the thoughts of people older than he.

And then it was the end of April, 1861, and Augustus Saint-Gaudens was barely thirteen. "I am sorry, my boy, but you must go to work," his father told him. "What do you want to do?"

This seems to have been an unexpected blow to a boy who had just begun to want to go to school. Augustus told his father that he would like to work at something that would help him to become an artist. There seems to have been no jeering comment about such a high ambition, or about so impractical an occupation. After all, much industry went under the name of art in the mid-nineteenth century, most of it profitable.

Those huge wrought-iron lanterns on Gramercy Park were made by a blacksmith but designed by an artist in the Venetian style. In the oyster cellars on Downing Street were "exquisite and voluptuous drawings" of partially draped females,[10] while over hotel bars where ladies were not allowed, oil paintings of undraped females were so large they must have been ordered from the artists by the yard.

Every New Yorker of any pretension to elegance required white marble statues of assorted gods and goddesses as well as portrait busts and oil paintings for his home. Mr. A. T. Stewart, his department store a success, was to build a marble mansion,[11] and had five life-sized marble statues in his hallway. Nothing was more satisfying to a successful businessman and his wife than white marble against Turkey-red curtains and carpet.

Cameos were statuary in miniature, in low relief rather than in the round. The most expensive cameos were cut in agate, different-colored strata of the stone used to bring out the design. Usually a head or a tiny figure was white, the background black or dark orange. It was possible, however, to show one figure behind another by using a third stratum of different-colored stone. Shell cameos were easier to cut, were thinner and more liable to break and inclined to be convex if large, owing to the contour of the original shell. They were less expensive, as a rule. All were set in frames of varying value, from solid gold with pearls and diamonds, to polished brass. Women favored classic subjects, a head of Apollo or a Venus trailing delicate veils that melted into the background. A lady would hardly consent to sit for a daguerreotype, these days, without a cameo pinned into the Venetian lace or even home-crocheted lace beneath her chin.

It is not surprising that Bernard Saint-Gaudens should have been acquainted with a French-speaking cameo cutter, said to be the best in New York. The man's name was Avet. He was a dark-skinned Savoyard with a great black mustache, a man of alternating black and cheerful moods who had never before taken an apprentice. But more orders were coming in from Tiffany and Ball, Black and Company than he could fill, so he entered into negotiations with the shoemaker. Terms were agreed upon, wages — when Augustus should be sufficiently trained to merit any — to be paid to Gus's father.

At first, Gus only polished stones for Avet to work on. Then he was allowed to rough out a design, and finally to finish a piece. Men wore cameo scarf pins of a sporting nature, a dog's or a horse's head. Gus cut so many lions' heads he could have done them in his sleep. Gradually, he was allowed to attempt more difficult work. Completed cameos were wrapped and entrusted to the apprentice, who carried them to Ball, Black and Company on Spring Street and to Tiffany on Fifteenth Street. The boy was thrilled by the splendor of these stores.

Avet was a hard taskmaster and Augustus said later that he suffered a kind of slavery but that he was grateful for habits of hard work which he acquired. He was constantly scolded, but his master's fits of depression came from some cause the boy never understood. On bad days his oaths rose from a "Nom de Dieu, de Nom de Dieu," until he was almost screaming as he pedaled furiously on his stone lathe, which worked more or less like a primitive sewing machine. At first Gus was frightened, but he soon got used to Avet's rages, and as his master grew angrier, Gus became cooler. The fit of anger always ended with a terrible "Nom de Dieu." as the master's fist came crashing down on his worktable, making all the little fine-edged instruments jump and rattle. Gus looked forward with secret pleasure to the moment of the crashing fist.

When in a cheerful mood, Avet sang — and very well, too, Gus thought. Even his rages had an orchestral quality, like the *William Tell* Overture. Then there were the good days when Avet took his apprentice hunting on Staten Island. They walked through narrow lanes, the master in the lead, carrying his loaded gun over his shoulder, hammers cocked. It was exciting, to put it mildly, for Gus to look into those double barrels pointed straight at him when the master strode down a hill. But it was the boy's gun that went off one day as he jumped down from a stone wall behind the master. Both barrels discharged within three feet of Avet's head and sent him leaping into the air, shouting curses. More peaceful were the holidays spent fishing off the docks near Fort Hamilton, catching eels or learning to swim among the rocks at the foot of Sixtieth Street.

Avet's one-room workshop was just north of Eleventh Street on Broadway. Gus had to be there at seven in the morning. There was a horse-drawn omnibus on Broadway, supplanted in winter by a huge four-horse sleigh, either of which he could have taken if he had had the fare. Since he had no money and often left home late, there was an obvious solution. It was called "cutting behind." There was always a crowd of boys hanging desperately onto the back of the bus, sometimes crowded off by bigger boys into the street. Gus was thin, not very big, but wiry and determined. The omnibus driver had a long whip which he flipped over his shoulder from time to time, giving a stinging lash to his hangers-on. It all added to the pleasure of the stolen ride.

As an apprentice, Gus was no longer free to run to fires or follow parades, but he managed to see a good deal of the drama constantly going on in the streets of New York. Avet's place on Broadway was on the first floor but well above the street level, in a former dwelling house. The room was tiny, but there were two windows, a stone lathe under each. Gus had the lathe at the window overlooking Broadway. It was a grandstand seat at times — not that the boy dared take his eyes from his work for long. In 1861, Lincoln was welcomed in New York, at least by those who had voted for him. Although only thirteen, Gus observed with an artist's eye. He said that Lincoln sat tall in the carriage.

Church bells had been ringing all over New York when Lincoln was elected, but the rejoicing was by no means unanimous in the city. In 1861 a group of merchants sent petitions to Congress, urging concilia-tion with the South. Mayor Fernando Wood suggested to the common council that Long Island, Staten Island and Manhattan Island should secede from the Union and form an independent state called "Tri-Insula."[12]

Then Fort Sumter was fired upon. One morning as Gus raced downtown to work, he saw cavalry horses "packed together in Madi-son Square, tied to trees."

2

THE CAMEO CUTTER

DISSENSION in New York City disappeared, at least for the time being, with the siege and fall of Fort Sumter. The Massachusetts Volunteers were the first troops to cross the city on their way to Washington, but news filtered through to the public so slowly, in spite of Morse's telegraph, that almost everyone was as surprised as young Saint-Gaudens to see the men bivouacked on Madison Square.

The troops came in the night, leaving the train at the New York and New Haven depot between Twenty-sixth and Twenty-seventh streets, just west of what was then Fourth Avenue. The Astor House, between Vesey and Barclay streets on Broadway, with its great hollow square, was made ready to receive the troops for breakfast. Then the men would march on down Broadway to the ferry at Fulton Street.

It must have been hard for Gus to leave Madison Square, suddenly alive with men and baggage, loud with shouted commands and the stamping of impatient horses. But he dared not be late to work. He had been at his stone lathe at a window on Broadway near Eleventh Street for some time when he heard the sound of marching men.

In the paper next day, Gus read of people packed "from side to side of the street, from wall to wall of the buildings." In front of the Astor House, they were silent as they waited. Then they saw the twinkling of bayonets above the heads of the crowd. Gus would have liked to be there to hear the drums roll and to see the crowd come to life. There was a roar of applause, the band playing "Yankee Doodle," but what the boy actually saw was more than he could have seen if he had been in front of the Astor House. Avet's shop was still on Broadway in a former dwelling house. From his window, well above street level, and before crowds had gathered, Gus watched sober-looking men, profile behind profile, rank after rank, marching by. It was a scene he would one day try to express in bronze bas-relief. Now, he was disappointed because the band was not playing, but he heard the men singing "John Brown's Body." He saw bayonets in the distance.

New York was not taken by surprise when their own regiment set out. Gus saw the great parade in honor of "Ellsworth's Zouaves," escorted by the entire New York City fire department. The Zouaves had volunteered from among the city's different engine companies and their astonishingly wide Turkish trousers and tight coats were a uniform devised by the firemen themselves. Men who had run to fires beside Lady Washington's White Ghost, favorite of Lispenard Street, and their former enemies from west of Broadway now marched together. A flag was presented to them by Mrs. John Jacob Astor when they deployed in front of the Astor House. George Templeton Strong, who saw the ceremony April 29, 1861, was critical of their style. "These young men march badly but they will fight hard if judiciously handled," he wrote.

Gus, who was probably not allowed to follow the parade down to Vesey Street, but only to see it pass his window, had no criticism. Later, he had a chance to see General Grant in slouch hat and on horseback, reviewing the Zouaves.

A man whom Gus must have remembered from Lispenard Street days now came into prominence. Lawyer Daniel Edgar Sickles, the congressman, was now General Sickles, having organized the Excelsior Brigade in New York, which he led in the Peninsular campaign. Young Saint-Gaudens said he saw General Sickles minus a leg, reviewing the troops in front of Niblo's Garden. This must have been after 1863, for General Sickles had his right leg amputated after he was wounded in the Battle of Gettysburg. His wife, the beautiful Theresa Bagioli, died young.

Not all memories of wartime New York were of parades and military reviews, however. On Monday, July 13, 1863, the draft riots began. From Cooper Union on Third Avenue at Eighth Street, to draft headquarters on Third Avenue at Forty-sixth, the streets were black with human beings who hung over the eaves of buildings, filled the doors and windows and packed the street. Police, armed only with clubs, were driven away or trampled underfoot. Houses were set on fire; Brooks Brothers clothing store at Catherine and Cherry streets was looted, as were other stores. Toward evening several thousand rioters moving uptown attacked the home for "Colored Half Orphans" on Fifth Avenue just above Forty-third Street.[1] Two hundred Negro children were hustled out the back door as the mob rushed in the front. The building was sacked, set afire in several places and burned to the ground.

The mob moved in upon the central police station on Mulberry Street. A Negro was caught and hanged on a lamppost. At last, two hundred police reserves arrived, outflanked the rioters, and the mob broke apart. When they left, Mulberry Street looked like a battlefield.

Augustus, fifteen the previous March, was astonished when his master Avet told him to go home early that day. Avet gave no reason. Gus went outside to find Broadway completely deserted at an hour when it was usually crowded. Doors were closed fast, and he saw no one to whom he could put a question. His steps echoed in the street. There was no one and not a carriage, cart or horse-car on Third Avenue when Gus turned into it. A moment later, however, he saw men with guns, running. It occurred to him that he'd better run. He pounded up the stairs to his family's apartment, where his mother took him into her arms.

All the family were there, his father, Andrew and Louis. For the second time in his life, Gus realized how much his mother loved him. She had been terrified lest, boylike, he might have been attracted by a crowd, might have stopped to see what the excitement was about, only to be trampled on or knocked out by flying rocks and swinging cudgels. All the shops above Twentieth Street were closed, the Saint-Gaudens shoeshop among them. As the day wore on, the family could see that there was a big fire over on Broadway, somewhere near Twenty-eighth Street. Soon there was another big fire to the east, said to be on Second Avenue. For once, the Saint-Gaudens boys were not allowed to run to the fires.

Although the Mulberry Street mob had been broken up, tough gangs roamed the streets most of the night. Mayor Wood, who had proposed the independent state of Tri-Insula, at first refused to ask the New York governor for help from the militia. Fire bells rang constantly, but about midnight a cold rain began to fall, dispersing the rioters.

The riots lasted, with sporadic outbursts, for four or five days. A total of 1200 people were killed before and after the state militia finally arrived. Later on it was strange to Augustus to see two cannon posted at Twenty-first Street and the corner of Gramercy Park. They were pointed east in the direction from which the rioters had come. There was no damage to the family shoeshop; it was too small to attract the rioters.

Bernard Saint-Gaudens, ardently antislavery, told the members of his Masonic lodge that they ought to admit Negroes. They refused, but he presided at the initiations at an all-Negro lodge. Thereupon his own lodge blacklisted him, so he joined the Negroes. Every day he read the war bulletins posted in front of Brentano's on the east side of Broadway near Washington Place — then he retailed the news at home. There was always a mob before the newspaper offices downtown and plenty of extras were hawked on the streets by shouting newsboys — but little reliable news.

In October, 1864, Augustus fought his own private battle. He had gotten used to Avet's constant scoldings, but one day the master came in after a lengthy noon hour. Gus had eaten the lunch his mother put up for him, as usual, and was back at work. But he had forgotten to sweep up the crumbs. Avet was in a particularly black mood and fired him.

Gus took off his overalls, wrapped them up and then walked uptown to his father's store. Both of his parents were there, at work. The boy told his story, feeling as if the end of the world had come. Within half an hour Avet appeared. Gus was sent on an errand during the interview which followed and when he got back he was told that Avet had offered to increase his wages by five dollars a week if his apprentice would go back to him.

Gus felt sure he could never get the same kind of work again and that he had lost three and a half years of his life along with all chance of ever becoming an artist. But he said he would not go back.

With his usual touch of humor, Saint-Gaudens told of the scene. "This was no doubt the most heroic act of my existence, if not the only one having any real style," he said. He was sure his father would be angry with him, then, he recalled "father's proud smile concealed in his mustache as I made my speech."

All was by no means lost. There was another man in New York, by the name of Jules Le Brethon, whose specialty was large shell-cameo portraits. All a gentleman had to do was to supply Le Brethon with a profile picture of himself — a silhouette would do — and Le Brethon would cut a flattering likeness on a shell to give to a lady. Gus applied to Le Brethon for work, feeling that he was lowering himself by engaging to cut shell cameos. But he spotted a stone lathe in the shop,

Saint-Gaudens at his cameo lathe, probably just before he left for Paris
(Courtesy of the Board of Trustees of Dartmouth College)

unused because no one knew how to handle it. Saint-Gaudens was hired immediately and Le Brethon discovered an unsuspected talent in his new assistant. Gus also could catch a likeness and cut a cameo portrait to please the most exacting customer.

Le Brethon was peculiar in appearance. He was very dark, with such a mass of bushy black hair that Gus amused himself by imagining that, as an immigrant, the cameo cutter had played the part of a freak for Barnum's museum. Temperamentally, Le Brethon was as different from Avet as day from night. He was actually kind to his assistant. Gus was given an extra hour every day to model in clay — Le Brethon teaching him how to make a portrait bust. This was so exciting that Gus swallowed his lunch as fast as he could and then devoted the rest of his lunchtime, as well as the extra hour, to modeling.

By this time Gus was studying nights in the drawing classes at Cooper Union. His father made shoes for the Cooper family, who lived on Gramercy Park, and one day Peter Cooper came into the shop — so the story went. He found young Augustus drawing a picture on a piece of brown wrapping paper. It showed his father's workmen at their benches, each man characterized by a few lines so that Mr. Cooper easily recognized them. Conversation followed and the result was that he personally helped young Saint-Gaudens to enroll and watched his progress with interest. "With such an incentive," Gus wrote later, "I became a terrific worker, toiling every night until eleven after classes were over in the conviction that in me another Heaven-born genius had been given to the world."

Instruction was free at Cooper Union. Gus was handing over good pay to his family, so he was allowed bus fare to work and to classes. Full of boyish dreams of glory, he stood on the outside platform of the bus where the fare was cheaper and thought that if the men standing with him could realize that a great genius was rubbing elbows with them in the quiet boy by their side, they would be much impressed.

Sometimes Gus and his two best friends, Herzog and Gortelmeyer, worked late together, then walked uptown, on and on till they reached Central Park, singing all the way. Along with money for bus fare, Gus had money for a seat high in the balcony at the Academy of Music or at Niblo's Garden. His memory for music was phenomenal, his voice a dramatic bass.[2]

One night as Gus and Gortelmeyer were leaving the huge brownstone building on Astor Place, they passed one of the various meeting rooms, where a debating society was having a fierce argument on the subject of slavery. The meeting had spilled out into the corridor and Gus and Gortelmeyer were laughing as they skirted the crowd. The Cooper Union policeman told them to be quiet.

"Shut up, yourself," Gus said, or words to that effect. He was told to clear out and although he was on his way, he said he would take his time. The policeman collared him and had him thrown into a cell in the Mercer Street police station, near Washington Place. Gus never forgot the horror of that night. To take the iron bars in his hands and feel that he could not get out — it was a nightmare. He slept not at all but watched men and women, drunken and cursing, being thrown into other cells in the row. Next morning he was taken to the Jefferson Market police court and herded into a pen with thirty or forty drunks, and held there until his father came for him. The policeman's account of what the boy had done was a lie from start to finish and Gus could see that the judge did not believe it. The boy was bound over to his father for one dollar to keep the peace. The policeman was indignant over the light sentence, but Gus found his father entirely on his side.

Thirty years later and largely owing to a sense of gratitude to Cooper Union, Saint-Gaudens was prevailed upon to model a heroic-sized seated figure of Peter Cooper to be placed in front of the building. Under a huge neo-Greek entablature upheld by Ionic columns designed by Stanford White in 1897, there sat the great man, sparse of hair but luxuriant as to beard, just as Augustus must have seen him. Gus himself was dissatisfied with this work, and it was certainly not his best, but it was good portraiture. There was a quizzical look to mouth and eyes, as though Peter Cooper might have been remembering the days when he built "Tom Thumb," the first steam engine made in America. It ran over tracks so winding and over grades so steep that Stephenson, the English engineer, said a steam engine could never make it. Cooper's "Tom Thumb" not only made it, but pulled a trainload of forty people at the dizzy speed of ten miles an hour. But later, Cooper's engine lost a race with a horse. All this was before Saint-Gaudens was born, and when Gus knew him, Cooper was the philanthropist, interested especially in science education, he himself having been to school just one year.[3]

During these student days, it must have been a relief to the Saint-Gaudens family when Augustus transferred from downtown Cooper Union to the National Academy of Design, next door to his father's shoeshop. In the autumn of 1866, the National Academy built a Venetian Gothic building with walls of alternate stripes of blue stone and gray and white marble.[4] The new building delighted Americans fresh from their travels in Italy, who felt that culture had come to New York. The Academy's palace was financed and owned by one hundred artists, one hundred associates and one hundred academicians. Naturally, the associates had been invited mainly because they had money to contribute.

For the first time in his life, Augustus met the recognized artists of his time. He was almost immediately allowed to join a life class taught by Emanual Leutze, painter of the immensely popular *Washington Crossing the Delaware*. Daniel Huntington, popular portrait painter and pioneer Hudson River School artist, advised students in portraiture. The emphasis was on art for art's sake, rather than art as a way of making a living, as it had been at Cooper Union. There were no tempestuous evening debating societies in the Academy building, nor a policeman suspicious of art students. By daylight, the imitation Venetian palace close to Madison Square looked incongruous enough, but at night the atmosphere was dreamlike, Gus said. The silence was broken only by the whistling of a defective gas jet!

Gus studied with fierce concentration, for this was the romantic world he wanted for his own. If the key to it lay in anatomy, he could and did study anatomy. Finding that the best books were written in French, he was thankful for his birthright — the ability to read the language. Meticulous studies of casts from the antique, drawn with infinitely fine-pointed charcoal, pencil or crayon, had to be approved by the teacher before drawing from the living model could be attempted. Most of the students hated this discipline, but Gus delighted in it. Compared to the exacting work at Le Brethon's when he cut cameos, this kind of drawing was play.

Drawing and painting were not his aim, however. From the beginning, his heart was set on sculpture, his hands demanded clay to work with. Although perfectly able to draw well, he later never finished a sketch properly, even to sell a client an idea for a statue. But he drew delightful cartoons, wonderful for their action expressed in a few well-placed lines.

News of the assassination of Lincoln reached New York on the night of April 14, 1865. Gus never forgot the scene in the apartment over the grocery store next morning, his father and mother weeping as his father read of Lincoln's death. They were at breakfast, all of them soon to be on their way to work. Gus was fortunate no longer to be working for Avet, because Le Brethon allowed him to watch the Lincoln funeral cortege from the roof of the old Wallack's Theater on Broome Street.[5] The President's body was carried to City Hall to lie in state, and Augustus joined the endless line of silent, slow-moving people that began down on Chatham Street and led eventually to the bier at the head of the staircase. "I saw Lincoln . . . and I went back to the end of the line to look at him again," he said.

Augustus admitted that he was so exhausted by cameo-cutting all day and drawing at night that his mother literally dragged him out of bed every morning and pushed him over to the washstand, where he gave himself a "cat's lick." Then she drove him to his seat at breakfast where he had tea and French bread with butter. He stumbled down the stairs and never really woke up until he was out on the street. Later, he regretted that he never had time to play, but he took fencing lessons at a fairly early age.

The fencing master was a Frenchman known simply as "Capitaine" — an old soldier with war medals which he wore on state occasions. Capitaine's father and grandfather had been fencing masters before him and he was proud of the tradition. His *salle d'armes* was a huge room in a building near Sixth Avenue and Twenty-sixth Street, where the walls were decorated with sabers, fencing foils, masks and plastrons. At one end of the room there was general athletic equipment. Fencing fascinated Gus, who was naturally quick of eye and fast on his feet. But it was not until later years that he learned that Capitaine must have been fond of him, for he called daily at the Saint-Gaudens' house when Gus was ill with typhoid. Capitaine saw that young Saint-Gaudens, besides being an ardent fencer, had more courage than brawn and more temper than muscle. He insisted on workouts with the wrestling teacher and was delighted when Gus became an expert at this more practical form of self-defense. "Dear Master and Pupil," Captain Nicolas would one day begin a letter to him.[6]

Fencing, wrestling and swimming, and in winter a little skating, were the boy's only recreation — aside from music. When he had no money for admission to the opera, there was good music to be heard in German beer gardens — even if he preferred coffee to beer. He felt superior to the other students at the Academy because he worked hard while so many were dilettantes playing at art to pass the time.

Gus had one cause of envy, however. Many of the art students had wealthy parents, able to supply money for foreign travel and even for study in Rome or Paris. At the beginning of the year 1867, the talk at the school was all of the Paris Salon. Some of the teachers and the more affluent students were going to see it as a matter of course. Americans as well as Europeans would exhibit, and no serious artist would want to miss it. Augustus seems not to have been aware that he talked about the Salon at home. His father asked him if he wanted to go, and without hope but with enthusiasm he said yes. "We will arrange that," his father said.

The money for the trip came from wages Gus had paid into the family treasury during his employment with Avet and Le Brethon. His father gave a large and hilarious dinner in honor of his son's departure. There was another banquet given by Le Brethon, an equally French affair with a tremendous surprise planned for Augustus. As he picked up his napkin, he found under it one hundred francs in gold. It was to pay for a trip to his father's village of Aspet in France.

During his last nights and Sundays, Gus modeled a portrait bust of his father — a charming, simple treatment of a round-headed little Frenchman with a small Roman nose, smooth contours of cheek and chin — and a big mustache. Later, he was to laugh at it as a mere boyish effort, but it had a style of its own. In the meticulous fashion of the National Academy, he drew a fine-line portrait of his mother, her eyes a trifle sad, her brow wide, cheeks hollow but delicately modeled — her mouth decidedly firm.

Le Brethon's banquet took place the night before Augustus sailed, in February, 1867. He would be ·nineteen in March. The ship was the *City of Boston,* his accommodations steerage, where he was "sicker than a regiment of dogs," as he put it. The ship docked at Liverpool, somehow he got from Folkstone to Dieppe — another stormy crossing — and on he went to Paris.

In retrospect, the departure for France seemed sudden and unexpected. Perhaps the nearly nineteen-year-old Augustus may not have been told of family plans until they matured. Letters had been written, however, to the Saint-Gaudens clan. Bernard, the youngest of the four brothers, had kept in touch with Jean, the oldest, who was still the village shoemaker in Aspet, and with François, now a contractor living in Montmartre, who prepared to receive nephew Augustus from America. Uncle François, on retiring from the army, went into politics in order to become an *entrepreneur de demolition,* or wrecking contractor. This was comparatively easy because Emperor Napoleon III was busily demolishing old Paris, flattening buildings, straightening winding streets to make the broad avenues for his gas-illuminated "City of Light." Louis Napoleon's urban renewal program was just about over, however, and Uncle François had not been able to tear down any historic landmarks for quite a while.[7]

Augustus Saint-Gaudens arrived from Dieppe by train, coming in at the Gare du Havre. Apparently no one had given him so much as a hand-drawn map of Paris. Carrying his carpetbag, which was immensely heavy because of his cameo-cutter's lathe, he set out on foot with his uncle's address, Avenue de la Grande Armée, in mind but with only the vaguest idea of where it lay. If he chose the widest streets and took the right direction, he walked a little over a mile, past the Madeleine, to come out on the Place de la Concorde. "I stood, bewildered by the lights of that square and of the Avenue des Champs Elysées bursting upon me," he said. The New York City boy, in his best clothes and lugging a huge carpetbag, surely looked like a yokel to Parisians. But his fluent French must have startled them as they directed him up the Champs Elysées to the Arc de Triomphe, where the Avenue de la Grande Armée begins. Even if his uncle lived close to the arch, this was a full two miles farther on. But it never occurred to Gus to take an omnibus, although he noticed that they had platforms outside, just as they did in New York, where one could ride second class. New sights met his eyes every step of the way. "Between the glory of it all and the terrible weight of the bag . . . I arrived in a mixed state of collapse and enthusiasm," Gus said. He was received, however, "with thorough-going French emotion."

For a while, Augustus was a welcome guest at his uncle's house. Two cousins, Pauline and Clorinda, made much of him and also tyrannized over him when they discovered that, in spite of his claim to sundry juvenile love affairs, he was shy with girls and had no sisters.

Having come to see the Paris Salon of 1868, Augustus presumably visited it at once. But he betrayed his unspoken purpose when he went around to apply for admission to the École des Beaux-Arts. This was not as easy as he had been led to suppose. More and more foreign students were flocking to the school and new rules had been made to favor the native French. Foreign students must understand French and speak it fluently. Gus had doubtless an odd accent, but he was a born mimic and soon spoke like a Parisian — when he wanted to. Drawings must be submitted and approved. Gus had brought his best work from the National Academy and there could be no question but that it was well above average. But the authorities at the Beaux-Arts had further requirements; Gus was told to see the director, and after much running around finally got an interview.

M. Guillaume was unusually affable, Gus thought, when he finally saw the great man. Augustus told him that he expected to learn sculpture in nine months and figured that his assets of one hundred dollars would be sufficient. The director smiled. There was one small formality; Mr. Saint-Gaudens could enter the École des Beaux-Arts only on formal application which must be made by the American minister. So Gus called on the minister. Again he explained his plan and again an official seemed kind. Gus would be notified when the application had been accepted. It was a decidedly less naive young man who was finally accepted at the École des Beaux-Arts exactly nine months later! This might not have been a mere coincidence. School officials may have assumed that the boy's one hundred dollars would be gone and that they had eliminated one more foreigner.

While doing all he could to get into the École, Gus also went around to look for some work as a cameo cutter. This was easy. He got a job right away with an Italian named Lupi who had a shop on the Rue des Trois Frères, near the top of Montmartre.

Having always handed over his wages to his parents, Augustus had no experience whatever in the handling of money. It seemed all right when Uncle François said he would take care of his nephew's cash for him. Gus lived at his uncle's house until, as he put it, his hundred dollars had gone through his uncle's fingers. The gold coins given him by Le Brethon for a trip to Aspet went the same way, and Uncle François was broke again. The American nephew was told that he had better get out.

Gus found a room next to Lupi's shop, and a modeling school which he could attend mornings and nights. Every afternoon he worked on cameos, but he begrudged the time and worked just enough to earn a bare living.[8]

The art school was in the Latin Quarter across the Seine, five miles from Montmartre, however, and Gus found he had neither time nor strength (on the small amount of food he ate) to walk ten miles a day. He took a room in the Latin Quarter, therefore, and at one time stayed with the son of an old shoemaking friend of his father's. Before long, his artist friend Herzog, from Cooper Union days, appeared and the two of them teamed up in the "very dirty St. Jacques quarter" in rooms over a perfume factory. The odor, delightful in small quantities, became too much for them when their rooms were drenched with it.

By now the process of moving had become a little more complicated than the mere matter of packing a carpetbag. The young men between them had two cot beds, two pitchers, two basins, a lot of books and a modeling stand, besides clothes and bedding. They hired a handcart and piled all this on it at night, dragging it through the streets at a time when no one would notice how little furniture they owned. They had found two nice rooms opposite the Collège de France on the Rue des Écoles, not far from the Panthéon, the Cluny Museum and the Sorbonne. A friend followed along behind the rickety handcart to pick up items that fell off it along the way.

Augustus promptly shared his room with the son of a wealthy shoemaker from England, of French descent, who had run away from home to escape going into the shoe business. This boy was penniless. They attempted to share Gus's cot, which was eighteen inches wide, but the boy was bigger and Gus ended up by giving him the mattress to use on the floor and taking the cot with bare canvas, where he nearly froze to death from the cold beneath him. This gave Augustus one more enlightening experience. He had learned not to take smiling Frenchmen at face value and not to rely on an uncle. But he would never hesitate to give shelter to a friend.

The school Gus found for himself, near the École de Médecine, was an excellent one, he said. There were about fifty students, seated twenty-five to the row in a small, stuffy theater. The model stood against the wall. Drawing students got all the front seats, with the fifteen or so "mud slingers" or sculpture students with their clay at the back. Here Gus modeled his first figures from the nude and considered that he laid a solid foundation for the future.

There were two professors of drawing, one who came on Wednesdays and the other on Saturdays. Jacquot, short, loud-spoken and exuberant, was the Wednesday man, who believed in heavy, vigorous drawing with bold strokes in thick charcoal. The other, Laemelin, was tall, thin and austere, advising pupils to draw lightly, carefully and firmly, avoiding sloppy effects in an attempt to show vigor. Gus took drawing as well as modeling, and because of his cameo-cutting experience and the training at the National Academy in New York, he tended toward the light touch. He was therefore praised on Saturdays and had his drawings ruthlessly criticized on Wednesdays. "You must draw freely with no fear of the paper," Jacquot would say, slashing at Gus's drawing with thick strokes. "There, fix that, my boy. Fix that!" He sprayed everyone with saliva when he talked.

Jacquot insisted on huge thighs and redrew Gus's drawings until the boy decided to play a game and give his next study tremendous muscles. It was no use. The criticism was the same and it was Gus's theory that Jacquot, being a heavy man, saw an image of himself in every model. Finally, Gus got the thighs as big as balloons. Jacquot caught on with a strange look in his wide-apart, crooked, china-blue eyes. He said it seemed the boy was trying to make a damn fool of him, and the other boys were delighted. But Gus, with that intuition he would always have, was suddenly sorry for the fat man and felt like a damn fool himself.

It was funnier when both teachers arrived on the same day by mistake. The quiet Laemelin wanted to know what all the noise was about on the other side of the room where Jacquot was roaring out his criticisms. It was Jacquot who had come on the wrong day, but he slapped his thighs and shouted with laughter. Some of the students got so noisy, the "gardien" threw them out into the night. Laemelin looked at the drawings he had corrected, now recorrected by his colleague, and pursed his lips. He was not amused.

Gus did so well at this school that he won the first prize and, with a few other students, was crowned with laurel. At the same time he received a big envelope with the seal of the United States on it. This was the notification that he had been accepted at the École des Beaux-Arts.

The procedure was to choose a master whose atelier the student wanted to enter, and then apply, submitting samples of work. Jouffroy was the most popular, because it seemed that it was always one of his pupils who received the Prix de Rome and other coveted prizes. Jouffroy was famous for his colossal statues representing the mercantile marine and the navy. He was commissioned under Napoleon III to ornament the entrance to the Pont du Carrousel.

Gus described the great Jouffroy in characteristic terms as tall, thin, dark, wiry with little, intelligent black eyes and a queer face in profile, his nose and forehead being all in the same line, except that his nose ended in a ball, "round, red and pimply." He was a sculptor of only moderate distinction and he worked in a strange fashion, his right hand pawing at the clay, while in his left he held a little wad of bread which he constantly rolled between his fingers.

Augustus applied, bringing drawings, to Jouffroy and was admitted in two days. He was the only American in the class until Olin Warner appeared, six months later.

It was the custom for a new student to stand to treat to the students already in the atelier. Fortunately for Gus, he knew another newcomer, Mercié by name, and they pooled their resources. They put on a grand spree, he said, and in the midst of the uproar, Gus was told to sing — by way of initiation. He favored them with the "Marseillaise," done in English with his mother's Irish accent. The students howled with joy.

3

STUDENT DAYS

"WHILE I was at the Beaux-Arts it was Hell generally all the time around the fellers, fighting, singing, throwing things etc. etc. and yet the three or four serious fellers kept right on, regardless," Gus said.[1]

If this was meant to indicate that Saint-Gaudens was a quiet worker, Alfred Garnier, his friend and fellow student, remembered otherwise. "Gus was one of the wildest, singing and whistling to break your eardrums," Garnier declared.[2] But he added that Gus worked with all his might.

Saint-Gaudens met Garnier at a small gymnasium near the Panthéon. They were about the same weight and equally fond of wrestling. The two Beaux-Arts students became friends after they were thrown about a dozen times into the perfectly black sawdust, which stuck to their sweat-covered bodies like glue. Then they would dash into the showers and the icy water that ran over them from open tanks in the attic raised a fog of steam until the globes on the gas fixtures along the walls were obscured completely.

Garnier went with Gus to the Bain du Louvre to swim — but not every day. Gus worked mornings at Jouffroy's atelier, afternoons at the stone lathe, so he went swimming at five A.M. He could be tempted, if a crowd of friends was going, to swim again later in the day. Garnier went principally to watch him. "Again and again, Auguste climbed to the top of the steps to dive, to disappear, to reappear — it was intoxication for him. No one else swam with such intense pleasure . . . he was the gayest of boys, . . . the most joyous person you could find," Garnier said.

Alfred Garnier lived with his mother in Paris and had never seen the ocean, so Gus proposed a trip to the channel coast of France when the summer vacation came. Dammouse, another student of sculpture, agreed to make a third if Gus and Garnier were sure they could pay their own expenses. Albert Dammouse was "prudent," his friends said. It was he who advised Gus to study under Jouffroy, the teacher whose pupils were the most likely to succeed.

Somehow, Gus and Garnier scraped up the money. The three boys took the train to Mantes, on the Seine, where there was a fine twelfth-century church with sculpture which they wanted to see. Then, shouldering packs, they walked to Rouen where again they remembered they were art students on tour. Vacation began when they reached St. Valery-en-Caux, a sea-bathing resort in a small harbor between high cliffs. Five minutes after they got there, they were all in the water.

There was a heavy sea running and people shouted at them to come back. A young man had drowned there the night before. They swam back, listened to the warnings, and the prudent Dammouse stayed on shore. But Gus looked back at the water and the temptation was too much for him — he plunged in. Afterwards Garnier admitted that he thought the ocean was always rough so he followed Augustus. Diving into the waves, whooping with joy, Gus swam "like a seal," his friend said. But something in Garnier's floundering efforts warned Gus and he turned back and towed his friend ashore, pretending that it was just a game. "I was personally timid," Garnier wrote, years later, "but brave to the point of recklessness when with Augustus, risking the wildest adventures, knowing we would succeed together." The boys walked along the coast from St. Valery-en-Caux northward, a distance of about thirty miles, swimming again and again along the way.

During the following winter Augustus discovered the Sunday classical concerts at the Cirque d'Hiver. All his friends flocked to Offenbach's light operas, but he was proud of his taste for symphony and only later in life regretted that in his youthful superiority he had missed most of Offenbach. However, there was drama at the Cirque d'Hiver one night when Monsieur Pasdeloup attempted to direct Wagner's *Flying Dutchman*.

There was so much opposition to Wagner that people came equipped with tin whistles. As soon as the leader raised his baton for the first bar of the music, catcalls and whistling by the audience began. "We could see the fiddlers fiddling away at a tremendous rate and evidently making a lot of noise, but in the overpowering uproar it seemed like a dumb show," Gus said.

Pasdeloup was a short, chubby little man, but that night he achieved dignity. He stopped the orchestra, began again — then put down his baton, turned to the audience, and they let him speak. The piece was on the program, he said. Those who didn't like it had not been forced to come. He was going to play it through and anyone who did not want to hear it had better leave at once. There were people on his side now who applauded until little by little the anti-Wagnerites gave way and the last half of the *Flying Dutchman* was heard in comparative order.

In 1869, Mercié, who had entered Jouffroy's atelier with Saint-Gaudens, won the Prix de Rome. This was the most valuable of all the prizes. It was given by the French government and entitled the winner to four years' study at the French Academy in Rome with an annual stipend of four thousand francs for expenses and exemption from military duty. Only French students were eligible at that time. There were other prizes, but Saint-Gaudens won none of them, for students a step or two ahead of their time are rarely prizewinners, at least in their youth. Gus had consistently good criticism from Jouffroy, so he may have been surprised as well as disappointed. In later years he accepted the time-consuming and often boring job as judge in the hope of recognizing some young sculptor with originality.

From time to time, Augustus received some paper money of small denominations in letters from his mother. It touched his heart because he knew the sort of economies she practiced in order to send them. Because of his regular work in cameos, he needed little help, and in 1869 the two friends Garnier and Dammouse planned a trip to Switzerland, asking Gus to go along. "We had scarcely spoken of it before Auguste wanted to be on the way," Garnier said. The prudent Dammouse again persuaded his friends to wait until each of them had money for expenses. Then there was the matter of equipment. Each must have buckled gaiters to go over boots, pants of tough material to stuff into the tops of the gaiters, a sort of brigandish sash in which to carry a knife, knapsacks and a flask slung by a strap.

Gus doubtless turned his stone lathe a trifle faster. Finally the boys had a hundred or a hundred and fifty francs between them — Gus couldn't remember which, but doubtless Dammouse could have told him. Garnier and Gus made Dammouse the treasurer, handing him their travel funds, "because we considered him more sensible than we were." Dammouse had "a little wallet in place of a heart and later he had bags of money," Garnier said. "But he kept us from doing some silly things. He was a charming boy, crazy with talent."

Gus was still living in an attic on the Rue des Écoles opposite the Collège de France. He got up early and quietly so as not to disturb anyone on the morning of his departure for Switzerland. He laced up his heavy hobnailed boots, slung his pack on his back, but it was so heavy it put him out of balance. Then he started down the first of five flights of stairs. On the top step his feet went out from under him and the metal flask, the cup hanging from his belt and the other paraphernalia jangled as he went down "on a part of his body not meant for locomotion." He made a tremendous clatter; then he approached the next flight cautiously, but the stairs had just been waxed from top to bottom of the whole house and his efforts to walk softly on tiptoe were disastrous again. People from the other apartments rushed out on landings. "Servant girls stuck their heads from kitchens on the re-sounding court." Gus had given himself a send-off.

It might have been Dammouse's idea to buy a third-class ticket on a crowded excursion train to Strasbourg, and when they got there, to sell the return half of the ticket, trusting to luck to get back to Paris another way. In Strasbourg, they chose too cheap a lodging, an old, unfashionable-looking hotel. During the evening the two French boys wrote letters home, while Gus went to bed early. Their plan was to hire one room having two beds, Garnier and Gus to share a bed. It had been decided that nightclothes would be superfluous in packs already too full, and when Garnier finished his letter and went to claim his half of the bed, there was Gus, his whole body covered with black spots as big as copper pennies! They were bedbugs, "piles and piles of them which mounted and descended all along the wall, while Gus slept just the same. We woke him up and the slaughter commenced which lasted till morning. Even so, we were all of us chewed," Garnier declared. "The marks on us lasted a fortnight."

Next day they visited Strasbourg Cathedral, admiring what they happened to like and disdaining what the guidebook told them to admire. Then, boylike, they forgot about art and architecture to climb as nearly to the top of the 466-foot spire as they could get, just for the view. They went swimming in the Rhine, then crossed it to drink beer in Germany. "It was always Augustus who enjoyed everything the most," Garnier said.

There was money enough for transportation as far as Basel, Switzerland, where the young men shouldered their packs. They had more or less of an itinerary in mind but apparently not so much as a sketch map. They wanted to see Lake Geneva (and swim in it, of course), so someone pointed out the main road where coaches climbed a distant pass. A few leagues out of Basel, in the bottom of a valley, a small river ran which they could see from time to time from the much higher road they were following. All of a sudden on the far riverbank they saw a castle which they stopped to admire. At a high window a woman appeared.

"Was she a woman or a young girl? From that distance, we couldn't tell," Garnier wrote, "but naturally a woman seen from a distance at a castle window by boys of twenty would have to be young and beautiful." The boys weren't sure that they would be noticed in spite of their wide-brimmed hats, bright sashes and what they hoped was a generally dashing appearance. But "this charming woman or young girl immediately waved a white scarf." Gus and Garnier imagined a romantic tale — she was a lady in distress, perhaps imprisoned by some cruel husband, and it would be brave and knightly to go to her rescue. Dammouse, the purse-carrier, brought them to their senses. He reminded the two wild romantics that they had a long way to go before they could hope to find shelter for the night.

It was, in fact, almost nightfall when the boys came to their first German Swiss village. Black clouds were gathering around the mountains and lightning split the sky. Some girls who were filling their pitchers at the village fountains ran when the students asked their way to the Hotel of the Bear, which someone had told them was the place to stay. Finally, they found it, a big, handsome wooden chalet at the top of a dozen or so stairsteps above a steep street.

Gus loved the place at sight. It was beautiful, large, clean and hospitable. Dammouse cautiously asked the price of supper and a room and then he, too, rejoiced. It was far less expensive than he expected. Not that Gus ever remembered anything about the rates — he was too much interested in the girl who showed them their room.

Garnier was equally charmed. "There was a young girl there — ah it was of that young girl that one could say that she only asked to be deceived. But let us hope she never was, it would have been a real misfortune, actually a crime. Such frankness, and so pretty too, such eyes — so totally charming! She was in service, coming from French Switzerland to learn German. She told us all this, coming right into our room with a confidence and an innocence which made us admire her."

Dammouse, who had been a medical student before he went to the Beaux-Arts, had a long talk with Augustus. He was astonished to find the American so ignorant and inexperienced with girls. In France it was different, he said, and this, at least, Gus had already noticed. Gus liked to look back on his life and describe himself as having been in love at least four times before he was twenty. Just before leaving New York he had taken a girl named Mary to a play called *Never Too Late to Mend*. That and two plates of ice cream afterwards put such a dent in his finances that he never asked her out again. He was also "terribly afraid of her," he said, but he made her a cameo and had it set for sixteen dollars by a friend who worked for Tiffany. He gave her the box containing the pin, told her he was going abroad next day, shook hands with her, and there was an end to that. Mary wrote to ask if they were "keeping company." Gus never answered the letter, but she consoled herself with someone else without too much delay.

At twenty, Saint-Gaudens was heart-whole, impressionable enough to remember a pretty Swiss girl for the rest of his life, but still too scared to go further than shaking hands with any girl.

The boys were up and away at dawn next day. Their flasks were filled with white wine, a tin box they carried in their knapsacks was filled with butter, and they were each given a long loaf of bread at the inn. Now the knapsacks bit into their shoulders and the heavy boots raised blisters. Each was too proud to admit such weakness until they sat down by a mountain brook to eat lunch. Then off came knapsacks and shoes. The box of butter was put into the ice-cold water, which proved equally beneficial to blisters.

Shoulders grew tough and strong, extra socks helped in hiking boots, and as always it was Augustus who enjoyed everything the most. When they reached the top of a pass there were mountain ranges, one after the other, on and on into the distance, and he said he had never had such a thrill since he had seen his first hills — on Staten Island!

Not surprisingly, they lost their way and somehow got into a ravine instead of a pass. Confronted by the headwall of the ravine after hours of climbing a steep road which they supposed was a shortcut, their road ended. It seems never to have occurred to them to turn back. A path led up the cliff, so they climbed it into an alpine pasture inhabited by a bull! Perhaps he looked more fearsome to city boys than he really was, for he let them circle around him at a respectful distance, and at last they found another road. But now it was nightfall and raining. Far below their road they saw a tiny cabin where a light was burning, and plunged toward it down a trail.

There was a bunch of juniper over the door, which meant that it was a hostelry of some sort, but dogs were barking fiercely and drawing nearer around them in a far from friendly circle, so they knocked at the door instead of pushing it open. "A horrible-looking woman" appeared and said, "The police are here." She seemed astonished when the young men looked relieved and came right on in.

A young police sergeant was sitting by the fire and the three Beaux-Arts students realized that the woman had meant to warn them. They had just crossed the frontier into France and she thought they were smugglers. Fortunately, the border guard was a pleasant chap willing to believe their story. He read the letter the head of the École des Beaux-Arts had written for them under the letterhead of the Ministry of Education, which told whomever it might concern that these were students traveling for study.

The hostelry had about three rooms. The boys were shown one where straw mattresses lay on a dirt floor, and were told not to shut the door because their hostess would have to go through their room to get to her own. During the night a great racket arose — dogs barking, men coming into the cabin, shouting. The boys made sure their knives were handy. But it was only a band of actual smugglers. The border guard had left and the hostess had signaled an all clear. The road the boys had been following was a smugglers' route.

They accidentally crossed the border again later, but this time they were grabbed by some French customs officers as drunk as pigs from sampling confiscated brandy. These men were in no condition to read letters or listen to explanations but would have thrown the boys in jail if they had not yelled louder than the drunken officers did.

When at last the boys arrived in Geneva, they all went swimming in the lake at once. Gus idolized water and had converted his two friends to his form of idolatry. Now even the prudent Dammouse was tempted into extravagance. So far, they had explored no glaciers. The place to go was Chamonix, where glaciers could be reached on foot. The distance from Geneva to Chamonix was over sixty miles, but ever since the days of Louis Agassiz, the Mer de Glace, on the north side of Mt. Blanc, had attracted visitors, even ladies with long skirts, climbing the ice. Train fare was expensive; prices at Chamonix were high. The boys were shocked to discover that they would be required to take a guide, but they made the climb and then were appalled at the amount of money they had spent.

After a desperate conference, while Dammouse counted their assets and figured ways and means, they decided to walk forty-two miles to the town of Bonneville, eat nothing but bread and cheese on the way and take a diligence from there back to Geneva. In that way they would have enough money left for the railroad ticket from Geneva to Paris.

As they left Chamonix a pouring rain fell. On went the boys, water sloshing in their shoes, broad hats dripping, clothes wringing wet. It rained from early morning until afternoon. At lunchtime the boys set their backs to a big poplar that only partially kept out the rain, and ate bread that was damp in spite of being protected by being slung under a knapsack. White wine was already a luxury of the past. They had taken to filling their flasks with milk and now they drank water, "of which there was plenty." Butter was no longer on their diet and they had only a bit of Gruyère cheese.

After lunch they went on in the rain. It was market day in a big town they passed through, but it was raining so hard that everyone was indoors or huddled under the tarpaulins that covered their market carts. At last the sun came out, bright and hot on the roadway. The boys came into a forest where they took off all their clothes, wrung them out and found linen still dry in their knapsacks, and also "cloth suits" they had brought along to wear in large towns.

On they went, "pretty tired" and not too happy over the prospect of a night in the open. Then from behind came a carriage with two passengers, a man and a woman. The carriage pulled up and the man said, "Are you the ones who went through the town where there was a market?" The boys said they were and that they had been walking all day. He offered them a lift to Bonneville, which they joyfully accepted. He was friendly, but the woman questioned them with suspicion. She directed them to such cheap lodgings that they realized she thought they were beggars. After a miserable night in Bonneville it was almost no trouble at all to walk to Geneva, only twenty miles away.

Again they swam in the lake. The return from Chamonix had cost less than they figured, so they gorged themselves with food and then took the train to Paris, "proud as Artaban." When they arrived and separated, each had one franc in his pocket.

Without his skill as a cameo cutter, Gus could never have stayed in Paris. A clever young artist might sell a sketch or two at shops like the D'Angleterre, a framer's on the corner of the Rue de la Seine. There was little any sculptor could do, since any clay model would have to be cast at least in plaster, and even that was expensive — metal casting prohibitive. Nevertheless, Gus sold a small bas-relief now and then — an "infant Moses," for example, to a pottery shop in the Passage d' Enfer, just off the Boulevard du Montparnasse. These trips to the cameo cutter's workshop, with now and then a stopover at a curio shop, gave Saint-Gaudens a chance to see fashionable Paris as well as the student quarter, which most of his friends never left. He was aware that Napoleon's "City of Light" was brighter, more extravagantly rich and contrastingly poor than ever before, but he was too preoccupied with art to think about either politics or economics. On first coming to Paris he discovered Plutarch's *Lives,* which he read with a passion equal to his schoolboy enthusiasm for the American Revolution. This was as close as he came to studying current history! Paris was entering a tragic period in the history of his own time, but Saint-Gaudens was about as unaware of it as the Emperor Napoleon himself when he stepped into the trap set for France by Bismarck.

On July 15, 1870, France declared war on Germany. Alfred Garnier, with another student, the painter Bastien-Lepage, was out on the Boulevard des Italiens and they "demonstrated against the idiots who were shouting 'On to Berlin,'" he said. Men urging war were "pigs and thugs, sure to hide out when real trouble began." The students started a fight and the war crowd "fell upon us, punching, kicking, hitting with sticks and we, with some bruisers who joined us, whacked away in the pile-up." Saint-Gaudens was not there.

About two weeks went by and then Garnier, but not Saint-Gaudens, went to the opera. For a curtain call a popular tenor came onstage carrying a French flag and sang "Le Chant du depart." "Everyone went wild, ourselves not the least," Garnier wrote — for this was the song the troops sang as they marched out of Paris. "I was wilder than on the day of declaration," Garnier said, but now he was ready to march on to Berlin instead of demonstrating for peace. Fifteen days later, he was in the field.

"Well — that's how it was. The war once started, I went my way and Auguste went the other," Garnier remembered. The circle of close friendship was broken as other French students joined the army and

Gus suddenly found himself a foreigner, the American, outside the pale.

During the summer of 1870, Gus made his headquarters at the little town of Lieusaint, about twenty miles from Paris.[3] His uncle François had a summer place there and possibly, if Gus had money, he was a welcome guest. Lieusaint was on a small river where there must have been swimming and it was comparatively close to the forest of Fontainebleau, made famous by the Barbizon School of painters. But Corot, Jean François Millet and the rest were no longer the young moderns, impressionism was pretty well accepted and people who painted out of doors were no longer considered crazy. Corot was seventy-four in 1870 and Millet fifty-six. Each had only five years more to live. Saint-Gaudens explored forest paths or climbed curious rock formations, alone for the most part.

Being so near Paris, Gus could afford to go and come, more or less like a modern commuter. His younger brother Andrew was in France. Gus did not say when Andrew arrived, but in 1870 he was head of a firm and making two hundred francs a month in a china factory in Limoges. Gus wanted to visit him and fortunately was given a stone-cameo portrait to do, for which he was to be paid a hundred dollars, an enormous sum to him at that time. When war broke out, the lady who had ordered the cameo left for America and Gus gave the cameo to her father to take to her. He had not been paid, but he was sure he had money coming to him, so he made plans to go to Limoges.

Gus was at Lieusaint on the third of September.[4] Allies had failed to come to the aid of France and as a military leader Napoleon III was a disaster, but young Saint-Gaudens had seen no dispatches. "I didn't know what was going on — the defeat at Sedan, the taking of the Emperor. I came back to Paris late, went to bed and put in some good hours next day."

Gus worked at Jouffroy's atelier, then packed a few belongings that night, planning to go to Limoges next morning. He was on his way to the railroad station when he saw crowds around a bulletin board. They were reading some proclamation or other by the Emperor, he supposed, but the ministry kept going back on everything they promised and he had no confidence in them. He bought a copy of *Le Siècle* and put it in his pocket to read on the train. About an hour out of Paris he took out the paper to find that the Emperor had been deposed and a republic formed, without violence.

Suddenly thrilled with the idea that France was now a republic like his own country, he resolved to go back to Paris and enlist. Lafont, a student he knew who lived in Limoges, would come with him, he felt sure, and they would enlist together. "Nothing would happen right away," he thought. There was plenty of time.

But when Saint-Gaudens went to see Lafont, the day after he arrived in Limoges, he found that his friend was already a member of the Tenth Regiment, "drafted by lot and expecting to be sent to the Army of the Loire." Gus went back to Paris alone a few days later, still planning to volunteer but still feeling sure there was plenty of time.

Women came crowding into the train at stops near Paris. They were weeping for their men at the war front. Gus began to think about his mother and how long it had been since he had seen her. When the train reached Paris, he saw battalions marching out of the city. Women were weeping in the streets. And waiting in Paris was an eight-page letter from his mother, pleading with him to come home.

"I know you love your mother and you know how much I love mine. Put yourself in my place. What would you have done? Just as I did, I'm sure . . . ," Gus wrote to Garnier.

In a box, Saint-Gaudens packed up his stone lathe which furnished him his livelihood. If he took anything else with him, he did not mention it, but long afterwards he still had Paris sketchbooks full of designs for sculpture he hoped someday to execute. Andrew had assured him that he could stay in Limoges as long as he pleased.

Before he left, troops from Brittany began to march into Paris by way of the Porte d'Orléans. They had no uniforms but wore peasant smocks. Among them, in utter confusion and dust, were droves of sheep and cattle being led to the Jardin des Plantes, in preparation for a siege of Paris. A line of fortifications around the city was being frantically repaired and strengthened. The defeated army of Mac-Mahon, those who had not been captured, bivouacked on the Avenue de la Grande Armée, in the shadow of the Arch of Napoleon Bonaparte.

Gus watched provincial troops marching to the railroad station at night on their hopeless mission to block the road to Paris. They marched better than the raw recruits, but many were drunk. All were singing the "Marseillaise." They seemed like "sheep being driven to the shambles. . . ," he said.

These battalions were defeated and Paris was invested on the 19th of September. Gambetta, escaping from the city in a balloon, attempted to win allies and raise more provincial troops, but in vain. Food, hastily assembled, gave out and starvation walked the streets of Paris. After five months the city surrendered.

Earning his keep by cutting cameos, and feeling far from happy, Augustus lived in Limoges about two months. And then he might be said to have awarded himself the Prix de Rome, for he borrowed a hundred francs from his brother and set out for Italy. It was November. Skies were dark, wind was chill as Gus made his way from Limoges to Lyons, where he had been told he could buy a low-priced ticket on a river steamer going down the Rhone to Avignon. But at Lyons they told him that boat service had been discontinued. Twenty or thirty Prussian prisoners of war were waiting for the train, peacefully smoking their porcelain pipes, more like family men than soldiers.

At Marseilles, Gus found he had just missed the boat for Civita Vecchia, the port of Rome. He had to wait there three days and he was followed once or twice the first day by suspicious-looking individuals. Mindful of his precious hundred francs (minus train fare), he left the tough port city and found a nearby village with a fine view of the Mediterranean. But he allowed himself nothing to eat except figs, chocolate and pieces of a huge pie given to him by his brother's lodging-house keeper. She was a fat woman, generous and good-hearted. This was all his food for the entire journey. The pie and a box with his cameo lathe in it represented his entire worldly goods. He hung onto the lathe box during the forty- or fifty-hour journey from Marseilles to Civita Vecchia. The boat, when it finally set out, encountered heavy seas and Gus, who was never a good sailor, "suffered the tortures of the damned," in his more lucid intervals catching glimpses of the sailors seated before his pâté, finishing all of it themselves.

Gus thought he was in heaven when at last he got on the train from Civita Vecchia to Rome. The train rolled smoothly, the air was soft and warm, in contrast to the gray, bleak weather of France; people were happy in contrast to the French, who faced war and disaster. He arrived in Rome in the night and went to the Via Sistina, where a friend was living. They told him his friend had gone next door. Gus found him making love to a beautiful girl and planning to spend the night with her. So he went back and slept in his friend's bed. Next morning he awoke "to the blessed charm of Rome," he said.

4

ROME

THE defeat of France was crushing and young Saint-Gaudens suffered in sympathy. But Italy profited by the breaking of French power. Ten years earlier, Victor Emmanuel II had been proclaimed king but established his court in Florence, since Rome, with the help of France, held out as a papal state. Now French troops were withdrawn and the King saw his chance. Remaining safely behind in Florence, he sent an army against Rome. Although the Pope made what he called only a moral protest, cannonading lasted five hours, the Roman walls were breached at the Porta Pia and the King's army marched in — greeted by cheers from the people and scornful silence from the nobility. When Gus arrived in November, 1871, Rome had been the capital of Italy for two months. He found a joyful atmosphere.

To be sure, the tourists were still staying away from Rome — lacking the adventurous spirit of Miss Harriet Hosmer, American sculptress, who went out to watch the cannonballs crunch into palace walls. From Saint-Gaudens' point of view, empty lodgings were all to the good, for it meant that rents were low. He found a friend he had known in Paris, by the name of Soares dos Reis, who had been sent to the Beaux-Arts by the Portuguese government and who was now in Rome to escape the war in France. They decided to take a studio together and found one, where the scent of flowers mingled with the sound of fountains in the gardens of the Palazzo Barberini. Hanging up a sheet, each went to work in his half of the studio, Soares to model a figure in clay which he called the *Exile*. It was to be a statue of Camoëns, a Portuguese poet of the sixteenth century.

Describing his friend's statue, "It was intensely melancholy, like Soares himself, and a beautiful work he made of it," Gus said. "I began a statue of Hiawatha, 'pondering, musing in the forest on the welfare of his people.' This accorded with the profound state of my mind, pondering, musing on my own ponderous thoughts and ponderous efforts." But Gus was no longer unhappy, as he had been in Limoges. He started singing the minute he entered the studio and never stopped till one o'clock, when he left to work on bread-winning cameos.

Gus sang just like a hand organ, going through a regular program, Soares declared. His repertory consisted of French songs popular between 1830 and 1850, learned from Avet and Le Brethon back in New York but long forgotten by fellow students twenty years later. Soares and Gus never quarreled, "which is saying a great deal, considering my ever-readiness for one," Gus remarked. Once in a while, however, when the singing got extra loud, Soares would "protest with an occasional 'Ouf.'"

Toward the end of December, Rome had the worst flood in two hundred years. The Corso was navigable in boats, shopkeepers lost an average of fifty thousand francs apiece, for the Tiber rose faster than anyone ever dreamed it could and, as the intrepid Miss Hosmer put it, people just sat down and waited for the Madonna to help them instead of trying to help themselves.[1]

The piazza in front of Saint Peter's, with its famous Bernini colonnade, was like a lake. No sound was heard but the lapping of the water and the beat of oars as men in great flat-bottomed boats tried to provision the city. Many days later, the Piazza del Popolo was still under water. The King's troops, awaiting the establishment of the new government in Rome, were encamped in the grounds of the Villa Borghese on the Pincio, the northernmost hill outside the walls of ancient Rome. Soldiers became sailors as they rowed around the streets, carrying provisions or rescuing people from crumbling buildings.

The Palazzo Barberini was on a well-drained hillside where Augustus and Soares could carry on their work. Gus had lodgings in what an elegant young lady from New York was soon to describe as "a low attic," but this bothered him not at all, since the top of the building was well above floodwaters. The flood affected him, however, in a way he was never to understand. Mosquitoes would soon be swarming in Rome, bringing the dreaded Roman fever, or malaria.

The warm Roman sun came out again, however, and Gus saw the entry of Victor Emmanuel into his new and at the same time ancient capital. The mud had been shoveled from the streets in the wake of the flood, and the streets were perhaps cleaner than they had been in two hundred years. From every balcony on the Corso bright-colored silks, family flags, tapestries and Persian rugs were hung to decorate the line of march. Good weather had brought flowers which were made into garlands to hang over doors and windows. Gus and his friends managed to get themselves invited to a balcony overlooking the procession, where they found flowers to throw into the carriages when the parade passed by.

At last, "up the street there seemed to be a cloud approaching us with an increasing rush of noise," Gus said. "As it drew near, we saw that the cloud was a tremendous storm of flowers. Then came a bewildering instant of wild enthusiasm from the people as the King was driven past at a very high speed, preceded and followed by a crowd of dragoons. As he flew by, we found ourselves in the height of the noise and confusion and the flowers. But in a moment the storm disappeared down the street like a tornado, diminishing in the distance. . . ."

The Romans were accustomed to the solemn processions of church dignitaries in their gilded coaches so this was something new. But the people loved it. The haste, as Gus remarked, was no doubt "lest someone favoring the Vatican should throw a bomb."

An older generation of American artists still lived in Rome, most of them preferring the old regime. They entertained lavishly in their rented palaces, fraternized with Roman nobility and lived more like Italian princes than like citizens of a republic. This, in itself, made them a sight for tourists.

Thomas Crawford, immensely popular during his short life, was now dead and his widow, the beautiful Louisa, was married to the painter Luther Terry. They lived in the Palazzo Odescalchi, Louisa's children being entirely on the side of the Pope's political party. One of the shells from the King's artillery exploded in the library at Odescalchi, ruining a collection of Etruscan vases.

The highest-ranking American sculptor was William Wetmore Story, fifty-five, occupying the fourth floor in the Barberini palace. He gave receptions in his huge rooms, sending his manservant each day to the Hotel Constanza to see who was registered. If a sufficiently important name appeared on the list, the servant returned with an invitation to the Barberini, where statuary was very discreetly for sale. Story's subjects ranged from his huge marble *Cleopatra Contemplating Suicide* to his parlor-sized *Little Red Riding Hood and the Wolf*.

Not all guests were prospective customers, of course. There were authors, for example, and Henry James, soon to come on the scene, was to be Story's biographer. Titled Italians frequented the American sculptor's parties, where food and wine were excellent. Story's daughter married a Medici. Doubtless Mr. Story knew there was a small flower-covered studio in his palace garden, but it would be too much to expect him to enter it and encounter a young American — Augustus Saint-Gaudens by name — at work upon a statue of Hiawatha.

Gus was aware of Mr. Story but equally uninterested in meeting him. Certain that truly great art belonged to his generation and no other, certain that he was being original and different, Gus was working on a statue which was an echo of Story, Crawford and the rest, except that his *Hiawatha* was worse than Crawford's best and better than Story's worst. The Saint-Gaudens *Hiawatha* was a very Roman-looking Indian, sitting on a rock, leaning against part of a tree decorated with English ivy. For modesty, Hiawatha had what looked like a Roman festoon of flowers across his lap. He wore his hair in long bangs over the forehead, long locks behind and a bun on top. A quiver of arrows leaned against the base of his tree.

Saint-Gaudens himself was the first to laugh at this youthful effort, but actually he had created a figure precisely in the style of the eighteen-seventies. American tourists were bound to like it and later, when he achieved his own style, he would be less easily understood.

Of course Gus had already looked up jewelers selling cameos. He found a man in the fashionable Corso, known as Signor Rossi, perhaps in honor of his big red beard. In March, 1871, Gus wrote to Garnier to report progress.

"I am earning a lot of money," he said. "I'm going to be able to have the figure I'm beginning this week not only cast in plaster but done in marble.

"They pay a lot more for cameos here than they do in Paris and they're a lot less demanding. Living is cheaper, models half as expensive as in Paris, studios etc. the same.

"Better still, I'm beginning to establish myself with some rich Americans and cameos for them are extra high priced."

It did Augustus no harm to have his studio in the gardens of the Barberini, a palace described in Baedeker's guide as "begun in 1624, completed by Bernini in the baroque style." All conscientious tourists would go to see it, sooner or later. His address was Number 4, Via San Nicolo da Tolentino. Studio-visiting was a favorite pastime among tourists, once they had covered the famous sights starred in Baedeker. After admiring the ornate Barberini palace, they could just come in at the Barberini garden gate to call on Saint-Gaudens.

Wealthy Americans loved to spend a winter in Rome, bringing daughters or other young members of the family to acquire culture. Young ladies, however seriously interested in improving their minds, soon discovered that two unmarried young sculptors had a studio in the palace garden. After attending a reception at the Palazzo Barberini so that they could say they had met the great Mr. Story, they found it even more cultural to call on the melancholy Mr. dos Reis and the American Mr. Saint-Gaudens, who was gay and not averse to going to parties after his work was done.

Inevitably, more than one American girl claimed to have been the first to sit to Mr. Saint-Gaudens for a portrait bust in marble. There was Eva Rohr, for example.[2] She was living in Rome, taking singing lessons, and she and her much older sister, Mrs. John G. Tuffs, had rented a house. They were daughters of "one of the five wealthiest men in America." Mrs. Tuffs was walking along the street one day when she saw a young man whom she recognized as the one who had made a shell-cameo portrait of her late husband. She spoke to Mr. Saint-Gaudens, explaining, when he didn't know her, that he had been "in his teens at the time."

Gus might well have remembered the portrait — it was almost full face instead of the usual profile and it showed a plump gentleman wearing a tall hat! Apparently it was designed to be displayed in a case like a daguerreotype rather than to be worn as an ornament. Mrs. Tuffs said she would like a portrait cameo of herself as a companion piece and Gus told her that he was now a sculptor with a studio of his own but that he had brought his cameo lathe to Rome and would be glad to accommodate her.

Mrs. Tuffs's youngest sister, Eva, appeared on the scene and it was decided that what she needed was a portrait bust of herself in marble. In the course of events, so the story goes, the two young sculptors gave a studio party and Eva Rohr went out into the kitchen of her luxurious home and baked two pies with her own hands to bring to the party. Gus returned the empty pie plates, having painted a Puritan girl on one and a boy on the other, labeling them John and Priscilla Alden. The painted pie plates became family heirlooms.

Eva had to leave Rome when her bust was finished in clay but not yet cut in marble. When it was sent to her the sculptor's name was carved on the base, and the words "Roma, 1872." There was also an "ornamental inscription" which read, "I'm neither lady, nor fair and home I can go without your care." It might be inferred that Eva had a poor opinion of herself and had also refused to let Gus see her home. But the lines are from the second act of *Faust* where Marguerita humbly refuses Faust's escort — Eva was taking singing lessons and quite possibly studying this popular piece. If Gus had a chance to see *Faust,* he doubtless added a selection to his repertory, to the further dismay of Soares dos Reis.

Although still shy with girls, Gus was learning fast and although he underevaluated his personal charm, he estimated the value of the location of his studio correctly. It was a very good idea to be opposite the Hotel Constanza.

At the Hotel Constanza, early in the year 1872, were Mr. Montgomery Gibbs of New York, his wife and his two daughters, Miss Florence and Miss Belle. Mr. Gibbs was a successful lawyer, now living in Paris and traveling through Europe with the idea of doing some guidebooks for Appleton and Company, publishers. He was also in a buying mood, commissioning oil paintings of foreign scenes — and in need of statuary for his parlors.

"I was in much distress of mind," Gus said at about this time. Rents were now rising in Rome, every room taken, and although he could make even more money if he made more cameos, Gus discovered that he could not afford to get his *Hiawatha* cast in plaster, not to mention putting it in marble. He explained this to the Reverend Robert Jenkins Nevin,[3] rector of Saint Paul's Anglican Episcopal Church in Rome since 1869. Nevin was forty-three years old, had seen four years' service in the Civil War as captain, then brevet major. In 1872, he was starting a Roman Y.M.C.A. "I was the last person in the world," Gus said, "to be associated with such an organization," but he liked Nevin, accepted an invitation to the Y.M.C.A. rooms, and to his surprise found a group of men and girls, students in Rome, most of them, and a good party going.

Still more to his surprise, Gus found Mr. Nevin at the door of his studio soon after — come to see the *Hiawatha.* The clergyman was delighted with it and returned almost at once — with Mr. Gibbs and the girls.

But Saint-Gaudens was not at the studio. Soares dos Reis did the honors with elegance and with generous enthusiasm for his friend's work. As soon as the callers were gone, Soares "rushed out to tell me of a rich American who had been to the studio and who proposed to help me," Gus wrote.

It was Miss Belle Gibbs who remembered that Soares had rushed out to "the low attic" — although she never saw the room where Saint-Gaudens was desperately ill.

Saint-Gaudens was in love with Rome. After working hard all day, he explored the city by night. Like all Americans, he thrilled to the Colosseum by moonlight, but he also discovered hillsides and gardens with ancient Roman fragments for ornament, where a lost world could be created, in his imagination, under the stars. Unfortunately, no one then knew the cause of Roman fever, although the two words in Italian, *mala aria,* showed that "bad air" — shortened to "malaria" — was part of the picture. Doctors noticed that patients who were out at night often came down with malarial fever, and concluded that it was "night air" that was bad and not just the daytime foul smell of certain alleys. Years would have to pass before the anopheles mosquito with its deadly parasites would be revealed as the culprit. It was no wonder that Augustus Saint-Gaudens fell a prey to Roman or malarial fever. The wonder was that he didn't die.

The fever was intermittent, of course, and Gus, with his youthful optimism, considered himself cured every time he felt a little better. He came back to his studio for an interview with Mr. Montgomery Gibbs. And Mr. Gibbs, on the 26th of February, 1872, confirmed the conversation in a letter from Naples.

"I write to say that I adhere to my purpose to purchase the statue of Hiawatha as I stated I would do at Rome. I will, on my return to Rome, in about two weeks, carefully reduce our arrangement to writing.

"My youngest daughter is now at a photographer's and will have the photographs with which you can commence the bust, in a day or two.

"I will try very hard to get your *Hiawatha* into Central Park at New York. I hope that you will work at it without cessation.

"On receiving your letter with your statement, I will arrange for sending you funds.

"I think I would like a good bust of Dante. Look out for a good copy.

"I hope you will be ready, on my return, to arrange for getting some small works into the studio.

"Please write me at the Hotel Washington."

So Mr. Saint-Gaudens was to work "without cessation" on the *Hiawatha,* and while doing that he was to begin a portrait bust of Miss Gibbs, go shopping for a bust of Dante and get small sculptures, as yet to be designed and modeled, into his studio. At the same time, of course, he was to prepare a statement showing the cost of casting the *Hiawatha* in plaster, then rendering it in marble, figuring in rent, food and lodging, price of marble, wages of workmen — and his own percentage of profit. Of all the requests, this was the nearest to impossible. The Saint-Gaudens family system of taking the sons' earnings and doling out a small allowance had given him no experience. He had scarcely if ever seen a financial statement and he had not so much as an account book of his own. Jotting down figures on scraps of paper all mixed with drawings of arms and legs seemed to him the proper procedure. Of course, he often lost the papers.

But Gus was boyishly jubilant. "To add to my delight, the Gibbs family, who were on intimate terms with Senator William Evarts . . . brought the senator's daughter, Miss Hettie, around to the studio," he said. She commissioned Gus to do copies of two Roman busts, Demosthenes and Cicero, for her father. He agreed to do them at once while working "without cessation," on the *Hiawatha.* Mr. Evarts, also a New York lawyer, was in Geneva as a member of the arbitration tribunal trying to settle the United States' claim for damages of $6,500,000 against Great Britain, caused by the Confederate privateer *Alabama,* built in Liverpool. Mr. Gibbs persuaded the senator that he needed to have his portrait bust done in marble by Augustus Saint-Gaudens and Senator Evarts promised to sit for it when he stopped over in Rome on his way home to America.

This was success! Gus never stopped to think about the time element, nor had he the nerve to ask for a good solid payment in advance. Both lawyers were not slow to remind him that he was young and could not expect to charge much for his work.

Contacts were obviously important if a young sculptor were to succeed and Saint-Gaudens was now invited to the receptions given by Mrs. Thomas Ridgeway Gould. Her husband was a self-taught American sculptor of great popularity at the moment. A Bostonian whose father had died when he was eight years old, he left school early, with his two brothers, to support themselves and their mother. They had a good business in New Orleans, with Thomas as the Boston representative, when the Civil War put an end to their firm. Whereupon Thomas, helped by "hints from artist friends," became a sculptor. Colossal heads of Christ and Satan, exhibited at the Boston Athenaeum, were greatly praised and he set out for Italy. Now about fifty-five, he belonged to the American artists' group in Florence, rather than Rome, but in 1872 his wife was playing hostess in Rome.

Mrs. Gould's parties were stiff and formal and the lady herself extremely executive. She took the lead in such worthy endeavors as a Christmas party for Roman orphans or an evening of parlor games for American students. Young people were organized to carry out her plans with precision while she kept a sharp eye on them as chaperone. Her letters to Boston friends were full reports, whether accurate or not, of the doings of all the young ladies and young gentlemen.

Needless to say, Gus did not like Mrs. Gould very well, but if the Gibbs girls wanted to take him to her receptions, he was agreeable. Concerts at the German Club were what he liked best. Evenings at the Café Greco, where only men (with the exception of the daring Miss Hosmer) went to smoke cheroots and drink black coffee, were also a cheerful diversion, and Gus was a welcome member of an international group of young artists who met there and talked of everything but art. After accepting politely Mrs. Gould's weak tea, Gus felt obliged to take the Gibbs girls to the Colosseum by moonlight, and after leaving them at their hotel, there might still be time to listen to a little German music and have coffee at the Greco on the Via Condotti.

It appeared to Mrs. Gould that young Saint-Gaudens was interested in Miss Florence Gibbs. Miss Florence was coquettish, but she was probably only practicing for bigger game. Augustus was being polite but had little previous experience with a young lady as a subject for a portrait, and eventually moonlight excursions set off another bout of Roman fever for the young sculptor.

About three months after Mr. Gibbs had agreed to buy the *Hiawatha,* he had news of a severe business recession in New York, panic on the stock market. "I am sure that the last thing of which I stand in need is a marble statue, particularly one of the dimensions of your *Hiawatha,*" he wrote to young Saint-Gaudens.[4] He did not go back on his first agreement, but he made a new proposal — to pay the sculptor's living expenses, "not to exceed about 150 francs a month," which must cover "the rent of your studio, the cost of marble and labor of workmen in completing the statue of Hiawatha." Mr. Gibbs would become the owner of the statue, paying the cost of shipping it to New York and promising to exhibit it for at least one year in public. He would sell it if he could, and if he got more than it cost and fair interest on money paid out, he would make a reasonable allowance to the sculptor.

Next, Mr. Gibbs took up the matter of the portraits. "You have kindly undertaken to make the busts of my daughters and some copies for my use on the same conditions as those arranged for *Hiawatha*. Of course, while you are engaged about them, your living expenses, marble and labor are to be paid and your work used as far as possible for your benefit in procuring further orders." The "labor" referred to was that of the studio boy, the plaster casters and those who pointed and roughed out marble for the artist to finish. Gus wouldn't make anything on the portraits of Miss Belle and Miss Florence, and there would be no chance for him to show them, even at the National Academy of Design in New York. There was the usual perfectly reasonable request for accounts. Money would be advanced "from time to time according to a statement of sums and times which you will make up," Mr. Gibbs wrote.

The proposition was generous from the lawyer's point of view and humiliating to the young sculptor, confident of his ability. Moreover, Gus loved his *Hiawatha* and hated to part with it. Something of this he managed to get into a letter. Gibbs replied, "My idea was that if I bought the figure I would be safe in selling it. If we were both its owners, we should clash and neither be at liberty to act." It had not hurt Augustus to indicate that he prized his own work, for Gibbs went on, "If, however, you see a fair opportunity to sell it, I shall not interpose."

And meanwhile, would Mr. Saint-Gaudens go around to see a painter named Carlandi? Mr. Gibbs had commissioned Mr. Carlandi to paint a picture of the Arch of Titus, but he needn't think he could charge eight hundred francs, because Di Castro would do it for that, including frame. "Mr. Carlandi, when he is as old as Di Castro, can get his prices" but not yet. To ask a young fellow artist to cut down a price was anything but a pleasant task to give Saint-Gaudens.

Then there was the matter of Mrs. Gibbs's parasol. Would Mr. Saint-Gaudens just go around to a few shops, looking for it? The parasol was bought at "Gagliardi's or some such name on the Corso not very far from the Piazza Colonna but near the Via Condotti." The parasol was "dark brown with ruffles, two caught up with small buttons — lined with white silk — short wooden handle." It had cost "14 francs and broke three days" after Mrs. Gibbs bought it. Mr. Gibbs had taken it back and a clerk who spoke French said he could have it mended that day and sent around to the hotel. It didn't come and now would Gus just get it and send it special delivery to their hotel in Venice!

Miss Florence wrote the next letter, not dating it other than "April, 1872." "Mother now refuses to receive the parasol," she said, and Gus was to go around and get the fourteen francs. She hadn't had time to get her photographs taken for Mr. Saint-Gaudens to use in finishing her portrait, but she'd do it in Vienna. Belle's "particular friend, the fattest Mr. Roosevelt," was in Venice, "much to her joy" — and they had bought "two lovely scenes," *The Doge Leaving the Ducal Palace* and *A Fisherman's Family on the Seashore Watching a Storm*, both "elegantly painted."

Mr. Gibbs himself had one more piece of advice for young Saint-Gaudens. "If I was a sculptor," Gibbs said, "I would follow Mr. Story and make good looking women, for they always sell." By the end of May the Gibbs family was back in Paris, referred to as "home." Mr. Gibbs had been consulting friends about putting the *Hiawatha* in bronze, instead of marble. He wrote that it would be cheaper. Mr. Saint-Gaudens was to "complete the statue right away and put it in plaster, in any case" and it would please him "to know that every stroke was being done under your eye," Gibbs added. "Mr. Evarts has no other thought than that you are making his busts of Cicero and Demosthenes. . . ." Evarts would want his own portrait done in July.

Five days later Gus replied, and the lawyer found that the artist, who had taken so many humiliating orders so pleasantly, still had a mind of his own. Gus had gotten a price from a bronze foundry in Florence and it was extremely high. Marble was cheaper. Moreover, he had modeled "certain forms and arrangements so that they acquire a certain effect in marble which would be quite lost in bronze." The Florentine founders also wanted two years to do the work; expert workmen in Rome would "point" and rough it out in stone as soon as they had the cast to work from. If done in bronze, "there are certain effects for the bronze, that would require a too great and radical change in the clay to be thought of now. I am certain the *Hiawatha* will appear to an immense advantage in the marble . . . ," Gus said. He wanted an immediate answer so he could go himself to the Carrara mines to choose a beautiful stone. He won his argument.

"Miss Belle's bust shall be finished in two or three days and I am highly satisfied," Gus told Mr. Gibbs. But he had had bad luck with the marble for the bust of Miss Florence. He had nearly finished it when a flaw appeared in the stone. This was one of the hazards most dreaded by nineteenth-century sculptors in marble. He would have to get another stone and begin over.

Gus asked the advice of Mr. Gibbs as to which of two antique busts of Cicero Mr. Evarts would like best. The choice was left to the sculptor and he copied the Capitoline Cicero because it would look better as a companion piece for the *Demosthenes*. Then, Mr. Gibbs discovered that the Vatican Cicero was entirely different, thin and bony, rather than heavy-set like the one called the Capitoline.

"Mr. Evarts has the idea, as many of his friends have told him, that he resembles Cicero," Gibbs explained. "Now Mr. Evarts is as thin as possible and if he sees the bust of a fat man, I am sure he will not accept it." Again, Augustus bought another piece of marble and started over.

Sometime in May, Saint-Gaudens must have written that he wanted to go to New York for a brief visit. He had heard that plans were afoot for a statue of Admiral Farragut and he thought he could get the commission for this big and important piece of work — after making a small model which he would submit to the committee in charge.

"Don't waste any time modeling a statue of Farragut," Mr. Gibbs replied. "Nobody will get that to do except a man who can intrigue at Washington. If there is the least chance for merit, and merit alone and not for politics, I will ascertain, and then you can make a model if you see fit. I know Senator Morrill who is on the committee and will write to him. Meanwhile I wouldn't waste an hour on a sketch, even."

Gibbs was much against letting Augustus go home even for a visit until all his orders in Rome were filled, but he added that "a round trip ticket good for a year can be had from Liverpool to New York and return for $120 to $140, first class on the best ship."

The *Hiawatha* was finished in clay on July 18, 1872. "In the last week I gave it quite another appearance, and I am sure you would be surprised to see it now," Gus wrote. "Miss Belle's portrait has also been even a greater success than I expected, in the marble. The marble on

Miss Florence's is one of the finest pieces I have yet met with and if the accessories (meaning her heart-shaped locket and the ruffles on her dress) come out as well as Miss Belle's — and there is no reason for the contrary, it will be finer, if anything, than Miss Belle's."

Saint-Gaudens was still determined to go to New York for a short visit, to see his family and to get some commissions, if he could. He had the stubborn streak necessary to those who are to accomplish their purpose in life, and he had not given up the hope of getting the job of doing an Admiral Farragut, one of his heroes. Of course he was not going to tell this last to Mr. Gibbs, but he had a delicate question to ask: Would Mr. Gibbs lend him fifteen hundred francs to get home on?

On July 8, 1872, Gus had assured Mr. Gibbs that he had plenty of money because, contrary to expectations, Evarts had given him an advance on the two copies from the antique. But now, after throwing out the wrong *Cicero* and doing another, the money was gone! Gus hoped to sell the discarded *Cicero,* but so far no one had wanted it.

Gus knew that Gibbs had expected him to put the *Hiawatha* in marble before he left, but he promised to make his visit short and finish the statue as soon as he got back to Rome. It was a tribute not only to his persuasiveness but also to his genius that lawyer Gibbs knew enough to give him the loan and let Saint-Gaudens go. Just before leaving, Augustus had another serious bout of malaria. The doctor urged him to leave Rome, and as soon as he could get out of bed, he took a train to Paris.

In Paris, Gus saw traces of the siege of the city. In all the principal streets, houses could be found with pieces knocked off by musket bullets and cannonballs; the Montparnasse railroad station was covered with these breaks while the iron shutters of some of the great department stores were so literally filled with bullet holes, they looked like sieves.

Gus was in Paris only a day or two, seeing to the setting of a cameo, looking up old friends. Garnier was back, safe and sound in his mother's apartment, but a painter of great promise, Regnault, had been killed in one of the last engagements with the Prussians. The "prudent" Dammouse had survived, eventually to become a notable ceramist. Gus went to Liverpool, took ship and, after a fantastically rough voyage, arrived in New York — unannounced!

5

ENTER MISS HOMER

AFTER recovering from the shock of realizing that the young man in his shop was Gus, Bernard Saint-Gaudens greeted his son in his most exuberant French manner. The nineteen-year-old boy he had last seen on the deck of a ship bound for Europe was now a young man of twenty-four with thick curly red hair and a delicate mustache, balanced by just the suggestion of triangular chin whiskers under his lower lip. Gus may have grown a little taller, but he was certainly much thinner than when he left New York. He had brought his stone lathe home with him.

The shoeshop was still close to the corner of Fourth Avenue and Twenty-third Street and the family still lived over a grocery store on Twenty-first Street. Gus dashed up the stairs to find his mother, who wept for joy and then said he looked pale. It had been a rough voyage, he told her. Then, before his father could arrange any joyful celebrations for his son with the Union Fraternelle Française or the Masons, Gus had an attack of Roman fever. Now he had to admit that he had been seriously ill in Rome, with a relapse in Paris. The doctor had probably never seen such severe malaria before, but Gus was now cared for by his mother, which was a different matter from being looked after by fellow artists, however kindhearted. He recovered his strength slowly and his spirits immediately.

Louis Saint-Gaudens, now a handsome, delicate-featured boy of eighteen, was rather at a loose end, Gus thought. Pronouncing his name "Lewis," he wanted to be typically American but was too shy to make many friends. It pleased Gus to discover that Louis wanted to be a sculptor and as soon as Gus was well enough, he unpacked his stone lathe and began to teach Louis to cut cameos. Louis showed exceptional ability and Gus declared he would take him to Rome and make something of him. Gus would gather in orders, Louis would cut

Photograph of Saint-Gaudens taken in Rome for his fiancée, Augusta Homer
(Courtesy of the Board of Trustees of Dartmouth College)

cameos and the Saint-Gaudens brothers would be in business. Except for a finishing touch or two to each cameo, Gus would be free to work on his big commissions; they would make plenty of money and send money home to their parents. Bernard Saint-Gaudens was always optimistic, but it was his wife who kept the accounts and told Gus of dwindling profits from custom-made shoes.

As soon as Gus was able to go out, he called on Senator Evarts, who was now living in his new house on Fifteenth Street and Fifth Avenue. The senator had received the two busts ordered of young Mr. Saint-Gaudens in Rome, the *Demosthenes* and the thin, so-called portrait of Cicero, copied from the antique. He had not had time to sit to the young man abroad as planned, but he was delighted with the ornaments for his new house and agreed to sit at once to Saint-Gaudens in the dressing room on Fifth Avenue. Mr. Evarts ordered a Psyche in pure white Carrara marble, to be done by the young sculptor when he got back to Rome.[1]

Mr. Evarts was rather short, very thin, his face almost hollow-cheeked. His was a well-known figure on the streets of New York as he walked along, wearing a very tall hat shoved to the back of his head. In cold weather he turned his coat collar above his ears so that he was an odd-looking gentleman, unlikely to be impersonated. But Mr. Lodge remembered that during Tammany-sponsored election-fraud days, Mr. Evarts, on going to the polls, was told that William M. Evarts had already voted.

"Has he indeed!" Mr. Evarts said. "Well, I hope he voted right."

Friends dropped by and approved the clay model of Mr. Evarts, who sat looking more like Cicero than Cicero himself. These friends were lawyers, all of them involved in one way or another in the breaking up of the Tweed ring. Whether they worked for the famous Tammany grafter, William Marcus Tweed, or against him, they all made money out of the lawsuits. Three of them decided that their features should be immortalized in marble and that Mr. Saint-Gaudens was the man to do it — cheaply, of course. Masses of long hair made Edwin Wallace Stoughton, adviser to Tweed, an interesting subject, Gus said. Then there was Charles O'Conor, proslavery lawyer also involved in Tweed cases, and Edwards Pierrepont, soon to become United States attorney general.

Mr. Pierrepont seems to have been the only client interested in having his wife immortalized also. Gus was commissioned to do a companion piece, the former Margaretta Willoughby of Brooklyn to be placed upon a pedestal alongside her husband.

The only lawyer friend of Senator Evarts's anywhere near the age of Saint-Gaudens was Elihu Root, twenty-nine at this time, also associated with William Marcus Tweed but not implicated in any scandal, as he constantly and indignantly declared. Mr. Root did not want a bust of himself, however — he wanted a Demosthenes and a Cicero, like those Senator Evarts so proudly displayed.

Bernard Saint-Gaudens had not been slow to let his Masonic friends know of his son's merits as a sculptor. A new Masonic building was going up on the corner of Twenty-third Street and Sixth Avenue. Mr. L. H. Willard, an old friend of both the senior Saint-Gaudens and Le Brethon the cameo cutter, commissioned Gus to do a larger-than-life-sized figure representing Silence, to stand at the head of the grand staircase in the new building.[2] And by the time Mr. Willard had talked things over with Gus, he found that he, personally, needed a marble sarcophagus to be copied from the antique by the young sculptor.

As Gus traveled about New York from house to house of his sitters, the city was changing before his eyes.[3] There was a thing called an elevated railroad in Greenwich Street — not like the first small experiment with a wooden cable car, but a train in the air with a steam engine belching smoke and sparks as it puffed along. People said the elevated was the coming thing, the "West Side and Yonkers Patent Railway" sure to make money. There was the "pneumatic subway" several blocks long, but this idea seemed hardly practical. Old houses built by Dutch early settlers had been cleared away and everyone seemed glad to see them go because there was going to be a bridge — all the way to Brooklyn. Towers for cables were about halfway up, but the bridge was much delayed because of a general strike in the building trades.

Gus found a studio of sorts on Wooster Street, in the area where he had once lived as a boy. Here he worked on a commission for the Adams Express Company's new building in Chicago. It was a big semicircular panel — a bulldog guarding a couple of safes with revolvers, bowie knives, etc., to help him out. This necessitated acquiring a fierce-looking but gentle bulldog which Gus loved. Compared to modeling whiskered middle-aged gentlemen, the job was fun and he enjoyed it — finishing it before he returned to Rome and writing later to ask how it looked when it was set up.

For Tiffany, Gus modeled a candelabra, the figure of an Indian dancing with knife and scalp.[4] It was to be rendered in silver for Gordon Bennett, who planned to award it as a prize in a race sponsored by the New York Yacht Club. This order, too, was finished and paid for in New York. Now and for many years to come, Saint-Gaudens found Tiffany a good firm to deal with.

The clay models which Gus made from his various sitters in New York would have to be cast in plaster, then shipped to Rome for rough-cutting in marble. The finishing he would do himself, taking both pleasure and infinite pains in the process. He sent his brother Louis "a month or so" ahead to Rome to receive the casts and get the work under way, paying his brother's passage, of course, and giving him expense money.

Gus felt richer than he ever would again, he said, looking back on this first return to New York in search of commissions. There was one detail he had overlooked, however, and this was the mere matter of cash rather than promises, some of them not even on paper. A lawyer was a gentleman surely to be trusted, he imagined, so he was not worried when only three of his clients, Mr. Evarts among them, gave him money in advance for expenses. And Senator Evarts, "no doubt without thinking," as Gus put it, gave him nothing on the order for the *Psyche.*

About a month after Louis left, Augustus sailed for Europe on the *Egypt.* He gave his mother two hundred dollars from his small fund of cash and never forgot how she "stood weeping on the dock" as the ship moved slowly away and the water widened between them. This was the last time he ever saw her and he said he had a presentiment, because she was far from well.

Still feeling rich and joyous, and of course generous, Augustus stayed in Paris awhile. He began to model a large sketch of the nude for his eventually fully clad *Silence* — a beautiful girl with her finger on her lips to indicate silence — whether Gus had ever known a really silent girl or not. Apparently he was somehow able to get his large sketch to Rome, because on October 15, 1873, he said he had studied very fine effects of drapery with real drapery on it. He had intended to come direct to Italy from Paris but was with some friends who prevailed on him to go to Vienna, he said.

One of the friends was the prudent Dammouse, companion of the Swiss adventure of earlier days. He could afford the trip because his "little wallet in place of a heart" was much better filled, even if he had not yet acquired the future "money bags" Garnier had foretold. Garnier wanted to come along and Gus in his opulence would have paid his way, but Garnier still lived with his mother, whom he felt he could not leave. Gortelmeyer, the friend from New York student days at Cooper Union, arrived in Paris, however. He was now a skilled lithographer, a well-paid occupation before the days of photographic illustration. It was this "long, thin, lank Prussian" with his elegant manners who was the friend to decide on Vienna, then Nuremberg, Munich, Venice and Leghorn as the most desirable route to Rome.

Nuremberg was a grand old place, Gus thought. It was like being brought back to the Middle Ages. But Venice pleased him best — what public squares, what statuary! New York ought to have statues like that. Over the main portal of Saint Mark's were four more or less recently gilded bronze horses. Probably young Saint-Gaudens had no idea that they were early Greek, brought from the treasury of Athens at Delphi. Bronze horses were a thrilling sight in any case, and many years later he was to acquire a plaster cast of the Parthenon frieze with plenty of horses in it.

At Leghorn, Saint-Gaudens talked with the American consul about buying marble for Mr. Willard's sarcophagus. Gus had asked Mr. Willard for an advance and had received five hundred francs, with five hundred more awaiting him in Rome. So it would be a good idea to get on with the sarcophagus, which Mr. Willard seemed in a hurry for!

Gus was surprised when the American consul asked him to dinner, sending a handsome private carriage for him, to take him along the sea road. Besides being American consul, Mr. Torrey was a dealer in marble and an agent for the transportation of statuary from Italy to New York. The gentleman saw a customer in the young sculptor, now beginning to be well known in Rome. Gus remembered the dinner with dismay. A platter of asparagus was passed to him by a resplendent butler who left it to the guest to cope with a curious sort of fork. Gus somehow released the prongs too soon and dumped a great forkful over his knees and onto the floor. It never occurred to him that it was the butler who should have been dismayed over being of so little use.

Rome was crowded, "every corner grabbed, and the hotels over-flowing."[5] The gentle Soares dos Reis, who had shared the flower-smothered studio in the Barberini Palace garden, had gone home to Portugal. Now in his opulence, as Gus put it, he not only took over the whole studio but sent for workmen to enlarge it, much to the delight of the titled landlord, who promptly increased the rent.

Mr. Gibbs had advised Saint-Gaudens to have some figures or groups of figures standing around in the studio to attract customers. Just before leaving Rome, therefore, Gus had made a small composition which pleased him very much. He called it *Mozart*. Gus imagined Mozart as a twelve-year-old boy who had jumped up from his sleep and seized his violin to play vigorously as if he had a sudden inspiration. Mozart's hair was all mussed up and he had his legs muddled up in sheets and he was supposed to be sitting on the corner of his bed. "I shall have it put in marble during my absence as I feel certain it will sell very well," Gus wrote to Mr. Gibbs. "It will also help to fill up the studio during the coming winter. If it comes out well I shall have it reproduced in a kind of galvanized silver, it being a very good size and the right kind of composition for that. . . ."[6] Gus was right about the popularity of this sort of thing. It would have delighted any New York dowager in Rome who had a marble-topped table back home in her parlor to put it on. But an attack of Roman fever had ended the *Mozart* for the time being.

As soon as he got back to Rome, Gus had iron supports set up on a small revolving model stand and began young Mozart all over again. He also began another, similar item — a Roman slave holding the young Augustus on top of a Pompeiian pillar and crowning him with laurel. Many years later, Saint-Gaudens commented on these early efforts. "Why under Heaven I made him [Mozart] nude is a mystery." But in the eighteen-seventies people wore layer upon layer of clothes while feeling pure and uplifted, surrounded by white marble figures having nothing or next to nothing on. The Pompeiian pillar in the young Augustus composition looked like the smokestack of a loco-motive, according to one of his friends, Gus said. Even this might have been popular with some railroad tycoon, had Saint-Gaudens ever finished it.

The bust of Florence Gibbs had needed about ten days to finish when Gus was ordered by his doctor to leave Rome, the previous winter. He now set to work on it — along with everything else, of course. Gus confessed to "a weak spot" in his heart for one of the Gibbs girls and judging by her rather flirtatious letter to him,[7] it would seem to have been Miss Florence.

Saint-Gaudens had been depending on Louis to cut enough cameos to earn the daily living for both of them. He had paid for the marble for almost all the work he had on order; Mr. Torrey had seen to that. So now he was short of cash as usual, in spite of one more advance from Montgomery Gibbs of a thousand francs. He was not worried, however, having got some very good orders for cameos, and Louis was doing beautiful work. There was the portrait brooch of Mr. Stoughton, for example. The huge head of hair had been picturesque indeed, carved in miniature from "a profile photo." Mr. Stoughton wanted it set in gold with pearls and paid Louis $150 for it — instructing that it be sent not to his home in New York but to his office. The Saint-Gaudens brothers speculated that it was intended to charm the old boy's mistress rather than his wife.

Then Louis had pneumonia. He was not expected to live, and Augustus was beside himself with anxiety. Writing to Mr. Willard[8] and asking for more money, Gus cautioned that nothing must be said to his parents about his brother's illness. On December 7, 1873, Louis was "only now commencing to get better," Gus wrote. "The illness has upset his system and he has to be very careful for a year and for three or four months he can do little or no work."

Fortunately, Augustus discovered a young man, Louis Herzog, wood-carver and artist, who was willing to undertake cameos. After a few lessons, Herzog could fill orders and later, Louis Saint-Gaudens wrote that "for several years there were four or five of us working at our lathes at jobs Gus procured for us."[9]

Free again to return to the modeling stand, "I am now working on the nude of your figure," Gus told Mr. Willard, referring to the *Silence* for the Masonic Hall. "I have modeled it just the same size and at exactly the same height as it is going to be placed." This meant that the *Silence,* supported by an iron post and crossbar under the clay, stood on a very high platform which Gus reached by climbing up and down a ladder, again and again. "I shall be ready for the drapery as soon as I get your answer to this," he added — explaining that he must have cash for a big block of Carrara marble.

Considerable correspondence ensued, as Mr. Willard wanted to know if the *Silence* couldn't be sent in plaster to New York and cut

Bust of Miss Belle Gibbs, done in Rome, 1872, when marble portrait busts were all the rage (Los Angeles County Museum of Art, Los Angeles, California)

there. Mr. Saint-Gaudens was shocked. He always worked on the
marble himself after the plaster had been measured by workmen in
Rome (armed with calipers to get the general form exactly right), then
"pointed" with small metal spikes to indicate where cutting should be
done. A great deal of marble would be cut away, thereby reducing the
cost of freight, Gus reminded Willard — an argument which appealed
to him.

Nevertheless, letters came and went slowly between Rome and New
York. Gus would have been desperate while waiting for replies, had
not ex-Governor Edward D. Morgan of New York arrived in Rome on
a visit. He called on young Saint-Gaudens at the studio in the Barberini Palace garden, took a look at everything — the busts of New
York lawyers being finished in marble, the nude *Mozart,* the pretty
Miss Gibbs wearing lace and a locket. He paid particular attention to
the big *Hiawatha,* being put into marble, it would seem. He departed — then summoned Saint-Gaudens to his rooms at the Hotel
Constanza.

Writing to Willard on October 15, 1873, Gus had said, "In regard to
my Indian, Gibbs kept putting off the putting of it in marble or bronze
so I told him it was important that I should get it to America as soon
as possible. He said he could not have it done now — and as he had
advanced me some money I asked him to allow me to commence with
the money I owed him. He accepted, but then I am now quite free to
sell it or do what I please with it." This was a remarkable piece of
financing.

"How much do you want for the *Hiawatha?*" Morgan asked. He
wanted it for his own use — not for Central Park, as Gus had hoped.
Vague as always about money, Gus soon forgot the price but thought
it was around eight hundred dollars. Morgan bought the *Hiawatha,*
and Gus, remembering the scene, supposed he danced with glee when
he got back to his studio.

Saint-Gaudens had a beautiful model by the name of Angelina, who
posed for the figure of Silence while he worked away on the nude.
Now that he was feeling rich again, he asked her to elope to Paris with
him. No money had come from Willard, so there was no hurry about
the drapery which he had promised to start. However, the beautiful
Angelina was "sensible," Gus said. She refused to go to Paris.

The next best way to celebrate Morgan's purchase would be to take
a trip with fellow artists. So Gus set out with George Dubois, land-

The HIAWATHA, *first large marble sculpture by Saint-Gaudens, done in Rome,*
1872 (Courtesy of the Board of Trustees of Dartmouth College)

scape painter, and Ernest Mayor, Swiss architect. "We took the cars
sometimes, the diligence frequently, donkey-back often," Gus wrote.
But they traveled on foot through the Calabrian hills, delighted to
believe that they might meet brigands and armed accordingly, with
big revolvers stuck in their belts. They were promptly arrested on
suspicion of being brigands themselves. To judge by a photograph,
Dubois, with his full beard, looked most like a brigand, Mayor a likely
suspect, but Gus, dreamy and absent-minded in the picture, could not
possibly have filled the part. The young men were locked up together
in a small room displaying a poster that offered a big reward for
brigands caught dead or alive. Somehow, they managed to talk their
way out of trouble but were told to put away the guns and carry
passports next time.

The goal of the excursion was Naples and Sorrento. Orange and
lemon groves filled the air with perfume. At Sorrento the artists hired a
boat and rowed themselves out to Capri, where a religious procession
was in progress, townspeople tossing flowers by the bushel over the
priests. Gus and his friends danced with Anacapri girls, and Mayor,
who was only about five and a half feet tall, chose an especially buxom
young lady. The girl wore white and it made Gus laugh to see little
Mayor, his face buried in her ample bosom as he danced around with
hardly more than his short legs showing.

Gus returned to a perfumed, flowering Rome in December — with
most unexpected snow to come in March. American visitors, especially
those who wanted to escape the Boston winter, had arrived to enjoy
the December sun. There had been Roman fever the previous year, to
be sure, but it was gone, they were told. Mrs. Gould was in her glory
with so many well-recommended winter residents to invite to her
receptions. On December 16, 1873, Augustus Saint-Gaudens went to
Mrs. Gould's — just to be polite and not intending to stay long. She
was fairly affable, having heard that he had come back from New York
with commissions.

There was a girl standing rather alone. Gus noticed her first because
she was taller than most girls, extremely slender and her regular
features had a sculpturesque quality. Unlike many tall girls, she stood
beautifully straight rather than stooping to conceal her unfashionable
height. She was not talking to anyone and her attitude might have
seemed haughty, except that Augustus sensed that she was shy.

Remembering Mrs. Gould's insistence on propriety, Gus looked

Saint-Gaudens seated between two hiking companions, George Dubois (left) and Ernest Mayor (right) (Courtesy of the Board of Trustees of Dartmouth College)

around for someone to introduce him, although his impulse was just to go up and talk to the girl. Vanderhoff, a painter, obliged, presenting Mr. Saint-Gaudens to Miss Homer, a painter and art student in Rome for the winter.

Watching her changing expression, her eyes, now blue, now almost black, and her air of anxious attention, Gus realized that Miss Homer was deaf but was trying desperately to conceal it. He hated the politely murmured conversation that was going on around them, anyway. Raising his fine, naturally carrying voice just a little, he was rewarded when Miss Homer responded with a beautiful smile.

She was trying to get up a ladies' painting class, she said, to share the expenses of a model and a teacher. There was Bompiani, for instance, who took pupils, but she had not seen him yet.

Well — Bompiani was a nice old gentleman, Gus remarked politely — but how about somebody younger and more modern? He knew Carrodi, a young Italian landscape painter who had done some good things for Mr. Montgomery Gibbs. Whether Carrodi wanted to take pupils or not, Gus didn't know. Would Miss Homer like to meet him? She thought she would.

Gus asked the girl what her first name was — not that he expected to use it on so short an acquaintance, but he would need to know her name and address in order to call for her to take her to Carrodi's studio. A young man never used a girl's given name (nor she his) until they were practically engaged — at least if the current novels were to be believed. Miss Homer said her name was Augusta.

Mr. Saint-Gaudens said his name was Augustus; they confessed that each of them hated the name. They laughed, and Mrs. Gould looked at them sharply, for such cheerful laughter was rarely heard at her receptions.

Vanderhoff hung around, having discovered that Miss Homer was quite handsome and rather more fun than he had supposed. Another young man drifted by and Miss Homer introduced him. He was Richard Ela, of Cambridge, Massachusetts, in Rome with his mother and his sister. They were all friends of Miss Homer and her family, and also of Mrs. Todd and her daughter Ella, with whom Miss Homer shared an apartment, Number 56 Via Barberini. Miss Homer looked pleased when she learned that Mr. Saint-Gaudens' studio was nearby.

On the evening of December 22, Gus called on Miss Homer. He was introduced to Mrs. Todd and Miss Ella Todd, and they were all, including Miss Homer, from Roxbury, Massachusetts. Probably Gus had never heard of Roxbury, which at that time was a pleasant country suburb of Boston. The Todds were unpretentious people with rather formal manners, who, like the Homers, considered themselves Bostonians. Augustus Saint-Gaudens may never have met anyone quite like them before, but he was unpretentious himself and he liked people. They were pleased with him, even if Mrs. Todd wished she knew who his family was. He was just a man with an anglicized foreign name who said he came from New York! She didn't know many New Yorkers.

The bell at the foot of the steep stairs tinkled and it was Mr. Ela and his sister Mary, come to call. Mrs. Todd brought out some wine and some little cakes. Augusta noticed that Mr. Saint-Gaudens did not like wine very much but was appreciative of cakes. Promising to escort Miss Homer to Carrodi's studio on December 24, Mr. Saint-Gaudens took his leave.

Augusta Homer was copying a picture of two boys at the Palazzo Doria Gallery. She had had the usual difficulty, finding the gallery closed for some Saints' Day unknown in most calendars, then waiting for a permit to copy there before setting up her easel. Now she spent each morning at the Doria, measuring carefully, drawing accurately if mechanically, the way she had been taught to do in Boston. An excellent eye for color and much practice made her one of the best among the copyists who were always to be found in all the Roman galleries, reproducing popular paintings to sell to tourists or to friends back home. The gallery was cold and damp, the sun shining outside, but Augusta was determined to earn at least part of her living if she possibly could.

Miss Homer came back from the gallery at noon as usual on the day before Christmas. She found Mr. Ela at the apartment, come to offer to take Mrs. Todd, Ella and Gussie "to Mr. Hooper's reception that evening." "We of course accepted," she said. There was also a note from Mr. Carrodi, inviting Miss Homer to the Christmas celebration given by the German artists' club at the Sala Dante.

At one o'clock, right on the heels of Carrodi's messenger, Mr. Saint-Gaudens arrived to walk with Miss Homer to the Italian painter's studio in the gardens of the Villa Medici. He evidently knew about the invitation because he asked Miss Homer if he might be her escort to the German Club party. Mrs. Todd and Ella assumed that they were included. There wasn't much he could do about that. He also suggested taking them to the Hooper reception but found that "Mr. Ela had gotten ahead of him."

During the previous winter, while Saint-Gaudens was in New York, Augusta Homer and her brother Joe were in Rome. They had tried to see the Medici gardens but found tourists were not admitted. "Mr. Saint-Gaudens had the 'open sesame,'" Augusta now wrote her family in Roxbury.[10] "It is the loveliest garden in all Rome — the day was warm as summer. We wandered about for some time, visiting the studio and going through a little wood where it was so easy to imagine some of the Medici plotting some foul deed."

Beyond the wood, there was "a little observatory where you have a most superb view of Rome — the snowy Alban Mountains and the beautiful country in all directions. I wanted to stay . . . ," but there was the German Club party in the late afternoon.

They had time, however, to sit in the sun and talk. Miss Homer told of her work as a copyist and Mr. Saint-Gaudens, so full of original ideas himself, felt sorry for her. He got tired of copying Ciceros and urged her to work from life — to study anatomy. In Paris he had bought a magnificent book on anatomy which he would lend her.

Mr. Carrodi was not interested in teaching a class of young ladies, but Gus assured Miss Homer that he could find someone else for her. All too soon it was time to wander back through the Medici wood — conspirators themselves as "Gus and Gussie," although it would never do to let anyone know they called each other by the name they shared.

"At a quarter before six Mr. Saint-Gaudens called for us," that same day, Augusta wrote. She and Ella Todd had been out to the flower market and Augusta had bought yellow tea roses. She wore her best dress, a delicate spring-green silk with a little shoulder cape she had made herself to go with it. She put yellow roses in her dark hair and where the cape met in front.

The German Christmas tree was "beautiful," Augusta said, but they got to the party too late for the music. Mr. Saint-Gaudens promised to take her to a German Club concert some other time. He found it sad that so much of the world of sound was shut away from a girl who loved music.

Gus went to the Hooper reception anyway and Augusta described it. "Think of going to a party in a palace once occupied by the Bonaparte family," she exclaimed, knowing how her family in Roxbury would love the details. The grand staircase was "gorgeous" and the clothes were "very fine." Everybody came out in their best. "Of course there was no introducing but I knew enough people to have a very nice time."

Saint-Gaudens went back to his studio where he was working on the drapery for his figure of Silence. He put "a rose between her breasts." But Mr. Willard proved a difficult client and rejected photographs of this model. Saint-Gaudens was obliged to "place the rose at her waist."

6

MAY I BE ENGAGED?

AUGUSTA HOMER was not a rich Boston girl, as gossips in
Rome, Mrs. Gould among them, liked to imagine. Her father
had been a merchant, the head of the firm of Homer and Fowle,
dealers in cotton textiles. He had once been prosperous, living in a big
Victorian house with porches and a mansard roof in the middle of a
tract which ran from Winthrop Street, Roxbury, through to Morland
Street. There were well-kept lawns where the five young Homers
played croquet; flower gardens, a grape arbor, vegetable gardens and
fruit trees. Thomas Johnston Homer, Gussie's father, had horses and
carriages and a staff of servants.

Furnishings were heavy black walnut for the most part, with here
and there a fine old family piece no longer appreciated save for
sentiment. Ancient four-poster beds had been relegated to the attic.

Among early Homers was John, a member of the "Honourable
House of Representatives of His Majesty's Province of the Massachu-
setts-Bay in New England," called the "Glorious Ninety-two," who
defied the King in 1768 — his name, therefore, being inscribed on the
Liberty Bowl made by Paul Revere. A more recent ancestor was
Joseph Warren Homer, born in 1775, who built himself a house on
Pinckney Street and had ten children, seven of them sons. Most
prominent among the sons was Sidney Homer, a bachelor, importer
and real estate owner whose operations, especially as a Boston landlord, brought him a fortune. His charities were many. He established
homes for aged men, for aged women, for destitute children and for
foundlings. He left money to the Massachusetts Institute of Technology, various hospitals and the Unitarian Society, and for religious
services at Music Hall. Unlike many philanthropists, he also left money
to his brothers and sisters and their children.

Thomas Johnston Homer, Sidney's younger brother, failed in busi-

Mary Elizabeth Fisher Homer,
Augusta's mother (Courtesy of
Mrs. Richard W. Crocker)

Thomas J. Homer, Augusta's father
(Courtesy of Mrs. Franz J.
Inglefinger)

The Thomas J. Homer house, Roxbury, Massachusetts
(Courtesy of the Board of Trustees of Dartmouth College)

ness through the dishonesty of a partner, it was said, and insisted on paying his creditors in full with his own private funds, rather than going bankrupt. He went back to St. Louis, Missouri, where he and his wife had lived when they were first married, and tried to salvage something out of the wreck of his business, but his letters to his family[1] indicated that there was no hope. Elizabeth, his oldest daughter, remembered that her father had written to tell her that she must now do all the dusting because the parlor maid must go. She was to help with the younger children, since they could no longer afford a nurse. Augusta remembered little about her father's prosperous days. She was brought up to count her pennies, never to spend any money unless it was necessary — and to keep careful accounts.

Horses and carriages were sold, but the horsecars went right by the house, an extra horse being needed to pull the car up the hill. Mr. Homer, when he returned to Boston, opened a small office in the Studio Building, where his occupation consisted mostly of administering his late brother Sidney's real estate business. He received under Sidney's will two thousand dollars a year for life — and for his wife's lifetime if he died first. Each of their children received five hundred dollars a year for life.[2] Augusta spoke of her annuity with pride and made it go a long way.

The family feared that there was one family inheritance Gussie had received but would gladly have done without. This was deafness. Gussie's Uncle George, when he was ten years old, began gradually to lose his hearing as the result of diving in the Charles River, some people said. Educated as a deaf-mute, although he could talk, he was sent to Hartford to study under Dr. Gallaudet. At the school he met Anna Maria Swift, totally deaf since she was three years old as a result of an attack of scarlet fever. Later, they married, and to their great joy, their son, Sidney, Augusta's first cousin, had perfect hearing and became a composer, many of his songs written for his wife, the beautiful Madam Louise Homer of grand opera.

A love of music and ability to study it evidently was a Homer characteristic — so George Homer's childhood deafness had been a shock to the family. Gussie studied music, but when she was a child she was susceptible to colds which always affected her hearing. Her father worried about this and sent her to warm climates, no matter how low the family funds might be. She formed the habit, early, of worrying about her health and of expecting someone, her younger sister Eugenie usually, to take her on a trip and look after her.

In 1869, Gussie's older sister Elizabeth, always called Lizzie, married Dr. Arthur Howard Nichols and went to live on nearby Warren Street, just across a cow pasture from her parents' home. In 1872, Augusta, twenty-four, went abroad with her brother Joseph, aged twenty-one. For Joe, this was the European tour considered essential to a young gentleman's education. He later started a school for the deaf. Gussie's journey was in search of a doctor who could do something about her loss of hearing.

After Joe went home, Gussie stayed in Europe, traveling with one or another of her mother's friends. She was in Rome most of two winters because she hoped to earn money by copying paintings in the galleries to sell at home. Her art teachers in Boston said she had talent and by careful management of her annuity money, she hoped to take painting lessons in Rome.

Augusta arrived in Rome in January, 1873, and began to go daily to the Barberini Palace Gallery to copy *Beatrice Cenci,* by Guido Reni. Her Baedeker's guide put a question mark after the artist's name and said that the picture was only supposed to be Beatrice Cenci, but this made no difference to Gussie. Hawthorne had described it; Americans still bought copies of *The Marble Faun,* bound in Rome with photographs of scenes supposed to have been haunted by Hilda, the American sculptor Kenyon and Count Donatello. They flocked to see the *Beatrice.*

For more than a month, Gussie "painted away for dear life." Then she took some friends from Boston to the gallery to see her copy of *Beatrice.* "While I am about it I may as well tell you that Miss Homer's copy of the *Beatrice Cenci* is said by a great many to be the finest thing they ever saw," Gussie wrote her family back home, half in fun, half in earnest. "Mr. Cook of Cambridge, who is quite a connoisseur, after sitting and looking at it for a long time, took back his first opinion which was that it was one of the three best and said it was *the* best; that I ought not to sell it for anything, that it must go to the Boston Athenaeum; that he should speak to Mr. Silsbee about it and that henceforth he should call me 'Hilda. . . .' Mr. Ayer said if it was in a frame, they scarcely should know it from the original."

Compliments had "not turned my heard quite around," Gussie added. She only repeated them because "it will please you all at home." She was sure she could sell her copy in Rome for fifty dollars but thought it would bring more in Boston. And she started another *Beatrice* right away which, in her own opinion, turned out even better than the first one. Meanwhile, she copied a *Sybil* at the Borghese Galleries, another popular subject sure to sell.

"My time is so short that I shan't attempt any lessons but do all the copying I can," Augusta wrote. By May 13, she was in Vienna for a consultation with Dr. Gruber, a famous ear specialist who, after testing her, agreed to take her case. Her father sent her money for the treatments because careful as she was, her annuity could not cover everything. For a while she felt sure that her hearing was improving. She went to a Strauss concert and also heard *Il Trovatore,* both of which she enjoyed immensely.

Then Dr. Gruber sent Augusta to another doctor and then to Salzburg to take the waters. The expenses at the famous health resort frightened Gussie and the mineral baths proved utterly useless. She returned to Vienna, wrote that Dr. Gruber thought she was better, but when she was back in Rome again in early December, she wrote her father a sad little letter. She marked it "private" because he was the one who was always so anxious about her hearing and he would understand. "I haven't the visit to Dr. Gruber to dread nor have I the hope of being better for the benefit was short-lived and I am no better. May I be no worse!

"I went to church this morning and altho' the room was very small and I sat way up front, I couldn't hear a word but when we sang 'Coronation' it brought back our Sunday evenings at home." Gussie was the one who played the piano and the whole family had gathered around to sing hymns. "But if I can't hear," Gussie said, "I can see and I think money spent on painting lessons will not be thrown away and I have about made up my mind to take lessons from Bompiani.

"I am very glad you settled the letter of credit and promise you I won't spend the money foolishly, although now that everything is in such a state at home, I feel as if I had no right to spend a cent over here. . . . Mr. Todd wrote that you said Uncle Sidney's property, although shrinking like everything else, gave you no trouble and I was so glad to hear it."

Gussie's father would have appreciated it if his sons had taken as much interest in financial affairs as Gussie did. Of course a girl was not expected to understand business, but Gussie and her father were much in sympathy.

Augusta had expected Christmas day in Rome to be lonely for her. She and Mrs. Todd and Ella agreed that they ought not to spend money exchanging presents, but much to her surprise, Mrs. Todd gave her a pretty pincushion and Ella gave her a knife, done up in ten different-colored papers and sewed into a blue silk case. "I had to give her two centimes so as not to cut our friendship," Gussie wrote.

Ella Todd and Gussie decided to give a Colosseum party for Dick Ela and Gus Saint-Gaudens on New Year's Eve. They invited other friends to make a party of four girls and four men to visit the Colosseum by moonlight and finish up the old year at the apartment on the Via Barberini. Gus accepted with alacrity. What did it matter if the doctor had cautioned him the previous year about going out into the *mala aria* at night. Everyone said there were only a few cases of Roman fever this year, anyway.

Augusta testified that the air was anything but bad. "It was a glorious night, clear and cold, but no dampness. We took carriages at the Piazza d'Espagna, an unusual luxury." Mrs. Todd had come along as chaperone but naturally did not attempt to climb all over the massive ruins. "We went 'way up to the very top and looked down into the arena and over to the Palace of the Caesars but the most beautiful of all was the glimpses thro' the broken arches." Gussie had brought her steamer rug to wrap around her when she sat on the cold stone, and it was probably big enough for two. She did not mention who climbed to the top with her but said, "We are going again, just we three with Mr. Saint-Gaudens when the moon rises later — to see it slanting through the arches.

"Mr. Saint-Gaudens was very polite and entertaining," Gussie added. "We next went to the Forum and the Capitol and tried to see the Tarpean Rock." Gussie had not been called Hilda for nothing and if Gus had not actually read *The Marble Faun,* he knew all about it. But Gussie explained for the benefit of her family, "We wanted to take a similar walk to that of Hilda and her friend. Mr. Saint-Gaudens mustered· all his Italian and we succeeded in waking up some half dozen people (one old fellow in his nightcap) who put their heads out of windows" — but no one would come to unlock the gate into the garden of the Casa Tarpea on top of the Capitoline Hill. "Sensible people went to see the rock in the daytime," they were told, so they went down "through the quaint old streets to the Fountain of Trevi." They looked at their "shadows in the moonlit waters and then all drank a handful. . . ."

The girls had decorated their apartment "with ivy and over the mantelpiece a large '1873–4.'" They served "cake, coffee and oranges and just as the clock struck twelve, down tumbled the little 3 and 1874 was here." They played "dead Commerce" and "old maid . . ." and after "laughing until we couldn't laugh any more, shortly before two o'clock" the guests went home.

Gussie was too tired to study anatomy next day, although she had been "going at it" ever since Gus brought her his book — all in French, which she read easily except that the names in anatomy were so out-landish that she had to use a dictionary. But she drew "a beautiful skeleton," and although she did not tell her parents whose anatomy book it was, she said she could keep it as long as she pleased.

Augusta Homer was not only conscientious but she worried over all sorts of things. In her diary she wrote, "Mr. Bradford called in the morning. Our silver was stolen." It was not that she thought that George Bradford, of Boston, a former beau of her sister Lizzie's, had taken "soup ladle, table and teaspoons." She "could not think how it was done," but she worried for fear she would have a big bill to pay to the landlord from whom she and the Todds rented the furnished apartment. This, like many of Gussie's worries, proved unfounded. Her painting lessons caused anxiety. Bompiani charged thirty-five dollars a month and the other ladies who said they would share ex-penses changed their minds. It amazed Augusta that Mr. Saint-Gaudens never seemed to worry about anything. He got her another teacher, a Frenchman named Bellay, and laughed when she said it wouldn't do "for her to go to a French studio alone." Monsieur Bellay had a class she could join, so the "lively" Mr. Saint-Gaudens had been right to tell her not to worry.

The holiday season lasted a long time in Rome. Mrs. Gould was having a Christmas party for children as late as January 7, and Gus agreed to go to the hall to help Augusta trim the tree — once he found out that she was not dragging him off to a prayer meeting!

They arrived at the hall to find "the ugliest looking tree" Augusta had ever seen. Mrs. Gould wasn't there, so "there was nothing for us to do but to roam around and talk," which suited Gus very well. "But after a while Mrs. Gould with the untiring Dominicans and some young men appeared. Such a state she was in! Someone had put things onto the tree without her knowledge so we all went to work taking them off."

Gus cut great wings out of gilt paper and Gussie sewed them to the backs of dolls to make angels. A most precarious high ladder was brought in and Gus climbed it to fasten the angels to the tree and put little wax candles on the branches. "Mrs. Gould *would* have candles everywhere and with her you must obey orders," Gussie said. They went back the next evening to see the tree — Gus to light the candles. He told Gussie he had "done his best to set the whole thing on fire." Once more Mrs. Gould heard laughter and saw Miss Homer and Mr. Saint-Gaudens talking together.

A Roman custom surprised Augusta. "This is the only place I ever heard of where gentlemen invite the ladies to call on them," she wrote her parents. On Saturday, January 3, she and Ella Todd went to "Mr. Saint-Gaudens' and one or two other studios." One of the studios was Carrodi's and the other belonged to William Gedney Bunce,[3] a fellow student with Saint-Gaudens at Cooper Union and already possessed of a Paris Salon prize for his painting *A Venice Night*. Augusta would one day know him well, but at present she mentioned only the Saint-Gaudens studio to her parents.

Mr. Saint-Gaudens was not there. A handsome but pale and diffident young man showed Augusta, Ella Todd and Mrs. Todd around. They saw "a large figure for some public building in New York, a fine bust of Mr. Evarts of New York which is being put into marble and a splendid *Hiawatha*." Since they had not been introduced to the young man, they had no means of knowing that he was Louis Saint-Gaudens.

On January 20, however, Mr. Saint-Gaudens came for Gussie to take her to his studio. "You people at home have really no idea what a sculptor's studio is and how sculpting is done," Gussie wrote her parents. "It's a perfect marvel to me how they do it and how, inside of a great block of marble is some beautiful work of art. They have little points which are driven in at certain places and so sure are the workmen here that apparently, with no sense at all, they make a perfect copy of the plaster cast before them. Very few sculptors do anything to their own work in marble. . . ." Mr. Saint-Gaudens of course was different, cutting marble with pleasure and confidence instead of being afraid to touch stone with a chisel.

Augusta was discouraged over her own painting. "I am improving in my working from life but at the same time seem to be losing my power of copying for they really are so different." She loved working from life and was tempted to take another month of painting lessons, although 250 francs seemed a great deal to spend when she might be making copies to sell.

In her letters home, Augusta mentioned other men besides Mr. Saint-

Gaudens. There was "a Mr. Frank Millet of the Harvard class of '69. He knows so many people that I know, it was real fun to see him. Of course Mr. Millet is an artist — who isn't here!" He was Francis Davis Millet, lithographer and future war correspondent.

There was a dance at the German Club, where Augusta discovered that Gus didn't dance at all and that Mr. Vanderhoff could not dance very well. Her younger sister Genie had written about the german, a popular kind of cotillion in Boston. It was unknown at the German Club in Rome. "How I would like to have a good dance with some-one," Gussie said — "but you never get any of that here."

Even if there were no germans, Augusta Homer was having more fun in Rome than she had ever had in her life before, and whether she knew it or not, it was all due to Saint-Gaudens. He and his friends were a happy young crowd, not given to worry, rarely concerned over making money. They worked hard but not necessarily during the business hours Gussie was accustomed to. They played hard, accepted any friend of Gus's as a friend of theirs. Saint-Gaudens was the one who worked and played the hardest of all.

If Gussie's letters home gave the impression that there was no one in particular she cared for more than another, her diary told a different story. She saw Gus nearly every night. On February 7, she went to walk in the Villa Medici garden with Mr. Saint-Gaudens. It was a "beautiful day — a rose-colored day." On the 22nd, "Mr. St. G. came and we went to the Forum and afterwards we two went to the top of the Colosseum and had a long talk." Gus called at the apartment next evening. After a reception at the Ticknors' he saw her home and they had "a long goodnight." Augusta began another letter marked "Pri-vate" at the top of the page. The date was February 8 and this time it was to her mother, not her father. "From what I have written you about Mr. Saint-Gaudens you will not be surprised to hear that things have culminated and the end of the thing is just this. Mr. St. G. is very much in love with me but the way he is situated now, he can think of nothing further. . . ."

Augusta had written more discreetly than she realized, however, for her mother was both surprised and anxious. Gussie was reassuring. "He is every inch a gentleman and there is an innate refinement about him. His treatment of me has been just what a noble man ought to do and I have told him that I think a great deal of him. . . ." Augusta continued with a reasonably accurate account of Saint-Gaudens' life to date, but she still did not know that he was born in Ireland and that his mother was Irish. To Bostonians, still overwhelmed with Irish immigrants, this would have been hard to take. That his mother had tried to make a good Catholic out of Gus, but with little success, was another point the Homer family was spared at this time. They knew an eminent Unitarian, then in Rome, and their daughter wrote that Saint-Gaudens was "firm in his principles and a great admirer of Mr. O. B. Frothingham, with whom he agrees in many things." This should have been the most reassuring of all Gussie's arguments, but it might have made Gus laugh.

Augusta was writing to ask permission to become engaged. She knew that if Gus had gone to Harvard, like Frank Millet, for example, consent would have been more easily given. "Mr. Saint-Gaudens' education in everything pertaining to art is complete," she wrote. "He occasionally makes mistakes in speaking . . . his history is much like that of any other self-made man who has worked his way up in the world by his own determination, talent and manliness. . . . He ranks very high here, is courted in every way but with it all is as unaffected and with as little conceit as a man could be. He says he is not at all accustomed to society but I never saw him make a mistake for his kindness of heart would prevent that. . . ."

Unconsciously, Augusta revealed a good deal about her own attitude and that of her parents when she wrote, "There is surely nothing against Mr. Saint-Gaudens except the social position of his parents and if they are good honest people who brought up their son to be what he is, that ought to be no objection. . . . All he asks for is fair play but you people at home have no idea what perfect frauds many of the sculptors are, most of the statues ascribed to them being modeled by some smart Italian in their employ. Still, Mr. Saint-Gaudens' talent is universally acknowledged and there is no doubt in his mind or that of all who know him that he must succeed."

Mr. Saint-Gaudens could not ask her to marry him at once, Augusta explained. "All the funds coming in to him now, and the amount is by no means small," with the exception of enough to live on, he planned to give to his parents. "His father and mother have always done for him, they are getting old and are not well off and now it is his turn to do for them." His two brothers were neither of them "inclined to help him take care of his parents. . . ."

Augusta had been wearing a ring of her mother's and "Mr. St.

Gaudens" thought at first that "some other man was ahead of him." He asked her about the ring "and now the damage is done," Gussie said. She told him "if it is not for his good he must not be with me, but there is no helping the matter now. . . ." Ever and always conscientious, "I don't mean to be a hindrance in any way to him," Gussie wrote, "so I try not to think how much I like him. . . .

"I don't know what your daughter Augusta has been up to but there are two other young men here in Rome who think entirely too much of me," she added. "But their trouble is nothing serious, I think — I am sorry for Mr. Saint-Gaudens and myself, but maybe it will all come out right in the end. He helps me much in my painting by his criticism and I believe I learn more from him than from Bellay. Of course he thinks it will be death to my art to go home and I'm sure I don't know what is best for me to do."

A wave of homesickness swept over Augusta. "Oh Mother darling, I want you now more than I ever did in my life before. Mrs. Todd is very kind but she isn't *you.*"

Two weeks later, on February 22, 1874, Augusta wrote again, this time to both parents. "Thirty years ago today since you two were married. Well, my hope is that many, many more years will go by happily and that if I am ever married, my life will be as happy as yours. . . .

"I want your and Father's advice and how can I have it when you are so many thousands of miles away. I am not *dead* in love, as they say, but perhaps I would be if I thought I ought." A letter from her father came at last, asking questions concerning Saint-Gaudens. She showed it to Gus and wrote, "Every question can be answered with a 'yes,'" and in addition, Gus had said, "'I like that letter and I like your father.'"

It was not until the first of March, however, that Saint-Gaudens wrote a formal letter to Mr. Thomas J. Homer. This did not indicate the reluctant lover, as it might seem. Saint-Gaudens, while climbing up and down the high platform to work on his heroic-sized *Silence*, had taken a bad fall. In addition to this, the Roman fever was upon him again. He had been walking in the warm spring nights in the rain with Augusta — rain bringing mosquitoes, as usual. Intensely cold weather put a temporary end to mosquitoes but not to chills and fever.

"As you know, I have been very attentive to your daughter," Saint-Gaudens began, "and I now come to ask your consent in gaining her

Photograph of Augusta Homer taken in Rome for her fiancé, Augustus Saint-Gaudens (Courtesy of the Board of Trustees of Dartmouth College)

affections and claiming her hand when I find myself in a position to do so with honor. . . ."

It was later generally supposed that Mr. Homer set the terms for his consent to his daughter's marriage, but this is not true. It was the sculptor himself. "I shall return to America in August when I hope for a large commission." There were to be three more statues in the Masonic Hall and he thought he could get the job of doing them. Talk of an Admiral Farragut was again in the wind, for New York, this time, rather than Washington, and in spite of Mr. Gibbs's warnings about politics, Gus thought he could get that commission, too. He made no specific statements to Mr. Homer, however, but simply said, "If I am successful and with your consent I shall claim Miss Homer's hand, immediately. If not, then I shall have to delay until . . . I can guarantee our future welfare. This, I think, will not be long. . . ." Gus asked consent "to my attentions to your daughter, leaving her completely free and binding her to nothing" and promised to call on Mr. Homer, "by your daughter's invitation."

Consent was forthcoming, but Augustus was ill "for five weeks" and Gussie was most unhappy. She sent him notes daily, violets on March 8 as a sign that spring had come, and the next day it snowed in Rome, and it snowed again a week later. The roofs were all covered with snow, something that had not happened for thirty years.

Taking pity on Augusta, Mrs. Todd acted as chaperone and took her to Saint-Gaudens' room to see him. Using the dreaded name "Roman Fever" for the first time, Augusta wrote her mother that Saint-Gaudens had had a "second relapse." In another letter marked "private" she was not going to pretend that she still called him "Mr. Saint-Gaudens." "Gus is very ill," she said. There was "no one to take care of him, no one to put on the poultices" which the doctor prescribed for the pain in his back.

No longer did Gussie pretend she was not "dead in love." In answer evidently to a letter from home, "Yes, Mother, I am afraid I am as bad as other girls in the same fix," she wrote. "I don't think he is perfection but I believe he would make me very happy."

The Homers wrote to tell Augusta she had better come home. It was going to be hard to say goodbye but she promised to find some lady to travel with from Rome to Paris and if possible someone going from there to Liverpool or from Le Havre to Boston. "Of course I shall not go away until Mr. Saint-Gaudens is better," she added. This was a new, more independent Augusta, but she signed herself "Your loving daughter who is trying to do right."

Augusta ended her painting lessons with Monsieur Bellay and began to copy a *Madame Le Brun* at the Santa Luca Gallery for Mrs. Ayer, one of her mother's friends. Fortunately, no American lady was leaving Rome for Paris at present — and Gus recovered somewhat from his bout of malaria.

They had their pictures taken, Gus looking "as if he were just going to sleep and as if he had not one particle of life in him," Augusta complained. "That is decidedly contrary to what he is." And she herself went back to the photographer several times because, although her pictures showed her to be a handsome, sensitive, rather sad young girl, they were not lighted properly, according to Gus, who could not see the real Augusta in them at all. On April 6, they took a carriage and drove to San Paolo and Tre Fontane, outside the walls of Rome. Afterwards they went to their favorite spot, the little observatory in the Villa Medici garden on the Pincio — "A beautiful afternoon and happiest day," Augusta wrote in her diary.

The following Saturday, she "got up early and met Gus at 8 o'clock." Again they drove outside the city walls by way of the Ponte Molle, across the Tiber. There were fine views and meadows where they stopped to pick wild flowers. "Mr. Ticknor," the American vice-consul in Naples, "was at the door when I came home, my hands full of flowers," Gussie said. "As he stood talking with Augustus while he was waiting for me to come down again, I think there was very little doubt in his mind as to the state of the case." But she wasn't ready to talk to people about her engagement — it was still too much of a private happiness to share.

Until it was time for her to leave Rome, Gus saw her every day. "I never expected that anyone would love me as much as he does," she said.

The 15th of April was their "last day in Rome." They drove "way out on the Via Appia . . . Gus gave me my ring."[4]

7

"YOUNG LION"

O N April 16, at eleven-ten in the morning, Gus took the train from Rome to Civita Vecchia, escorting Augusta and Miss Amey Goodwin, the girl she found to travel with. They arrived at the port of Rome at one P.M. and drove to the wharf. Gussie had a huge trunk containing, along with her wadded dolman, her Roman overdress and other items of clothing, her copies of paintings done in Rome. Each copy had a seal from the gallery to prove it was painted on the spot and not copied from a copy. Gussie had packed with care, but when she got to Paris she found that the *Madame le Brun* was spoiled because the paint had not dried sufficiently.

The boat did not leave till late afternoon. Miss Goodwin was tactful, leaving Gus and Gussie alone together as much as she could, but the return train for Rome left at three in the afternoon. "It was hard — that parting," Gussie wrote in her diary.

Going by boat and then by train, it took a full week to get to Paris, and another week went by before a letter from Gus could reach Augusta. "I am working like a young lion," he told her. He had promised to come to Paris to see her once more before she sailed for home, but almost immediately she began to worry for fear he would not be able to make it. The *Hiawatha* "commenced in marble" seemed to go well — then flaws in the block of stone appeared. If they were deep, the statue would have to be roughed out again in a new block of Carrara. But on the 26th of May, 1875, "Gus came," Augusta wrote, "and after a while we went off together." The marble for the *Hiawatha* had turned out to be clear because the flaws could be cut away from the figure. Gus took his girl to the Parc Monceau, a "beautiful little park" she had never seen before, frequented by French families with their children. Augustus was not in the least "Frenchy," as Gussie had assured her parents, but he loved Paris and knew restful places to show a girl accustomed to walking briskly across Boston Common. "In the evening to walk, etc.," Gussie said, her diary always most discreet. "I was so happy to see him again."

The next morning they went out to do a few errands together. To her mother Gussie wrote, "You need not expect much from me in the way of shopping, for my heart and my head are not in it, at all." She would try to get Genie's gloves and parasol and for herself, she was having a black silk dress made. As she told her mother, "There is not the slightest prospect of my being married for a year or two, still a handsome long black silk will last a long, long time."

Augusta and Amey Goodwin shared a room on the Rue de Castiglione and took their meals at a nearby pension where Annie Homer[1] and other Bostonians already lived. In the afternoon Gus and Gussie "had a nice time in my room," Gussie said, making no mention of Amey Goodwin. In the evening they went walking in the romantic Luxembourg Gardens.

As a conscientious tourist, Gussie had recently visited the graves of Molière and Racine at Père Lachaise cemetery — "a very forlorn place," she said. But Gus took her to Versailles where they "walked through a lovely little wood and park to the Grand Trianon." And then, next day, "went to the Salon but we did not feel in the mood for it," so they went back to Gussie's room. On Sunday they "stayed at home all day and were as happy as possible."

Although Augusta had already been given her ring, a cameo, Gus seems not to have been satisfied with an Italian setting for it. Having managed to arrive in Paris with money in his pocket, perhaps he had the cameo reset. In any case, on Monday, June 1, "Gus brought me my ring which is beautiful," Augusta wrote. She wore it now, and always.

Tuesday, June 2, was the last day. They "went to the School of Fine Arts" where Augustus showed Gussie the studios, the various haunts of his student days. Old friends were off on their own, students no longer, but the place itself was changeless. How would it be if they lived in Paris instead of Rome after they were married?

But now it was time to go to the Cunard office and then back home. At the railroad station "they would not let Gus go to the train with me and the parting was oh so hard," Gussie wrote. The train "left Paris at 3:45 P.M."

Gus returned to Rome by way of Carrara and the marble quarries, where he discovered that the work he had ordered done on the sarcophagus for Mr. Willard was unfinished. He reached Rome on June 21 to find a draft on account from Mr. Evarts. Evarts also wanted a cameo — of himself, it would appear. Gus sent the Evarts bust to New York and wrote anxiously, "I hope the portrait pleased you. A Mr. Barnard and a Mr. Ward and several others saw it here and spoke highly of it to me. I am very desirous that you should see it in the right light previous to placing it in your apartment. I believe I have already explained how to arrange it just as it was in the room where I modeled it, the lower half of the window darkened and no other side lights on it."

Always careful of other people's money rather than his own, Gus asked Mr. Evarts how many pedestals he needed, at about two hundred francs the pedestal. Orders for the *Demosthenes* and the *Psyche* would soon be sent and pedestals could go with them, free of duty. At last, Mr. Evarts replied. The portrait "arrived this summer when we were all in the country and I preferred to leave it unopened until we were back in town. A few weeks ago we opened the box and found the bust in perfect order and we were delighted with it." He needed only two pedestals, one for himself and one for the *Psyche*. And he enclosed a draft on Baring Brothers for fifty pounds.

Mr. Evarts was now "expecting the rest of the work you are doing for me and shall be happy to send you the balance that will be due you on learning how much it is." As usual, the rendering of accounts would be extremely difficult for Saint-Gaudens. Mr. Evarts, in his letter, wished him the prosperity he so well deserved, but it would be a long time coming.

Rome was prosperous, however. Two big hotels were being built and there were sidewalks everywhere. The city was like New York, Gus observed — "There is so much pulling down and building up." But the price of marble increased, and wages also, so that the cost of producing statuary was rising all the time. "I expected to return to America with a goodly sum in my pocket," Gus wrote to Mr. Willard, in connection with the statue of Silence for the Masonic Hall. But at the moment he was completely out of money.

Miss Brewster, a correspondent for a Boston paper, had seen the *Silence* and had written a flattering notice of it, which Gussie promptly sent to all her friends and relations. It was the first press notice of any importance Saint-Gaudens had ever had and he was delighted. But it didn't butter any bread. From New York, Mr. L. H. Willard wrote that he had suffered business losses.

Augustus was longing to get to America, to see Gussie and to land that big commission that would make their marriage possible. "They are making arrangements for several statues in Washington," Mr. Montgomery Gibbs wrote him in December. "If you were here you would stand a chance for some of the work. Mr. Evarts and others would help." Gibbs was returning to Europe, but would be back in New York by April, ready to "do all in my power for you," he added.

Augusta went to New York to visit a friend named Carrie. She wore her "black silk with Roman over-dress and fixings and they all thought it very handsome," she told her mother. "A young artist, a Mr. Flagg, came calling and we had a delightful evening." But Gussie could not help remembering New Year's in Rome where all her guests were artists. She sold one of her pictures to Carrie for twenty-five dollars but thought she could get $150 for a copy of *Beatrice Cenci*.

She called on Mrs. Bernard Saint-Gaudens. This she had dreaded, but it "was not bad at all and I need not have worried in the least about it. Mrs. Saint-Gaudens received me very cordially and I soon felt quite at home with her. I think Augustus looks a good deal like her."

Gus finally sailed for the United States from Le Havre on board the *Silesia*. During his brief stopover in Paris, he received a telegram from his brother Louis in Rome. He learned "the dreadful news" that his mother was dead after a painful last illness. Her death was a great shock to him because Gussie had seen his mother less than two months previously, when she seemed well. It was to a desolate home that Gus came on March 8, after a long and rough voyage.

Before leaving Rome, Saint-Gaudens consulted with Henry Lowe, an American banker in Rome, concerning remittances he would soon be sending from New York. Gus owed the banker for work in progress, but there was money promised which would more than cover all indebtedness, as soon as the commissions were shipped to New York. Lowe therefore was able to pay the rent on the studios and pay the Italian workmen regularly.[2] Blanco, a fellow sculptor, was to keep an eye on things and Louis Saint-Gaudens was to attend to accounts — and cut cameos. It seemed as though everything should go well and Gus was sure of getting new commissions as well as final payments on previous orders.

Gus went to live with his father and to drum up trade. And now he discovered that the business depression in New York was serious.[3] After the panic of 1873, bank deposits had fallen off a hundred million dollars and there were business failures all over the country. Railroad bonds were still in default. "My darling girl," Gus wrote, "I must have more time to procure orders here." So he would go to Boston "Friday or Saturday, no matter what turns up." Augusta had written that there was a competition for a statue of Charles Sumner to be set up in the Boston Public Gardens and Gus thought he would try for it, provided he could find a cheap studio in Boston where he could also live, to save room rent.

Miss Augusta Homer would not be in Boston to greet him — Gus already knew that. She had had her usual severe cold with increased deafness and the Homers had sent her to Aiken, South Carolina. But her family was waiting at 59 Winthrop Street, Roxbury (or Boston Highlands, as they called it), for their first glimpse of Mr. Saint-Gaudens.

Genie, Augusta's younger sister, ran to the head of the stairs when Gus pulled the bell handle. She let her mother go down to the parlor first, of course, but she heard his voice, which she said was "thrilling." Peeking over the banisters, she thought him handsome.

Mrs. Thomas J. Homer had an abrupt, almost harsh manner with which she concealed a generous heart, as Saint-Gaudens explained later to those less perceptive than himself. He saw through her matter-of-fact manner at once. And she, although doubtful and perhaps prepared not to like him, loved him almost at sight. Augustus had not been seated long in the Homer front parlor before he found that there was a spare bedroom he might as well occupy. Mr. Homer, coming from his office in the Studio Building, soon announced that he could arrange a place for Saint-Gaudens to work in the same building, at 110 Tremont Street.

Gus began a clay model, two and a half feet high, to enter in the competition. It showed Sumner "seated in his senate chair looking up, his head thrown back and a little to one side, as if he were about to rise and speak in earnest debate." The Homer family thought it "full of action."

Meanwhile, however, Gus needed to be gainfully employed and it was fortunate for him that Henry Hobson Richardson was building Trinity Church in Copley Square in Boston. Richardson had been a slim, elegant youth with plenty of money when he graduated from Harvard and went to Paris to study architecture. Then the Civil War wrecked his father's New Orleans cotton business. Lack of funds forced young Richardson to leave the École des Beaux-Arts, but he got a job in a Paris architectural firm. When the Civil War ended he came back to the United States, where he struck a remarkable winning streak in competition for church buildings. His first, for the First Unitarian Church in Springfield, Massachusetts, meant so much to him that he stood outside the building where the judges deliberated, and his eyes filled with tears when they told him he had won. In quick succession came the Brattle Street Church in Cambridge and then Trinity in Boston. Richardson could marry the Boston girl he had been engaged to since college days, and her Boston friends helped him, it was said.

Now Saint-Gaudens was helped by his Boston girl's parents — to meet Richardson, who gave him a job. Saint-Gaudens was invited to dinner at Richardson's house in Brookline, where the walls of his dining room were painted blood-red. Gus admired the big oval dining table made of black oak and made friends with the "round-faced, expectant children." Richardson, now much overweight, wore a bright yellow waistcoat and ordered a magnum of champagne for his guest. Gus was appalled to discover that he and Richardson were supposed to drink it alone.

Richardson had a painful stammer which caused him to talk in a series of explosions. He explained that both the wine and the cheese were forbidden him by his doctor — he just wanted to honor his guest; but Gus said the diet didn't seem to bother the architect, who drank practically the whole magnum by himself.[4]

"Some day we'll have you do rows and rows of statues for the façade of Trinity," Richardson promised Saint-Gaudens — but right now there was a little painting to be done.

Gus found himself working for John La Farge, a man with whom he was to be associated from time to time for the rest of his life. Thirteen years older than Saint-Gaudens, La Farge was also born in New York City with French the language of his home. But unlike the Saint-Gaudenses, both of La Farge's parents were French, and, unlike Gus, he was educated privately by tutors. His father, after an adventurous career in the French army and navy, escaped to Philadelphia, then settled in New York. He had the Midas touch, succeeding in shipping, banking, real estate and the hotel business. When his father sent him to France, La Farge did not bother to enroll at the École des Beaux-Arts but took private painting lessons and traveled, teaching himself history of art in museums all over Europe. He was now engaged in

decorating the interior of Trinity Church with murals in the Romanesque manner to accord with Richardson's fortresslike design in
brownstown, rough cut.

Gus could draw very well indeed if he had to and he could render a
saint in a sculptural style to look more or less like antique mosaic.
Genie remembered going to Trinity to meet Gus and riding home with
him in the horsecars. She was vague about what, exactly, Gus was
working on but thought it was "*Saint Paul*, the large figure at one side
of the chancel arch." La Farge was hard to please, but it was a job —
and Gus needed one.

The competition for a statue of Charles Sumner was won by Thomas
Ball, of Boston, the sculptor of the equestrian *Washington* already
standing in the Public Gardens. Two prizes of five hundred dollars
each were also offered, but one of them went to Martin Millmore, a
pupil of Ball's, and the other to Miss Anne Whitney, who had a
handsome studio on Mt. Vernon Street, Boston, and whose seated
Sumner was eventually placed in Harvard Square, Cambridge.

The loyal Homer family still loved the Saint-Gaudens plaster model
of Sumner, so "full of action." It was "too full of action," Gus declared,
laughing later at this early attempt. He gave the plaster cast to the
Homers.[5] It was painted gray to simulate stone and ornamented their
parlor mantel until somebody broke it years later.

Meanwhile, Gus went back to New York in an unhappy mood, never
again to enter a competition. He hired a studio in the German Savings
Bank building, 314 Fourth Avenue, on the corner of Fourteenth Street.
He had a commission to do the portrait of the president of Yale College, going to New Haven where Theodore Dwight Woolsey sat to him
for what was described as "a marble half-statue."

Saint-Gaudens modeled a beautiful, sensitive face, the play of light
and shadow subtle to a degree. The hands were exquisite, but the
president's academic costume was cut deep into the marble with an
extravagance of detail which doubtless pleased the sitter and the
public of the period.

The Homers put Gus in touch with Mrs. Joseph Ridgway, who
commissioned a portrait medallion of her late husband for three
hundred dollars. Mrs. Ridgway, who had also lost her daughter, then
set sail for Germany with her son-in-law and a grandson. The ship
sank and they all drowned — a terrible tragedy, because this wiped
out the family; a minor tragedy for Gus, since it took him about a year

Portrait of Theodore Dwight Woolsey, President of Yale University, in the entrance foyer, Woolsey Hall (Yale University Art Gallery, gift of Hon. Edwards Pierrepont, Yale 1837)

to collect two hundred dollars for work already done on a portrait that no one now wanted.

Somehow, Gus managed to send Henry Lowe, the banker, 1275 lire. A letter from his brother Louis assured him that the *Hiawatha* would leave Rome on the 24th of April. Gus hoped his other works were on the same steamer, because money due on them would clear up all his debts in Rome.

Then disastrous news began to come from Rome with every mail. Louis Saint-Gaudens had been unable to stand up to the responsibilities of looking after his brother's affairs. Perhaps it was at this time that he began to drink more wine than was good for him. He failed to answer letters and then finally wrote in remorse to "Dear Father and Gus. I am exceedingly grieved at the harm I caused you by bolting away and spending so much money, but I am an ill-fated cuss and all that I appear to be able to do is to cause harm and tribulation and consequently am disgusted with myself and perhaps the sooner I kick the bucket, the better."

Two Italian creditors had attached the statue of Silence. Blanco (who was supposed to look after things) had departed for Chile, having drawn 180 lire from Saint-Gaudens' account with Lowe. Gus had two studios by now, but neither could be given up to save money because the lease on each ran until the following year.

Saint-Gaudens wrote frantically to Lowe, making over the statue to him and giving him power of attorney to act for him. Lowe replied that he was leaving Rome with his family to spend the summer in the mountains. His lawyer had told him that the sale of the *Silence* could take place at any time by order of any of the creditors and that the document Saint-Gaudens had sent was useless.

Lowe had taken money from the Saint-Gaudens account to pay himself, first of all, for whatever charges he could conjure up. Then he paid other creditors in full on a first come, first served basis until all the Saint-Gaudens money was gone. Creditors made a run on Lowe as soon as the word got out, but many of them got nothing.

Saint-Gaudens managed to send a draft of about seventy pounds sterling to Lowe through Duncan, Sherman and Company — a firm which promptly failed. In what was certainly an understatement, "I am not in luck," Gus said.

It gradually dawned on Gus and his creditors that Lowe had not just taken a vacation, he was gone for good. "You must arrange with your friends to advance money on your works," was Lowe's parting shot. Without Saint-Gaudens' permission, he had approached Dr. Henry Shiff — but the doctor had gone off to Paris without a word, Lowe said.

This must have been the ultimate blow for Saint-Gaudens. In the first place, he admired Dr. Shiff, who was older than he. It would have embarrassed him to ask the doctor for help, but to have someone else do it was humiliating. And now it seemed as though Dr. Shiff didn't care anyway and Gus was in New York without a soul in Rome to stand by him.

But Dr. Shiff returned from Paris almost immediately and went right to work in Saint-Gaudens' behalf. His help was like a raft to a drowning man. He told the Saint-Gaudens creditors to let the young sculptor's work go to New York. They would never get a cent by attaching the statues, but if Saint-Gaudens could deliver the orders, they would be paid in full. Five cases of Saint-Gaudens' work arrived at the Customs House in New York and among the items were two copies from the antique, the *Antinous* and the *Apollo,* which would bring in seven hundred dollars.

Dr. Shiff found two young men, artists, who would also help. The first was Chevalier, a French genre painter who had escaped from France after being condemned as a member of the Paris Commune of 1871. Chevalier was to look for reliable workmen to finish the *Silence.* The other young man, Defelici, was to pay the workmen, now that Blanco was gone. Gus agreed to send the money from the *Antinous* and the *Apollo* directly to Defelici. "Although I am not very fond of him, I trust him fully," Gus said, and he wanted to spare Dr. Shiff "trouble and difficulty."

As to the painter, "I do not distrust Chevalier, still, he has debts himself and I do not know him so much 'au fond' as Defelici." Not surprisingly, Gus had lost some of that faith in human nature that Garnier, in student days, had found so charming a trait. But the two young men worked hard for him.

Dr. Shiff wrote reassuringly about Louis Saint-Gaudens. The boy just wasn't practical and didn't understand the value of money, the doctor explained. It was a friend of his, a young man named Smith, who had led Louis astray, but Smith had now left Rome. Gus replied that he was glad to hear that his brother had "heart," which was better than a head for figures any day.

As for Louis, "I work night and day in your behalf," he wrote to Gus. "*Silence* leaves by steamer from Leghorn 4 September."

"If it is so that you can help me, you know better than I how grateful I should be . . . ," Gus had written to Dr. Shiff. Their friendship lasted through the doctor's lifetime and Dr. Shiff was able to help Saint-Gaudens more than once.

Dr. Henry Shiff had been born in New Orleans, his father a Hebrew and his mother a Catholic. He was educated in France, served as a surgeon in the Confederate army during the Civil War, then came to New York where he practiced medicine for a short time before retiring to Rome and Paris. It was at the Café Greco, in Rome, that Gus met him — that much loved rendezvous for artists, writers and talkers.

Eventually, Saint-Gaudens modeled a bronze portrait of the long-bearded, benign doctor. He inscribed the medal playfully in Latinized Italian, "to my friend Doctor Henry Shiff, aged forty-seven, lover of toads and the stench of Rome; philosopher and dilettante of the Fine Arts, and enamored of cat-like types." In the medallion, a little frog opposite the inscription gazed admiringly up at the doctor, and one of the meanings in Italian of the word for frog could be freely translated "curmudgeon."[6]

In spite of his troubles, Gus still believed that "hard work and courage would bring him out all right." The weather had been beautiful in New York, but Gus was homesick for Rome, no matter how badly the Romans had treated him. In his New York studio, he turned on the water faucet so that he could hear it dripping like a Roman fountain in happier days. The building superintendent found this out and was appropriately incensed.

There was one bizarre incident. Edmund Palmer, a young sculptor Gus had known in Rome, now had a studio in the same New York building. He asked Gus to help him make a life mask of a client, but Gus refused, saying it was a tricky process which only an expert should attempt. Palmer went ahead — then came tearing into Saint-Gaudens' studio, yelling for help.

Palmer's client was lying on a sofa, mumbling angrily, a mass of plaster all over his face, which Palmer could not get off. Fortunately, there were "the usual quills" in the victim's nose or he would have suffocated. Gus helped chop away the plaster. The poor man lost some of his eyelashes but was otherwise unhurt. His name was Henry Ward Beecher.

Gus had actually watched an experienced person make a cast from life in Rome. On his itemized bill to Willard concerning the cost of the *Silence,* he had included the bill for the casting of the beautiful Angelina's legs. Sculptors collected such casts for their studios as a historian would collect reference books.

When at work and when the work went well, Gus still sang. A day came, probably during the summer of 1875, when a young architect by the name of Stanford White came up the iron stairs of the German Savings Bank Building.[7] He heard someone singing loudly in a fine bass voice, the notes without words being the Andante from Beethoven's Fifth Symphony. This was followed by the "Serenade" from Mozart's *Don Giovanni,* with raucous words in French that White had never heard before. He knocked at a studio door, the singing stopped and Saint-Gaudens appeared.

In telling the story later, Gus said that White was a great lover of music and assumed that the sculptor was also a musician. Gus had heard the Andante only from Le Brethon, the cameo cutter. As to the words for the "Serenade," they had been made up by a fellow student at the Beaux-Arts. This in itself was sufficiently remarkable to interest Stanford White.

White, five years younger than Saint-Gaudens, was born in New York City, his background somewhat similar to that of Richardson. Having inherited a fortune, White's father devoted himself to music, became a cellist and composer, and also a specialist in the study of Shakespeare. Then the family iron works failed and Richard Grant White turned to music and literary criticism for a living.

There were two sons, Richard Mansfield and Stanford. Stanford showed unusual aptitude as an artist, but John La Farge told him there was no money in art, and at nineteen White entered the architectural office of Gambrill and Richardson. White worked on Boston's Trinity Church, felt that his efforts were not appreciated and irreverently called Richardson "the Great Mogul."

White and Saint-Gaudens were friends at sight[8] and it did not take White long to discover that Gus had done some painting for La Farge at Trinity. La Farge was at work on the decorations for the interior of the new Saint Thomas's Episcopal Church on Fifth Avenue at Fifty-third Street. La Farge was now painting two huge canvasses, *Christ Healing the Sick* and the *Resurrection,* to be fitted to the walls of the chancel as murals. Between the paintings there was to be a large plain cross surrounded by a bas-relief; the subject, angels adoring the Cross. A sculptor had not yet been chosen to model this bas-relief. It must be done by young Saint-Gaudens, Stanford White insisted, but La Farge hesitated. First, he gave Saint-Gaudens some work to do on the King tomb in Newport. Again, as at Trinity, La Farge was not easy to please. He had drawn a design which the sculptor was supposed to follow exactly. Gus worked in La Farge's studio on this but hated mere copying. La Farge sent him to Newport to confer with Mrs. King, who wanted acorns in the design of foliage and flowers. Saint-Gaudens told her she could have them. La Farge said they were inartistic.

To his surprise, La Farge found that young Saint-Gaudens was stubborn. Gus thought Mrs. King should have acorns if she wanted them and he ended by designing some to put in the bas-relief ornamentation. They looked well, after all, so La Farge finally approved.

White came around to Saint-Gaudens' studio with another proposition. Edwin Denison Morgan, now ex-governor of New York and a senator, wanted to build a family tomb. White had designed something very handsome for him, with a great many angels carved in marble, standing as caryatids to support a cornice all around the walls. Saint-Gaudens would be the man to do the angels. Gus made sketches in clay for the Saint Thomas bas-relief, *Angels Adoring the Cross,* and eventually got the commission from La Farge. He also made clay sketches of angels for the Morgan tomb, which White was delighted with.

Morgan, after breaking several dates with the young sculptor, arrived at last at the studio over the German Savings Bank. The tomb was beautiful but too expensive, he declared. He had told White he would pay $12,000, but White had come up with a design for $26,000. Now Morgan would pay no attention to other designs but said he believed he would do nothing at all for the present — because times were hard. When things looked better he might have the more elaborate mausoleum.

During these constantly discouraging and almost disastrous months, Saint-Gaudens never lost sight of his main objective — to get the commission for a statue of Admiral Farragut which was to be put up in Madison Square, New York. Money was being raised for the project and a committee had been appointed to choose a sculptor. Saint-Gaudens' first move was an excellent one. He asked permission of Farragut's widow to do a portrait bust of her husband from photographs. She agreed, supplied the pictures and became interested in the young sculptor. As the clay model progressed, she was amazed at the fine portrait work. She would try her best to influence the committee in his favor.

Gus modeled a figure of Farragut, probably about half life-size. Someday his studio would be so crowded with visitors that he could hardly work, but now the problem was to get anyone to come to see what he had done. He wrote to Augusta, asking advice about proper behavior in developing social contacts.

"Last night I called on Mr. Stoughton," he said. "He was engaged but Mrs. Stoughton was not and she received me very nicely. . . . I told her I had come to see Mr. Stoughton about the committee on the *Farragut* and while I am on that subject, is it my duty to call when I have never been invited? Is it the right thing to do? They were always very nice to me and invited me to that grand reception of theirs but never any further — that is why I told her I had an object in calling."

Mrs. Stoughton told Gus that they knew General MacDowell, another member of the committee, very well. She took a memorandum and promised to ask the general to call at the Saint-Gaudens studio the next time he came to New York. She herself would also call with pleasure, she said, and also go to see the *Hiawatha* as she had been invited to do, by Mrs. Morgan.[9]

Gus went next morning to call on Mr. Gibbs, who told him to get letters of introduction to ex-Governor Dix from "Mr. Evarts, Mr. Pierrepont, etc." — in other words, to invoke the names of the lawyers Gus had immortalized in marble.

"So you see, things go bravely on for *Farragut*," Gus told Augusta. He had no time for real love letters, but she was his "darling girl," his "own darling Dimply."

"Our separation will not be a long one, depend on it darling," he wrote. "Your own fond, loving Gus who loves you so truly, deeply and well will come and take you in his arms and we shall never be separated after that, again."

But Augusta, once more ill with colds, was again to be sent away to a warm climate. And before long, the friends who promised to help Saint-Gaudens advised him to give up hope of the Farragut commission.

8

PARIS APARTMENT

LATE in December, 1875, Augusta Homer and her sister Eugenie set sail on the bark *Azor* out of New Bedford, Massachusetts, bound for Fayal, the Azores. The sailing vessel was "entirely different from a steamer," Gussie wrote, describing the ladies' cabin. "We each lay on our shelves and shouted to the people on the other shelves. The dining table was between us and Genie could pass me up my meals as I lay on my shelf."

The voyage was so rough that "the crockery was rolling and crashing and everything that could slip away or break loose, did." The coal hod broke away nearly every night and went slam-bang across the cabin each time the *Azor* rolled, or up and down the cabin when the boat pitched. The bark sprang a leak, but passengers were told, with grim humor, that the sailors continually manned the pumps "for amusement."

Safely ashore after a thirteen-day voyage, Augusta described the scene outside her balcony with "Pico right across the bay, towering up out of a cloud, its snow-capped summit shining in the sun."

"My throat seems better," Gussie wrote, "although of course I don't hear any better — but that I have ceased to hope for." As soon as she felt strong enough, she carried her paints and canvas out to a knoll near the boardinghouse where she and Genie lived. But Fayal was not half as paintable as Italy. People were friendly, but most of the fellow boarders were elderly invalids and by April Gussie was describing herself and Genie as "still prisoners on this island."[1]

If Gus could only get that Farragut commission, Gussie wrote her parents, he would take a steamship from New York to Rome via Fayal, where he would join her. The idea was enough to frighten the Homers of "Boston Highlands," although they knew that a legal marriage, somewhere or other, was part of the plan.

Augustus was doing his best. Stanford White had made a drawing six feet high, of a pedestal for the *Farragut,* and Gus made a scale drawing of his statue to go on top of it in his studio. His design for the statue was now cast in plaster and he had another model in clay, showing a different pose. The Farragut bust was also in his studio, "so I have quite a battery for the Committee when they come," he said.

Alexander MacDonald was "after the *Farragut,*" Saint-Gaudens heard. From Ohio, twenty-four years older than Gus, and an established New York sculptor since the end of the Civil War, "he is a very energetic and compelling man and I don't like him as an antagonist. Nevertheless, he has no model," Gus wrote.

Early in the game, friends had sent Saint-Gaudens to see John J. Cisco, head of the campaign to raise funds for the *Farragut.* Cisco was a wealthy New York banker and real estate operator, but described by the pleasant-mannered George Templeton Strong as "growing more and more arrogant." Cisco appeared to favor Saint-Gaudens but said there were still not enough funds on hand. Gus was advised to make an estimate of cost and he came up with twelve thousand dollars.

Ex-Governor Edwin Denison Morgan told Saint-Gaudens to talk to "Montgomery, Secretary of the Farragut Commission." So Gus went to New Haven, where he received the worst blow to his hopes. "From my conversation with him, it is evident that he is using every effort to obtain the Farragut commission for Palmer, his cousin," Gus reported back to Morgan. This was probably Edmund Palmer, who had covered Henry Ward Beecher's face with fast-hardening plaster! Cisco had been passing Saint-Gaudens' confidential offer around and Gus felt sure that "Palmer, knowing my position and being known to the Committee, will take me at a disadvantage."

Augusta's parents finally let her come home in mid-June and Gus went to Boston to see her, but it was a discouraging summer, an autumn of slim pickings, with Gus giving modeling lessons to help with expenses. Morgan got a commission in Washington for Gus — to copy a portrait bust of Chief Justice Taney for seven hundred dollars. The original bust was by William H. Rinehart, a friend of Gus's who had died of tuberculosis in Rome, Augustus sitting up with him many nights.[2] Rinehart had left money to help young sculptors. Gus was required to make a perfect copy of a portrait modeled when the Justice was young. It took him well into the spring of 1877 to collect the money due, because friends of Taney's said the bust didn't look like the Justice — as an old man!

The *Silence* arrived from Rome at last. Gus had it loaded on a dray at the wharf and taken to the Masonic Hall, but he was angry over the way the workmen in Rome had finished the hands — so he finished them further before he would have the statue set up. He still disliked the drapery which Willard had insisted on. It should have been treated in a broader manner, he felt, and he resolved never again to let a client dictate to him against his better judgment.

Gus wrote cheerfully to Gussie about steady work for Tiffany, but he thought he might go to Washington to look for something important. Congressmen seemed fairly free with big commissions for statues of themselves, if possible, or failing that, of local heroes back home.

Then, in December, 1876, when all hope of the *Farragut* for New York was gone, the Honorable Edwin D. Morgan announced the news. Gus had won the commission by the skin of his teeth. The vote of the committee was six to five, in his favor.

Saint-Gaudens' saw this as a turning of the tide in his favor. Very shortly, Governor Dix got the contract for him to do a statue of Robert Randall, for the Sailors' Snug Harbor on Staten Island." In the spring of 1877, La Farge finally decided to let Saint-Gaudens do the reredos for Saint Thomas's Church, the subject, angels adoring the Cross, already chosen.

Augusta Homer wrote at least one and perhaps all of her wedding invitations in her own hand. Addressing the Reverend Oliver P. Emerson, who was eventually to marry her sister Eugenie, Gussie said, "I hope you are to be in Boston and vicinity before long for I am to be married on Monday, June 4, [1877] at seven o'clock and it would give me great pleasure to see you here, then. We are to be married at home and expect to sail for Europe very soon afterwards. . . ."

An elderly Homer relative, signing herself "Cousin Lizzie," described the proceedings. "It was a lovely wedding and dear Gussie had such an exalted look during the ceremony (I could see her unobserved behind my fan)."

Cousin Lizzie was thrilled because, as she put it, "Augustus kissed me — just quietly by ourselves as we had a parting word alone in the back entry. It was a pledge of cousinship which I am proud to have claimed of him — it was the spontaneity of the act — and to an old grey-head like me."

Mr. La Farge, with his curious heavy-lidded eyes, the pince-nez, the French manners, was there, but Cousin Lizzie was dying to know if the pretty lady in beige with velvet trimming was his wife or his daughter.

The wedding was enlivened by the presence of young cousins of the bride. One boy, Sidney Homer, the future composer, had an unforgettable memory of the occasion because of a bet. He bet with other juvenile relatives that the minister would get mixed up in the names Augusta and Augustus. Sidney won![3]

The bride and groom went directly to New York after the wedding, but their ship, the *Abyssinia,* did not sail till June 6. There was time for Bernard Saint-Gaudens to gather his friends for one of his joyful French celebrations. "Please do up a large piece of wedding cake, perhaps one-fourth of a loaf," Gussie wrote to her mother, "and send it to Mr. Saint-Gaudens, Number 314 Fourth Avenue, for him and Andrew." She had been ashamed "of the little we had brought with us which was so crushed I didn't like to give it to them."

In London, Mr. Montgomery Gibbs and Miss Belle called on the bride. But the bride and groom hurried on to Paris because the Salon would soon be over and Gus didn't want to miss it. On June 21, the day after the Salon closed, Mr. and Mrs. Saint-Gaudens started house- and studio-hunting. They wanted a home of their own, a studio was essential — and they wanted to save money. In a summary of her accounts, Gussie told her father, "When I left home I had $2821 and when he left home Augustus had $3300." It was a respectable amount of money for a sculptor and his wife to get started on and Gussie was determined to account for every cent and make the most of it. Perhaps the most valuable wedding present she received was her father's promise to take care of money due Augustus on his commissions. He would have to deal with reluctant committees unwilling to part with funds, but Gus and Gussie had someone on their side who would see that proper payments were made.

By the 6th of July, the first Paris apartment had been found. It was on the Boulevard de Pereire near the Avenue des Ternes, "on the extreme edge of Paris." There was a view of the city wall and open fields beyond, although the Arc de Triomphe was only about three blocks south. "You know, there is a railroad that runs around the city of Paris, just inside the fortifications," Gussie told her parents. "It is thirty-four miles around the city which is walled and surrounded by a moat." She thought she would take the trip someday, but meanwhile it was a pleasant walk to the Parc Monceau, where she carried letter paper and sketchpad.

The Saint-Gaudenses were required to pay six months' rent and taxes in advance and repaper one of the rooms at their own expense. Suspicious of a couple without any furniture, the landlord unpleasantly remarked that all his other tenants were people of property, *rentiers* living on invested income.

Maybe the previous tenants had been *rentiers*, Gussie remarked, but they lived like pigs. "Do you remember what it was to go to housekeeping with not a blessed thing but table cloths and silver spoons? Not even an old rag to clean up with?" But there was "plenty of water in the kitchen," a convenience she had not found elsewhere. She hired a man to help, but before the cleaning process was over she was in "such a state with flea-bites," she could "scarcely write or think."

Seven huge packing cases arrived from Liverpool along with Gussie's "steamer chair, big trunk and valise." She and Augustus made a dining-room table out of a small packing case, stained brown, with the lid of a larger one for the top. Another packing case became a sideboard and Gussie made curtains to hang on rings and to pull across the window at night — light brown, with a fringe of dark green and black. There was material left for a cushion for the steamer chair. With twenty-two dollars, the money being a wedding present, they bought a Persian rug which covered the whole floor.

A green cloth over the table, touching the floor all around, turned the dining room into a parlor and Gussie considered further decoration. She decided to copy a Rembrandt head at the Louvre, frame it, put it on an easel and stand it in the corner, draped with dark brown. Augustus had an Indian bow and quiver which he doubtless acquired while doing the *Hiawatha*. He liked it for a decoration for his studio, but Gussie appropriated it for the wall of the apartment and she bought a house plant "like a begonia, only larger." The whole effect was just what the eighteen-seventies would call "artistic." "I don't know how it strikes other people but I am very well satisfied," Gussie wrote.[4]

Of course the bride's first dinner party had its embarrassing moments. "Katy Appleton and Miss Spalding," both from Boston, were the guests. The maid brought in the meat course before the fish course and when questioned about it in Gussie's best French, explained that they would have to eat the meat now because the fish wasn't done.

"Augustus keeps racking his brains all the time to think of something good and original for his *Farragut*. He ought to succeed, he is trying so hard," Gussie wrote. He had hired a studio, much larger than his New York studio, but it cost the same. It was just off the Rue de Faubourg Saint Honoré, not far from the apartment, so that he could walk home for the customary noon dinner — and then go back to work as late in the afternoon or evening as the light would serve his purposes.

Gussie made big white cotton curtains for the studio and Augustus set up an easel for her in a corner where the light was right. Together they arranged a still life for her to paint — a brass plate, some books, a fan, etc. — "nothing too difficult," but "a pretty combination in color." She got on with it very well. Two artists, working side by side — this is what she had dreamed her married life would be. It was a jolt to have to remember to put down her brush and go to market. What should they have for dinner? This eternal question bothered Gussie for the first time.

Much as he would have liked to get at the *Farragut*, Saint-Gaudens had smaller commissions acquired in New York to attend to first. He and Gussie drove around Paris for three days, looking for just the right marble for the tomb ordered by Mrs. King of Newport. They were in a Paris that tourists never saw and Gussie enjoyed it — but it was time-consuming. Then there was the "Montgomery medallion," "a portrait bas-relief to go on the wall of the Church of the Incarnation" in New York, in memory of the Reverend Dr. Henry E. Montgomery. Gus was "still fiddling over it," Gussie wrote on August 14 — evidently not appreciating the minute changes being made. It was cast by the first of September in a beautiful golden shade of bronze which Saint-Gaudens had evolved with the help of the Paris bronze foundry. This was a departure from the customary dark brown, a "modern" note in the coming rage for the color of gold.

Visitors from America came to the studio and Augusta put down her paintbrush to welcome them — and report their comments. The rector of Saint Thomas's Church, the Reverend William F. Morgan, who "knew Dr. Montgomery very well," pronounced the likeness perfect. And Phillips Brooks, on vacation from Trinity Church in Boston, had supposed that he never met Dr. Montgomery but "remembered seeing him" after looking at the portrait medallion.

The really big job going on in the Saint-Gaudens studio was the reredos for Saint Thomas's Church. There were to be four nearly square bas-relief panels on each side at the base of the cross and a band of cherubs' heads across the top. In September, 1877, when American visitors stopped by on their way home, Saint-Gaudens had completed two panels; one already cast in a special kind of plaster, one still in clay.

Six of the panels contained two angels each. They looked like lovely young American girls with big wings — serious, innocent and sweet. In fact, they had a strong resemblance to Augusta, whose profile Gus could study as she sat at her easel. Of course, Gussie had "never *really* posed for him," as her two very proper sisters were to insist when the Saint-Gaudens nude *Diana* for Madison Square Garden became famous.

"Indeed a good angel is leading you toward the rewards of signal excellence in art," Dr. William F. Morgan said after seeing the first two bas-reliefs for his church. Writing from his Paris hotel just before sailing for New York, "Pardon me if I again urge all possible dispatch consistent with justice to the work," Morgan added, taking most of the pleasure out of his praise. He wanted the whole panel of bas-reliefs in New York and in place by the first Sunday in October.

After they were modeled in clay, then cast in a kind of plaster that Gus was assured would last as long as those done during the Renaissance, the panels had to be painted before leaving Paris. "It is an immense job," Gus wrote La Farge in mid-September. "From seven in the morning until eight at night, six of us are at work besides the other men employed in drying the plaster so that it may be painted on, immediately." Two days and a half was all the time he allowed himself for each panel. The men who did the plaster casting "could only help me in putting on masses of clay and getting everything ready," Gus said. "I tried to have them do some of the work but it was beastly and I had to do it all over."

On the 16th of September, Gus was "working like sixty" — coming home at noon for a hurried dinner and then going back to the studio till half past eleven at night. "A young American artist, Mr. Low has commenced today to help him," Augusta wrote. "Mr. Low hasn't a cent and for a week past we have invited him to dinner and I expect he will dine with us for the next few weeks or so."

Will H. Low was indeed to be a guest, sleeping at the studio, eating at "the little apartment," as he described that first home Gussie was so proud of. Will Hicok Low came originally from Albany, New York, but had been making a living as an illustrator in New York City since he was seventeen. At the age of twenty he decided to study in Paris and become a great painter. With good luck and enterprise he succeeded in persuading a famous opera singer to pose for him in her costume as Lucia di Lammermoor. She was "Madame Albani" and she consented because she too was from Albany, by way of French Canada, and had chosen her stage name accordingly. Low painted a handsome picture, doing full justice to the satin folds of her train. He won a silver medal at the French Salon for another picture costumed in the period of 1820, but by 1877 he was down on his luck, his pictures were no longer sold and he had given up his studio. But he had a gift for friendship, idolizing first Robert Louis Stevenson, whom he met in Paris, and Augustus Saint-Gaudens, who gave him a helping hand.

Low described Saint-Gaudens at work and said that the figures in the relief were life-size and that he thought Gus had done them without practice sketches—being unaware of scraps of paper covered with drawings of angels and of the working and reworking of the first two panels. Low was astonished when he saw the clay come alive under the sculptor's hands while Gus talked as he worked, first in French, then in English. This impressed Will Low because he had come to Paris under the delusion that he would be able to speak French just by being in France. Will's French was the joke of the Quartier Montparnasse, where he lived.

Saint-Gaudens wrote, assuring La Farge that Low would just put on paint as told — not at his own discretion, because La Farge knew that Will Low was not a very good artist. Gus indicated exactly where he wanted clear shades of blue, where faded rose and dull gold. Low climbed the tall ladder, when all the panels were set up in the studio, and Gus called out, "Make that shadow dark. No. Darker. Now a high light," as Low worked away. "There was a kind of vague showing of different colors in the dresses of the angels," Saint-Gaudens told La Farge in explanation of what he was trying to do.

At last the painting was done; the cross, plain dull gold, the angels "grave and harmonious," although more colorful than anything as yet seen in any New York church. Saint-Gaudens had the whole reredos set up in his studio, the skylight curtained to give the effect of dim light in a church. He and Low brought candles, cleaning out the stock of all the little neighborhood shops, lighted them in front of the great bas-relief and opened the big studio doors on the narrow alley leading

to the Rue de Faubourg St. Honoré.[5] By this time it was late at night
and the street was almost empty, but the few passersby stopped to
stare. An old woman dropped to her knees at the entrance to the alley
and took out her rosary.

"Do you like it?" Gus asked her when she got to her feet again.

"*Mon dieu, que c'est beau!*" she exclaimed. At first she had thought
she was seeing a vision from heaven.

In an exalted mood, Gus saw his work "packed, baled and sent off"
on September 20. He sent La Farge a long letter — "I make no pre-
tense of it as a piece of sculpture, that would be ridiculous. Consider
the time I had . . . all made since August 23. Do not judge the panels
as they come out of the box. They are in some cases hideous, seen at
close range." Gus wanted judgment suspended till the panels were in
place on the wall of the church, and assured La Farge that the effect
had been imposing in his studio.

Now there was nothing to do but wait for letters from New York.
Gus visited a few museums with Gussie. "As usual, after I have been
to places of that kind, my head is in a whirl," he wrote. "I feel as if I
had come across a gold mine and then again, I feel that I am very
small potatoes."

There was time, also, for meetings to organize the Paris group of
young artists for the American Art Association. Just before leaving
New York, Saint-Gaudens had met a man who, with Stanford White,
was to play an important part in his career. This was Richard Watson
Gilder, editor of *Scribner's Monthly* magazine and later of the *Century*. Saint-Gaudens was "going down the stairs of the 14th Street
Building" when he saw Gilder coming along the street — slender, full
of energy, with intense dark eyes. He was with an artist Gus knew.
There were introductions and all three went up the stairs to the studio
where the Farragut model was on display, along with other work.
Gilder liked what he saw.

Gilder was interested in starting a new organization for young
artists. They would have rooms and an annual show. His wife, the
beautiful Helena de Kay, was an accomplished artist who would work
for the new organization along with Walter Shirlaw, muralist, and
Wyatt Eaton, portrait painter. Would Saint-Gaudens join? With a
great many other things on his mind, Gus paid little attention. He still
admired the National Academy of Design, with its Venetian palace,
and a member of the hanging committee had invited him to send his

Roman Slave Girl Playing with a Child to their annual show. "A Sketch in Plaster," Gus called it. Then back it came, with word that there was no room for it after all. Gilder had invited Saint-Gaudens to call on him, so Gus went right around.

On a Saturday in early June, he rang the bell at an iron gate leading to a flagstone walk bordered by flowers. The Gilders had a small studio apartment, once a carriage house, at 103 East Fifteenth Street.

"It was noon and I was at home for lunch," Richard Watson Gilder wrote.[6] "I ran down to the gate and I can tell you there was a high wind blowing. Saint-Gaudens was 'mad as hops' because they had just thrown out a piece of sculpture of his from the Academy exhibit and he was ready to go into a new movement. I told him to come around that evening." Gilder got hold of Walter Shirlaw and Wyatt Eaton and that evening they founded the Society of American Artists; Shirlaw, president; Saint-Gaudens, vice-president; Eaton, secretary, and Helena de Kay Gilder, a mere member willing to do most of the secretary's work. They changed the name to the American Art Association at the next meeting. Louis Tiffany joined at a third meeting and said he knew where he could raise some money.

In Paris, Saint-Gaudens joyfully took on the job of getting young American artists to join and send work to New York for the first exhibition. Up to this time, Gus had never shown his father's passion for organizing clubs and for belonging to clubs already functioning. But now, on October 12, 1877, after his Saint Thomas angels had been sent to New York, he wrote Mrs. Gilder, "I got a meeting together last Sunday evening." The American artists living abroad became associate members of the new organization and many remembered that gathering as a milestone in their lives. Thirty-eight American artists joined. They wanted "to select among themselves a jury to accept or reject works sent from here." They said they were "in dead earnest" and "wanted an excellent and strong show and that in acceptance or rejection of pictures absolutely no partiality was to be shown." Of course, this would be difficult to achieve, but the young artists had faith in Saint-Gaudens and wanted him to head their jury. They also wanted their show to "commence before the Academy and lap over it!"

"The young fellows can't have any orders if they don't have any medals and they can't get medals if they break from these fellows," Saint-Gaudens wrote, "these fellows" being the artists who clung to the styles of 1820. They saw, in the new association, a chance for recognition, and of course they never supposed that their new ideas would soon seem conventional.

The Saint-Gaudens studio became well known as a place where young artists could get together at night and Gus, in his efforts to help them, became well known himself, a point he hadn't thought about.

Weeks went by, while Saint-Gaudens worked for the success of the American Art Association and continued to hope that the reredos would please La Farge. Finally, in November, La Farge wrote a long letter, first damning the Saint Thomas angels with faint praise and then angrily holding forth about the difficulty of installing the bas-relief panels. "I did all I could and three weeks of work was spent; it cost me nearly what I paid you to make all these alterations," La Farge wrote — and then came to his real cause of complaint. "Besides this, I had to cut my picture which . . . was very disagreeable to my artistic feeling and to my personal feeling also, as I had given you the principal place it was a bore also to have my place injured."

The papers more or less took up this theme. But it was Richard Watson Gilder to the rescue. He had an "engraving" of the angels made for the midwinter number of *Scribner's* and commissioned Clarence Cook, an art critic, to write an article about them. Helena Gilder wrote to Gus, telling just how the angels looked to both the Gilders. "Really, there is in your angels something religious which we never see in modern churches. Their religious dress is so pure and, so unsentimental. . . . I say we because Mr. Gilder, my brother, Mr. Eaton and I all feel the same way. . . ."

Wyatt Eaton wrote from an artist's point of view. "Two things are talked of at present in New York. The American Art Association and the decorations of St. Thomas' Church. I can't tell you, St. Gaudens, — how much I am delighted. I am sure you don't know — and I question if your friends in Paris know how good your things are. . . . I have never seen any sculpture so well managed for similar circumstances, light and distance. Seen from the nearest point, the work is all that could be desired without any sense of lack of detail — the important forms are simple and massive, which makes the expression expressed by gesture to be intensely felt. From the extreme end of the building nothing is lost. On the contrary I believe that very quality is still stronger." This praise from a professional artist was gratifying, but it must have pleased Gus just as much when he began to get letters from people who only wanted to say that they thought the angels were beautiful. Even La Farge said, ". . . it is universally liked . . . it has such simple feeling. . . ."

Augusta, however, had an anxious thought that would cross her mind more and more often as time went by. Speaking of Will Low, "Gus will pay him liberally for his work and with all the expenses on them I fancy the 'angels' won't pay very well except as a card!" Gussie was unconscious of any incongruity in describing an immense reinforced plaster bas-relief as a "card," or advertisement — she was just worrying about the budget. After all, she was the one who bought the food. "Why wasn't I taught to select meat?" she asked. The veal had been much too fat as well as too expensive. And would her mother please send the recipe for "Parker House Soup."

Not only were profits from the Saint-Gaudens angels negligible but La Farge failed to send money due. Mr. Homer, for the first time but by no means the last time, wrote polite but firm letters, and amounts due on account were sent. "Over a thousand dollars" was eventually collected. "I am much obliged to you, Mr. Homer," Gus wrote. " 'Much obliged' expressed very mildly how much I thank you for all you are doing and have done for my finances."

Usually, it was Gussie who wrote all the letters home, but on September 26, while she was "wrestling with preparations for a dinner" for the much loved Dr. Shiff, now in Paris, Gus took over a letter she had begun, and described her to her parents. "I wonder whether she has told you what a regular 'puddin fatty' she is becoming. She eats more, sleeps more, talks just as much and is a thousand times less nervous than I have seen her in three years. You write splendid letters to her and the best part for her as advice, is when you tell her 'don't work too hard!' She is inclined that way but still, as I said before, she's a pretty good girl. She manages to be occupied all the time and I wish we could fix it so she might be able to paint more.

"She can give you lessons in cooking, if you wish any first rate soups, first rate mackerel, first rate anything in fact and too much of all. There's nothing to complain of in that tho' — I'm fond of plenty and she takes care of the inner man splendidly."

Gus described a new and larger dinner table he had manufactured out of a door that he had previously used to model two of the angels on, plus another packing case for a base. "It's quite an imposing piece of furniture with its white cloth, silver spoons, plates, salt cellars etc. all like an army drawn up for the battle — ready for the onslaught" —

a dinner for six. He and Gussie were a little dashed when the "Boston Highlands" Homers seemed shocked because there was still no proper dining-room table.

Gussie found a French dressmaker to make over her Boston clothes. Her striped silk she had "pleated to cover all but the gray stripe in front," then "let out like a fan on the sides" with a "long train behind." Revers of garnet velvet ran from waist to hem of the "very long skirt which hangs splendidly." This was to cost six or seven dollars, while the gray dress her father liked so much, "dyed a handsome dark green," was to have a "saque" lined with blue and green plaid to go with it, the whole thing to cost fourteen dollars. Then Gussie blew herself to a new dress bought at the Magasin du Louvre, ready-made but fitted to order. "The waist" was a plain habit-shaped basque, a little low at the neck but fitting beautifully, the overskirt plain with the exception of two stitchings, the underskirt "broad, with pleating." The dress was "long and when looped up," was drawn across the front. It was black with a black velvet collar because Gus said he liked her in black — and it cost twenty dollars.

In spite of the fact that Augusta was well and strong, full of delight in her new clothes and going out to parties as well as giving them, it was understood that she was too delicate ever to spend a whole winter in a cold climate.

Separation from her from December till spring was what Gus was trying to face when he wrote her father. Should they both go to Rome or should she go to Rome while he stayed in Paris?

"The production of good work, regardless of everything else is what will be taken into consideration," Gus wrote. "This sounds hard and in fact it is hard . . . but it is now or never for me." He had a motto pinned up where he could see it every morning: "The time to be carefulest is when you have a handful of trumps." "The great thing is to make a good work out of my *Farragut* and when I reason, 'Where do I run less risk of making a bad statue' — France is the answer."

But Gus found that he could not part with Gussie — so they went to Rome together. On the 10th of January, 1878, Augusta wrote a long letter to her parents. She and Gus had found a furnished apartment in Rome — Number 23B Via San Nicolo da Tolentino.

9

ROME AND RETURN

SAINT-GAUDENS was completely happy to be in Rome, after "dark, sloppy Paris." He was in love with this glorious place — "such sun and light as there is here!" he exclaimed. "Italy has a greater charm for me than ever and I should not be surprised if I remained here all the time I am doing my work."

Gussie was equally happy. They had a large bedroom and parlor "with a great window where the sun poured in from eight o'clock in the morning until half past two or a little later," she said. Of course the furnishings were hideous, but she had expected that. She had worked hard in Paris, packing up belongings, some boxes to be stored and sent for later, some to be forwarded at once. From the huge trunk that traveled with them by rail and by boat, she took Mrs. Moseley's afghan to throw over a corner of the sofa, and books, candlesticks and photos, to make the apartment homelike. They expected a box in a day or two with rugs and curtains. A little defensively, Gussie remarked that it was a good thing they hadn't bought furniture in Paris. The packing-box dining table and sideboard had now reverted to their original packing-box state.

The apartment cost thirty dollars a month "with service," but there was no kitchen — only all the hot water they wanted for tea or coffee. Meals were downstairs in the same building "and they generally warm up whatever soup was left from dinner and it's very good for breakfast," Gussie thought. Although fuel was expensive, they had a coke fire in the grate of their huge marble fireplace every evening.

Defelici, the artist who had helped Saint-Gaudens when the Roman marble cutters were intent on robbing him, came often to the apartment. Other artist friends appeared. French was the common language and Gussie astonished herself by "talking French all the time." She told the artists they only came to get warm, but they laughed and urged her to believe otherwise. This was what she had imagined life would be like, married to Saint-Gaudens and living in Rome. But of course poor Gussie still worried about money.

The beautiful flower-smothered studio in the Palazzo Barberini gardens was just down the street — but it belonged to someone else now and was not for rent. All the studios that would do at all were taken, except two, and the rents were much higher than in Paris. "We never anticipated this difficulty," Gussie said. One studio had belonged to Margaret Foley, an American sculptress who had just died. Gus went to see Miss Clarke, her artist friend, about renting it. The price was fair, but Miss Clarke would not commit herself till she talked to "Miss Howitt," another maiden lady of advancing age. So Gus had to take a much overpriced studio for a whole year.

Saint-Gaudens went on a search for belongings of his that he had left in Rome. He found two roughed-out but unfinished busts, Gussie's little copper teakettle she had given him when she left Rome four years previously, and her painting of a model in peasant costume. He did not say where he found them — perhaps in some dusty corner of his former studio or in some pawnshop. He finished the busts and sent them to the United States. "Please say to Father that he will very probably receive $350 from Miss Merrick and $150 from Miss Bull, minus the freight," Gussie wrote. "We have received no news from La Farge," she added. Of course she meant that no money had come, but she hoped a payment had been sent to her father.

In spite of his best efforts, the Italians got the better of Gus when he signed the contract for a studio, Gussie told her father. All the previous week the "lazy workmen" had not been working and Gussie found it trying to patience and pocket. But by the 1st of February, Gus was installed, was pegging away at his *Farragut* and singing as he worked. He was trying "to strike away from the stuff we have in America," he wrote to White, but it was "hard work with our infernal modern dress. . . . When you come over I want to talk to you about the pedestal," Gus added.

Saint-Gaudens soon had a small sketch for the *Farragut* which Gussie thought would be the one he would finally select. But he wanted to try out other ideas before starting on the five-foot model, which later he would enlarge to ten feet, he told her.

Gus hung his wife's painting in his studio, although Gussie protested on the grounds that it wasn't good enough. He arranged a corner of the studio for her painting kit and at last found a model the right size to fit the Farragut uniform which had been loaned to him along with sword and cap. There was a fine-looking old man among the models for hire, whom Gus wanted Gussie to paint. But first she thought she ought to make some duty calls among the Bostonians who had come to Rome for the winter.

"Such a quantity of ladies with daughters I never saw together," was Gussie's comment to her brother Joe. "A young man here would be a godsend."

By far the most interesting Americans were Julia Ward Howe and her daughter Maud. Her "European tour was undertaken for dear Maud's sake," Mrs. Howe said. Gussie was thrilled to meet "Mrs. Howe and Miss Maud" at Miss Brewster's reception. But Maud, now twenty-four and a famous beauty, "riled" Saint-Gaudens "pretty effectively by her vanity and affectation." Poor Maud was not entirely to blame. She was constantly praised and certain relatives, other than her mother, had insisted that, with her beauty, she could and should marry for money. But a young artist, Jack Elliott, gifted but penniless, was desperately in love with her, and Saint-Gaudens knew Jack. Years later, Maud Howe Elliott and Jack were to become good friends and neighbors of Mr. and Mrs. Saint-Gaudens'.

The chief tourist entertainment in Rome in 1878 was rather macabre. King Victor Emmanuel II died January 9 and Gussie, with ladies from Boston, went through the gardens of the Quirinal Palace and up the long staircase to the grand salon, which was hung with crimson brocade. The sides of the room were lined with great candles and the King's body, "crowned and dressed in royal robes, was seated on the throne." Gussie was shocked.

By the 10th of February, the Pope was dead, and Gussie, with some of her mother's friends, went to see the body lying in state, "the soles of his feet against the grille at St. Peters so that people could kiss his feet." Gussie was shocked all over again.

Augustus was good-natured about the Bostonians who came to the apartment to call and to mingle uneasily with the artists. "There are always several of your cousins here," he wrote his mother-in-law. "For that matter, I've found that every American lady or gentleman we meet is connected in some way with the family. I believe, if we were wrecked on a desert island, my spouse and myself, and if a year after another fellow was wrecked on that island, we would find, after a few moments conversation, that he was related to the Homer family or that he went to school with you or Mrs. Nichols [Gussie's sister Lizzie] or Father Homer . . . and the rest of the time . . . on that desert island would be occupied by the two, Gussie and he, in telling about new engagements and the death of this person and the birth of that one; of incidents that occurred at the Roxbury germans and so on, until some ship would come by, commanded by some member of the family, to save us."

Saint-Gaudens was hard at work on his Farragut sketches in clay when he had great news from Stanford White in New York. Times were good again; ex-Governor Morgan had been making money. (His fortune was to be estimated at eight or ten million dollars.) So White went back to him about the design for a family tomb, which he had rejected. White told Gus about the interview. "Enclosed you will find a very rough and very bad sketch traced from a hastily finished-up drawing of Morgan's tomb. The *Honorable* Morgan, I should say. . . . Oh he is a most honorable gent indeed! He has gouged me out of half my commission and what end of the horn I will come out before the thing is finished, I am sure I don't know, confound the man. The commission always charged on a monumental work is from 10% to 25% according to the size and cost of the work. He said he wouldn't give more than 5% to any man etc. etc. My first inclination was to pick up my hat and bid him good morning, but I remembered I was poor and young and had run into debt to get abroad and that it might interfere with you — so I told him I would think the matter over — which I did and swallowed my pride and principles and accepted his damned 5% — which by the way is not on the total cost of the monu-ment — but on the cost minus your work, which is also somewhat unfair. . . ."[1] So White would have to take his commission on the sculpture not from Morgan but from the amount Gus was to receive — which was $8000. "I may ask you to give me a hundred or two dollars," White said. "I do this because I shall have to superintend the putting up of your work. . . ." But "in no case will I listen to your paying me anything unless you make a little pile for yourself."

The work Saint-Gaudens was to do included eight figures, four in high relief and four in low — a band of angels around a column; four little symbolical figures at the angles of the superstructure — all for $8000 minus a hundred or two. But Gus began to dream of bands of angels with no thought of money entering his mind.

It was Gussie as usual who kept the accounts and worried about cash. "Mrs. Saint-Gaudens has copied my account for expenses," Gus wrote to La Farge at the end of January. This was for the King tomb for which Saint-Gaudens had bought the marble in Paris, advancing the costs, including the wages of workmen to cut his design. Under prodding from Mr. Homer, La Farge had paid for the Saint Thomas angels, but Gus was still out of pocket for the King tomb in Newport. La Farge finally sent "drafts for $100 and $200" not to be "drawn on him for thirty days," but Gus "could not make use of them in Rome," so back they went to the United States for Mr. Homer to take care of.

Gus and Gussie were on their way "to Miss Brewster's party" when the porter handed them a letter at last. They "opened it under the street lamp" — but there was no money in it! Finally, on March 1, "the check Father sent to Augustus" was found. It was in a letter at the studio and Gussie spied it, behind a plaster cast on a bracket beside the door. The postman, seeing no one in the studio, had stuck it there at least ten days earlier.

Rejoicing greatly, Gus and Gussie took American friends to see the Colosseum by moonlight. Next, they hired a carriage and drove out on the Campagna because spring had come and they both said they had never seen Rome so beautiful before. They got out of the carriage at "a huge unknown tomb" with people living in a hut above it, "hens and children scratching around close to the edge of the great circular top with no railing whatever at a height of at least fifty feet."

The mountains surrounding the plain were still covered with snow, but the sun was warm. They watched shepherds tending their sheep, staying there "a long time with Rome at their feet." Writing to her mother, Gussie said, "There has not been one death of Roman fever in Rome for two years, and Dr. Nevin, the Episcopal clergyman said there had been but three cases among the visitors. . . ."

In March, Saint-Gaudens replied to White's letter — in the facetious vein the two friends always used. "You would have received this love song ten days sooner," Gus said, if his old friend Mr. Fever had not made him a two-week visit. Gus was not fond of Mr. Fever, made faces at him, gave him horrid-tasting medicine to eat, but still Mr. Fever hung on. Gus tried to get away from him by going up to the mountains, but Mr. Fever followed. Old Man Fever was probably tired now because he visited Gus for only a short spell morning and night. Gus thought Mr. Fever was just as boring as he, himself, was in telling all about it.

Saint-Gaudens hated to leave Italy but dared not stay through the summer, because of malaria. He confided to White that Italy gave him mixed feelings. "All those glories of the Renaissance" made him determined to do something good himself, while at the same time this ambition seemed hopeless. His brief enthusiasm for the neoclassic was behind him and Saint-Gaudens was a Renaissance man now and forever, but Italy was his lost paradise.

Gus and Gussie left Rome together. On March 26, Gus was back in Paris, but Gussie was traveling with friends to Nice and Monaco. Her "throat was so very well" and she "never had a cold," so it was decided that she should stay longer in a sunny climate. Gussie had grown strong since her marriage, but her insistence on constant care of her health, a habit acquired in childhood, would not add to her future happiness.

Gussie assumed there would be a new Paris apartment waiting for her in April, but there was nothing of the kind. Her husband met her at the station and explained that he had been too busy working on the Paris International Exposition to go house-hunting or look for a studio. He had been appointed one of a jury of three to accept the work of American artists to be shown at the Exposition. La Farge had urged him to take the appointment because it would help "establish" him.

At the head of the jury was David Maitland Armstrong, now forty-two, former consul to the Papal States and at present Director of the American Department of the Paris Exposition. In a letter to Gus he made it clear that he was going to be the boss. "Bierstadt offered a picture here," he wrote from New York. "It was refused. He had sent it to Paris and will try to get it in there. . . . Look out for him. He shall not get it in but do not let it be known, as we do not want to make a martyr of Bierstadt. There is another horrible painter who has made a ghastly daub which was rejected here. He says he will get it in Paris through you. This man is Carl Gutherz of St. Louis. Look out for him. Do not make any promise to artists. You have no right to do so and it will give you trouble." D. Maitland Armstrong, as he signed himself, said he spoke "so plainly" from friendship, but it seems unlikely that Saint-Gaudens had made any promises anyway. "I shall have absolute control of the hanging," Armstrong added. There were to be eighty-four pictures from America and forty from Paris.

"I do not want any statuary in the gallery," he continued. He and Saint-Gaudens were only slightly acquainted, although he later claimed early friendship, and somehow Gus put up with his dictatorial manner. It was just one more proof of that gift for diplomacy that Saint-Gaudens possessed.

Gus told Gussie that he had seen a place he thought might do for a studio. It was on the Rue Notre-Dame-des-Champs, a little street curving between the Boulevard Raspail and the south end of the Luxembourg Gardens. Built originally as a dance hall, the building had been used as a printing establishment for a Paris publisher, but it was empty of presses now, a huge place "with quantities of windows in the roof."

"Gus thinks this skylight would be very like the light out of doors in which he could model his *Farragut* as he likes," Gussie wrote, putting a sculptor's problem in layman's language. The rent was four hundred dollars a year.

The place had a balcony which, with characteristic generosity, Gus let other artists use, free of charge, of course. As usual when things went well, Gus sang, and Maitland Armstrong thought the song must have "startled even the waltzing Parisians." In a mellow bass would come the words:

> *You secure the old man*
> *I'll bind the girl*
> *Once aboard the lugger, she is mine.*

All the artists, painting or just lounging around, would join in the song. Gus took time out to model a bas-relief of Maitland Armstrong and another of his daughter, Helen.

On April 22, 1878, Augusta announced that they had taken "a lovely apartment in a most delightful location, the only objection being the price, 1400 francs a year with taxes." The address was 3 Rue Herschel, and Gussie drew a little map, showing it running east from the south end of the Luxembourg Gardens to the Boulevard Saint-Michel. It was the only house on the south side of the street, with nothing opposite to cut off the view. They were five flights up. Gussie was worried about the high rent, but Mr. Armstrong was going to live with them. "Having his room here of course lessens our rent," Gussie said, "and we find him a delightful companion and many a pleasant hour will we have on our balcony this summer with this great garden at our feet and Paris in the distance. . . ."

Gussie drew a little plan of the apartment. The parlor, overlooking the Rue Herschel, the Luxembourg Gardens and beyond, had two windows and a balcony. Next to it was a good-sized bedroom — Mr. Armstrong's. Behind it was the kitchen and behind that a small bedroom, for Gus and Gussie, with a window overlooking a court with a pretty garden. There was a small dining room across the entrance hall from the parlor.

Armstrong assured Gussie that she would have to pay twice as much for such an apartment in New York and she argued with her New England conscience to the effect that they must be "in a nice quarter where we would not be ashamed to ask anyone" because Gus, as one of the jury for the Exposition, would have important people to entertain.

Off to the "Hotel Druot" went Augusta — that wonderful warehouse where secondhand furniture, rare antiques and even priceless paintings were to be found by collectors. Gussie bought some Louis Sixteenth armchairs, carved, gilded and covered with cordovan leather — except that she did not know what to call the stamped gold leather which at one time was gold-embossed but, excepting on the back, was now all worn off. "We are delighted with them," she said. Then there was the "fine old chest, the front all handsomely carved and the wood almost black with age." They told her it was "of the time of Charles the Ninth and if so it is nearly three hundred years old." Gussie didn't really care how old it was; she and Gus just liked it — and it was cheap.

Seeing Oriental art for the first time at the Paris International Exposition, both Gus and Gussie fell in love with it. They got a "fine old Persian embroidery" for the parlor table and Japanese matting to put on one of the walls. Eventually, Gussie painted an interior of this much loved Paris apartment, showing light from the window, well handled. She promised to send the painting home to Boston "if it is good when it is done" — which it was.

But as usual, Augusta had very little time. It was good to paint when Gus "was off all day" — he and Mr. Armstrong "deep in their jury business with no time or thought for anything else." Gussie heard "nothing but pictures, hanging, jury, commissions, etc."

The Exposition of 1878 opened and artists who had come to Paris to see their own work flocked to call on Saint-Gaudens and his wife. Gus and Gussie were invited by wealthy art collectors to dinner at famous restaurants or "under the stars" in the Champs Elysées. They saw "Paris under the gas light" — the equivalent of the Colosseum by moonlight, it would seem — but without the deadly mosquitoes.

Frank Millet, whom Gussie had met in Rome, was back from a trip to the Orient. He had a studio on Montmartre, furnished with divans and hanging lamps, with musical instruments, weapons and other souvenirs strewn about. When he gave a party, he wore Oriental costume and played the bazoo. It was all exciting, with invitations requiring reciprocal entertainment, of course.

Gussie gave a tea and a reception. They took down the doors between the hall and the parlor, and "draped" the doorways to make more room. "Cake, tea and wine, that sort of feed is the custom here," Gussie explained to her mother. "They all stayed till nearly twelve and my rooms were pretty full. . . . I wonder when I shall ever do any painting again."

Toward the end of June, there was news from New York. Stanford White would soon be on his way to Paris, "and who do you think is coming with me — even McKim!" he wrote. "I am tickled to death. He is coming over for but a six weeks trip but still it is perfectly jolly. . . ."

Gus knew Charles Follen McKim[2] well because they both loved ice cream! It was during that dreary summer in New York before his marriage that Gus met McKim at a favorite ice-cream parlor on a hot summer evening. They were both red-haired, so the Three Redheads — White, McKim and Saint-Gaudens — were to meet in Paris.

McKim was a year older than Gus, a shy, rather quiet man with an excessively high forehead accentuated by the loss of most of his red hair on the top of his head. He was named in honor of Charles Follen, famous professor of German at Harvard and a man of ardent anti-slavery convictions. McKim's Pennsylvania parents sent him to the Eagleswood School, run by Theodore Weld, an abolitionist. But McKim did not become a social reformer. His mother, a Quaker, urged him to be kind and gentle, which he was. His father sent him to the Lawrence Scientific School, but the École des Beaux-Arts was where he wanted to go, and he made it in 1867, but the Franco-Prussian War drove him home, as it had sent Saint-Gaudens to Rome. Although they never met as students in Paris, Saint-Gaudens and McKim had plenty of common experience to talk about over their ice cream in New York. McKim had worked on the plans for Trinity Church in Boston but he had an office of his own by 1872, and by the time Gus met him, he had married Annie Bigelow of New York and Newport and had a little daughter about two years old. The reason for McKim's sudden decision to go abroad was that his wife had left him, taking their child. It was the result of "malign influences," according to discreet report. McKim's friends said he had been framed and there was no question but that he was brokenhearted — especially because his wife took their child and never let him see her again. When his wife finally died, his daughter came to live with him. Described by his friends as "a merry, cheerful companion," Charles McKim was at this time the observant but silent member of the redheaded trio meeting in Paris. He was on the scene when an incident concerning Saint-Gaudens and his Farragut statue took place. It was a tale to be repeated again and again, with variations, by others who were not there.

One July day, McKim and White burst in on Saint-Gaudens at work in his studio. They wanted him to go with them on a trip to Southern France. He said no, the Farragut Committee were coming to look at his sketch. They went away. Coming back later, they found Gus "whistling."

"Evidently the ladies were pleased," they said.

"No, they weren't pleased," Gus told them. "If they had been I would know it was bad!" But Gus still wouldn't take time off for the trip. He wanted "the boys" to see the statue. This time, White and McKim stuck around. Fellow artists came by, looked at the plaster statue and said, "Saint-Gaudens, you have given Farragut your legs!" There was a slight outward curve.

Saint-Gaudens "carefully lifted the head" off the statue, "tipped the figure over on the floor, where it shattered into a thousand pieces. 'Come on,' he said to White and McKim, 'I'll go to Hades with you fellows now!' "

Gus loved a dramatic scene, so something of the sort must have happened, but even the account attributed to McKim was somewhat apocryphal. There was another reason why Gus decided to take a trip. An invasion of Homer relatives was due in Paris, now that Gussie had such an attractive apartment. She tried her best to protect her private life and her ever-disappearing funds. "Please say to Lizzie that I am afraid she thinks I am going to do more for her than I am," Gussie told her mother. "She can sleep in the dining room and use my great closet with the window in it for a dressing room. I shan't even buy a wash bowl, for everything of that kind is dear now. She can use mine. The beds I shall hire."

The servant's room on the top floor of the building was occupied by Louis Saint-Gaudens. He had turned up in Paris after a long absence when no one in his family knew where he was. A letter from Bernard Saint-Gaudens in New York, dated November 11, 1878, was addressed to both his sons. "I had vowed not to write before having another from Louis, who, like the child in the parable, has come home, — that is to say, he has returned to the right road which he should never have left. Let him imagine now the anxiety I have suffered all during the time he left us without news of him."

Then addressing Louis directly, "But anyway I forgive you provided you keep to the plan which is proposed for your future; for I tell you, my dear son, that you will find no rest for your soul save in work — that is the real source of well-being. Work lifts the soul to God and gives strength of will that nothing can shake." Augustus had promised to send Louis to the École des Beaux-Arts.

In spite of Gussie's remarks to her family, Lizzie came to Paris, also her brother Tom and a friend named Harry. Her sister Eugenie followed. Augustus had his "small *Farragut* cast in plaster" before the invasion of Roxbury relatives, so it must have been the five-foot plaster sketch he smashed — not the ten-foot plaster model still to come. He set out for Southern France with White and McKim on August 2.

White listed twenty towns that the Three Redheads visited, and commented on each.[3] At Beaune, for example, they "came across two very attractive and inseparable things — good wine and pretty women." They bought a bottle of "old Beaune" which they drank on the train, having a compartment to themselves, and "became quite tight before getting to Lyons."

There was a passenger boat going down the Rhone, a trip "rarely made" by tourists. "The boats go but once a week and it is sometimes dangerous," White said. The river current was very strong, the paddle-wheel steamer just barely able to cope with it. In due course they ran aground on an island. "There is immediate uproar, everybody shouts, the engineer leaves his engine and rushes on deck, the captain jumps off and violently endeavors" to push off the steamer, 275 feet long with two hundred passengers on it. The Three Redheads were not dismayed — McKim had rushed off the boat at one of the river stops and invested in two bottles of sparkling wine. Finally, the force of the river swung the boat loose.

Saint-Gaudens now wore the elegant pointed beard that was part of his cartoon signature. It looked so well that White began to grow a beard, but his was a round face, his cheeks fat. He looked like "a revolving sun on the half-shell," he said, and sadly shaved off the beard, leaving a ferocious-looking red mustache. McKim, who was said to affect the grand manner, remained content with his small, neat, somewhat drooping mustache.

"It is really a business trip," Gussie wrote her parents. "Mr. McKim wants Augustus to do some bas-reliefs on something that he's going to be architect of. . . . Augustus feels he has learned a great deal from traveling with his architect friends."

In September Eugenie Homer arrived. She was a cheerful person whose dramatic entrance, laden with all sorts of packages, led Augustus to call her "Bundles." Gussie had found a room for her in a nearby pension, but, judging by the cartoons her brother-in-law sent home in Gussie's letters, Genie brought chaos to the Rue Herschel apartment. She was now twenty-four years old. Gus had always liked her and recently she had grown to be quite a pretty girl.

In 1874, when she was twenty, Genie had taken one of the Harvard College entrance examinations for women. She wanted to go to "the Annex," the future Radcliffe College, and a cousin of hers wrote all about it to Oliver Pomeroy Emerson. He had been the Reverend Mr. Emerson since 1871 and it was said that he had been in love with Genie since she was fourteen. "Let me relieve the tension of your mind by saying that 'the long agony is over' and the lovely victim is serene," Mr. Emerson was told. "Genie was very tired, but cheerful like her usual dear self." Professor Greenough, who gave the first day's examination in "German and English Literature," told her she had done very well, so far.

Mrs. Charles D. Loring of Mt. Vernon Place "opened her large cool parlors and each noon" had refreshments ready for the seven brave girls taking college exams. She "urged their lying down to rest" at noon between sessions each day. "Tuesday was devoted to algebra" and the next morning to writing a composition "on an unknown subject." Professor Greenough was "happy to tell Miss Homer that" she had passed the examinations satisfactorily. Doubtless Oliver Emerson, the thirty-nine-year-old clergyman, congratulated Genie appropriately, but his

own suit was not to prosper for a long time to come. Genie arrived in
Paris in 1878 without a Radcliffe degree, after all, but perfectly heart-
whole and fancy-free.

McKim had gone home, and White was in Rheims when he summoned Saint-Gaudens to come at once to see the famous thirteenth-
century sculpture on the west façade of the cathedral. Genie wanted to
go too.

Gussie "looked me over and decided that if I had a bonnet instead
of a hat and wore a plain gold ring on my left hand it would be
perfectly proper," Genie said.[4] So after "working hard," altering a
dress of Gussie's to fit and concocting a bonnet, Gus and Genie took
the afternoon train.

White went to the station to meet Saint-Gaudens. "Imagine my
astonishment to see him sail through the R.R. station door with his
sister-in-law on his arm!" White wrote.

"Such a jolly time as we had in our (St.G's and my) room! I ordered
a bottle of champagne which she positively refused to taste. Instead,
she roasted apples and chestnuts in the fire. She is the most self-possessed young lady I ever came across. A Boston girl; and we had a
tremendous row on the subject of women's rights. She quietly paid me
off by darning my socks and sewing buttons on my shirts, in spite of
my most earnest protests. In fact she is a brick — and what is more,
awfully pretty."

Genie, on the contrary, said the scene was "a little parlor" in a
commercial hotel and that it was the men who roasted apples on a
string while she mended White's socks. She didn't mention the champagne. Early in the morning she went with Gus and White to the
cathedral. The intense concentration with which the two men studied
five hundred or more carved figures in the great recessed doorways
was beyond her. Many of the figures were headless, but Gus and
White "spent money lavishly for photographs of details," so that they
all had to travel third class to Laon to look at more twelfth- and
thirteenth-century sculpture.

An old verger with a flaring torch led them up into the strange
towers of the church to see some curious carvings of oxen. Genie went
along, bonnet, long skirts and all, but she enjoyed the perilous climb
fully as much as the queer-looking animals. Then White went back to
Rheims with only a few sous in his pocket; Gus and Genie went on to
Paris, equally broke.

White eventually returned to Paris. "I have been asked to dinner by

Mrs. St.G., and expect to go under the table with St.G., Bunce and Dr. Shiff about two in the morning . . .," White wrote. On Christmas Eve, he went out with Gus to buy presents and decorations for the apartment.

They all went out to the boulevards to be part of the gaiety and then, at midnight, to Saint Sulpice to hear Jean-Baptiste Faure, leading baritone at the opera, sing "Noel."

At the Christmas dinner party next day, it was discovered that Stanford White had brought mistletoe along with the other Christmas greens and hung it in the middle of the parlor.[5] In vain, White tried to get Genie under it. But after dinner, served by Gussie's full-time servant, and presumably after plenty of wine, it was time for play-acting. Louis pretended to harness himself to the armchair where Genie was sitting. He pranced appropriately. White said he was the footman on the coach, and pushed the chair around the room — then under the mistletoe.

Genie said she escaped when Stanford White tried to kiss her. She probably did — because he didn't tell the story. But on the other hand — years later, she didn't want to tell the story either.

10

THE *FARRAGUT*

STANFORD WHITE fully intended to go to Italy as soon as the Christmas festivities were over, but two months later he was still in Paris, working in Saint-Gaudens' studio, sleeping on a cot there and taking his meals at the apartment. The pedestal for the *Farragut* had taken possession of his mind.

"It is to be a high circular stone seat," Gussie said, but she warned her family not to tell because "it is by no means decided upon." This last was certainly an understatement. White changed his design as often as Saint-Gaudens remodeled his clay. It was almost the end of February when "they put the whole thing up in paper so as to get the proportions." The circular seat had been discarded for a wide ellipse, the back still high to give room for large bas-relief figures representing Loyalty and Courage. Gussie was sure they had arrived at a satisfactory result, but again she was wrong.

After White went back to New York, he redesigned the pedestal several times, coming up with more "parabolic, bucolic or any other kind of olic curves than a Greek temple ever had," he said. He sent Augustus "exact dimensions." Gus went to work to model bas-reliefs to fit, only to receive new dimensions by the next mail.

White was still in France, but taking another excursion, when Gussie set up her easel in the studio again. She painted a portrait of the studio boy, discovered that she could catch a likeness and went to work on Mrs. Farlow, wife of an expatriate doctor and a friend of hers. To her delight, Dr. Farlow said he liked the portrait and would buy it. He sat for his own portrait, which also turned out well. Gussie asked her husband if he would have accepted her portrait of Mrs. Farlow for the American Painting Gallery at the International Exposition the previous year. He said yes. Feeling "quite set up," she dared not press her luck by asking him if he would have "hung it on the line."

Dressed in her "brown studio-dress" and with pen in hand instead of brush, "It's strange," Gussie wrote, "how little idea people have that Augustus must be left alone to work and he is very much bothered by visitors at all hours." Washing his clay-covered hands in a pail of water, he would come to greet his callers. "He can't turn them out. He isn't made so."

"Another knock at the door. This time it is a man who wants to know if the citizens of the Rue Notre-Dame-des-Champs may be allowed to hold a mass meeting in this studio!"

Life in Paris was by no means all work and no play, however. Father Homer's Christmas check had been more generous than usual and Gus and Gussie went to the opera often. *Pré-aux-Clercs* was Gus's favorite. They went to symphony concerts on Sundays, but Gussie was inclined to let Gus go without her to the theater, "what with my deafness and the French language," she said. Dressed in her black silk Paris gown, her head "wrapped in black lace," Gussie went to a fancy dress ball at the Opera House with Gus, in his "dress suit with a crush hat" — and domino mask. The Place de l'Opéra was brilliant as always with gaslight, some of the girls' costumes were "short of material" and there was "skylarking in the corridors" too improper to describe to Boston relatives — but Gus and Gussie stayed till three-thirty A.M., enjoying what Gussie called a "very gorgeous" sight.

The large Christmas check from the Homer parents lasted until the 21st of March, when Gussie happily described an antique liquor cabinet from Brittany, "carved all over the front," two feet high by two feet long, with little doors, "in perfect condition in spite of its age." It's by far the nicest thing we have," she said. She was going to keep sheet music in it, for she had hired a piano. Gus had bought a flute, "and toots all his spare moments."

This happy letter was followed, just ten days later, by one in which Augusta told her parents that her husband had been very ill. "We sent for a French doctor as being the nearest," she said. "Later we called in Dr. Farlow and Dr. Shiff but neither could take the case as they are not practicing physicians so Sunday night we sent for Dr. Allen Herbert. Gus's suffering was so intense that it was all Mr. White, Louis and I could do to take care of him, night and day. The doctor came every day until yesterday and will be here today. The trouble was inflammation of the intestines extending to the stomach." There was

recurrent fever along with recurrent pain; the treatment was morphine — and arsenic.

Augusta always had a succession of maidservants to report on,
knowing that her mother enjoyed such details. Berthe, the paragon
who could cook and serve seven-course dinners, had departed.
Theckla had arrived just in time to help when Gus was taken ill. She
cooked "an old hen for broth," which was all he could eat, and Gussie,
full of enthusiasm, said the "new girl" could "get up the simplest thing
in the best style . . . a first class cook."

But Gus's uncle had sent them "half a cask of grape wine" from the
Midi (which they paid for). They kept the cask at the studio and
Gussie walked across the Luxembourg Gardens with bottles for Gus to
fill. The bottles soon seemed empty, however, and before long the
"lady-like girl" was drunk, particularly at dinnertime. Meals were
hilarious. "I tell you, we had high old times," Gussie said. And after
dinner, the soup tureen, glasses and everything would be on the floor
of the kitchen. Silver was lost — then recovered in the bottom of the
soup kettle which every proper French cook keeps on the back of the
charcoal stove. Then Theckla left and the silver went with her, never
to be recovered.

By the middle of April, Saint-Gaudens, White and Gussie were in
Saint Germain-en-Laye, twenty miles from Paris, on a bluff overlooking the Seine. They went "to see if the bracing air would make Gus
feel himself again." But it rained and this summer residence of ancient
French kings did not live up to its reputation. Returning to Paris, Saint-
Gaudens worked on bas-relief portraits of his friends — most of them
artists, John Singer Sargent among them. This was recreation for him,
but he was bothered by his *Farragut*. He found it "hard work to
satisfy" himself.

All the Roxbury relatives had gone home except Genie, who had
been traveling in Italy. White made her a list of great sculptors whose
works she must see — ending with Augustus Saint-Gaudens. His fame
was less of a joke than anyone thought at the time. In August, Genie
decided to go to Switzerland — Gussie to go with her.

Accordingly, Augusta acquired a costume in the latest style. Her hat
was of a "shape called 'The Gleaners.'" Broad-brimmed, worn on the
back of the head and faced with cardinal-red satin, it was "romantic,"
Gussie said, and Gus agreed. Mrs. Farlow, her former sitter for a
portrait, helped her make "a navy blue waterproof" into a dress, "very

scant and short," with which she would wear colored stockings. Gus promised to meet her in Switzerland after Genie left for home. He allowed himself to be persuaded to go to northern Italy with White — who was also soon to return to America.

It was frightfully hot in Verona, Gus said. But he found early bronze doors replete with angels with big wings, and tombs even more elaborate than the one he was at work on for ex-Governor Morgan. Best of all was the great fourteenth-century equestrian statue *Can Grande*, his battle helmet slung on his back, grinning happily from his casque and chain-mail gorget. The horse was also armored, a visor over each eye, giving a comical look that was most appealing. Glorious drapery swept backward from the horse. "What can you do with modern costume!" Gus mournfully exclaimed, not for the first time. But to do an equestrian statue — that was his dream, whether he said so now or not.

"My Italian trip has been a great thing for me," Saint-Gaudens felt sure, although he had to "race around," somehow getting to Carrara to select marble for the Morgan tomb. He bought Gussie "a lovely Venetian lamp on a curious wrought-iron chain" to hang in the center of their parlor in Paris.

Gussie received a telegram that her husband would arrive at Château d'Oex, in Switzerland, on August 6, by diligence. She had already been out to get a better room because hers was so small "and the partitions too thin." They had three days — the first time in their two years of marriage that they had been away together just for a good time. Then Gus left his wife to complete her "water cure and to enjoy cream" which they put in great bowls on the table. She was very thin. She stayed in Switzerland until the end of September, returned to Paris but went at once to nearby Cernay-la-Ville, "because they say that after taking the baths one should rest in country air."

Gus again told her that he "felt like a young lion" — an expression he liked to use.

Stanford White arrived in New York the 6th of September. Three days later, he went into partnership with McKim and Mead, to form one of New York's most famous architectural firms — McKim, Mead and White. McKim was the conservative member, Mead the man with the money — and White the genius. They hired George Fletcher Babb, who had been White's instructor in architecture when White was a paid student in the office of Russell Sturgis in New York, ten years earlier. Silent, almost unknown to outsiders, was Joseph Wells, whose devotion to the Renaissance was equaled by his love for music. He and Saint-Gaudens were to be especially compatible on both counts.[1]

It was evident at once, from White's letters,[2] that the new firm wished that he would forget about the pedestal for the *Farragut*. But White said he would not see many such chances to work in an entirely artistic spirit, "unhampered by the — well — the small Hells that encircle us on every side — women who want closets, for instance."

The partners might reproach him, but White was going to do a pedestal for Saint-Gaudens every time he felt like it, the *Farragut* pedestal being only the first of many. But prices for stone and stone-cutting had gone up twenty-five percent. The lowest bid White could get on the *Farragut* pedestal from Fordyce and Browning, contractors, was $2700. So White wrote to Cisco. "The statue, owing to Mr. Saint-Gaudens' illness and the impossibility of erecting it during the winter, will be some six months" late, White began. He knew "there must be some interest owing on the fund for the statue which could be added to the $2000 already allowed for the pedestal."

White was in Cisco's office by appointment, but Cisco mistook him for a stone contractor. White was furious and Cisco said, "Ah, dear me," several times. No more money was to be had and as for asking about interest on the Farragut fund — it was an impertinent question.

White departed, got a letter of introduction from his father, Richard Grant White, and went back to Cisco, who then sang a different tune. They had $2450 above the $9000 total left in the Farragut fund, Cisco said, and he offered personally to give $50 extra and thought ex-Governor Morgan might chip in with $100. "He then bade me good morning and told me to see Governor Morgan and get his advice." Cisco remarked that Morgan was "Mr. Saint-Gaudens' friend."

"So I marched off with joy in my soul and had hard work to stop myself from writing you a high-cock-a-loring of a letter. . . . Alas, I did only too wisely — or rather I won't say 'alas' for who cares for Morgan. . . . He immediately got on a high horse and acted in a most outrageous manner, misunderstood everything I said, and in fact would listen to nothing. 'The Committee wouldn't guarantee a cent.'" was Morgan's last word.

Saint-Gaudens offered to take the cost of the pedestal out of his commission and not only donate his designs but cut them himself free of charge. "My dear boy, what are you thinking of!" White replied.

White went back to his office, "drank a brandy cocktail" before Fordyce came in again with his estimate. Thus fortified, White told the contractor to reduce his bid or "never to darken the doors of McKim, Mead and White offices again."

Fordyce came in next morning with "a sort of yaller green blue stone" which he said was the "grandest" stone on the market and offered to make the pedestal out of it for $350 less.

"He swore it was as strong as Blue Stone and to prove it picked up a sample of Blue Stone, hit the two together and smashed his own stone into a thousand splinters — convincing, wasn't it?" White wrote.

Next came a discussion of a site for the statue. Madison Square had been the choice right along, but ever since 1858, when he was appointed architect in chief of Central Park, Frederick Law Olmstead had been arbiter of everything to do with all New York City parks and statues.[3] He had already told White that Saint-Gaudens could have any site he wanted but that Madison Square was "a sort of shiftless place" which would give the *Farragut* no prominence whatever. Blissfully unaware of future traffic problems, he preferred "the intersection of Broadway and Sixth Avenue."

But Gus had always loved Madison Square since his boyhood days when it had been suddenly and dramatically the bivouac for men and horses in the Civil War. Then there was the later elegance of Delmonico's restaurant and the Fifth Avenue Hotel. "The principal objection to Madison Square is the reflection [of light] from the Fifth Avenue Hotel," Gus wrote. New York was still gaslit, just like Paris, but in a few months Broadway would be the first street to be electrically lighted. "The statue must be unveiled in the afternoon," when there would be no reflections. But "Go for Madison Square," was Gus's verdict.

On November 14, 1879, Augusta watched the process of enlarging the life-sized *Farragut* to heroic size, or eight feet, three inches, not counting the plinth, which was four and a half inches more. The big clay model with iron straps and supports inside it was surrounded with scaffolding so that the men who had come to "point" it could swarm up and down with their calipers, measuring the life-sized model and transferring the enlarged measurements to the eight-foot clay. Seven large kerosene lamps "had been brought in so that the men could work at night. The statue was growing into shape" — looking "very mammouth," as Gussie put it, and she thought it was "much finer" than it had been in life-size. Gus was overworking, of course, driven by a fire of excitement as his dream took shape. The doctor gave him "iron and arsenic pills."

Gussie had a part in it all. "I have been modeling some on the sword hilt and feel quite elated that I can do something of the kind," she said. A week later, she was "making the braid on the sleeves of our *Farragut*." The statue looked pretty much finished to her, but she supposed "Gus will work on it until the middle or end of next month. Mr. Godwin (Parke Godwin's son) is modeling a little at the studio now and Augustus likes him very much."

She handed over her letter to her husband, and Gus wrote, "Gussie wants me to add something to her letter." So he put down "$2 + 2 = 4$" several times and made a cartoon of a thin girl dragging along a fat, protesting one and wrote, "This is Gussie taking a walk with Genie."

On December 12, Augusta told of record-breaking cold weather in Paris. There was "great difficulty keeping warm" and almost all the fuel they could get had to go to the two studio stoves to keep the great clay statue at the right temperature. The whole family took turns watching the stoves at night, lest the studio boy fall asleep and the statue freeze. Augusta, considered by her family as "delicate," said she had never felt so well.

But the snow was "fifteen inches deep"; the railroad and the river were blocked so that food and fuel supplies dwindled. "The law does not allow the horses to be shod with anything but smooth shoes on account of the asphalt pavement underneath the snow and the poor horses go slipping and straining and then do not get over the ground nearly as fast as one can walk and it takes three or four horses to do the work of one. The few horse cars that are running have six horses instead of two. Quantities of men and women are employed shoveling with little bits of shovels and it's very slow work." Augusta watched it all through Boston eyes and marveled that she had seen but one sleigh, and a fancy one at that. It was probably from some museum! She thought one snowplow could do the work of fifty men — not realizing that there was no such thing as a Paris snowplow.

They had "a little shindy" on Christmas Eve, just the same — two men, Howard Lombard and Mr. Minot, to dinner and nine more guests, including Mr. Godwin, Mr. Longfellow and Jack Elliott, to come in the evening. They "took up the rugs, opened the doors from parlor into dining room and hall which made a fine place for dancing.

Annie Ingersoll played splendidly for waltzing and Howard Lombard, for a Virginia reel."

The cold continued. There was talk of "blowing up the ice in the Seine with dynamite," but all the Christmas Eve guests came calling — the men bringing flowers for Gussie and Genie. With Gussie at the piano, Gus tooted on his flute. These were the last happy times in the Rue Herschel apartment.

Gussie was dismayed by "the perfidiousness of the French people in the way they have acted with us in this apartment business," she wrote. Their lease was soon to be up and the rent had been raised beyond their means. When they failed to renew the lease, men "invaded the apartment," looking for damages and charging an outrageous sum for small scratches and flaked paint. Gussie packed a huge box to send home, discovered that it was too heavy to be carried safely down five flights of stairs, so transferred the contents gradually, armload by armload, then repacked and sent the box to her husband's studio to be crated. Other boxes followed; then, with trunks and valises, she and Gus went back to the Pension Saint Joseph on the Rue Notre-Dame-des-Champs. They would have a large, sunny parlor, bedroom and kitchen and a place for Berte, her Paris servant, on the second floor.

The move was not accomplished until March, however, and meanwhile Augusta was often at the studio. "My poor sword that I spent so much time on proved to be a trifle too small so now I am making it all over again," she said. Part of the modeling was in wax instead of clay and "Augustus is going to show me how to make some straps for my sword. I got my hands and everything all over wax. . . ." Even after her lessons, "It is slow work," Gussie discovered. "The wax is so easily put out of shape."

On the 27th of January, sheets were put up behind the *Farragut*, the photographer took pictures and on Sunday, Saint-Gaudens invited guests to the studio. Nineteen great bags of plaster were stacked against the wall, molding was to begin at once, plaster casting to follow.

Guests were enthusiastic. There was an impressive quality about the Admiral — his heavy coat blowing aside, his face with a seaman's look of searching the horizon. In the former printing shop, now a studio, fellow artists looked up in awe, sensing the drama of impending battle at sea. Models for the pedestal bas-reliefs were also on view and there was something new about them. Loyalty and Courage were handsome women in Greek drapery, as all symbolic figures were supposed to be, but the wind in their hair, and the extremely stylized ocean waves, combined to form a decoration neither Greek nor Renaissance but modern for its day and new to American sculpture. Eventually, it would become part of the much imitated Saint-Gaudens style.

There were newspaper reporters among the guests. Gus was positively superstitious about having any publicity before the *Farragut* was done, and he had a hard time restraining them. "Mr. Whiting of the *World*" sent a letter to New York anyway, on the grounds that Saint-Gaudens had forgotten to tell him not to. It would take Richard Watson Gilder to explain gently but firmly to Augustus that the gentlemen of the press would be his best friends if he would let them, and that genius without publicity simply would not be recognized.

Spring came early. "Paris is full of violets now," Gussie wrote in March, "Everyone seems to be wearing or carrying a bunch and you meet handcarts full of them."

In April, at the Salon, a lady "dressed in black lace, strangely fashioned, was seen in one of the galleries. She was small, her step and carriage slow and queenly. . . . She was a dazzling blond, somewhat restored and not beautiful as one saw her near — the striking part of her costume" was that the upper part of it, or the "yoke," was made entirely of fresh violets. She was Sarah Bernhardt, and no wonder Gussie found her strangely fascinating.[4]

Gussie herself wore duchess lace purchased with Christmas money from home. She dressed in white this spring and also wore violets.

The heroic-sized *Farragut* in clay had been covered with plaster. This thick covering, carefully sawed apart and cut open, would become the mold into which the new plaster would be poured to form the cast, but on March 10, "*Farragut* met with a serious accident. In getting him down from the scaffolding he came too heavy on his legs and cracked the mold of one of them. It gave the molder two weeks extra work to cast it and Augustus extra work to finish it. . . . There seems to be no fault to be found anywhere. Twenty men were working to get the poor fellow off the scaffolding with ropes, rollers, etc. It was immensely heavy, probably twice as heavy as the plaster statue after it is cast . . . and much heavier than the bronze!"

Augustus had a recurrence of his "spring illness," probably the long-term effects of his severe malaria. The doctors called it "neuralgia of the stomach," giving him morphine and this time applying a mustard plaster, so that he also suffered from a "great blister." He drew cartoons of himself seated miserably in a chair, a blanket over his head to ward off chills. In another he was walking bent almost double because of "a blister as big as a 25 foot front house lot on my 'stummick' that resembles a prairie fire," he wrote. He said that the drawings had "cheered Goosie up a little" and she was smiling.

On April 16, the *Farragut* went to the foundry. Saint-Gaudens had been working on the plaster cast, refining, improving it. New molds would now be made, bedded in sand and locked in wooden forms. Preparation was so slow and careful that nearly a month went by before "the body of *Farragut*" was ready to be cast. Augusta went with her husband to watch the process.[5]

The alloy of copper and tin known as bronze was mixed in different proportions to give differences in color and Saint-Gaudens had already checked with the foreman at the foundry to get a color he liked. The casting of the *Farragut* was to cost $1200 and Gus had chosen the best firm in Paris, whose work he had seen and admired. There was no light in the great stone building save the glare of the furnaces. Men wore leather aprons and heavy gauntlets made of carpet on their hands and forearms, strips of carpet lashed over their legs. Thick, cloth-visored caps were pulled over their heads and silence was the rule.

A big crucible was set in glowing coals. A man stirred the metal and at a signal the stirring stopped and the head founder stepped forward, leaned over the glowing furnace to look at the white-hot metal. The time was right. With tongs, lifting with both hands, he set the crucible on the earthern floor for a moment. Two men stepped forward with their carrying bar. They lifted in perfect unison, carried the crucible to the waiting mold and poured "a strong, even stream of liquid fire."

Almost instantly, the air was filled with smoke and sparks. The mold was allowed to overflow and a man with a poker knocked off the extra metal before it hardened. Few people were allowed to watch a bronze casting in a foundry because the slightest distraction might make the men pour badly. A crucible might also break, spreading liquid metal on the floor. "It was quite exciting," Gussie said, putting it mildly. She was surprised that the actual bronze casting took so short a time.

A month later, the lower half of the *Farragut* was ready for casting, but now there was disaster. The molds were not properly locked into their sand-lined forms, and "on account of a piece of forgetfulness on the part of three of the men, the thing was a failure and the mold destroyed. The bronze was superb but it all ran through."

Sick at heart, Saint-Gaudens went home at half past two that Saturday afternoon and told his wife that the founder "could not get another mold done before the end of July."

Gussie was frightened. A short time previously, she had written her mother that she was expecting a child. She had wanted to have a family someday but she had been willing to wait. Then, much to her surprise, she had "gotten into this fix," as she put it to her mother. Vague plans for coming home suddenly became settled decisions. Although Mother was not to tell anyone, she and Gus would be home in June — Gussie to visit her parents "if you will have me," Gus to look for a studio and living quarters in New York.

But now there was this delay. You could explain matters to the Farragut Committee, but the course of nature in producing an infant was impervious to argument. The child would not be put off and Gussie was determined to be at her parents' home with the doctor on call when the baby came. Gus agreed with her. He had missed being born in the United States by a few months and he wanted his child to be a native American. Should he go home with her then, and return to superintend the finishing and crating of the *Farragut,* plus the shipping of other work, thereby "losing a month's time, making three trips across the Atlantic and spending $200 extra"? — this last being Gussie's worry, not his. Or should Louis go home with Augusta? But Louis had been working for his brother, "modeling beautifully" while attending the École des Beaux-Arts part of that time. Gus needed him. Should they cable Mrs. Homer or Genie to come to take Gussie home? What a pity that Genie had already left. It never occurred to them that Gussie could travel alone. "I never spent a more unhappy afternoon," she said, "for all the alternatives seemed so bad."

That evening they went together to the bronze founder — a middle-aged man and probably the father of children. He understood, he said, perhaps remembering his own state of mind over the coming of his first child. He would "have the statue done and ready for Mr. Saint-Gaudens to see it" on the 9th of July.

Sunday morning came and Gus and Gussie went to see Dr. Shiff. He said it would do Gussie no harm to cross the ocean during the first two weeks of the seventh month. "The seventh month cannot begin until the 17th of July, probably a week or so later," Gussie told her mother.

She wanted to know what she should buy in Paris and bring home "for the little Saint."

While the molders were at work and with considerable hesitation over the hundred-dollar extra cost, Saint-Gaudens decided to exhibit a plaster cast of his *Farragut* at the Paris Salon of 1880. He specified that it must be placed "at the height of ten feet, as it was modeled," and that light must come from above, since it was designed for the open air. When he went to the Salon to see it, he found it "on a pedestal not over two feet high" and hidden away under the shadow of a balcony while, as Gussie put it, "the whole center of the building was taken up by those who have already had medals." He managed to get his statue raised to five feet, "after days of trying but the light came from the side . . . and the effect wholly changed, much to his disadvantage." Gus was bitterly disappointed but not surprised that the *Farragut* received only an honorable mention.

But Saint-Gaudens also sent a collection of his portrait medallions, getting up at half past three in the morning to finish his medallion of Bastien-Lepage. This young French artist was about to leap into fame with his painting of *Joan of Arc Listening to Voices.* The Bastien-Lepage medallion was one of the most attractive of the Saint-Gaudens portraits and Gus received another honorable mention for his medallion exhibit.

A collection of Saint-Gaudens bas-relief portrait medallions was shown in New York and London, and about two years later, Bastien-Lepage wrote in French to Augustus to tell him that "la Princess de Galles" had seen his work at the Grosvenor Gallery and was much impressed. "She asked your name and wants to meet you and to possess some such jewel as those medallions which you have shown." He said he hoped that Saint-Gaudens could profit by "this incident," but Gus never bothered to cultivate Alexandra, Princess of Wales.

Gus wrote Mr. Homer, happy to tell the news of his honorable mentions and of orders for medallions. He was hard at work on a small model for the Robert Richard Randall statue, the other large commission he had received just before leaving New York — and on the Morgan angels, a commission already causing more trouble than it was worth.

During those last weeks in Paris, Augusta went shopping with money sent her by her father. She was already imagining a New York apartment, and bought a "large, handsome Japanese rug . . . thick and soft . . . and big enough to cover the greater part of a bedroom." She and Gus both fell in love with "a Japanese table . . . curiously lacquered . . . with bamboo legs that come out so it can be easily packed. It was at the Great Exposition," but they "got it at quite a bargain because of a few insignificant scratches."

The bronze founder was better than his word. The second pouring was a success; the huge statue was crated and sent to New York in time for Gus and Gussie to sail from Le Havre on the 3rd of July. They had been Parisians for three years — in many ways the happiest years of their lives.

11

NEW YORK STUDIOS

THERE was a joyous welcome for Gus and Gussie at Number 59 Winthrop Street, Roxbury. Mrs. Homer and Genie fussed over Gussie because of her so-called interesting condition, bringing her cushions to lean on and asking her every few minutes how she felt — or so it seemed to Gus. Business talks with his father-in-law were all to the good, but after a few days Gus left for Albany with a sense of escape.

Richardson still felt sure that there was a big commission for Saint-Gaudens in decorating the interior of the New York Statehouse, and at first Gus wrote that his trip was successful. He would do designs in mosaic, surrounded by borders of fruit and flowers in bas-relief — not that he liked such work, but it would pay well. When he realized that he was being given a runaround by politicians who had no intention of giving him anything, he managed to make it sound funny in letters to Gussie.[1] And when his old friend Will Low got the job, he was genuinely pleased. He set out for New York, sure that opportunity awaited him in his own city.

Louis had come home with Gus, as planned. Their father was still living over the grocery store on Fourth Avenue, but their brother Andrew was there now with his wife and little daughter Marie. There was no room for Gus and Louis, so they moved into William Bunce's studio. This was fair enough, since Bunce had lived in the Saint-Gaudens studio in Paris at the time when Stanford White lived there too.[2] Bunce was the painter, in love with Venice, who worked on-the-spot sketches into easel pictures full of sky and water effects, with yellow the dominant color. He used too much yellow, in the opinion of Saint-Gaudens and Stanford White, so one day they sent Bunce on an errand and then wiped the yellow paint from his picture, getting it all over their clothes. It seems possible that they might have been sampling a little of that Saint-Gaudens wine from Southern France, but when they arrived at the apartment late to dinner they told Gussie that Bunce had just been "having a yellow day."

Bunce, a gentle person, made no protest, but now he had his revenge. His paintings were immensely popular. He had a fine studio, welcomed Gus and Louis with open arms, eager to befriend his friends. There was already one cot in the studio, so Gus got hold of another and Louis wrote to Gussie, asking her to send him his gray blanket. Bunce was a bachelor and so it might seem as if the three young men had returned to carefree student days. But New York was not Paris and what Gus really wanted to return to was an apartment of his own — and Augusta.

The hustle and noise of New York bothered him at first. The elevated railroad had now been built as far as the Harlem River, steam engines in the air a sight to see. High-wheeled bicycles competed with horsecars, private carriages and livery hacks.[3] Young bloods took pride in tooling a coach-and-four through Central Park while the employees of breweries displayed just as much skill, driving six pairs of horses over the cobblestones, downtown. There was only one studio building. It was on West Tenth Street and was designed by Richard Morris Hunt. La Farge had his quarters there and at one time so did a cousin of Gussie's, Winslow Homer. But in 1880 there was no space in it for rent. Gus saw a place nearby with two little bedrooms attached, where Gussie could come to live with him "quite respectably" before their child was born. Gussie wanted to do it, but her mother said it wouldn't be "wise."

Gussie was homesick at home — a state of mind her mother could never understand. Gus and Louis were not eating properly, Gussie felt sure, and she thought they ought to arrange to take regular meals with their father, paying board of course. Her French father-in-law always had "good things to eat," she wrote. And how about a walking trip in the White Mountains for Gus and Stanford White? They ought not to stay in the city all through the hot summer.

Sitting in the armchair her mother had placed in the bay window for her, Gussie looked out on Winthrop Street. "Keep your head cool," she wrote. "Just this minute I see two gentlemen going by with umbrellas for the sun, so see that you have your *high* hat and an umbrella too."

Augusta's mother reminded her that after the baby came, she would have no "strength" — a favorite word with Mrs. Homer. Gussie began to assume that she would be practically an invalid for months, but by the middle of August she began to hope that Gus would find an apartment. "Of course we shall want nothing before January, if I am well enough to do light housekeeping then," she wrote. "When I do go in January there will be a nurse and baby in train. How you will groan at the number of packages! You will count us all over — four live packages including yourself, carpet bags, bundles, trunks, shawl straps, and you will say.'come on!' and start off with the *umbrella* in your hand and we will follow with all the packages including baby. . . . Then, when you get us on the train, you will count us all over and forget how many you ought to have, then the conductor will come and you will present him with one ticket for the crowd and wonder why he wants more. Then the arrival in New York. You will send the nurse by District Telegraph, the baby by telephone and me by Elevated R.R., then you will slowly plod along on foot, wondering how you, the great American sculptor, could have gotten yourself in such a scrape."

Gus finally found a studio on the corner of Fifty-seventh Street and Sixth Avenue. It was in a new apartment house all of seven stories high, called the Sherwood Building, and he took the whole of the seventh floor. All around were empty lots, some with squatters' huts, but people like Stanford White, with wild ideas about the future of New York, said that someday upper Fifth Avenue would be fashionable and Fifty-seventh Street quite elegant. Gus agreed. He signed a lease to run from the 1st of September, 1880, to May 1, 1881, for $58.52 a month. The first job was to enlarge the bas-relief figures for the *Farragut* pedestal and he got himself a model to sit for Loyalty and Courage. If Gussie teased him about his future role as father of a family, he got right back at her with equally affectionate good humor. "Did I ever tell you what a lot of handsome female models there are here?" he asked. "A great many more than in Paris and all of them have that rare thing — fine breasts."

Gussie remained unperturbed. "When you come next time I am afraid you won't be able to put your arm around me for I am growing very important I can tell you. A fish wife is nothing to me," she wrote. She had been anxious because she felt no signs of life, but in August she knew that her child was very much alive and she called him "Kickey." "I have commenced some little clothes for Kickey and I enjoy working on them very much. You have no idea how much I love the little thing — and my husband," she wrote, about a month before her baby was born.

Dr. Howard Arthur Nichols, her sister Lizzie's husband, was Gussie's doctor, seemingly intent on making a naturally thin girl produce as large an infant as possible. Gussie was required to drink pale ale at bedtime, but the first time she tried it she declared that she dreamed of snakes. They let her change to half a bottle of lager instead.

Gus proposed partitioning off a part of his studio in the Sherwood Building to make two rooms to live in, and Gussie said the idea was "splendid." There was a restaurant on the ground floor and she wanted Gus to ask what they would charge for furnishing two people and a servant with two meals a day; "breakfast of meat, oatmeal, coffee or cocoa or tea and bread and butter — dinner of soup, meat, two vegetables and some kind of desert." Gus was to get prices by the week and by the month and find out if it would cost too much to have their meals served upstairs in their own rooms.

Remembering Paris, Gussie asked if there were some hotel nearby where they might get a bedroom and parlor, as an alternative to living in the Sherwood Building. They might hire a nurse for the baby "by the month."

But hotels were yet to be built so far uptown as Fifty-seventh Street and when they finally appeared they would be expensive. Grand Army Plaza at the foot of Central Park would be the site of the first Plaza Hotel building, a rough brownstone semifortified chateau with towers. "Marble Row" was in process of construction, the first white marble French-style chateau already gleaming like a new false tooth among dingy brick and brownstone on Fifth Avenue. It served successfully as a decoy for a rich man's housing project.

Saint-Gaudens must have found prices high, even in the modest Sherwood Building restaurant. For a while he and Gussie played with the idea of building themselves a house and studio on one of the vacant lots in the neighborhood. Stanford White would have been delighted to design it. The Chapins, friends of Gussie's who had seen much of her in Paris, built a house on Fifty-seventh Street and Gus went to see it.

"Close to the studio, . . . it is very nicely and sensibly arranged, for that matter the best of the regular block houses I have ever seen," Gus reported. "It's Mr. Chapin's own plan. The outside is horrible, particularly in these days of pretty good architecture but Mrs. C. thinks it's very good."

Gus and Gussie consulted Thomas J. Homer and Gussie wrote out her father's advice. "He says the way would be when you have decided exactly what you want, for you and Mr. White to go to a builder, show him what a simple thing we want, how plainly we want it done, no ornamentation, no wall papers etc. and then offer him a certain percent on his money. Father thought 8 percent would be about right but since we want a studio, we might have to offer 10 percent on the builder's money — that to include taxes. Father knows a great deal about such things. . . . Uncle Sidney's estate owns a great deal of real estate and he has the management of it. He thinks you are right in thinking you could get something for $1500 a year or less." It was an alluring dream and Gus and Gussie enjoyed it — while it lasted.

Meanwhile, Saint-Gaudens was living on hopes instead of cash, as usual. John J. Cisco made one more typical move. He told Saint-Gaudens that the money due on completion of the *Farragut* would not be paid until the statue was in place and unveiled. Unveiling was put off till spring and Gus had to explain matters to his wife. "It will take two weeks to build the foundation — four weeks must be given it to settle before putting the monument on it and two weeks more" to set up the carved pedestal, "bringing us up to the end of December" — not a good month for unveiling.

The Park Department caused further delay. They said that the Farragut pedestal, as designed, would encroach an inch or so on legal sidewalk space. Mrs. Farragut told Saint-Gaudens that she thought all the delays had been contrived so that inauguration might take place after the election and Gus suspected that she was right.

Gussie asked her father to look over the Farragut contract and Mr. Homer found that Cisco had no right to withhold payment, but former General Dix, who had always been Saint-Gaudens' friend and could have brought pressure on Cisco, had recently died. Ex-Governor Morgan was angry because the Morgan family tomb was not done yet, and refused to help. "Cisco might hang on to the money for the next ten years," Gussie thought despairingly, and meanwhile her husband had to pay storage and insurance on the completed *Farragut*. They must put off their dream of building a studio apartment even if they could find a builder to put up the money.

But in the midst of gloom, the Fifty-seventh Street studio became a scene of triumph. La Farge told Saint-Gaudens that Cornelius Vanderbilt II was going to need some decorations for his new house, now being built at Fifty-eighth Street and Fifth Avenue, opposite the future Plaza Hotel. Estimates for the work Saint-Gaudens might do were "between 16,000 and 20,000 dollars," Gus told Augusta. Gus began to wait anxiously for George B. Post, the architect, to "call on Mr. Vanderbilt and make the offer."

Never dating a letter but writing during the autumn of 1880, "Mr. Vanderbilt called this morning with Mr. Post," Gus reported at last. "We talked about what I suggested to be done with his hall, he seemed pleased and is to call again shortly as he has but little time left. He [Vanderbilt] is a man of about 30 and very simple and inconspicuous."

Vanderbilt and his architect departed, but La Farge stayed on with Saint-Gaudens until very late that night. "The studio is a cheerful place, and with White and La Farge and Louis and a little whiskey mixed in, we had a good time," Gus said. The celebration seems to have been a trifle premature, but for once optimism was justified. Vanderbilt came across with a commission for all the carving for his great entrance hall. Saint-Gaudens was to model two caryatids to support an enormous mantel shelf and design the mosaic that went over it.[4] He was not expected to do actual stone and wood carving himself, but Mr. Post would find artisans, most of them Italian, whose work Gus was to superintend. What really pleased him, however, was the modeling of Vanderbilt family portraits to go in some of the wall panels. The subjects were young Cornelius and George Vanderbilt, Gertrude Vanderbilt, William Vanderbilt and Cornelius Vanderbilt I. The child Gertrude, later Mrs. Harry Paine Whitney, would be one of the most appealing of Saint-Gaudens' portraits. Gus and his brother Louis were also to work with Mr. La Farge on models for the superb ceiling that La Farge had designed for the main dining room.

On September 23, 1880, "Don't worry about my being blue," Augusta wrote her husband. "I don't indulge in such nonsense now-a-days and am feeling well, bright and happy — as handsome as life and twice as large." She looked out of the sunny guest-room window and saw a neighbor wheeling his baby in a carriage. "I wonder how it will look," she said, "to see the 'Old Sculp' wheeling the Young Sculp." The following day, September 28, Augusta had a son.

Genie had been given the job of telegraphing to her brother-in-law when the baby arrived. She had already devised a code. If the baby should be a boy, they were going to name him Henry, in honor of Dr. Henry Shiff who had been such a friend to Gus in Rome and to both Gus and Gussie in Paris. So Genie was going to telegraph, "Long life, Prince Hal, Queen Mother doing well."

But Genie got excited, although she said afterwards that the telegraph operator mixed up the message. Augustus got a telegram saying that he had a "little Queen daughter" and took the next train for Boston, thinking that he was going to see his baby girl. There was great rejoicing in any case, but somehow the name Henry didn't seem to fit the baby now that he had arrived.

Back in New York again, Gus addressed Gussie as "Well, ole Kotz" and wondered whether she were well enough to read his letter. He thought someone would probably read it to her — "so I won't tell you what a darling little hen you are and what a sweet honeysuckle and what a May Rose . . . ," he said. "I won't send you a Pullman car full of kisses nor a Sound Steamer full of hugs. No — No!"

Gus had had a letter from Gussie's mother, to which he referred. "I hear you are getting along well and have turned into a Provision store for the supply of Napoleon Bonaparte. See here, I want that child *named something* if it is only 'fried potatoes.'" And how did Gussie "like the role of being a figure of 'Abundance' or 'Charity' a la Dubois?" Signing himself "Pater" with his own profile caricature, Gus wanted to know if the baby was "as ugly as ever? Is his nose as big and his hair as black?"

Augusta assured her husband that the baby was as *pretty* as ever and getting prettier every day — but his name still remained in question. So Gus called the baby Julius Caesar and asked if he were President yet. He was preparing "three boards" of his bronze medallions for the "Boston Exhibit," which would provide him with a good excuse to come to Boston again to see Gussie and his boy.

After the "Boston Exhibit" was over, the Museum of Fine Arts in Boston asked Saint-Gaudens for a copy of the medallion of Rodman de Kay Gilder for their permanent collection. This had been done in Paris when the little boy was two years old. The Homer family was jubilant and Gus himself admitted that he was "sot up" about it. Since the museum directors had asked him to put a price on it, he wondered how much to charge.

"At first we all thought the Museum should pay a hundred dollars," Gussie wrote. Then the Homer family got to thinking about the honor of having a Saint-Gaudens medallion in that astounding brick and marble edifice in Copley Square. What if the trustees wouldn't pay that much? Gus had better charge only fifty dollars.

Gussie had not lost her habit of thrift, however. "My darling Old Kotz," Gus wrote her, "I was glad to get your postal card. What have I done with the 20 dollars? Well, now really I don't know, all I can recollect is plenty of ice-cream, oysters on the half shell, minstrel shows and puddin' for a couple of days." But at the end of his letter he stopped teasing her. "It was a fib; the ice-cream, the oysters. . . I didn't use the 20 dollar gold piece — the identical piece is in my pocketbook where I placed it the day you gave it to me." Gus drew a big grin on the profile cartoon of "Pater, his mark."

Almost a full month after her baby was born, Dr. Nichols, or "Arthur," as she more often called him, let Gussie get out of bed for the first time. "It did feel so good to put my feet on the floor again," she said. She was allowed to walk across the room with the help of a nurse but not to sit in the rocking chair. Another month went by and Gussie wrote, "I have my hair waved as you like it. I have my pretty wrapper on and I am going downstairs to dinner." By the middle of December she was at last allowed to go out of the house and to lead the life of a normal, healthy young woman.

But in December, Augusta's father caught cold. She went to his office to do some work for him, and on December 19, he was "still sick in bed and can talk very little with me on account of my deafness," she wrote sadly. Mr. Homer sent a message to Gus. "I have a secretary now," he was able just to whisper.

"I am doing all his trustee business for him," Augusta explained. "Yesterday I met his co-trustees, Warren Emerson and Homer Pierce, at Father's office to sign checks etc. . . ." Next day she went again to her father's office, "to meet a lot of people," and she went "to the bank for checks. It makes me feel badly to see poor father. Arthur thinks he will be better before long but he will have to be careful all winter. . . . When he gets better I will talk with him" about the Morgan contract. Gus had asked advice and Mr. Homer said the contract was "a simple one," but that Gus ought to finish up the Morgan job.

On December 21, "Father's symptoms have changed," Augusta wrote, "and now he has pneumonia. We have a nurse. . . . At present we need not feel seriously alarmed about him." Flaxseed poultices had been prescribed and Augusta was making them for the nurse to put on her father's chest to relieve congestion. "The house is pretty sad, so don't come, will you, darling," she wrote. "My own dear husband, take good care of yourself. There seems to be so much sickness everywhere."

Thomas J. Homer died on Christmas night, December 25, 1880. He was sixty-seven years old and seems never to have experienced a previous serious illness. Augusta's grief was scarcely greater than that of her husband, who also dearly loved her father. Neither of them realized all his loss meant to them at first, for both Gus and Gussie had depended on him to fight their battles, to guide them with his good judgment and to stand behind them in all times of trouble.

Actually, Augusta had more natural business ability than either of her two brothers, or so it would seem. But it never occurred to anyone to teach her anything beyond mere procedures concerning her annuity. The other trustees gave her no help — a woman was not supposed to understand finances. Having no one to reassure her, Gussie fell back on her childhood training in rigid economy. She could save money but she was always afraid of spending it.

The baby was named Homer, in memory of Augusta's father, with Shiff for his middle name. On January 2, 1881, Gussie wrote her husband, "My plan is to go [to New York] the latter part of next week. The day I start, I shall send you a telegram so that you may secure a room definitely. . . . Be sure the room you get for us is warm and sunny and see about milk for the baby in time." Gussie was especially anxious about milk — she thought it must always come from the same cow or the baby would have the dread cholera infantum, fatal to so many infants.[5] She did not say just how Gus was to arrange for a special cow, but he would surely try to do his best.

On the 24th of February, Henry Hobson Richardson summoned Saint-Gaudens to Boston. He addressed his letter to the Sherwood Building, for Gus had found no better place. "I have arranged about the Shaw Monument," Richardson wrote. "When can you come on to see the committee, Messrs. Atkinson, Lee and Forbes?" Here was the big commission that Saint-Gaudens needed. All the wood carvings in baronial mansions would not build his reputation the way a public monument would, in this age of admiration for statues in the park. The job in question was a memorial to Colonel Robert Gould Shaw, the young Bostonian who died at the head of his Negro regiment that he had recruited, during the Civil War. Fifteen thousand dollars was the sum offered for the sculptor's services, and at the time, this seemed not only adequate but magnificent.

Looking back on these days, Saint-Gaudens wrote of himself in his usual slightly sardonic vein. "I, like most sculptors at the beginning of their careers, felt that by hook or by crook I must do an equestrian statue and that here was my opportunity." He drew a handsome pen-and-ink sketch of a hatless young officer, sword in hand, gazing at the spectator with a commanding air and reining in a pawing steed with beautifully arched neck. Behind the equestrian was a high masonry screen bearing a long inscription, plus an ornamental tree. This screen was the only part of the design which would identify it with the actual *Shaw Memorial* when it was completed.

When Gus finally met the committee, he learned that the Shaw family "objected" to his sketch. The young colonel had not been a great commander and only men of the highest rank should be so honored as to sit high in the air in bronze on a bronze horse. It would be "pretentious." Saint-Gaudens was very much cast down, but if the Shaw family thought he had given up his idea of an equestrian, they were wrong. "I fell upon the plan of associating Colonel Shaw directly with his troops," Gus said. He filled the great semicircular screen not with an inscription but with marching men, wonderfully modeled in low relief, middle relief and high relief. Young Shaw on horseback was to be almost in the round, looking forward over the heads of his men — riding to his fate.

The contract was not actually signed until 1884 and Saint-Gaudens said he would get the work done in two years. He now took a new studio at Number 148 West Thirty-sixth Street. It was a low building, formerly a painters' supply shed and at some time or other a stable. Gus practically rebuilt it, as one thing led to another and he partitioned off two small rooms, put in a new floor and added toilet facilities. He had a huge skylight cut, a sort of bench built around the walls of the big room, the whole place painted white. The "great white studio," people called it, and it was to be his headquarters for the next fifteen years. He set up the *Shaw,* which grew in conception and in actual dimensions until it filled the whole end of the studio and was finished not in two years, but in thirteen. He could have done a small relief panel such as the Shaws expected, for the sum of money promised and in the time required, but the dream of what he wanted it to be possessed him. He had to set it aside again and again for work that would bring in ready money. The *Shaw* became "a labor of love."

On the 26th of May, 1881, the Admiral Farragut statue was at last in place in Madison Square. "A day as calm and serene as Farragut himself saw the statue of the great commander unveiled," said the New York *Herald.* "The attending circumstances were brilliant, the

Preliminary sketch of the SHAW MEMORIAL (Courtesy of the Board of Trustees of Dartmouth College)

crowd great, the stands filled with the best citizens of the Metropolis. . . .

"A great quantity of camp stools and park benches were ranged about the statue in the northwest corner of the square and a cordon of Park Police preserved this space for those who had been favored with invitations. The statue was veiled with flags of the United States and the State of New York. A little to the left and in front of it was the speaker's stand while still farther to the left was another stand for especially invited guests. On the opposite side of Fifth Avenue was erected the last and largest stand capable of seating nearly a thousand people. Bunting greeted the eye in every direction. . . .

"There could not have been less than ten thousand people in the vicinity of the statue during the ceremonies, without estimating the hundreds of ladies and gentlemen who viewed the proceedings from the windows of the Brunswick and Delmonico's and other neighboring buildings."

On the guest stand were John J. Cisco and Joseph H. Choate, chief speaker, along with four generals, five admirals, two commanders and the park commissioner. On another stand were Mrs. Farragut and her son, Loyall Farragut. The sculptor was not mentioned!

"Armed marines and other sailors" were applauded as they marched in the parade, because Tunis was in the news. The band of the First Artillery of the United States Army played lustily; the "howitzer battery" from the navy yard fired a salute. After many speeches, Admiral Melancton Smith "pulled down the flags surrounding the statue"; the Navy Jack was pulled up a staff on the speakers' stand. "Cheer after cheer went up from the crowd as they looked upon the splendid bronze, where Admiral Farragut stood above them as if in life, as if he could hear their plaudits and the notes of 'Columbia the Gem of the Ocean' as they rang through the leafy square and the booming of the cannon which began at that moment to fire seventeen guns — the Admiral's salute."

One would suppose that John J. Cisco or perhaps William R. Grace, the newly elected mayor of New York, had created the statue. But the New York *Herald* had an early-rising reporter whose story, without a by-line, appeared on May 26. "As the sun rose at half past four, yesterday, the sculptor, Augustus Saint-Gaudens, drew off the coverings that concealed his heroic bronze statue of David Glasgow Farragut, the first American Admiral, and saw for the first time on its

The FARRAGUT, *Madison Square, New York City (Frick Art Reference Library)*

pedestal, to which the stone-cutters were putting the finishing touches, the work which will do much to make him famous. At seven o'clock, after photographs had been taken, — it was again shrouded until the hour of its unveiling in the afternoon. Then the monument took its place in the very front rank of the few fine ones in the country. . . . Farragut stands thoroughly dominating the magnificent stone pedestal . . . as if on board his ship in time of action. The pose is remarkable for its naturalness, its supreme quality of just arrested motion. . . .

"The treatment we believe seen for the first time in this statue, though used in the works of the Renaissance, is the light gilding of all that is gold or gilt in the uniform, sword and belt. . . . This realism is remarkably effective and by no means obtrusive, the slight gold coloring telling finely in its picturesque contrast to the deep, rich natural tone of the bronze. . . ."

Both Saint-Gaudens and Augusta must have been there — somewhere in the crowd, to see "our *Farragut*," as Gussie once called the statue. She must have been thrilled as the sun glinted on the golden sword and the braid she had worked so hard to perfect. Most certainly, she and Gus were at the Gilders' at a dinner party in honor of the success of the *Farragut*. The Gilders had been in Paris while the *Farragut* was being modeled and Gilder always proudly claimed that *he* had posed for Farragut's legs. "Gee Gee de Saint Gee" was Gilder's nickname for Saint-Gaudens, and he was having an article written about him for the *Century* magazine.

It was around midnight when the Gilder party broke up. Gus and Gussie walked up Fifth Avenue with William Webster Ellsworth, a fellow guest and secretary of the Century Company. They came to Madison Square and "as we approached the statue, we saw an old man standing in front of it. I think his hat was off," Ellsworth said.

"Why, it's Father," Saint-Gaudens exclaimed, going over to the man. "What are you doing here at this time of night?"

"Oh, you mind your own business! Haven't I a right to be here?" Bernard Saint-Gaudens said in a gruff voice.

They "understood and left the old man standing there in the moonlight."[6]

12

SUMMER IN NEW YORK

IN 1877, just before his marriage, Saint-Gaudens had been proud to receive his second commission for a public statue in a park. This was for a Robert Richard Randall, to overlook the water from Sailor's Snug Harbor on Staten Island. But the *Farragut* crowded Randall out of the sculptor's mind. Then, just before leaving Paris, Gus managed to model a four-foot figure of Randall, merchant privateersman. He had it cast in plaster and sent to New York.

At the Fifty-seventh Street studio, after collecting commissions through La Farge with which to pay the rent, and after finishing the *Farragut*, Gus set up his *Randall*. He would have it ready for enlargement in two weeks (with another payment due him), he felt sure. But somehow, the costume he had devised for Randall didn't look right. The Homer family and their friends connected with the Charlestown Navy Yard had searched old records for him. Genie had sent sketches to Paris, indicating what a privateersman at the time of the American Revolution might have worn aboard ship. Now Gus remembered some illustrations he had seen in magazines in New York. He had admired the good drawing. Most of the subjects were either pirates or privateersmen and the illustrator's name was Howard Pyle. Gus wrote to him, asking how he could get hold of a costume.

Five years younger than Saint-Gaudens, a Quaker who had studied art in spite of family opposition, Howard Pyle was just beginning to succeed after a hard struggle. *The Wreck in the Offing*, a double-page spread in *Harper's Weekly* in 1878, had proved a turning point in his favor. The two men were destined to be friends, but mainly by correspondence, because Pyle hated New York as much as Saint-Gaudens loved it, and he was now living in Wilmington, Delaware.

"After considerable difficulty I have gathered together material for having a costume made up for myself," Pyle wrote, "but as I am using it at present I cannot send it to you as I would be glad to do." He enclosed what he called a crude sketch — actually a delightful pen-and-ink drawing. Pyle suggested that Saint-Gaudens could buy "a rough striped jersey . . . in any gentlemen's furnishing store." And "as to head-gear, a style very commonly worn, especially by the American sailor, was the Mediterranean skull-cap, striped or plain colors." Saint-Gaudens "could ask for a French nightcap in any furnishing store."

Gus sent Pyle a sketch of his *Randall* and Pyle replied, "I was not aware that you had any special merchant in mind. The merchant captain *did* most probably wear baggy trousers." Captain Marryat had written that "a certain captain's loose trousers were split in a gale of wind." Pyle said he would be happy to have Saint-Gaudens use any of his illustrations but that "what they lacked in quality may be made up in quantity like New Jersey champagne."

Gus continued to find it difficult to visualize Randall, a man who was not only a successful privateer but who gave his large farm, located just above the present-day Washington Square, to aged sailors and the orphans of sailors. Would this man, whose father also had been a sea captain and shipowner, dress like a city merchant or like a seaman? Gus changed his model to his satisfaction at last and hired a vacant machine shop at 125th Street and Eighth Avenue, in which to have it enlarged. He put in "a big north light" at his own expense and hired "two of the most experienced men to enlarge it." Then Gus went about his other business, trusting these men to measure carefully, point after point, setting the metal spikes in the huge mass of clay to correspond exactly with the points in the small model. Six months went by. Then Gus went to look at the finished figure and found it hopelessly wrong. The top half was larger, in proportion, than the lower half. "The work was pulled down, the year's rent paid and a thousand dollars lost," Louis Saint-Gaudens said later. Gus began all over again in the Thirty-sixth Street studio.

When the Randall commission was first awarded, Augusta spoke of "making money" on it. She visualized a married life similar to that of her parents, with savings, the result of careful economy, put into conservative stocks and bonds to provide for a secure old age. Now, as the *Randall* continued to cost money, she began to hope only to break even. The *Robert Richard Randall* was completed at last in 1884.[1]

Gus and Gussie found an apartment, downtown at 22 Washington

The ROBERT RICHARD RANDALL (*The Sailors' Snug Harbor, Staten Island, New York*)

Place. Their friends the Gilders lived on Union Square, eight blocks north, and Helena described the Gilder living room. There were "great shelves for casts and books and nails for everything." The Gilders had been given a hammock for a wedding present, which was slung "across one corner of the room with a beautiful leopard skin below it." Helena Gilder continued to paint, stopping only briefly when each of her seven children arrived. Gussie had no hammock at 22 Washington Place, but she had red cushions in a bamboo chair. Two tapestries and the gold lacquer table reminded her of her Paris rooms, but she reserved no place for easel and paints. Gussie's New York apartment looked like the home of an artistic woman but not that of a woman artist. While living with her parents, she had proposed entering a contest for a design for a Christmas card, in the hope of winning a hundred dollars. Apparently nothing came of this and now she devoted herself entirely to the infant Homer. She had put away her paints forever. Her husband's Thirty-sixth Street studio was too far away for her to visit often and she was never again to say "our statue" of any of his work, as she had of the *Farragut.*

While in Roxbury, Gussie had bought a desk, for which the dealer tried to charge five instead of four dollars as agreed upon. She made him stand by his bargain. Her mother gave her an "old fashioned high-post bedstead" out of the Winthrop Street attic. It had belonged to Gussie's grandfather, "was enormous," with four solid-mahogany posts, the footposts carved. Gussie made a cover for it out of "plush."

Augustus Saint-Gaudens had been a New Yorker when Washington Square was Washington Parade Ground. The Seventh Regiment drilled there, which would have been a fine sight for a small boy — if he had been allowed to venture so far uptown. The neo-Gothic crenelated building between Waverly Place and Washington Place was still the home of the University of New York and next to it, on the Square, was the red-brick and stone Reformed Dutch Church, equally Gothic and battlemented. A few Greek Revival town houses, with pleasant front yards and small backyard gardens, faced the Square, but Stanford White had yet to design the Washington Arch, an ornament for a gracious residential section. The apartment where Gus, Gussie and Homer were to live for the next eleven years was higher than most neighboring buildings. They were "seven flights up,[2] a hard climb," and of course there was no elevator, but the rooms were sunny and there was a view.[3] Washington Square was a safe place for a little boy to play.

Portrait medallion of Homer Saint-Gaudens, aged seventeen months, by his father (Courtesy of the Board of Trustees of Dartmouth College)

Not that Gussie and Homer would ever be in New York in summer. Grandmother Homer's big house, her orchard, vegetable garden and large lawn, made Roxbury seem much more desirable. On July 1, 1881, Gussie, the nursemaid Mary and Homer had left Roxbury for the Pleasant Beach House, Cohasset, reached by stagecoach. They had gone to stay there three days, but two weeks passed. "We went so long without troubles," Gussie wrote her mother, "and now our turn has come." At Roxbury was her sister Lizzie Nichols, with three little girls, Rose, Marion and Margaret. Their only brother, Sidney, had died July 6, 1881, at the age of six. Sidney's illness was diagnosed as diphtheria, but the other children and Lizzie had not been ill. They had been visiting at Rye Beach, New Hampshire, at the house of Mary Abbey Jenness, and "the water in her well became polluted."

Saint-Gaudens was not the only man left alone in New York in summer. Will Low was among the others. "During the summers when our women folk had sought the sea or the mountains and the men were left in town, there were few corners of the city where we did not penetrate," he said, writing of himself and Gus, whom he referred to as "our greatest sculptor."

"These were the palmy days when Harrigan and Hart were producing 'The Mulligan Guards' Ball' and 'Squatter Sovereignty.'" It did not take much penetrating of corners to find the Theatre Comique where Harrigan and Hart produced their shows — it was on Broadway, facing one end of Washington Place. Irish "greenhorns" were the butt of all the jokes; Irish actors played their parts to the hilt and had everyone roaring over the slapstick comedy. The Irish themselves were smart enough not to be insulted, but to capitalize on the buffoonery.

Among his friends back at the studio, Gus loved to put on a scene of his own with pantomime, fully as funny as anything at Harrigan and Hart's. It was "the winning charm of the Celt" plus "the Latin-exuberance of Provence . . . that drew him many friends," said Will Low, feeling called upon to explain!

The studio concerts began in 1882 and no one who heard them ever forgot them. It all started, Gus said, because Joseph Wells, Francis Lathrop and he discovered good music at "a little beer saloon opposite Washington Place on Broadway." Joseph M. Wells was a brilliant but temperamental designer at McKim, Mead and White. Francis Lathrop was a painter whom Gus first met in Boston when both of them were working on Trinity Church.[4]

There was music on the violin by a bald-headed man who played with feeling, on the clarinet by his son, who blew without any. A third performer banged away on a piano. What struck Gus and his friends was that every now and then this trio played better music than the sort of thing usually heard in a beer saloon. Since the place was closed on Sundays, Gus asked the three performers to come uptown to the Thirty-sixth Street studio and give a concert. The musicians were only too glad to earn a little extra money. Gus invited sundry artists and writers, whose wives were away, and everybody chipped in on expenses.

But Wells was a perfectionist whose second gift was music, and he thought they could do better with the entertainment. The next year he negotiated with the "Standard Quartette" consisting of men from the Philharmonic Society, directed by Theodore Thomas. Thomas had brought the Philharmonic to "artistic heights," people said, but his musicians were nonetheless eager to earn extra money. Gus and his friends now organized an informal club, the members to pay the string quartet twenty-five dollars for each Sunday concert.

Programs were printed on a small card, that of April 17, 1884, being typical:

1. Quartette (No. 1 in G)	*Haydn*
2. Quartette (in C No. 17)	*Mozart*
3. Quartette (Opus 18, No. 4 in C minor)	*Beethoven*

Gus attempted to act as treasurer, but he got mixed up in his accounts. One year he was sure he had a surplus and promised to use it to give "the fellows" a dinner. Then he found he had a deficit instead and got "a little mad at Wells," who said he wouldn't chip in on the dinner.

"Smoking concerts," they called these Sunday afternoons at the big studio on Thirty-sixth Street. Although the concerts were started as a summer entertainment, the "Standard Quartette" now performed from October to May. Ladies might now have been invited, but they were not.

"We sat or reclined at our ease on the divans which ran along the walls of the studio," Low said. But there were forty men in the club and not all of them could lie down. A photograph shows that folding chairs were brought in. The none-too-clear picture has Stanford White well up front, Richard Watson Gilder farther back and Saint-Gaudens near him — among the many other bearded or mustache-adorned gentlemen.

At this time, in 1884, Augusta was in Halifax, Nova Scotia, with Homer, a nursemaid and her mother. It was her second long stay under the care of a Dr. Fitch, who was attempting to cure what was diagnosed as a floating kidney. He prescribed exercise, drugs such as twelve drops of arsenic a day, tonics of iron and phosphate, and what was, to judge from her letters, a pessary. "Dr. Fitch put in the supporter yesterday," she wrote her husband in June, 1883, during her first summer in Nova Scotia, "but I do not think it is right." She was in great pain.

"I take five minutes walk at 10, 12, 2 and 4 — then lie right down. The rest of the time must be passed either sitting bolt upright in a straight chair or lying on my side. . . ." Gussie hoped to be cured by the end of summer, but Dr. Fitch kept putting off the day of her return home. "May some good come of it all. I will do exactly as Dr. Fitch says and bear all the pain as well as I can but if this is not a success I think I shan't try any more," Gussie wrote. Dr. Fitch was persuasive, however, and she had returned for a second unhappy summer.

Gus wrote his wife that he missed her keenly. He told her that he dreamed of being with her family "somewhere" when a beautiful naked girl came to sit beside him "on the sofa." He heard the strains of Beethoven's *Pastoral* Symphony — the girl leaned over, "undulating exactly to the cadence of the music," and he felt she ought not to do that right in front of his mother-in-law. Gus did not bother to interpret this dream, but he told Gussie to ask Dr. Fitch when she could have a visit from her husband.

"I tried to think how I could ask him," Gussie replied rather pathetically. The days of frankness concerning sex had yet to dawn.

"I think you are very well as you are," was Dr. Fitch's answer. "Tell him to come the middle of August." When August came, the doctor proposed September, and finally November.

Of Homer, Gussie wrote, "The little fellow is a great comfort and pleasure but almost past managing. It takes physical strength, which I haven't, to make him mind."

Gus wrote a series of letters for Gussie to read to their child. They were stories of his own boyhood in New York and Homer loved them. But a greater contrast could hardly be imagined. Homer Saint-

Bernard Saint-Gaudens, his son Augustus, and his grandson Homer (Courtesy of the Board of Trustees of Dartmouth College)

Gaudens never went hungry in his life. He was waited upon by his mother, his grandmother and his nurse Mary, these days, and he had a "temper fit" whenever he felt like it.

Doings at the studio filled Saint-Gaudens' determinedly cheerful letters to his wife. There was the classic supper party when everybody came wearing a toga, bare feet thrust into sandals, wreaths of laurel on every head. Tall, florid and increasingly heavy around the waist, Stanford White made an especially noble Roman. Of course, since it was summer, all the ladies were away and if the artists invited some models just to make the scene more authentic, Gus did not mention it.

Plans were afoot for a Lincoln monument in Chicago and this Saint-Gaudens wanted to do more than anything else. "I suppose this will reach you on the eve of your departure for Chicago," Gussie wrote, dating her letter June 19, without the year but most probably in 1883. "Good luck to you and stand up for your rights as the man at the head of his profession should do."

It was good news to Augusta when her husband decided not only to go to Chicago but to continue on to the West with Stanford White. Of course Gussie was a little anxious about the apartment. She had left their maid Anne in charge — would Anne take her vacation at the same time? If so, Gus was to "ask Anne to take the red cushions out of the big bamboo chair" and if the boxes with the rugs in them are "in that little room they had better be brought down to the apartment. That little room has no lock worth anything. There should also be bolts on the back door and the front door leading into the main hall." Presumably, Gus did as he was told; then he and White set out.

Richard White, Stanford's older brother, was in New Mexico. Dick met Gus and Stan at the train at Engle at 3:45 A.M. sometime in August, 1883. They were to wait four hours for a stagecoach, so the proprietor of a primitive hostelry showed them where they might get some sleep — and Gus began his adventures.

White and his brother were in one room, Gus in another, "which opened out on the wild prairie." There were two beds, on one of which lay two men, one inside the sheets, the other on top of the blanket. "Couldn't do any better — Hobson's choice," the proprietor muttered. The room smelled of kerosene. Gus lay on top of the empty bed, taking off only his coat, shoes and pantaloons, he said. He couldn't sleep, because for two days he had seen nothing but rough looking characters armed with knives and revolvers, and he knew that Engle was called "an irresponsible city." There were only four shanties in the city, besides the hotel.

Gus heard "some kind of a shaking of chains — then a slight rustling sound outside in the yard." Suddenly, a woman's voice cried, "John, the store is on fire!" A glance at the window showed "a red reflection and suddenly the three of us were tearing on our clothes," Gus said.

Within three feet of where they had been sleeping was the store, burning fiercely. "It was a strange, weird sight — the grand solemn prairie, the faint dawn, the bright stars and a great piece of destruction going on. Then suddenly, crack — crack — crack!" Cartridges inside the store were going off. "Away blazed the cartridges like a battle with occasional louder and smaller bursts — and there we stood, a few men in the lurid light. . . ." No one could go near the store to save anything and it burned to the ground. Gus saw that there were "a couple of captured bears in the yard," which explained the rattle of chains he had heard just before the fire broke out.

The four-horse stage left at seven that morning. Other passengers were two Irish-Scotch speculators looking for mines, two miners and a boy. They rattled across the prairie into the most God-forsaken country . . . past Fort McCrae, the scene of the Indian massacres "which might have been committed yesterday, so terrible-looking was the place. . . ." They crossed the Rio Grande by a ford in a dirty brown river where they "drank the muddy waters and changed horses at a picturesque Mexican village at one P.M."

This was the end of the stage journey. Gus, Stan and Dick White now "got on two horses and a mule that White's brother had led to the place two days before from his camp 25 miles off." They rode under a broiling sun, saw no one except a Mexican boy with a revolver, down in a gulch with two dogs. "It was a splendid ride and one which I shall never forget," Gus said. "White showed us the bones of a horse, shot by Indians two years ago, the owner and his family" having been found murdered a short distance away. "It was sensational."

They were in the mountains now and the going was rough. They finally "struck water at the foot of the gorge where the mine was." The sun had set and they "urged the animals through the darkness, trusting them for the path." Out of the darkness a voice called — "Hello Dick? Here's some mail for you." But Dick said he'd come for his mail the next day and the three went on, till finally they pulled up in front of Dick White's log cabin. Dick "made a fire in the stove, made some hash, some tea — some *licking* [good] soup — and in a little while I was rolled up in a blanket in a kind of bunk with White likewise, over me, and Stan on the floor," Gus wrote.

They visited Dick White's mine — which he didn't seem to be in too much of a hurry to work — and a mine worked by "four fellows" who were in the hundred-foot hole they had dug, night and day, working in shifts. Gus liked the miners, "a sanuine crowd they are, the whole of them and hard-working, hairy, uncouth, horny-handed," one an "old Tennessee Confederate captain, good-natured, jolly and whole-souled."

Jerked venison of a deer killed a week before "tasted like a salt mine and felt like rawhide." Gus and the White brothers went on an exploring and hunting trip, to get another deer. They slept around a campfire and took shelter under a big pine tree, when it rained. After the shower the night was "superb," but the experience was "such a novelty" that Gus couldn't sleep.

And then it was back "in the same stage" to the rail line. "We tore away . . . very fast, we thought . . . and at last when we were going up hill we got on top of the stage, when I very shortly found that the handsome driver was tearing drunk. We tore down the hill and several times we were within an ace of being thrown over. Finally, I got mad and told him" to be more careful. The driver mumbled something and slowed down a little, but the farther they traveled, "the more drunk he seemed to get. . . . He couldn't seem to get the idea of putting the brake on while going down hill, but put it on just when the need for it was over, so that the four horses could hardly make the next climb. At the top of the hill, he would release his brake." Somehow, the stage reached the plain. The horses were "tearing along at a full gallop" when the stage driver suddenly turned to Gus and said, "I was never so sleepy in my life. Wouldn't you like to try?"

He handed over the reins to Gus, who said he had his "fingers nearly torn out" because he hadn't any gloves. After a while the stage driver was induced somehow to take over the driving again. They reached Engle and went "duck shooting till dark. I didn't shoot any more ducks than I did deer," Gus confessed.

The story of the western trip was written to Gussie aboard trains, in hotels, on scraps of paper illustrated with cartoons by Gus.[5] Homer confiscated most of the pictures but asked his mother to explain an odd little drawing at the bottom of a page. She told him it was a kiss. On October 4, when her husband was in New York again, "You don't know how I count the days until we get there," she wrote.

13

THE MORGAN TOMB DISASTER

IN January, 1884, Miss Bessie Springs Smith's engagement to Stanford White was announced. White had met her in 1880 just after he had written to Saint-Gaudens, "You no catchee me marry!" Genie Homer heard rumors that Miss Smith, of Smithtown, Long Island, had refused White, two years later, and she wrote to Gus, asking all about it.

Saint-Gaudens came as close to telling his sister-in-law to mind her own business as he ever did. "I would not refer to it, if I were you," he said. But Genie was unwilling to take the hint and when the news of White's engagement came out, she was ready with further questions which Gus answered circumspectly.

"Yes, Miss Smith has been on the tapis, so *rumor says,* for two years," Gus now admitted. He thought Bessie was "about twenty-one." She was actually only nineteen — seventeen when White first met her. "I believe that White laid siege to the girl's heart but unsuccessfully — then went to the mines — came back I suppose cured — but meeting her again, the flame broke out again and the second siege was, as you say, a victory and an easy one I suppose." Gus paraphrased *Othello* — Bessie "loves him for the dangers he has passed."

Bessie was the youngest daughter among Judge Lawrence J. Smith's thirteen children. She was descended from "Bull Smith," a man to whom the Indians gave all the land he could ride around in a day on his wild bull. The whole Smith family loved the legend in spite of antiquarians who took pains to disprove it.

As his gift to the groom, Saint-Gaudens dropped all paying commissions and began a portrait of the bride. His bas-relief of the children of Prescott Hall Butler was already much prized by Mrs. Butler, who was Bessie's older sister, and Bessie was delighted to sit to the sculptor in wedding array. After making several sketches with a pointed modeling tool on a tablet of clay, showing a thin young woman in front of a

Portrait of Miss Bessie Springs Smith, fiancée of Stanford White (Photo from
AUGUSTUS SAINT-GAUDENS *by Charles Lewis Hind, London, 1908, by cour-*
tesy of The Bodley Head, London)

mirror, arranging her veil, Gus left out the mirror and came up with one of his most interesting portraits, of a girl who could not possibly be called beautiful. The design was reminiscent of a Greek stele, a plaster cast of which he had in his studio, except that Bessie was not drawing a veil across her face to symbolize death — but away from her face as though at the culmination of the marriage ceremony. The raised hand and veil were exquisitely modeled, Bessie's eyes were lovely, but Saint-Gaudens was too honest not to portray lips that were too thin, the line severe and uncompromising. He thought her cold and so he showed her to be — in cold white marble which not even the warm gilded frame designed by White could change.

At the time of their western trip, Gus had borrowed money of Stan. What with Augusta's board and doctor's bills in Halifax along with regular bills at home, he had not been able to pay his debt and this worried him. He proposed not only to model Bessie free of charge, as a gift to White, but to pay for the cost of rendering the medallion in marble as well.   "You must not pay for any cutting of the medallion," White wrote. "If I dared — I should insinuate that, in spite of your long nose, I did not believe that you had the slightest idea of how much you owe anybody or anybody owes you — but I don't."

White enclosed some figures showing the debt to be about $450. Then he put down, "marble — cutting of marble" and so on, writing slantwise all across the sheet, "Settled by God, in full payment."[1]

No one among the fifty-seven guests ever forgot the cartoons Gus drew for the menu card at White's bachelor dinner. Most of them showed the architect wearing the beard he grew in Paris; the one he said made him look like "a rising sun on the half-shell." No one forgot the wine at that dinner — nor the "impromptu dancing" by F. Hopkinson Smith, artist and author, and Loyall Farragut, son of the admiral. It was a glorious blowout, supposed in theory at least to be the bachelor's last wild party.

After the wedding on February 7, the bride and groom set out for Europe on what was to be virtually a shopping spree lasting six months.[2] Bessie bought clothes while Stan bought stone carvings discarded when French chateaux were modernized. He collected fine old statues thrown out of provincial churches to make room for brightly painted plaster casts, and he bought palace furniture from tax-poor Italian noblemen to sell to Americans with tax free incomes. A "mosque-full of antique tiles from Constantinople" was lost when the freighter the tiles were shipped on was wrecked on a reef off Bermuda.

New York without Stanford White was dreary, Gus soon discovered. In order to pay expenses, he took on commissions for portraits in bronze, which could be produced at little expense and in a short time, compared to statues for a park.[3] The only trouble was that he could not turn them out as mere potboilers but invariably became interested in catching the character as well as the likeness of his sitter, producing a work of art on which he lavished hours before he would let it out of his studio. Harvard University acquired a Saint-Gaudens bas-relief of Professor Asa Gray — his hair in disarray, his beard beautifully curly, a quizzical expression to mouth and eyes. Josiah Gilbert Holland, former editor with Bowles of the Springfield *Republican* and editor of *Scribner's*, had died in 1881 and Saint-Gaudens did one of the first of his many portraits from photographs. The problem here was to tell the truth and at the same time satisfy admiring relatives of the deceased, but Saint-Gaudens did justice to the luxuriant mustache of a gentleman of solemn mien. Children were difficult, but their portraits were among Saint-Gaudens' best.

"I have two dogs in the studio and that's about all I can attend to besides two little models," Gus wrote to Gussie in 1884. He was doing the "Schiff medallion" in marble — a little girl, Freda, "in her eighth year," holding by the hand her brother Mortimer, "in his seventh year." Their father was Jacob Schiff, New York financier and railroad magnate. The children seemed to be setting out on a walk together, into a child's world all their own. The little girl held on to the collar of a beautiful dog which Saint-Gaudens said was a "Scotch deerhound." The dog was part of the background, well subordinated yet essential to the composition. As always, it was in the pose of the subjects that much character was expressed, and even the dog told a story, the curve of his head seeming to say that he loved and protected the children. He looked as if he really belonged to them, but he did not — he belonged to Gus.

Saint-Gaudens had been to kennels to find just the right dog for a model and brought two into the studio on trial. He fell in love with the deerhound and bought him. This double or perhaps triple portrait, including the dog, was "almost finished" in 1884, but it was actually dated 1888 and perhaps not completed to suit the sculptor until then. The Luxembourg Museum in Paris eventually acquired a bronze replica, while the marble original was presented to the Metropolitan

Portrait of the children of Jacob H. Schiff, reproduced in marble from the original bronze especially for the Metropolitan Museum of Art (The Metropolitan Museum of Art, gift of Jacob H. Schiff, 1905)

Museum of Art by the childrens' father when he became one of the
museum's trustees and a generous benefactor.

The popularity of bas-relief portraits by Saint-Gaudens was a surprise to C. Lewis Hind, a British art critic who described how a bronze
medallion looked, "usurping the place of a picture in a modern
drawing room." He was the guest of the Prescott Hall Butlers on Long
Island and saw "the relief of the Butler children in its rightful place in
the house of the mother of the two little boys whose young beauty it
perpetuates." Saint-Gaudens had done this portrait in 1881 at the
Sherwood Building studio, showing Charles Stewart Butler, aged four,
and his brother Lawrence Smith Butler, dressed in Scottish costume,
the older boy's arm protectively around the shoulders of his brother.
The bronze was "enclosed in the hammered oak frame designed for it,
hanging on the wall of a panelled room above a wood fire which cast
reflections on the patina of the bronze. No picture could seem more
suitable to the place, or give a more enduring pleasure than the surfaces of this low relief, hiding and revealing themselves under the
influences of the ruddy light from the fire and the pale light from the
window."

Augusta and Homer, with Homer's nurse, had left New York at the
first hint of hot weather. They went to Grandmother Homer's house in
Roxbury, collected that lady with her trunk and carpetbag and headed
for Halifax. Gussie once more put herself into the hands of Dr. Fitch,
who continued his treatments: the painful support for her so-called
floating kidney, the arsenic drops, the tonics and the weird diets. Anne,
Augusta's general housework girl, was left at the New York apartment
to keep house for Mr. Saint-Gaudens.

Reports from Gus were not slow in coming. One night "at two A.M."
he was "awakened by a thunderstorm and a furious pricking sensation" which he thought must somehow have been caused by that
mysterious force, electricity. He lighted the gas — and discovered that
he was being eaten alive by bedbugs. "The battle lasted an hour," in
the course of which he killed eighteen. "Then I laid me down to
sleep — praying God to give me sleep," he said, "but survivors renewed the attack." He moved to another bed and was attacked there
also.

Anne's cooking was even worse than her housekeeping — if such a
thing were possible. Gus drew a chart with a rapidly descending line
to indicate the "level of the cooking" the day his wife left and the far

lower present level. There was a point indicated which showed "the level that ordinary animals such as horses, dogs, etc. feed on," but Anne's rate of achievement sank far below that to a point marked "arctic food such as Louis and I get every night when we get home." But for the fact that he got a good noon meal at a restaurant near the studio, Gus thought he would not go home any more but "leave Anne to the unhappy fate of eating her own cooking."

This was all very funny, but Augusta's pride as a housewife was hurt and she could not believe that the servant she called "my trusted Anne" could be quite such a total loss. Gus was to give her money, tell her what he wanted to eat and have her get better food at the market. There were suggestions concerning poison for bedbugs and disinfectant for the toilet, of which Gus seems also to have complained. These were orders a highly temperamental artist-husband would hate to bother with, but Gussie said that Anne was really "a remarkably good girl" compared to some of the servants their friends had. It took her four years to lose faith in Anne, but in 1888 she discovered that "my trusted Anne, whom I had loaded with benefits, was and has been probably for years pilfering from me — to use the mildest word."[4] It took Gus fewer then four years to form the habit of staying at the studio or elsewhere rather than at home, when Gussie was away.

In August, Bernard Saint-Gaudens was taken ill. "Poor old man, he looks very badly," Gus wrote. "It sends a pang through me every time I see him. We have decided to send him back to his village as he is always talking of it. . . . He will stay as long as he cares to and the desire of his life will be satisfied." The elder Saint-Gaudens planned to pay his own way. His shoe business was practically at a standstill, but recently he had taken to changing paper money into gold pieces which he kept under his pillow at night. "He would get savage when we discovered them," his youngest son, Louis, said — and recalled the story of his French grandmother who had been upset when her box of gold pieces had been discovered under her bed.

Bernard was scheduled to leave New York for Boulogne in September, to be met by a cousin and taken to his native Aspet in the French Pyrenees. But by the middle of August "the cholera has developed itself in Aspet, his village, I see by the papers, so we won't let him go of course," Gus wrote. They didn't dare to tell the old man, but they figured that he would put off his trip of his own accord.

The elder Saint-Gaudens had remarried and Gus, who had been

especially close to his mother, resented the young woman who took her place. It was decided to send Louis to the country with his father, letting "the girl run the store, I suppose with her lover, who is there nine-tenths of the time," Gus said bitterly. Augusta tried to calm him. "That young woman is his wife," she wrote. "When your father gets well he will make her behave. You don't have any proof about the men who hang around her and it would be a great scandal if anything were done about a divorce."

Bernard Saint-Gaudens never returned to his beloved Aspet. He recovered his health to a certain extent but soon closed his shoeshop. His favorite haunt became his son's studio and nothing more was said, at least in letters, about the young woman who was his second wife.

Work on the Vanderbilt commission, celebrated by Saint-Gaudens and his friends with joyous libation, dragged on until it became merely a chore. The marble caryatids, finished fairly soon after the commission was received, resembled sweet-looking young girls with a tired air easily explained by the job they had to do, holding up the huge marble mantelpiece.[5] Saint-Gaudens executed the family medallions with pleasure, however, and with his usual sensitive touch.[6] But the tops of panels had to boil with acanthus leaves surrounding heraldic beasts; diamond shapes superimposed on squares had to be edged with egg-and-dart or bead-and-reel moldings; ribbons rippled in oak; there were festoons and garlands. Gus used this sort of thing in his medallions but always sparingly and with restraint. Restraint was the last thing Vanderbilt wanted, and to save his sanity, Gus hired assistants to carry forward this part of the commission. He began to gather around him the corps of men and eventually one or two women who would proudly add "pupil of Saint-Gaudens" to their list of art experiences when fame overtook them.

Among the first was Frederick William MacMonnies, studio boy at seventeen, prizewinner in Paris within a few years. Discovered as a wood-carver on the Vanderbilt job was Philip Martiny, whose later statues could almost be said to overpopulate the Library of Congress in Washington. Comparatively unknown and unsung was René de Quélin, who did not hesitate to sing his own praises as he told of scenes in the Saint-Gaudens studio, beginning in 1881. That was when he said he arrived in the United States and "walked uptown in New York from the Battery to Union Square, to see what it was like." He met Saint-Gaudens, claimed acquaintance from student days in Paris and there was an exchange of news. De Quélin was looking for a job; Saint-Gaudens was sick of designing Renaissance decorations in oak and even having to carve them himself when workmen failed to suit him. De Quélin said decoration was right in his line, and he was hired on the spot.

He was "much attracted to MacMonnies," de Quélin said, describing the studio boy as "pale, thin, gaunt and anemic-looking — seeming better fitted to be a patient in some good sanitarium in a more congenial climate." He overlooked the fact that MacMonnies was also as brash as he was brilliant, but took the credit of discovering the boy's talent. According to de Quélin, Mac was supposed to do nothing but prepare clay, cover models, run errands and stoke the fires.[7] Then one morning Saint-Gaudens came in to find a handsomely designed decorative panel. "Who did this!" the master exclaimed. It had been modeled by MacMonnies, given his chance by de Quélin, who helped Mac after hours.

The story is obviously false, because MacMonnies had already studied nights in the life class at the National Academy of Design — helped to do so by Saint-Gaudens. Mac's parents objected to his becoming a sculptor; Saint-Gaudens helped them to understand. "My relations with Mac are such that I see everything he does in very much the same way that a mother contemplates her boy," Saint-Gaudens wrote.[8]

But the story told and embroidered upon by de Quélin concerning the master's studio rages had a little more foundation in fact and became an often-repeated Saint-Gaudens legend. "One morning Saint-Gaudens came into the studio ranting as Masters will, finding fault with everything and everyone," de Quélin said. "Saint-Gaudens, like a mighty Zeus, hurled maledictions and anathema with Olympian wrath" until everyone took refuge under the high platform where the *Shaw Memorial* stood in preliminary form. De Quélin was too brave to hide, according to his own account.

The landlady who owned the frame building Saint-Gaudens had built over for his Thirty-sixth Street studio lived next door, de Quélin said. She came in every morning to dun him for the rent. It was MacMonnies's "duty to keep accounts" but there was one custom de Quélin did not seem to know about. Saint-Gaudens always paid his assistants first, but when he could not meet his payroll, the assistants would "borrow" whatever small portrait medallions were lying around and pawn them, counting on redeeming them before the master missed them.

Visitors constantly distracted Saint-Gaudens now that his *Farragut* had made him famous, just as the papers predicted it would. Because of her health and because of Homer, Augusta could no longer sit in the studio, receiving people and keeping them out of his way. Accordingly, Gus used one of the two rooms (already partitioned off) as a reception room, building a platform there, where work could be placed on exhibit. Louis used the other from time to time. Each room had a couch or bed of some sort and because of the discomforts of Anne's housekeeping, Gus had a place to spend nights, which suited him very well. Since the sound of visitor's voices distracted him, the partitions were exceptionally thick.

All during the summer of 1884, Gus was trying to find time to visit Augusta in Halifax. They were both lonely. Gussie thought she could hire a cottage where Gus could "work in the top rooms if a skylight were put in." This was "an excellent idea," Gus said. But Dr. Fitch vetoed the plan. "For specific reasons that Mr. Saint-Gaudens will understand," he was not to see his wife until September — if then.

Gus described his state of mind, writing to Gussie on August 9. "When I am in the full spirit and enthusiasm of work, I don't care a cent for the country and curse the fate that makes me torment myself as to when or where I shall or shall not get to see you," he said frankly. "When I am doing the drudgery of my profession, then I curse the work that detains me from the country and the family, and, taken all together, this great distance does neither myself nor my work any good. . . . I shall get off when I can although it seems absurd to go to the north pole in September when I dislike the cold as much as I do."

Gus seems to have suggested that Gussie ask Dr. Fitch to report on her case to a Dr. Lee of New York so that she could have treatments at home and end their constant separation. But nothing came of this. Gussie wrote out her impression of what Dr. Fitch said, but another doctor would not have found it clear enough to be helpful.

"Spirit and enthusiasm for work" came to Saint-Gaudens when he modeled the angels for the Morgan tomb. They were beautiful young girls, as he portrayed them, not tired like the Vanderbilt caryatids but full of the joy of Resurrection morning. They held archaic musical instruments in their hands, their hair was soft about their faces, their robes delicate, their wings big enough to have brought them down from heaven.

"You have probably seen by the papers the calamity that has happened," Saint-Gaudens wrote to Augusta on August 26, 1884.

The Hartford *Courant* told the story. "On August 21, disaster struck the Morgan tomb project, now almost finished. One of the most extraordinary fires on record was the one at Cedar Hill Cemetery last Thursday night. The elaborately sculptured column crowning the Morgan Mausoleum . . . would have been completed in a few weeks and would have been one of the choicest pieces of sepulchral work in the country. . . ."

The tomb itself was already built of gray granite in a heavy style, with short, stumpy columns having more or less Byzantine capitals. It had solid bronze doors, and windows of Tiffany glass in geometric designs. When Stanford White had first approached Saint-Gaudens on the subject of the Morgan tomb, White was still working for Richardson. The completed tomb might be described as Richardson railroad-station style in miniature. Ex-governor Morgan, who had infuriated White by constantly trying to get more than his money's worth, now occupied this last earthly home of his.

Morgan had objected to the cost of the two huge blocks of marble which Saint-Gaudens had traveled to Carrara to select for him. He had questioned every item of cost submitted to him and ordered the marble brought up the Connecticut River on the ice, it was said, because transportation by sled was cheaper than by barge. In February, 1883, the former governor died, unhappy because the angels Saint-Gaudens was modeling for him were not yet rendered in marble. He left an estimated eight to ten million dollars to his heirs and a debt of five thousand dollars still due the sculptor.

Saint-Gaudens went to Hartford in October, 1883, "and sublet the cutting of the cross and the angels to Albert Entrecs of this city," the paper said. "Four other skilled workmen began to chisel the design furnished by Saint-Gaudens who frequently visited the project — now and then taking chisel in hand. He felt that the angels were his best work" and it was said that he fired one of the stonecutters for carving carelessly.

"Gradually the two stones, towering twenty-five feet above the tomb, yielded to the efforts of the artisans. . . . A temporary structure was erected around the shaft to protect the workmen from the weather."

The "three angels at the base had been roughed out" and in August, 1884, "Saint-Gaudens himself planned to put a finishing touch to his work."

Around eleven o'clock on the night of the 21st, the cemetery custodian "from his cottage at the entrance gates" saw a blaze high on the hill "at the farthest point of the cemetery."[9] There was nothing the custodian could do to save the sculptures when he arrived, breathless, to find a flaming torch over the Morgan tomb. There was a great deal of straw, packing for the marble and the casts of the angels, inside the wooden shelter. Everyone connected with the work was questioned, but the police came up with no one suspected of arson. A family living just outside the cemetery limits said they had slept through the whole thing. The papers mentioned "a tramp" seen loitering in the vicinity, but no arrest was made, although the rumor persisted that a dismissed workman had set the blaze.

"My whole work in utter ruin . . . ," Saint-Gaudens wrote Augusta. "I don't know what I am doing — I can't write — you know all I know," from the papers.

Of course it was the loss of the angels that Saint-Gaudens minded most, but he had been counting on the five thousand dollars still due him and he was afraid that the Morgan heirs would not only refuse to pay this but would "want their $3000 back" — money already spent on contractors. "What is to become of the matter I don't know and I dread to think of it," he said. "None of my lawyer friends are in town."

Mark Twain, who lived in Hartford at the time, exclaimed, "Who would have dreamed of a fire in a cemetery! Of course Saint-Gaudens had no insurance."

A day or two after the cemetery disaster, "young Evarts" told Saint-Gaudens that he was "absolutely not responsible for the fire," and that the Morgan executors were willing to pay him $3800, a $1200 deduction having been made for the amount of work not accomplished.

Saint-Gaudens still had plaster-cast duplicates of two of the angels in his studio. The third one he would have a good deal of trouble fixing up, he thought, "after searching for and retrieving only a few calcined pieces out of the ruins" at Hartford.

There was one more blow in store. Ex-governor Morgan's widow decided that she did not need three angels and a cross for her husband's tomb. She paid what the lawyers said she owed and that was that. Gus had assumed that he was to do over the angels for her, and his heart was broken.

The mood of despair speedily gave way to elation, as would always be the way with Saint-Gaudens. The committeemen who had invited him to Chicago to talk about a Lincoln statue in 1883 had suggested that he enter a competition. Remembering his defeat in the Boston competition for a statue of Charles Sumner, he refused. Now that committee had had a chance to think this over and they offered a Lincoln commission outright. Gus telegraphed the news to Gussie.

"Three cheers for the *Lincoln*," she replied. "We shall have *one* decent statue of Lincoln anyway."

14

COUNTRY OF LINCOLN-SHAPED MEN

THERE was no commission that Saint-Gaudens wanted more than this chance to do a Lincoln. He would have liked to go straight to Stanford White who could be relied on to rejoice — and design a handsome pedestal with background and approaches guaranteed to set off a fine statue — but White was still in Europe on his honeymoon, not due to return to New York until autumn.

On September 8, 1884, at five P.M., Saint-Gaudens and McKim went down to the barge office at the docks to greet the returning bride and groom. "After much standing around in the dirt and some bustling about by a mob of howling cabmen and policemen in the most disorderly confusion," they were hailed by Prescott Hall Butler who had driven in from Long Island with White's mother, Mrs. Richard Grant White. He led them "through a mess of carriages to where the two Mrs. Whites were, Junior and Senior." Gus was surprised by a change in Bessie. "She looked quite pretty and less hard than I have known her as yet."

They all shook hands and then the coachman flicked his whip and the carriage with the two ladies rolled away in the direction of Long Island. Saint-Gaudens and McKim "struggled and waited and finally shook hands with White over the rail in the interval of furious running after trunks lost in the confusion ten times greater than that outside the building. We waited around on the Battery till nine o'clock for him."

Dick White, who had returned from New Mexico, and Prescott Hall Butler joined Saint-Gaudens and McKim, but before long Butler thought he ought to go home to his family. When Stanford White finally found his friends, they "took dinner at Solari's," lingering over the fine wine. Marriage was not going to change White's habits very much. The next evening he dropped in at Saint-Gaudens' studio. "It was like champagne having him around again," Gus said.

On the modeling stand, White saw a handsome statue in process of completion. It was to be named the *Puritan,* but it would always be called "Deacon Samuel Chapin" in Springfield, Massachusetts, its destination.

Chester William Chapin, banker, president of the Boston and Albany Railroad and promoter of other railroads, had commissioned the *Puritan.* Reputed to be the wealthiest man in Springfield, Mr. Chapin liked to recall that he began his career in transportation by driving a yoke of oxen belonging to his brother. He next drove stage coaches and began buying up stagecoach lines, Connecticut River steamboats and steamers plying Long Island Sound. Where some men might have seen the railroad as ruinous competition, Mr. Chapin recognized the rails as a new opportunity and put his money in them.

The Chapins knew Augusta Homer's family before she married Saint-Gaudens. Chester W. Chapin, Jr., and his wife were living in Paris when Gus and Gussie furnished their favorite apartment overlooking the Luxembourg Gardens. Mrs. Chapin and her generous gifts were often mentioned in Gussie's letters home. A sewing machine from Mrs. Chapin was used to stitch the big white curtains for Saint-Gaudens' studio; Japanese teacups, acquired from the International Exposition, gave just the touch of elegance to Gussie's tea parties. It was while Augusta was in Roxbury, awaiting the birth of her child, that Gus went to Springfield to talk over the Chapin commission.

"I suppose you will use old Mr. Chapin's head for the statue," Augusta wrote.[1] But Gus had a different idea. He made a bust of the younger Mr. Chapin, his friend from Paris days (whose wife's portrait he had done while still in Paris). The bronze statue, twelve feet tall, was to represent a Chapin ancestor, Deacon Samuel, who, in 1642, left the town of Roxbury to settle new territory on the Connecticut River. There was no known portrait of this pioneer, but Gus argued that young Mr. Chester W. Chapin, square-jawed, with wide, determined mouth, might resemble his ancestor.

Saint-Gaudens hired a model, muscular, well-proportioned and over six feet tall. His name was Van Oertzen. Gus took him to Springfield where ladies of the Chapin family had found woodcuts and antique paintings to show the proper Puritan costume. A "tailoress" was summoned to make a flowing cape, buttoned coat and knee breeches to fit the big model. Unfortunately, Van Oertzen looked stronger than he was. One day when he came into the Chapins' house he fell in a faint in the hallway. The ladies couldn't move him and had to call the gardener and the coachman, as well as the doctor.

Saint-Gaudens made preliminary sketches, showing Deacon Chapin, hatless, against a background of masonry. Eventually the statue was free-standing and immensely effective, with a high-crowned, broad-brimmed hat.

Early stages of studies for the *Puritan* in the studio on Fifty-seventh Street were going on when George B. Post came in, bringing a young boy by the name of Charles Dana Gibson. The boy, then aged thirteen, had a remarkable aptitude for cutting silhouettes, freehand, out of paper — his subjects, such as animals with clothes on or children at play, all imaginative and original, although suggesting Kate Greenaway's popular children's books. The boy's parents were willing to give him an art education if his talent seemed to justify it. Saint-Gaudens was supposed to encourage Gibson or not, as the case might be.

As far as Gus was concerned, it was just one of those irritating interruptions. He told Van Oertzen to take a rest from posing, listened with half an ear to the Gibson boy's story, and pulled some paper silhouettes out of an envelope the boy handed him. They were not bad, he thought, although it was hard to see what they were for. "Did you do these?" he asked. Young Gibson said yes. Pointing to the big model sitting in a chair, "Do him," Saint-Gaudens suggested.

Presumably Gibson had paper and scissors with him. He set to work, never having had a model before. Observers said the "striped stockings seemed to hypnotize" the boy. Actually, the model wore stockings knitted in vertical ribs, all gray, as befitted a Puritan, but the figure was difficult, nonetheless. Gibson did a pretty good job. Intrigued, Saint-Gaudens learned that the boy's forte was imaginary figures, and told him to cut some. Gibson obliged with a boy sitting on a log, fishing. Saint-Gaudens was remembered as having called the next shot — a boy on a donkey. Then he ordered another boy behind the first before the silhouette was done. The red-haired MacMonnies, glad of a chance to quit whatever work he was doing, joined the group to watch the fun. Saint-Gaudens still had no idea why Charles Dana Gibson had been brought to him but assumed that the boy needed a job. He was hired to run errands.[2]

Gibson did not last long. He was sent to the architect's office one day to get a tracing, important dimensions of some panel or other for the Vanderbilt mansion, marked in pencil. He got the small scrap of tissue paper, then walked back to the studio, enjoying the sights of New York and absent-mindedly folding and rolling the paper into a wad in his moist hand. He delivered the mauled, illegible drawing to Saint-Gaudens and was fired, "with oaths, curses and abjurations," it was said.

Charles Dana Gibson developed his peerless pen-and-ink technique at the Art Students' League in New York. By the time he was twenty-one he was in Paris, already famous as a feature illustrator for *Life,* at that time a magazine of humor and satire. He met MacMonnies, "costumed for a ball as a diver," and doubtless helped "fill his rubber suit to the neck with beer and wine" when MacMonnies took his helmet off. Gibson married the most beautiful of his Gibson Girls, Irene Langhorne, of Virginia. His satirical drawings of New York society with its newly rich, its proud parents of humble origin in search of a European title for a beautiful daughter, appealed to Saint-Gaudens, who often encountered such people. The two men became friends in later years, laughing together over their first meeting.

Saint-Gaudens moved his half-sized model of Deacon Samuel Chapin down to his Thirty-sixth Street studio. He thought he might be able to finish it in Nova Scotia while spending the summer with Augusta, but Van Oertzen, the big model, refused to go there — and Augusta's doctor refused to let her husband visit. The *Puritan* was well advanced when Stanford White returned from Europe, and he set about designing a simple but handsome pedestal for it. After visiting Stearns Park in Springfield where the statue was to stand, he proposed a marble bench and a bronze fountain further to ornament the park.

The older Chester W. Chapin had died in 1883 and Saint-Gaudens might have supposed that the matter of the statue would be dropped. Young Mr. Chapin, however, was all the more interested in having the heroic-sized bronze as a memorial to his father, as well as to the famous ancestor. He liked the idea of a seat and a fountain.

But soon the *Puritan* was temporarily set aside and there was another armature on the stand, half life-sized, with clay soon covering it to take the shape of a man, this time in modern dress. This was the "Standing *Lincoln,*" so called because Saint-Gaudens later created a seated statue of Abraham Lincoln.

The contract between "Augustus Saint-Gaudens of New York City, sculptor," and the Chicago committee acting "under the will of Eli Bates, deceased," was signed on November 11, 1884.[3] The statue was to be "not less than eleven feet in height . . . of the best statuary bronze." As usual, the sculptor must pay all costs, including "a fitting and proper pedestal" — but not including "foundations for the statue below the surface of the earth . . . in Lincoln Park."

The Chicago Committee bought the services of "America's foremost sculptor" for $30,000 with only $500 payable on signing the contract. Saint-Gaudens was to receive "$500 on the last day of each month in which the greater portion" of his time had been spent in "preparation of the model for the use of the bronze founder," and "$750 on the last day of each month devoted *exclusively* to such preparation, up to a total of $7000." It would always be a moot question as to what constituted "the greater portion" of his time to an artist who punched no time clock but was mentally at work while walking down the street, or listening to music, or apparently just doing nothing. There would be days when Saint-Gaudens would work in his studio at fever pitch for hours on end, then turn, exhausted, to another project to renew his inner fire. Committees would never understand.

An amount sufficient to bring the total of all payments to $8500 would be paid when the model was finished and ready for the bronze foundry; $7500 when the statue was finished in bronze; $6000 when the statue and pedestal were delivered in good condition in Lincoln Park, and the final payment of $8000 "when the pedestal and statue" were "in place and finished. . . ."

The committee left the door open to award another commission, which they eventually authorized — "a seat designed and constructed," for another $10,000. But this had to be finished within three months after the statue was ready. Here was White's enthusiastic promotion at work. Stan leaped at the opportunity to design something handsome — a huge circular seat with inscriptions, flights of stairs and spheres in bronze. Richard Watson Gilder was asked to select passages from Lincoln's speeches and to compose inscriptions ornamenting the outside surface of the stone seat. Of course White changed the dimensions of the panels almost as often as Saint-Gaudens changed and improved the statue itself. Draftsmen sent Mr. Gilder wrong measurements now and then, so that he was forced to cut or expand his carefully chosen wording. Gilder complained mildly.

Saint-Gaudens had been studying Lincoln, reading his speeches, learning all he could about the man, his own boyhood impressions of Lincoln etched upon his memory. Photographs were plentiful; there was a life mask, a death mask and a cast of Lincoln's hands. The life mask, John Hay told Saint-Gaudens, was made "sixty days before Lincoln was shot." Hay had been a young private secretary to Lincoln.

A life mask showing Lincoln before he let his beard grow was made by Leonard Willis Volk.[4] He was a protégé of Stephen A. Douglas's and the sculptor of a colossal Douglas for Chicago, plus heroic statues of both Douglas and Lincoln for the State Capitol in Springfield, Illinois.

Volk gave the life mask he had made and also casts of Lincoln's hands to his son, Douglas Volk, a painter studying in Paris. The young man didn't want them, so he handed them over to Wyatt Eaton, a friend and fellow student with Saint-Gaudens at the National Academy of Design. But Eaton didn't really want the casts either and if Saint-Gaudens could use them, he was more than welcome.

Gilder saw the casts lying on a table in Eaton's studio, asked about them and was shocked to hear how these priceless relics had been casually handed around among the artists. He got up a committee to head a subscription list to buy them and present them to the National Museum in Washington. Subscribers would receive copies in plaster or in bronze, depending on the size of their donations, the names of substantial donors to be inscribed on the bronze replicas. Saint-Gaudens undertook to superintend the castings and inscriptions. There were thirty-three distinguished names on the subscription list, Henry Irving and the sculptor J. Q. A. Ward among them.

Augusta hoped that she had regained her health and she never returned to Dr. Fitch in Nova Scotia. She wrote of pleasant social activities to Rose Hawthorne Lathrop, daughter of Nathaniel Hawthorne, whom she had known in Boston and who, with her editor husband and artist brother-in-law, lived near the Saint-Gaudens' New York apartment, at least for a time. Augusta planned a dinner party for the Gilders, she told Rose. She worried — but it went off smoothly. She chose Thursday to be "at home" to serve tea to anyone who might call.

"Thursday being my day," Gussie said, "a good many people put themselves to a good deal of trouble to call" — it pleased her because it was a measure of her husband's success. But she had few intimates and missed Rose, who had temporarily moved away. Rose must come to visit. "I am surely stronger and would enjoy walking with you," Gussie wrote. "No pleasure in life is greater than a walk and a talk with a friend. Ideas and sympathy seem to come in the open, although a bright fire and a cozy room without interruption is not to be despised. . . ."

In April, the question of where to go for the summer came up. Charles Coatsworth Beaman, early patron and continued good friend to Saint-Gaudens, made a suggestion. The Beamans had discovered a tiny, almost deserted village on the east bank of the Connecticut River, Cornish, New Hampshire, by name. From the rocky, practically untillable hillsides, Mount Ascutney could be seen to the west, the high, symmetrical wooded cone beautiful at all seasons and in every light from dawn to twilight. Abandoned farmhouses and farmlands were for sale cheap and Mr. Beaman, a smart lawyer of genial temperament, knew a bargain when he saw one. He bought a summer place for himself and his family, and other houses and acreage as they came on the market. To Saint-Gaudens he offered an old brick house, once an inn, then a house of ill fame, according to legend. Saint-Gaudens could have it and plenty of land to go with it for what Mr. Beaman had paid — which was five hundred dollars.

Gus and Gussie took the train to Windsor, Vermont, with Mr. Beaman.[5] The weather should have been beautiful, but it was not. It was a dark and rainy day when a country carryall met them at the Windsor station, rattled them over the covered toll bridge to New Hampshire, then turned north at river level. After a short distance the carryall entered a mountain road running east along Blow-Me-Down Brook. The horse slowed to a walk, carriage wheels grated on loose stones and the horse's hoofs sloshed in mud. Forest trees arched overhead, making the dark day seem darker. Finally they came to a clearing on the left, an abandoned hayfield. Behind the remnants of a stone wall stood a gaunt old house.

End walls, supporting two chimneys each, rose high in a primitive Dutch effect, but fanlight and sidelights at the front door and a fanlight over the side door were in the New England tradition. Five of the nine windows across the front had their original small panes. The four windows at the right of the front door had been replaced by large-paned glass in country-boardinghouse style. Inside there were large rooms each with a fireplace. A straight stair led up to what might have been a ballroom of sorts in the days when young people went sleigh-riding out to a tavern to eat and dance. Shoddy partitions had long since been thrown across the big room.

The house looked "so forbidding and relentless," Gus said, "that one might have imagined a skeleton half hanging out of the window, shrieking and dangling in a gale, with the sound of clanking bones."[6]

The only thing Gus liked about the place was the barn. It would make a good studio — with a skylight put in. It was big enough to hold both a heroic-sized *Lincoln* and an equally heroic "Deacon Samuel Chapin."

Saint-Gaudens described his feelings about the country at this time. He had been a boy of streets and sidewalks. Country excursions were all to the good but after a few days of fields and woods he grew tired of them and longed for his four walls and his work.

Gussie wanted to buy the place. She could smell the fresh earth coming to life in the cold April rain and she was a born gardener, like her father. Ever since her father's death, her brothers had been selling off the family land in Roxbury until the lawns, orchards and gardens surrounding her old home were eroded away into house lots. This was a process going on everywhere in Roxbury, a town that could no longer be called "Boston Highlands" and lay claim to borrowed elegance. The last time Gussie visited her mother, her brothers were not at home, her sister Genie sat in her father's chair and Gussie could hardly control her tears. She needed not just a New York apartment but a place of her own.

"I was for fleeing at once and returning to my beloved sidewalks of New York," Gus wrote, "but Mrs. Saint-Gaudens saw the future of sunny days that were to follow."

Mr. Charles C. Beaman, reading the minds of his two prospects like the born salesman that he was, made the clinching statement. "There are plenty of Lincoln-shaped men up here," Beaman said.

Knowing also how to bide his time, Mr. Beaman suggested that the Saint-Gaudenses could rent the place indefinitely for a modest sum — making alterations to suit themselves, at their own expense, of course. They took the house for the summer.

Back in New York, Gus invited Gilder to come to look at the first version of the "Standing *Lincoln*." Richard Watson Gilder had the qualities of a fine editor, one of them being the gift of asking a question that would make an artist or writer clarify his own ideas and evolve new ones without loss of self-confidence.

"What do *you* think of Lincoln?" he asked Saint-Gaudens.

"I take him to be a good man, a benevolent, kind man called upon to take a great executive office," Gus replied.

"How about a prophet, a poet, a dreamer — called upon to take a great executive office?" Gilder suggested.

"What else can I read of his?" Gus exclaimed, and Gilder "loaded" him "with more of Lincoln's writings." Saint-Gaudens began to think about those Lincoln-shaped men of New Hampshire. The idea of packing up the present model of the *Lincoln* and the "Deacon Samuel Chapin" as well and finishing them in Cornish might not be so bad, after all.

The Cornish adventure began on a note of anxiety, however. Saint-Gaudens described what happened in a letter to Dr. Homer Emerson, his wife's cousin. Illustrating his letter with cartoons of horses, "Gussie trotted out her old war horse the other day and with champing of bit and flying of mane, proceeded to pack up — things did hum, as you can imagine." She was getting ready to leave for Cornish, putting rugs and sofa cushions away in mothballs, deciding what to take to New Hampshire and packing wooden boxes to be sent by express.

"Now she is down with what Dr. Lee said was pretty near a miscarriage," Saint-Gaudens went on. "The old war horse is stabled and old 'Worry Bones' has been trotted out — only the mare 'Worry Bones' has a mate now and that's me. I'm a little nervous about the trip to Windsor and the possibility of a miscarriage or a pull-back such as this." He wanted the name of a reliable doctor and there was none in Cornish. Did Dr. Emerson, of Boston, have the name of a doctor in Claremont, ten miles away, or Hanover, fifteen miles up the Connecticut? Gussie "hoped to get off at the end of the next week and would like to be armed before going, if she could."

Gus told Dr. Emerson that "the arrival is expected about December first." Perhaps Dr. Emerson "as one of the fraternity of doctors" gave the name of Dr. Fred L. Morse, of Windsor, Vermont. In any case, Dr. Morse eventually became a wise and good friend to Augusta, to whom she often turned in time of need. She recovered from the "pull-back," however, and did not see any doctor until she was back in New York in the autumn.

Augusta went to Cornish ahead of her husband. By the time he arrived, she had everything ready for him. The new skylight dispersed the shadows in the old barn, revealing huge hand-hewn beams and sending spiders scurrying to cover. The old brick house looked decidedly more cheerful with blinds added, doors and window trim freshly painted white and a small wooden porch with a neat railing and wooden steps, at the front door. These improvements represented Augusta's first encounters with village carpenters and established her reputation as a hard bargainer — and a lady it was difficult to argue with because she was hard of hearing.

"I was thirty-seven at the time it dawned upon me seriously how much there was outside of my little world," Saint-Gaudens wrote, looking back on his first summer in Cornish. In July, 1885, he left his New York studio with misgivings. With him was his brother Louis, his assistant Philip Martiny, Martiny's wife and little daughter Blanche and Frederick William MacMonnies.

MacMonnies, in 1885, had just won the National Academy of Design's first prize and was soon to be on his way to Paris, where he would receive the Prix d'Atelier, the highest prize open to foreigners. Prize after prize was to be his, some of his work good — some of his later figures of men so exaggeratedly muscular, his women so voluptuous, that they all looked as though made of rubber and inflated like balloons. MacMonnies had a passion for festooning his otherwise naked heroes with assorted fruit and flowers. Although twenty-two years old, he was still regarded as a boy prodigy when he went with Saint-Gaudens to Cornish during the summer of 1885. Later, as he turned more and more to the all-too-popular flamboyant style, while Saint-Gaudens continued to simplify, the two men differed seriously.

Martiny, five years older than MacMonnies, had already studied sculpture before coming to the United States with little or no money in his pocket. He too went to work for Saint-Gaudens in 1880, was married the following year, and although never the prizewinner that MacMonnies was, he would receive not only the commission for the statues in Washington, D.C., but also for decorations and figures for the Carnegie Library, and in New York, the commission for the Chamber of Commerce groups. Naturally, MacMonnies and Martiny were rivals. Rejoicing in the popular acclaim for his bulging, flower-bedecked figures, MacMonnies said that Martiny created but one figure and then used it over and over, just changing the position of hands and feet and putting Saint-Gaudens drapery on it. Critics were to say that Martiny "improved decorative sculpture in America." What MacMonnies did to American taste in sculpture was at least not permanent, which is about the best that can be said for it.

These assistants, plus assorted dogs and a steady stream of transient guests, came to Cornish, New Hampshire, by way of Windsor, Vermont, diverting the natives, who thought "the New Yorkers" were half crazy. Mrs. Saint-Gaudens had already brought two servants with her from the city. It was probably at about this time that she acquired the cook whose excellent efforts continued in the Saint-Gaudens household for many years. The cook's name was Augusta! She was always addressed as Augusta, while her employer continued to rejoice in the name of Gussie.

Mr. Saint-Gaudens, with his French appreciation of good food, won the heart of this amply proportioned lady and they became conspirators. The cook bought Jersey cream from a local farmer, made delicious ice cream which she assured Mrs. Saint-Gaudens contained only milk and was therefore not an extravagance. As time went by, the assistants lived in boardinghouses in the vicinity of Cornish but took their noon meal at the Saint-Gaudens house. In her never-ending but losing battle to keep down expenses, Mrs. Saint-Gaudens developed a formula for offering the young men a second helping. "You don't want any more, do you?" she would say. The reply was inevitably to the effect that more would be most welcome. If, somehow, the available supply ran out, a quiet visit to the cook paid off. It was not unheard-of to find Mr. Saint-Gaudens among the kitchen-door applicants for second helpings.

A horse was hired from a neighboring farmer, a vehicle of sorts acquired. A hired man, whose stubborn, independent ways Gussie did not in the least approve of, took care of horse and garden. "A good horse can be had for $7.50 a month and a man for $15.00 a month with board," was the way Gussie put it. That her husband put the man before the horse, liked and got on beautifully with the natives, did not help matters.

Life was not always peaceful in the country — not with the Scotch deerhound to break the monotony. At the foot of the hill was a horse-breeding farm, a Mr. Barker in charge. Every day at dusk Mr. Barker, in a high-wheeled racing sulky, drove a big stallion up the hill past the Saint-Gaudens house. He was driving back again one evening when the Scotch deerhound dashed out into the road, barking and leaping at the horse. The dog was only a pup, Saint-Gaudens said by way of excuse. "In one moment horse, driver and buggy were mixed up in . . . confusion, the horse rearing and plunging, Barker on the ground, the dog dancing around . . . leaping in the air."

Louis and Gussie rushed out and shouted to the man to drop the reins. The sulky was smashed, but Mr. Barker clung to the reins, refusing to let go until he was finally thrown clear. They carried Mr. Barker, bleeding and covered with dirt into the house and asked him why he had hung onto the reins. "I was afraid to let the horse go for fear he might kill someone," Barker said.

"Ever since, I have touched my hat to Barker, a man of the right stuff," Saint-Gaudens wrote. Barker "was a veteran of the Civil War."

It is to be hoped that somebody collared the dog and eventually taught him better manners. Saint-Gaudens made no mention of that, but told what happened to the horse. "The stallion tore down the road for two miles with the shafts burying themselves in his sides." He was on the main road now, at river level, and came to the covered toll bridge across the Connecticut. There was a sign over the entrance to the bridge which said, "Walk your horses or pay two dollars fine." So "the horse walked peacefully across" and allowed himself to be caught.

Saint-Gaudens and his assistants put in long hours under tension in the excitement of seeing things go right in the old barn — now the studio. Then there would come a day when it would be time to stop work. Saint-Gaudens would announce a holiday for all hands. It was one such day when he and the assistants climbed into a wagon and had the man drive them to Cornish Flats, another almost deserted village about five miles down the Connecticut River valley. They were off to look at an erratic boulder that might be used for a soldiers' monument if carted away from its hillside resting-place and set up in town, properly inscribed with the names of Cornish Flats men who died in the Civil War.

"We formed a conglomerate crew, garrulous and joyful during the drive," Gus said. "At the foot of the hill we arrived at the entrance to what we noticed was a deserted farmhouse. We climbed past it, over gateways and fences and tramped across a field filled with flowers." The boulder was at the top of the hill.

The men sat down to rest and the talk turned to speculation as to how many from the tiny village below them had marched off to the Civil War, never to return. "One guessed a certain number, one another." At the end "our silent driver, who was perched on top of the rock, said, 'There were twenty-eight men died from this here town.'

" 'What do you know about it?' we asked.

" 'I was one of the volunteers,' the driver said.

"We turned down the hill and entered the empty house. The doors were all open, everything was gone. . . . Over the fireplace someone had scratched with a piece of charcoal, 'Good-bye, old home.' We came out and went away."

When Saint-Gaudens brought his final version of the "Standing *Lincoln*" back to his New York studio, Richard Watson Gilder came to see it again. A change had come over it, Gilder saw. He thought perhaps Saint-Gaudens had "thrown the head down a little, giving that contemplative look which is so fine and so characteristic of Lincoln."

15

THE "STANDING *LINCOLN*"

SAINT-GAUDENS had fallen in love with the country of Lincoln-shaped men. He said he accomplished more during his first summer in Cornish than in all the previous hot summers in New York, so he decided to buy the old house with its acres. But Mr. Beaman had changed his mind about selling. He had small children and it occurred to him that when they grew up, one of them might want the place, but Saint-Gaudens could have it almost indefinitely, at a nominal rent. It would be a long time before any of the Beaman children would be old enough to look for a summer home. Meanwhile, Gus would be putting in improvements at his own expense.

Gus stayed in Cornish until November, enjoying his first New England autumn. Sometimes skies were as soft as the Italian skies he loved, sometimes they were as bright blue and hard as Italian faïence. Maples flamed among dark hemlocks on the flanks of Ascutney, then gradually faded into the colors of old tapestry. Cornish was the place for painters, Gus told his friends during his various sorties to New York and return. Friends flocked to visit him, many of them negotiating with Mr. Beaman for an abandoned farmhouse and barn to rebuild into a home and studio.

When snow lay on the upper slopes of Ascutney, when leaves fell and bare branches etched a black and white picture and river fog filled the valley, it was time to go. The sheet-iron stove, fired till it was red-hot, no longer warmed the old barn. The brick house was chilly, no matter how many fireplaces were kept full of burning logs all day and most of the night, then lighted early by the servants, who cared little for rising in the dark to set fresh wood over hot coals.

From the comfort of the New York apartment, Gus wrote to his sister-in-law Genie Homer. "Gussie is at the piano, playing to Homer, he must be put to sleep now with themes and melodies from Beethoven. Oh, he is like his Aunt Bundles — takes the cake."

Here Gus paused to draw some cartoons. A thin girl, (Gussie) was falling into the arms of a fat girl (Genie) and under the picture it said, "This is Gussie and you. It's a libel on both of you. You are not punchin' the life out of each other but 'tis only a representation of your appearance in the entry of the 4th floor of 22 Washington Place to pay us a visit, in reply to the invitation which I hereby extend." Gus drew a hand holding out a scroll with words printed on it as follows: "Mr. and Mrs. Sunkittens request the pleasure of your company at this Shebang as soon as you damn please."

Perhaps in reference to Genie's arguments in favor of woman's rights, Gus went on to say, "I haven't been able to attack you for a long while and I'm thirsting for your blood." He needed all the rest of the sheet of writing paper for a cartoon of himself in fencing position, brandishing a long sword over his head. On the other side of the paper he wrote, "Dear Genie, Gussie says, 'I don't think you've written enough about her coming, somehow or other.' Now, if I've got to cover this paper with ink in order to impress on your brain that we would very much like to have you come and pay us a visit, and that we sincerely mean it, why then I will see you and Roxbury in — no, I'll stop there." And he printed in increasingly large letters, "KUM, oh KUM, KUM ON."

Of course Genie came. They always gave her a good time in New York, taking her to the theater and trotting out bachelors for her. Now that White was off the list, it was Charles Brewster, an attractive young lawyer, who was Genie's escort. Genie also expected to go on duty as Homer's attendant along with the nursemaid — because Augusta's second child was due in about a month. The first hint of trouble was told in a letter to Rose Hawthorne Lathrop.

Even though Rose was Augusta's most intimate friend, it would have been indelicate to put anything down on paper about an expected child. Gussie merely mentioned her "gout" which the doctor told her was the cause of the painful swelling in her feet. She did not want Rose to tell anybody about "this little indisposition" because she "had been well so long now" that she "could not bear the hint of being sick at all."

A letter from Dr. Frederick L. Morse, of Windsor, Vermont, written on April 17, 1888 — or about two and a half years later — explains the

Saint-Gaudens as a "fickle bird."

Saint-Gaudens makes fun of himself
during a painful illness

As a fencer, Saint-Gaudens brandishes his sword

As "the Sculp," Saint-Gaudens liked to present
himself in Roman toga, laurel-crowned

so-called gout. "I will say nothing of your first mis-hap for I've no patience left when I think of your days of local, not to say general poisoning." Augusta did not bear a living child. Growth of the fetus had ceased, no one knew for how long a time, and Augusta, as a result of that "general poisoning" Dr. Morse mentioned, was ill all winter. Genie took care of her sister while the girls' mother arrived to super-intend the seven-year-old Homer. Saint-Gaudens took refuge in his studio where he often spent nights as well as days.

Augusta's hearing, which had been diminishing, was now much impaired and there was a new development which she referred to as "the noise in my head." A letter from a Boston specialist, written to her New York doctor, a copy of which she kept, gave the medical name of her trouble — "Tinnitus." Gussie heard the sound of the circulation of her own blood while sounds from the outside world scarcely reached her. The specialists whom she consulted could do nothing but recom-mend tonics on the ground that she was anemic, and suggested rest in bed, although when she was lying down the volume of inner sound increased. Severe tinnitus is described as "almost maddening."

Because she sincerely wanted to be well, Augusta haunted doctors' offices more and more. She was fortunate in becoming the patient of Dr. William Mecklinburg Polk, a Southerner who had intended to enter West Point.[1] He was seventeen when the Civil War broke out and it was said that no soldier took part in more battles and skirmishes than he. His father, a bishop, became a Confederate general and was killed at Pine Mountain. William was a captain when the war was over, then superintendent of an Alabama iron works, where a doctor he met inspired him to study medicine. He had graduated from the College of Physicians and Surgeons in 1869, and when Augusta met him he combined the teaching of obstetrics and gynecology at the University of the City of New York with a rapidly growing private practice. Eventually, he became Dean of Cornell University Medical School and head of the gynecological department. Friends said that "his understanding of womankind and his diplomatic management of their ailments was almost miraculous." Augusta Saint-Gaudens cor-roborated this statement and described her own attitude toward Dr. Polk. "There is a magnetism in his presence which makes your own feelings clearer. I think he is, above all, a good, inspiring listener."

Gus was not a good listener. Although he brought no bulging brief-case home from the office, he brought his work home from the studio in his mind. He tried to tell Gussie not to worry so much about her health, about Homer's (which was excellent) and about money. But words intended to be affectionate and consoling sounded otherwise when shouted to a woman who was deaf. Augusta would misunderstand a phrase or argue a point not even brought up in the conversation. They discovered that they were both high-tempered. They loved each other, but neither was able to make the other happy.

Arriving at the studio in a state of nervous tension, Saint-Gaudens steadied down as soon as his hands touched clay. To this the assistants and studio boys attested, along with descriptions of his studio rages. Work was his salvation these days and during the years 1886 and 1887 he completed two major commissions. On May 22, 1886, "I show my *Puritan* on Monday afternoon and would be glad to see you and yours," Saint-Gaudens wrote to Richard Watson Gilder — a similar invitation going to other friends, the writers, musicians and artists who made up New York's intellectual circle.

In the reception room at the Thirty-sixth Street studio, there were two sets of curtains to hang behind the platform — black velvet if the work were in plaster, white if it were in bronze. Ladies were invited and Gussie, if she felt well enough, would be there to sit behind a tea table decked out with the white Japanese cups Mrs. Chapin had given her. Wine and cake would be served at the reception as well as tea — a Paris custom Gussie had explained a trifle anxiously to her mother. Now, in New York, it was very much the thing among Americans who remembered Paris days with nostalgia, and this mild form of the future cocktail party gave New York's art colony the feeling that they were being Continental. Such gatherings were not fun for Augusta anymore, however, because of her loss of hearing. She imagined that people avoided talking to her — and perhaps they did.

Soon, however, the whole Saint-Gaudens family plus servants and assorted studio assistants were off for Cornish. Gussie felt better and devoted her energies to entertaining her husband's friends and her own relatives — and to having improvements made, such as the piping of springwater into the house. Gus continued to complain that the old house looked gloomy, and as seasons came and went, his efforts were directed to the building of terraces and white-painted pergolas framing a perfect view of Ascutney. Italian gardens became the rage in Cornish and eventually provided Maxfield Parrish with those fairy-tale landscapes for his illustrations and murals. Parrish included portraits of local people, his friend the carpenter or the handyman perhaps becoming Peter in his picture of "Peter, Peter, pumpkin-eater," for example.

One humorous friend of Saint-Gaudens' said that the sculptor's grim old brick house, with its white pillars in front, looked like an elderly New Hampshire farmer with a new set of false teeth. Another said that the house, encircled with Italianate pergolas, looked like a New England old maid struggling in the arms of a satyr.[2]

During this second summer in Cornish, Saint-Gaudens was working on fountains, one to go to Lincoln Park in Chicago, to be called *Storks at Play*, which he always referred to as "by Saint-Gaudens and Frederick MacMonnies" — the other for Springfield, Massachusetts, as part of the setting of the *Puritan*. Genie was recruited to help in the matter of models for fountains. "I want a bass, a trout and a small salmon — no matter how small the latter and no matter how large the former," Gus wrote her.

He sent ten dollars which should cover the cost of the fish "and two seats in the parlor car for Windsor," one for Genie and one for the fish basket. "You would have a gloriously lonely time of it in the car all by yourself with only the accompaniment of the flies that must necessarily accompany dead fish," he told her. Gus drew three fish, one biting another's tail, one mournful and one laughing. Then he relented. Genie could send the fish from Boston by railway express and he hoped she would have money enough left to buy a flower for herself and a plant for her sister Lizzie. Genie could not come to Cornish because Lizzie Nichols was now the family invalid requiring her services.

George de Forest Brush, at this time a painter of American Indians, arrived to visit Saint-Gaudens.[3] Although there were nine beds, "all but one with woven springs," Gussie took pride in saying, there was no room for Mr. Brush, so he built himself a teepee on Saint-Gaudens' land, about a hundred yards from the house. This he preferred anyway and his teepee was a work of art. Brush was a little over thirty, as yet unmarried. His father had been a doctor in Tennessee and George had been sent to live among Indians in the West, in the hope that an outdoor life would improve his health. He painted Indians not as brutal savages but as people in tune with their wilderness life; his backgrounds of stream and woodland being particularly beautiful. Perhaps because of his sympathy with Indians who had been deprived of their land, Brush became an ardent supporter of Henry George, champion of land reform and the "single tax." A huge electioneering portrait of Henry George as candidate for mayor of New York City ornamented the George de Forest Brush teepee.

Gus, his assistants and guests loved to spend an evening with Brush. If Brush were in the mood, he would dance his "Indian dog-dance" for them. But there was one uncongenial member of the group. He was Thomas Wilmer Dewing, eventually an immensely popular portrait painter. Some of his portraits were vague, not quite impressionistic, but fuzzy enough to flatter a homely woman. He must have been given to experiments with pigment, because it was said that his "beautiful portrait of Mrs. Saint-Gaudens turned black!"[4] Right now, Thomas Dewing hated Henry George and fierce arguments broke out in the Brush teepee.

George de Forest Brush did not return to his Cornish teepee the following summer. He married a beautiful pupil, Mary Whelpley, and Mr. Beaman built them a cottage. "Assembled" would have been a better word for it, because a "corn barn and a pig pen were put together to make it." Later, after living in a tent temporarily, they hired a big house in Cornish, but after a few years George de Forest Brush decided to give up Cornish as a summer home. Everybody there seemed to take sides on politics and on almost any other subject that came up, he said. He became one of the leaders of the Dublin, New Hampshire, art colony with its painters Abbot Thayer and Joseph Lindon Smith. They were happy in their admiration of Monadnock, a mountain of their own. Rarely would a Dublin artist admit that Ascutney could be as beautiful, nor would Cornish artists grant Monadnock equal praise. George de Forest Brush gave his teepee to Homer Saint-Gaudens to play in.

Dewing returned to Cornish, but Saint-Gaudens remarked that "Dewing is doing very little up here." He nevertheless painted a portrait of Mrs. Beaman in payment for "a charming little place much more cosy than mine," Gus said. Dewing's wife, Maria Oakey Dewing, began to lay the foundation for her reputation as a painter of flowers from her Cornish garden and as a writer for women's magazines.

As Saint-Gaudens remembered it, the summer of 1887 saw the spectacular end of the George de Forest Brush teepee. A group of seven or eight artists and their guests planned an evening picnic. "It turned out to be dismal, grey weather but nevertheless we went down, lit the fire, whereupon I believe Dewing's deep design showed itself,"

Gus said. "He reasoned unconsciously, 'if I can get all these chaps as well as myself full of fire-water, nature will do the rest.'

"He was right, for after having eaten all that was proper and drunk more than was necessary, we danced with glee around the teepee." Someone put too much wood on the fire — and the teepee, and the portrait of Henry George which was still inside it, went up in flames.

Although polling more votes than Theodore Roosevelt, Henry George failed of election as mayor of New York. In 1887, he was candidate for Secretary of State on the United Labor party ticket. George Fletcher Babb, onetime instructor of White in the office of Russell Sturgis, was designing pergolas and altering studios for Saint-Gaudens. He was a frequent visitor at Cornish, an incurable punster and practical joker. Babb hunted around the ruins of the teepee, found fragments of canvas — once the electioneering portrait of Henry George — and retired with them to his room, having borrowed scissors, needle and thread from Augusta. He was "mysteriously at work" for some time and then emerged with little rosettes (a popular form of political badge), each with a solitary tack hanging from the center. "The single tax badges were put in our lapels and we pranced over to Dewing's," Gus said. Dewing thought that Saint-Gaudens had devised the caper, but as a matter of fact, Gus had no time for such elaborate fooling.

During the summer of 1887, Saint-Gaudens had reluctantly left Cornish for Marion, Massachusetts, on Buzzard's Bay. This sleepy former shipbuilding town was still reached only by stagecoach after a tedious train journey. Henry James said that as "a sedative influence," the "toneless air" would "minister to perfect rest." Gus had little use for toneless air, but the Gilders had a summer place in Marion which they loved as much as he loved Cornish. Stanford White had helped them remodel an old stone building, formerly an oil refinery and later a plant for converting seawater into salt. White designed a huge chimney with a capacious fireplace, making the square stone building into a studio where Helena de Kay Gilder could paint and where her husband could read manuscripts late into the night. Their main house, described by Henry James in *The Bostonians* as "shingled all over, grey and slightly collapsing," was the favorite meeting place for many distinguished guests, from Richard Harding Davis to Okakura, Mrs. Jack Gardner's Japanese protégé. In 1887, the charming Frances Folsom Cleveland, recent bride of Grover Cleveland, was visiting the Gilders.

Saint-Gaudens had been summoned to do a portrait in bas-relief of young Mrs. Cleveland, who sat in an armchair on Mrs. Gilder's model stand and turned her pretty profile to the sculptor. Richard Watson Gilder was on hand with a camera to photograph the scene.

Gus begrudged the time spent away from his Cornish studio, but he knew that Gilder was doing him a favor by arranging a sitting with a lady who was much in the news since her marriage to the President of the United States. Cleveland, who had been a forty-nine-year-old bachelor, had been the victim of a smear campaign concerning his relations with a woman. Gussie, who was becoming more puritanical year by year, said she didn't see how a nice girl could marry a man about whom there had been so much scandal. Cleveland had told his political enemies to "tell the truth" and Gus said it was about time the nation had an honest President. But Mrs. Cleveland proved a difficult subject. She couldn't hold a pose!

On October 20, 1887, a brief notice appeared in the papers.[5] Under a Chicago dateline, the New York *Times* announced that "the statue of Abraham Lincoln, which is to ornament the southern entrance to Lincoln Park, was placed in its permanent position this morning." The "Standing *Lincoln*" had been cast in bronze and shipped by freight to Chicago. There would be no more changes, no more requests that the man who was the Lincoln-shaped model should stride over Cornish roads again in the broadcloth suit copied for him from Lincoln photographs. Creases, folds caused by actual wear had been molded in clay, cast in plaster and would now have to remain in bronze for all time.

Saint-Gaudens, his marble *Hiawatha* almost forgotten, now belonged to a strictly American school of artistic thinking as opposed to the concept of American heroes in Roman togas so dear to the heart of a previous generation of sculptors. As time went by, Saint-Gaudens would simplify his work, but already he omitted some details, emphasizing others to achieve a harmony in contemporary costume which his imitators could never quite understand. As to the deeply contemplative look, the bent head — this was a portrait of Lincoln that would seem right, for years to come.

Definitely more interested in statistics than in art, however, the *Times* reporter announced that "the statue, which is bronze, weighs over 2000 pounds. The casting, which was done by the Henry Bonnard Company of New York, was a very delicate piece of work as the chair and the figure of Mr. Lincoln and the heavy base on which both rest, were cast all in one piece."

Saint-Gaudens modeling the portrait of Mrs. Grover Cleveland in Mrs. Richard Watson Gilder's summer studio (Photograph by Richard Watson Gilder; courtesy of Miss Rosamond Gilder and the Board of Trustees of Dartmouth College)

Next day, the New York *Tribune* remarked only that Mr. Saint-Gaudens' statue of Lincoln was "put in place in Chicago." But the *Tribune* took occasion to put the *Times* in its place on the subject of reporting events concerning art. "The way many newspapers report the unveiling of statues suggests the question whether the sculptor is as important a person as the bronze founder. The latter's name is apt to obtain prominent mention for obvious reasons while the sculptor cannot be found even in the list of 'distinguished visitors. . . .' The casting of statues is a most interesting industry and the manufacture of artist's colors is also interesting, but it is not yet usual to mention the manufacturer's name in describing a picture and to ignore the artist."

The house in Cornish must have been closed earlier than usual in 1887 because, although the sculptor's name was far from prominent in the Chicago papers, one small item seems to indicate that the whole Saint-Gaudens family went to Chicago. "The sculptor sat on the dais, unrecognized, his wife and child by his side," said the Chicago *Tribune* on Sunday, October 23, the day after the unveiling. Perhaps Genie also climbed aboard the Pullman bound for Chicago, because toward the end of the list of ticket holders to the grandstand was a "Miss Homer."

Saturday was not a pleasant day in Chicago. A chill wind from the lake swept over Lincoln Park and everyone who came to the unveiling carried an umbrella. The New York papers said that five thousand people were in the park, but the Chicago *Tribune* declared that there were ten thousand and that it was "the biggest crowd since the Chicago fire. . . . Long before 2:30 o'clock, the hour of the beginning of the exercises, every street-car that passed the park brought a crowded load of passengers. People came on foot and in carriages."

Mayor Roche arrived "shortly after, joined by Mr. Saint-Gaudens, the sculptor," but it took another half hour for "members of the city council, the county board," a long list of judges, a general and his staff to appear and be seated. After the mayor had seized his opportunity for a political speech, the chairman of the board of trustees eulogized the donor, Eli Bates, a poor boy from Springfield, Massachusetts, who had made good in Chicago. While the eulogy was going on, "little Abe had been sent up to the foot of the statue," according to the New York *Times*. The Chicago *Tribune* came a little closer to the truth about "little Abe" and then described the scene. Abraham Lincoln, son of Robert T. Lincoln and grandson of the President, was "fifteen years

old." He had "modestly taken his place among the halyards and amid
the roar of cannon, the triumphant strains of national airs, the cheers
of thousands and the tears of many, the colossal bronze was unveiled
. . . while the gray heavens became aglow with a mild silvery light.

"A thirty-eight gun salute now commenced, the band-master once
more waved his baton, the crowd cheered and it was several minutes
before the speeches could continue." But there was another cause for
delay, other than cannon, band music and cheering. Two ladies had
driven to the park "in their cart," had found a good place to pull up,
not far from the statue — but their horse did not care for thirty-eight-
gun salutes. The horse "began rearing and plunging through the
crowd" and "tried to jump over the fence but became entangled in the
wires." The lady who was driving him was "thrown over his head but
was not hurt." The other lady jumped out of the cart, but the fence
"had to be cut before the horse could be released. Men and women
stampeded toward the stone terrace which surrounds the monument"
and the police finally persuaded "Battery D" to stop firing.

Homer Saint-Gaudens, now seven years old, must have had a good
view of ladies, horse and cart, finding an unveiling more within his
range of interest than he expected. Then the oratory began again, but
by the time the Honorable Leonard Swett arose, "the crowd, as well as
Mr. Swett were suffering from the cold and that gentleman did not
attempt to ornament his speech with oratorical flourishes" — as the
Chicago *Herald* put it.

Saint-Gaudens felt relief and perhaps a letdown when it was all
over. He said he was not sure whether the people came just to hear the
band play and the guns go off or whether they really cared about
Lincoln and saw the statue as he did — as a tribute to a great American. But the press, for all the lyric writing popular at the time, gave
impressive reports. The statue was "a labor of love, on the part of the
sculptor" and this was a phrase concerning Saint-Gaudens that would
often be used in connection with his work as the years went by. The
statue "proved that classic drapery is not indispensable to artistic effect
in sculpture, nor theatrical accessories to make the human form seem
somewhat divine. . . ."

The Saint-Gaudens "Standing *Lincoln*" was one of the best loved of
his statues. Many bronze replicas in various sizes were made and
placed in schools and colleges. A full-sized replica was to stand in
Parliament Square, London, and at this unveiling schoolchildren were
to sing Julia Ward Howe's "Battle Hymn of the Republic."

On Thanksgiving Day, in 1887, the statue of Deacon Samuel Chapin was unveiled in Stearns Park, in Springfield, Massachusetts. Again the skies were gray, but this was a simple ceremony, devoid of brass bands and military salutes. People just walked over to Stearns Park from the white-steepled First Church on Court Square, where they had attended a service, or came down the hill from other churches, at least three of them built by Richardson. Chester W. Chapin, whose face in bronze looked out from under the broad-brimmed hat of his ancestor, presented the statue to the city. His little daughter, Pauline, and her cousin, Chester Chapin Rumrill, pulled the cord to bring down the flags around the statue.

An "official history," perhaps written by a member of the family, said that "after the conclusion of the exercises on Stearns Park, an old fashioned stage-coach-and-four bore an animated party swiftly over the four miles to Chicopee Street for a reunion at the old homestead. There in the great dining room, by a cheerful fire in the old broad fireplace, with shining andirons and crane and pot hooks and trammels, twelve persons sat around the table and feasted on the generous viands. . . . Present at the dinner was Augustus Saint-Gaudens who had traveled to Springfield for the history-making occasion." This was the sole mention, by anyone, of the name of Saint-Gaudens.

Chester W. Chapin and a group of Springfield businessmen had a plan — not yet called urban renewal. They visualized new buildings and a theater to face Stearns Park which would become a handsome focal point in the city. Nothing came of the project and, as Saint-Gaudens said, "the quarter of the city was poor and in a few weeks the boys had destroyed everything in the way of vegetation in Stearns Park."

"Everything in the way of vegetation" included white birches set out along two sides of the park and a pine hedge all around it. In 1887, "Deacon Chapin would not have found the atmosphere a strange one as he looked out upon the park," according to the Springfield *Republican*. And yet it seems possible that he might have been surprised to see, directly in front of him, the pink granite seat designed by Stanford White and the Saint-Gaudens bronze fountain "cast in the shape of a world sphere, flanked by bronze tortoises to represent the four seasons of the year." The Indians would have been surprised too.

Twelve years later, the statue of Deacon Chapin was moved to Merrick Park on State Street just below the Public Library. Saint-Gaudens was not happy about the new location, because he had

The PURITAN, *Merrick Park, Springfield, Massachusetts (Photo from Museum of Fine Arts, Springfield, Massachusetts)*

designed the figure to be seen at street level and now it stood on a knoll — too high above State Street. But the *Puritan* is forceful on this spot. The impression of motion is striking as Deacon Chapin seems to sweep forward, great cloak blown back, a huge Bible on his arm. The pink granite seat, much chipped, and the fountain, minus two of its tortoises, were relegated to other city parks.

In "Deacon Chapin," Saint-Gaudens had created another much loved statue, replicas of which were sought after. In 1903, the New England Society of Pennsylvania commissioned a full-sized replica for Philadelphia. But Saint-Gaudens could not bear to send a mere copy to so important a city. He made changes so that both Philadelphia and Springfield, Massachusetts, would have an "original." The *Pilgrim*, as the Philadelphia statue was called, was not a portrait of Chester W. Chapin. The face of the Philadelphia *Pilgrim* was long and narrow, the "New England type," Saint-Gaudens called it. The Bible was reversed, the pilgrim carrying its spine forward instead of showing great metal clasps over the leaves, as in the Deacon Chapin statue.

There were other changes and then, after the *Pilgrim* had been set up in Philadelphia ready to be unveiled, Saint-Gaudens decided that the pedestal was too high. His passion for perfection overcame all considerations of cost. "I wish nothing said about this," he wrote, knowing that the sponsors were satisfied. "I mean to go ahead and do it; my men will appear with a derrick, and when everything is ready, lift the statue off, cut the pedestal and proceed with the work. . . . The charges will be 'on me.' "

The year 1887 had been notable for the creation of two public statues destined to become famous and to rank high on the list of the sculptor's life work. It was also notable for a private project which Saint-Gaudens undertook just for the pleasure of it. This was the portrait medallion of Robert Louis Stevenson. "I was never much of a reader," Saint-Gaudens said. But he had discovered Stevenson's *The New Arabian Nights,* was delighted with it and read all the other books by Stevenson that he could get his hands on. Then it turned out that Will Low actually knew Stevenson personally — had been a fellow student in Paris with him. Late in September, 1887, Stevenson came to the United States and Gus asked Low if he could fix it up for the writer to sit for a bas-relief. Low could and did arrange it.

Thomas Russell Sullivan,[6] of Boston, had just made *Dr. Jekyll and Mr. Hyde* into a drama for Richard Mansfield. It opened in Boston on the 9th of May, was a success, and it was playing in New York when Stevenson came to the United States with his wife, his mother and his stepson.

After a brief stay in New York, Stevenson made a visit to the Fairchilds in Newport, Rhode Island.[7] Much to his embarrassment, the cold he had caught on shipboard grew worse — but his hosts made it clear that he was no trouble at all to them and the beautiful Maud Howe brought him flowers. He lay "full length on a couch, wrapped in a scarlet dressing gown, smoking endless cigarettes," Maud said.

On September 23, 1887, Stevenson was back in New York City, writing to his publisher, Sidney Colvin. He was "awaiting the arrival of a sculptor (St. Gaudens) who is making a medallion of yours truly and who is (to boot) one of the handsomest and nicest fellows I have ever seen," Stevenson said. The Saint-Gaudens medallion showed him propped against pillows in bed, a rough blanket on his knees. He was smoking one of those "thin wisps of cigarettes" which he rolled himself — and he was writing a letter.

After describing adventures on his sea voyage and his delight at being offered seven hundred pounds for twelve articles for *Scribner's* magazine, Stevenson said, "Here I was interrupted by the arrival of my sculptor. I withdraw calling him handsome; he is not quite that, his eyes are too near together; he is only remarkable looking and like an Italian cinque-cento medallion. I have begged him to make a medallion of himself and give it to me."[8]

16

THE "GOD-LIKE SCULPTOR"

SAINT-GAUDENS worked in Robert Louis Stevenson's room at the Hotel Albert on Eleventh Street and Will Low never missed a sitting. He felt sure that his conversation put Stevenson at his ease so that Gus could get a better likeness. There were five sittings of two or three hours each. One day, the talk came around to the nude in sculpture. Saint-Gaudens said that he had never had time to do a nude statue but that he would if he ever got the chance. Will Low quoted Emerson:

> The sinful painter drapes his goddess warm
> Because she still is naked, being dressed:
> The God-like sculptor will not so deform
> Beauty, which limbs and flesh enough invest.

Stevenson promptly adopted the phrase "God-like sculptor" and this was his name for Saint-Gaudens henceforth, in letters sent from Saranac, New York, or Valima Plantation, Upolu, Samoa.

"My episode with Stevenson has been one of the events of my life, and I can now understand the state of mind God gets into about people," Gus wrote. He drew a cartoon of himself on his knees to Stevenson who wore a saint's halo. In a book which Stevenson had given to Saint-Gaudens, the author wrote,

> Each of us must have our way
> Mine with ink and yours with clay.

The bas-relief was nearly finished, but Gus needed more time to model the long slender hands. Stevenson left for Saranac, promising further sittings on his return. His wife, Fanny, had gone ahead to negotiate with Dr. Trudeau, famous specialist in the treatment of tuberculosis, and she had taken a frame house on a hilltop near the sanatorium.

Stevenson's health improved at Saranac although he thought the cottage with its view of a river "pretty bleak." As for a view of the lake, he cared nothing for it because, as he told Henry James, "I like water (fresh water, I mean) either running swiftly over stones or else largely qualified with whiskey." He continued to rejoice over the large sums of money he was to receive in America, compared to his British contracts. "Good Lord, what fun! Wealth is only useful for two things; a yacht and a string quartette. For these I would sell my soul," he said.

By April, Stevenson was back in New York, this time at the St. Stevens Hotel which his friends now called the "St. Stevenson." Fanny was soon on her way to San Francisco where she would buy the yacht *Casco* in which they would sail for the South Seas. But meanwhile, Gus came to the hotel to continue modeling the portrait bas-relief and mentioned that he was also doing a bust of General William Tecumseh Sherman. Both Stevenson and his wife wanted to meet the general, so Gus said he would try to arrange it but warned that the general was now "a little dotty."

Gus broached the matter to General Sherman at their next sitting. "Robert Louis Stevenson?" Sherman asked. "Was he one of my boys?" Gus explained that Mr. Stevenson had written *Dr. Jekyll and Mr. Hyde.* Sherman had evidently seen the popular play. "Well, *he's* no fool. Let him come," General Sherman said.

Saint-Gaudens brought Mr. and Mrs. Stevenson to the hotel where Sherman was staying. After being kept waiting awhile, they were shown into the general's room. He was lying on a sofa and Fanny Stevenson sat on the end of it. Sherman liked her. She was a forthright American who had lived a pioneer life in California during her first marriage; a woman "all blood and guts," as Saint-Gaudens is said to have described her.

Sherman began to explain to Fanny Stevenson "the difference be-tween sabre-cuts and bullet-wounds — how sabre-cuts make you look done-up without doing you much harm, but a bullet went into you, '*Zip!*' And Sherman leaned forward and dug his finger into Mrs. Stevenson."[1]

Now Sherman remembered that he had another guest. He turned to Stevenson. "Were you one of my boys?" he asked. After that, "things were rather perfunctory for a while" until Stevenson got Sherman to talking about the Civil War. "They soon had maps out before them" — becoming friends when it was clear that Stevenson already knew a good deal about the campaigns.

By the middle of May, Stevenson was in Manasquan, New Jersey, being looked after by the faithful Low.[2] The bas-relief, one of the most beautiful Saint-Gaudens had ever done, was practically finished, but he was not quite satisfied with the hands.[3] Taking Homer, now nearly eight years old, with him, Saint-Gaudens went to Manasquan to take a cast of Stevenson's hands. Stevenson wrote a letter which he gave to Homer, dating it the 27th of May, 1888.

Dear Homer St. Gaudens,

Your father has brought you this day to see me, and he tells me it is his hope you may remember the occasion. I am going to do what I can to carry out his wish; and it may amuse you, years after, to see this little scrap of paper and to read what I write. I must begin by testifying that you, yourself, took no interest whatever in the introduction, and in the most proper spirit displayed a single-minded ambition to get back to play, and this I thought an excellent and admirable point in your character. You were also (I use the past tense, with a view to the time when you shall read, rather than to that when I am writing) a very pretty boy, and (to my European view) startlingly self-possessed. My time of observation was so limited that you must pardon me if I can say no more: what else I marked: what restlessness of foot and hand, what graceful clumsiness, what experimental designs upon the furniture, was but the common inheritance of human youth. But you may perhaps like to know that the lean, flushed man in the bed, who interested you so little, was in a state of mind extremely mingled and unpleasant: harassed with work which he thought he was not doing well, troubled with difficulties to which you will in time succeed, and yet looking forward to no less a matter than a voyage to the South Seas and a visitation of savage and desert islands.

Your father's friend, Robert Louis Stevenson.

Saint-Gaudens and Stevenson never saw each other again, but this was not the end of their friendship nor of their correspondence.[4] Five years later, when Stevenson was settled in his house, Valima, in Samoa, he addressed his "God-like Sculptor" in the most delicate manner" to suggest three commissions. "No. 1 is for a couple of copies of my medallion, as gilt-edged and high-toned as it is possible to make them. One is for our house here. The other is for my friend, Sidney Colvin."

The second request was rather an odd one. Stevenson wanted Saint-Gaudens to design an alphabet, to be cast, gilded and equipped with pins on the back. The walls of his house in Samoa were of "varnished wood of a dark, ruddy ˙color." They needed brightening and he thought it would be a wonderful idea to spell out the names of guests in gold letters on his walls, or to arrange "festive mottoes" or humorous remarks which could be changed from time to time. Having no idea of the amount of work involved, he suggested that Saint-Gaudens adapt "some exquisitely fine clear type from some Roman monument," then get a "manufacturer to take the idea" because it would surely sell "in your land of wooden houses." Stevenson visualized all his American friends — Low, Gilder, Thomas Russell Sullivan and the rest — pinning up gold letters all over their living-room walls. Saint-Gaudens obliged with some samples of beautiful gold letters together with an estimate of what it would cost to have a whole anagram set of them made.

The bas-relief arrived safely in Samoa, but Stevenson had built his house high on a hill, reached only by a primitive track. Heading his letter "Valima, September 1889," Stevenson told of difficulties neither he nor Gus had foreseen. "I had determined not to write to you till I had seen the medallion, but it looks as if that might mean the Greek Kalends or the day after tomorrow. Reassure yourself, your part is done, it is ours that halts in consideration of conveyance over our sweet little road on boys' backs, for we cannot very well apply the horse to this work; there is only one; you cannot put it in a pannier; to put it on the horse's back we have not the heart. Beneath the beauty of R.L.S., to say nothing of his verses, which his publishers find heavy enough, and the genius of the God-like Sculptor, the spine would snap and the well-built limbs of the (ahem) cart-horse would be loosed in death.

"So you are to conceive of me, sitting in my house, dubitative, and the medallion chuckling in the warehouse of the German firm for some days longer; and hear me meanwhile on the golden letters.

"Alas! they are all my fancy painted but the price is prohibitive. I cannot do it. It is another day dream burst. Another gable of Abbotsford gone down, fortunately before it was builded, so there's nobody injured — except me. I had a strong conviction that I was a great hand at writing inscriptions, and meant to test my genius on the walls of the house; and now I see I can't. It is generally thus. The Battle of the Golden Letters will never be delivered. On making preparation to open the campaign, the King found himself face to face with invincible difficulties, in which the rapacity of a mercenary soldiery and the complaints of an improverished treasury played an equal part." Stevenson asked Saint-Gaudens several times to tell him how much the sample letters cost so that he could pay for them, but Gus would never do this.

It was not until the following July that Stevenson wrote Saint-Gaudens to announce that "the medallion has been at last triumphantly transported up the hill and placed over my smoking-room mantlepiece. We have it in a very good light which brings out the artistic merits of the God-like Sculptor to advantage. As for my opinion, I believe it to be a speaking likeness and not flattered at all; possibly a little the reverse." He also thought the verses which Saint-Gaudens had used as part of the design looked "remarkably well." These were lines which Stevenson had written to Will Low, beginning,

> *Youth now flees on feathered foot*
> *Faint and fainter sounds the flute*
> *Rarer songs of gods and still*
> *Somewhere on the sunny hill*
> *Or along the winding stream*
> *Through the willow flits a dream*
> *Flits but shows a smiling face*
> *Flees but with so quaint a grace*
> *None can choose to say at home*
> *All must follow, all must roam.*

There were three stanzas to this poem plus a final couplet, the panel of lettering requiring infinite pains in execution. Gus gave Will Low a copy of the Stevenson medallion which Low had built into the "chimney-piece" in his studio.

That people would gladly pay several hundred dollars for a replica of the Stevenson bas-relief probably never occurred to Saint-Gaudens. But Tiffany came up with a proposal to sell Saint-Gaudens replicas

Medallion of Robert Louis Stevenson, one of many versions of this best loved of Saint-Gaudens' bas-relief portraits (Courtesy of the Board of Trustees of Dartmouth College)

and Gussie was all for it. They wanted to be sole agents, which they were until Doll and Richards of Boston also received permission to sell. Gus couldn't be bothered with these details, so Augusta took over the business, which gradually became a substantial source of income and of satisfaction to her — although she never allowed herself to be overoptimistic. To New Englanders, optimism was a form of "flying in the face of Providence."

Augusta also helped her husband in the matter of letter-writing, as she had done since their first married years in Paris. It seems to have been in 1887 when Saint-Gaudens received a letter from Henry Adams — the result of conferences with La Farge and Adams, but puzzling to the artist. Gus sent it to Gussie who was in Roxbury, visiting her mother.

Marian Hooper Adams had died on the 6th of December, 1885. She was a woman of great charm, as her letters to her father clearly show, but she and her sister had been taking care of their father during his last long months of painful illness. The strain was too great for Mrs. Adams who suffered from melancholia. She seemed to be recovering but suddenly took her own life. The shock to Henry Adams was profound, for, to judge by her letters,[5] she had been a happy, congenial companion to him, a delightful Washington hostess, her wit no less brilliant than his but never caustic. Possibly she had reason to fear a lingering death, becoming with years an incubus rather than a help to her husband. Inevitably, there were those who had been hurt or angered by the sharp-tongued Adams and who said that his wife took her own life to escape him.

Henry Adams set out on a series of journeys to far places, but before he left he appointed a committee to handle the funds for a monument. "I think your idea of finding out if the Adams committee really want a serious monument and making a sketch if they will pay for it, is a good one," Augusta advised her husband. "How would it do to write to Mr. Clemens and find out? Of course it would take a good deal of time to think up the subject unless you were sure of doing something at the end of it. But you know best about it all. Of course another thing is to find out how much money they have to spend and surely there must be some idea. . . . In writing, you might say something like this. 'The subject you propose is a very indefinite one. Give me something definite either as to the amount of work you expect or the sum of money you wish to expend or the magnitude of your ideas on the subject.' "

Gussie said she would try to write the letter and send it on for Gus to copy — and change as he pleased, of course — and send to the committee. It made her happy to be able to help, even though she no longer set up her easel in her husband's studio, was no longer a fellow artist and had not touched a brush for years. She still hoped they might have a family of children.

But in the spring of 1888, disaster once more overtook Augusta. Again the only record of it seems to be in her correspondence with Dr. Fred L. Morse, plus a few references in letters from Rose Hawthorne Lathrop. On April 7, 1888, Dr. Morse wrote, "From all your symptoms as detailed in your letter it is my opinion that you are pregnant. Of course the time elapsed since you wrote me may have proved you not to be; but the weight of evidence is in favor of your being so. I am glad you are in the care of a cautious and skilled physician. I hope he will direct your daily life very strictly and minutely for the present. I would not use the electricity on any account — unless he applies it himself."

On April 30, "Your letter of yesterday is at hand. I am very sorry for you. It is too bad," Dr. Morse wrote. "There is no question that so far as foresight goes, all was done to avert the catastrophe that could be done. . . . When Dr. Polk discovered that 'all growth had ceased' . . . that fact settles all such questions as 'Could more have been done.'" Dr. Morse tried to encourage Augusta. "Many times, nature makes an effort at the close of the child-bearing period and enables a woman to bear a strong child," he told her. Augusta was forty. "Of course I want to tell you how much I sympathize with you," the doctor added. "I feel your sorrow very deeply."

Rose Lathrop wrote, "I could hardly believe my eyes when I read that you had been through such a disappointment again. I do not see why or how it is. I suppose it is absurd for me to have an opinion; but I cannot help feeling that with the condition which is so natural, you would gain the requisite strength. . . ." Rose's only child, a boy, had died about the time Homer Saint-Gaudens was born and she seems never to have had even the hope of a child since. "After all, I cannot help envying the possibility that hovered over you," she said. "Motherhood is so wonderful . . . that when a good woman brings another child into the world, the homilies of scientific men who tell us the world is not large enough for us all . . . go for nothing." Rose never wrote about the tragedy of her private life, but her husband, George

Lathrop, had had to battle with alcoholism and even blamed her famous father for his own lack of success in life. He had been "overshadowed" by the Hawthorne name, Lathrop thought. They both became Catholic converts in the hope that this religious experience could help them mend their lives. After her husband's death, Rose Hawthorne Lathrop became Mother Alphonsa, head of Rosary Hill, the hospital for people with cancer who had no means to pay for care. Augusta marveled at the devotion to nursing and the hardship Rose endured while living among the poor in New York. Rose and Augusta saw each other rarely after Rose took the veil, but they remained friends for life.

During Augusta's illness, after her second miscarriage, it was Genie to the rescue as usual, with Mother Homer to take care of Homer who was more than a match for her. Saint-Gaudens wrote to his sister-in-law, not dating his letter. The letter would seem to refer to this period, but it also summed up the situation during all of Augusta's years of ill health.

"Now that you are gone I'm going to put down on paper, what I can never say to a person's face — how grateful I am to your devotedness to Gussie. I want to write it down and I want you to put it in your heart. I think I have never shown gratitude during your presence here, but somehow or other, what with Gussie's sickness and my impatience, I doubt that in all that time you were here there has been more than an hour or two of natural quiet living. I know you have not seen my best side and I feel the necessity of apologizing all the more in that I have seen your best side. You have developed since we were both together in Paris, into a bully woman and I do hope, for some good fellow's sake, you will get married and make him a bully wife. . . .

"There is another thing that I wanted to write and which has its absurd side when one says it. I don't suppose I'm made for a nurse but I'm not the brute that I sometimes appear to be. My rudeness to Gussie at times is intentional. I believe that way of dealing with her might succeed in quieting her, at least with me. I found that sometimes, for short periods in our married life, it worked well. But then again, my rudeness often is simply brutal impatience at her instability and my conscience pricks me more than I have courage to show. I do the best I can to control it. Here I am speaking out when I only meant to write a word. I want to say, and I repeat it, that I appreciate deeply and thank you earnestly for what you have done for Gussie and me.

When Gussie comes back well, then you will come on too — and there will be sounds of revelry by night. I mean you shall have fun — fun — fun and no rubbing and bundling etc." Gus added cartoons to the spare page of his letter — a stout girl labeled "Genie before she went to New York to take care of her sick sister" — and a thin girl, labeled "Genie Homer after her sick sister got through with her."

Once more, as so often before, Augusta was off on a journey for health, but the phrase "when Gussie comes back well" in her husband's letter expressed his hope and love for her. If neither had cared for the other, they might have gone their separate ways for good, because wounds were deep when they reacted in anger, but there was compassion on both sides which held them together.

On September 20, 1888, Augusta wrote to Rose Lathrop from Switzerland. She was a lonely woman and told Rose that she treasured her letters "as I do none others but my husband's. . . .

"Homer is almost too much for me and needs the firmness that his father can give him," Augusta said. "I suppose a boy's school would be the best thing to teach him to curb his impatience but I cannot send him away from me." Gussie was going home so that the boy would be "where he can fear his father's displeasure." She had steamer tickets on the *Servia* for New York, for October 20. Her mother was with her as usual.

Writing from New York to Genie and dating his letter October 20, 1888, "Gussie sails to-day. Hooraa," Gus said.

As soon as the "Deacon Chapin" was taken from the studio and sent to the foundry, Saint-Gaudens began the *Adams Memorial*. It was to be placed in Rock Creek Cemetery, Washington, D.C. He had written to Henry Adams, "Do you remember setting aside some photographs of Chinese statues, Buddha etc. for me to take away from Washington? I forgot them. I should like to have them now. Is there any book *not long* that you think might assist me in grasping the situation? If so, please let me know so that I might get it. . . ."

Later, Henry Adams seemed to take pride in believing that he never told the sculptor what he wanted. He must have laid down some restrictions even if he made no recommendations. Gus wrote, "You asked that, in whatever was placed back of the figure, the architecture should have nothing to say and above all that it should not be classic." Stanford White was doing the architectural work with Saint-Gaudens, as usual, and he resisted all temptation to produce columns and porticoes, but at the top of a plain stone rectangle, he designed a narrow classic cornice. Would this be all right? Saint-Gaudens was anxious in behalf of White and also, for a different reason, in his own behalf.

"I should like to have you see the face of the figure in the clay," he wrote to Adams after he had been working for some time. "If it were not for that part of the work I would not trouble you. But the face is an instrument on which different strains can be played, and I may have struck a key in a direction quite different from your feeling in the matter. . . ." Although Mr. Adams was in the United States between journeys, he refused to come to look at the clay model but delegated to La Farge the job of giving final approval, both as to stone background and bronze figure.

This time there was no need of the long, almost indecipherable letters such as La Farge had written to Saint-Gaudens in Paris. Now he had only to walk over to the Thirty-sixth Street studio. As a young man at work on his first commissions, Saint-Gaudens had answered La Farge's letters politely — and then he had done as he pleased. Now with three major works behind him, it would be safe to assume that Saint-Gaudens still did as he pleased.

To many, the *Adams Memorial* was the finest thing Saint-Gaudens ever achieved. The face — which Henry Adams refused to look at in clay — was remote, stern, yet mysteriously beautiful in bronze. The figure is sometimes described as wearing a hooded cloak. Perhaps that is what it is, but the stark simplicity of flowing line, of light and shadow, is all that matters. Once more, Saint-Gaudens seems to have turned to the theme of his favorite Greek stele. The arm of the figure is raised as though to draw the veil of death, but the hand rests lightly against the woman's face. She has withdrawn but she has not said farewell.

Henry Adams and Saint-Gaudens became friends although each complained of the other. Saint-Gaudens was disappointed when Adams refused to look at the clay model and Adams grew extremely impatient as time went by and the figure was not finished. Adams made a long journey with La Farge, to Hawaii and the South Seas. The two men stopped off in Samoa to see Stevenson, and Adams wrote from Samoa in January, 1891. "On arriving here, I found a bundle of letters . . . all very satisfactory except in regard to Saint-Gaudens. . . . Apparently both Saint-Gaudens and White are afraid to write to me, perhaps it is best they should not. I should either have to leave their letters unanswered, or express myself in a way that would do no good. White knows already my feelings on the subject and I think Saint-Gaudens may suspect them, if no more. So I will continue my silence, as far as concerns them and wait and see where they are coming out. At times I begin to doubt if Saint-Gaudens will ever let the work be finished. I half suspect that my refusal to take the responsibility of formally approving it in clay frightened him. Had I cared less about it, I should have gone to see it as he wished. . . .

"From the first, I told Saint-Gaudens that he should be absolutely free from interference. The result is, that after nearly five years, I am not certain that his work will ever be finished, although contract after contract, one more binding than the other, has been signed without question or discussion on my part."

Adams, in his autobiography, written in the third person, told of the impact of the Saint-Gaudens figure when it was finally in place. "His first step on returning to Washington took him to the cemetery known as Rock Creek, to see the figure which Saint-Gaudens had made for him in his absence. Naturally every detail interested him; every line; every touch of the artist; every change of light and shade; every point of relation; every possible doubt of Saint-Gaudens's correctness of taste or feeling; so that, as the spring approached, he was apt to stop there often to see what the figure had to tell him that was new; but, in all that it had to say, he never once thought of questioning what it meant. He supposed its meaning to be the one commonplace about it — the oldest idea known to human thought. He knew that if he asked an Asiatic its meaning, not a man, woman or child from Cairo to Kamchatka would have needed more than one glance to reply. From the Egyptian Sphinx to the Kamakura Daibuts; from Prometheus to Christ; from Michael Angelo to Shelley, art had wrought on this eternal figure almost as though it had nothing else to say. The interest of the figure was not its meaning, but in the response of the observer. As Adams sat there, numbers of people came, for the figure seemed to have become a tourist fashion, and all wanted to know its meaning. Most took it for a portrait-statue, and the remnant were vacant-minded in the absence of a personal guide. None felt what would have been a nursery-instinct to a Hindo baby or a Japanese jinricksha-runner."

Quantities of letters came to Saint-Gaudens, expressing admiration for the *Adams Memorial*. Poems were written about it, one by Hilde-garde Hawthorne, granddaughter of Nathaniel Hawthorne. Richard Watson Gilder ran an article on Saint-Gaudens in the *Century* and received permission to use drawings or photographs, provided Adams's name did not appear. Gilder asked Adams if the statue had a name. "My own name for it is 'The Peace of God'" Adams replied. ". . . a real artist would be careful to give it no name that the public could turn into a limitation of its nature."

Mrs. Barrett Wendell wrote in her diary[6] on May 5, 1904 that she, Saint-Gaudens and John Hay were at Rock Creek Cemetery, Washington, D.C., looking at the *Adams Memorial*. "I was deeply impressed and asked Saint-Gaudens what he called the figure," she said.

Perhaps by 1904, Saint-Gaudens was ready to commit himself. "He hesitated and then said, 'I call it the Mystery of the Hereafter.'

" 'It is not happiness?' Mrs. Wendell asked.

" 'No,' he said, 'It is beyond joy.' "

On February 26, 1906, Wayne MacVeagh wrote Saint-Gaudens, "I was asked the other day to ask you if you ever formulated any expression of what you intended to represent by the memorial to Mrs. Adams in Rock Creek Cemetery."

Gus replied, March 3, 1906, "It is difficult to say just what I intended to express. Perhaps 'The Peace that Passeth Understanding' is as near to it as I can get in words. I feel as if it could only be expressed by music."[7]

The *Shaw Memorial*, commissioned long before the *Adams*, was progressing during 1889. Gus was at work on the horse for the young hero to ride. Many sculptors hired some other artist whose specialty was animals to do horses for their equestrian statues. But not Augustus. He became fascinated by horse anatomy, delighted with the challenge — and pleased with the excuse to buy a fine horse.

Beckwith, a painter, spoke of having to ride the horse out in Central Park while Gus ran alongside, observing action, making wild-looking sketches, and having "Beckey" rein in, trot the horse, then canter. It all began while Gus was still in the Sherwood Building, Beckwith remembered,[8] but Gus was now working in the Thirty-sixth Street studio and the horse was kept in a nearby stable, brought to the studio every morning — and mounted on a special model stand while Gus worked in clay, direct from life. The horse did not exactly care for this part of his duties.

The ADAMS MEMORIAL, *Rock Creek Cemetery, Washington, D.C. (Photo from* AUGUSTUS SAINT-GAUDENS *by Royal Cortissoz, Boston, 1907, by courtesy of Houghton Mifflin Company, Boston)*

Meanwhile, the Reverend Doctor James McCosh, President Emeritus of Princeton, was coming to the studio for sittings. Saint-Gaudens was designing a high relief of this gentleman whom he described as a "tall, handsome, refined figure in his academic robes." The contract was for $12,000 paid by the Princeton class of 1879.[9]

The first time the Reverend Doctor arrived, he found the sculptor's father already in the studio. There was a comfortable couch, where the elder Saint-Gaudens could lie down and watch his son. He usually fell asleep very shortly. When Dr. McCosh arrived, Gus introduced the two elderly gentlemen, noting with amusement the contrast between them. His father was short and stocky and spoke with a strong French accent. The President Emeritus of Princeton, square-chinned but long and lean otherwise, spoke with a Scottish burr. "How old are you?" Gus's father asked him without much preamble.

Dr. McCosh, taking his pose beside a small lectern, smiled gently and said, "Guess."

"Eighty-six," the elder Saint-Gaudens decided.

"Not quite so old, guess again," Dr. McCosh suggested. Gus began to model the gentle smile on his subject's face, evidently unaware himself that Dr. McCosh was actually not yet seventy-eight.

Dr. McCosh asked the elder Saint-Gaudens about his native Southern France. "Father delightedly and effusively told him of the charm of the south, the blue sky, the oranges, the figs, the sea, the gentle weather. . . ." Dr. McCosh listened with just the right expression of private amusement, which Gus transferred to clay with satisfaction.

Finally, in his broadest Scotch, Dr. McCosh told the sculptor's father that the figs, the grapes, the oranges, were all very well, but for his part he preferred "the gooseberry — finest of all fruit." Bernard Saint-Gaudens was so shocked and also exasperated that he turned his back on the eminent gentleman and began reading a newspaper.[10]

Dr. McCosh was enjoying his first experience of retirement and he wanted to get his sittings to Saint-Gaudens over with early in the morning so that he could pursue his metaphysical studies. His *First and Fundamental Truths,* a revised edition of his *Intuitions,* appeared in 1889. As Gus put it, "He wanted to pose early and I wanted him to pose late so that I could have a good three or four hours" on the Shaw horse "before I began with him."

The doctor, after more than thirty years of teaching, was accustomed to having his own way, so one morning he appeared early. The

Portrait of the Reverend Doctor James McCosh, President Emeritus of Prince-ton University (Courtesy of Princeton University Archives)

big gray horse was in the studio. Gus told President McCosh he was welcome to wait and watch the work if he liked. The scene was one Saint-Gaudens always remembered.

The horse stood on one side of the studio next to the wall with a man hired to keep him there and make him hold his pose. The studio was a wonderful place for sound — as musicians and audience discovered during the studio concerts. It now reverberated with "the pawing and kicking of the resentful animal." The sound was like a rockslide in mountain country during a storm. Gus was working on the large clay model and had "an arrangement of boxes" he would climb on, "so that between the stamping of the horse, the shouting and cursing of the man who held him and my own rushing up and down from the horse to the model and from the model to the horse, the studio was far from a place of rest."

Dr. McCosh agreed to wait. "He sat down in one corner without seeing my father, who was already asleep in the other." And then, in spite of the volume of sound, Dr. McCosh also fell asleep. "The snores of my father, vigorous and strong," were in contrast to the "gentle, academic snores" of the President Emeritus, Gus recalled.

The two elderly gentlemen slept peacefully until the horse had finished his sitting to Saint-Gaudens! Then the big double doors of the studio were opened, the man from the stable mounted the horse and with "a final pounding and standing-on of hind legs within two feet of Dr. McCosh," the horse dashed out of the studio and off to the stable for his oats.

Not even the ensuing silence awakened the two old gentlemen. Finally, Gus decided that he must wake Dr. McCosh or there wouldn't be time for his sitting. "Dr. McCosh, you have been having a nap," Gus said.

"Oh no, not at all," the author of *Intuitions* replied. "Not at all. I have been waiting for you."

17

DAVIDA

IN 1880, the Commonwealth of Massachusetts granted some of the Back Bay reclaimed land in Copley Square to the City of Boston for a public library. The new building was to face Richardson's Romanesque Trinity Church, now complete with rounded arches and massive central tower. In Copley Square to the south of this stood the Museum of Fine Arts, bringing Venice to Boston in alternating stripes of different building materials just as, in New York, the equally particolored National Academy of Design contributed Venetian Gothic uplift to the vicinity of Madison Square.

Naturally, the contract to build the new library in Boston was a plum every firm of architects scrambled for. In 1887, McKim, Mead and White won the commission. Richardson had died the year before and the vogue for neo-Romanesque was dying, although a church by Richardson would be a source of boastful pride to many a devout parish for years to come. Neo-Venetian Gothic was yielding the palm to Spanish Gothic, but neo-French and Italian Renaissance was what the public wanted now. With the award to McKim, Mead and White, the Renaissance was invited to come to Boston.

Saint-Gaudens was summoned to look over the site, a mud flat, and to talk over a plan for two groups of statuary, one on each side of the main entrance of the future building. Gus spoke plaintively of being caught on the train in heavy snow. But his journey was a fruitful one and he returned jubilant to his New York studio. The figures he was to do would be allegorical and as "ideal" as he could make them.

On December 10, 1888, Gus wrote to McKim. "In reply to your questions as to the time necessary and the mode of payment in the event of my executing the groups for the Boston Library, I should wish $20,000 the first year and $30,000 each of the remaining four years, the final $10,000 on the entire completion of the groups. I should agree to furnish them in either bronze or marble or stone and the payments to be made in installments as the work progresses, as is usual in all my contracts."

Gus made rough clay models showing his ideas for the two groups, but evidently McKim thought that only an artist would understand them. "I regret very much that the larger sized sketch is not the thing to show your committee," Gus told McKim. "I have made an earnest attempt to remedy it in the direction necessary but it is an utter failure. To make it as you wish would take as much time as to make a new set of sketches." Gus admitted that he hated preliminary clay sketching. He was sorry, but "I have no right to take the time. . . . It troubles me because you desire it so much and I desire so much to do the work."

Saint-Gaudens got the contract anyway. The sculptor of the *Farragut*, the *Lincoln* and the Springfield, Massachusetts, *Puritan* was the man the Boston Committee wanted. They liked his idea of having "on one pedestal, Labor, represented by a man seated between two female figures — Science on one side, Art on the other, and on the other pedestal a male figure of Law in the middle, with female figures of Religion on one side and Force or Power on the other."

Then, just as everything seemed settled and terms agreed upon, the mayor of Boston decided that all this art was much too expensive and cut the Saint-Gaudens figures out of the library building budget. Saint-Gaudens' feelings must have been mixed. His studio was full of unfinished work; the *Shaw Memorial*, for example, commissioned in 1880, was less than half completed. The Shaw horse, beautifully modeled in clay, threatened to collapse, clay being anything but a permanant medium. Gus took to spending nights at the studio because of his anxiety over the horse — or so Gussie thought. He had the horse cast in 1889; the wonderfully effective background of marching men was still to be designed.

Yet, disappointment over the loss of the Boston Library groups was keen. Then, in 1892, "the Mayor has of his own accord put back Saint-Gaudens' sculpture, which he had cut out of the estimates, the loss of which would have been more or less of a surgical operation," McKim wrote. "Saint-Gaudens' scheme for the groups of seated figures at either side of the front doors is worthy of the best period of Greek art. The bronze doors are also given back to us. Hurrah!" Gus rejoiced and echoed McKim's hurrah.[1]

Left to right: William Rutherford Mead, Charles F. McKim, and Stanford White (Magonigle Collection, New York Public Library)

Sketch of one of the two groups intended for the Boston Public Library. The sketches were cast in bronze, after the death of Saint-Gaudens, for the Freer Gallery of Art, Washington, D.C. (Courtesy of the Smithsonian Institution, Freer Gallery of Art, Washington, D.C.)

The next move in the campaign to make Boston neither Puritan nor Irish, but Renaissance, was to see that the interior walls of the new library should be decorated like the walls of a Medici palace. John Singer Sargent, in Boston in 1890, agreed to take the job of decorating the upper staircase and he began with the end wall. Instead of a Spanish subject which he first considered, he painted his *Frieze of the Prophets,* one of the best loved of murals.[2] People flocked to see it. Before long, no American home of any cultural claim would be without a framed sepia photograph of one or all of the prophets.

The scheme of having murals was McKim's, and to Saint-Gaudens goes the credit of acquiring the services of Edwin Austin Abbey for the "Distribution Room" in the library, where the Abbey *Holy Grail* series opened the eyes of Bostonians to glowing color. The catalogues were then kept outside the room. After finding the required reference, the reader entered the Abbey Room, filed the slip at a window and then sat down on a high-backed mahogany bench to wait — and to enter into the magic world of *Le Morte Darthur.*

Edwin Abbey was four years younger than Saint-Gaudens. Born in Philadelphia, he studied art at the Pennsylvania Academy, and at the age of eighteen got himself a job as illustrator for *Harper's Weekly* in New York. The work was grueling, a staff of draftsmen often working together on a big wood block, cutting away at it from morning till late at night to meet a deadline for the magazine. After five years of this, Abbey quit because *Harper's* would not raise his pay from thirty-five to forty dollars a week. He set himself up as a free-lance illustrator, his first illustrated book being Dickens's *Christmas Stories.* In 1876, he was invited to return to *Harper's* for a magnificent fifty dollars a week — which he accepted.

Two years later, *Harper's* decided to send Abbey to England to do a series of sketches at Stratford-on-Avon. Abbey acquired another good commission from *Scribner's,* and *Harper's* gave him a farewell breakfast at Delmonico's and sent him to his steamship in a four-in-hand coach.

Abbey managed to prolong his stay abroad by means of various European assignments, collected during brief visits to New York. Sometimes he made his home in England in the little village of Broadway, where his close neighbors were Sargent and Henry James. In New York he frequented the Tile Club, along with Stanford White and Saint-Gaudens. Abbey was a genial, lovable person, and he and Saint-Gaudens became fast friends.

In 1890, Abbey, now about thirty-eight, became engaged to Mary Gertrude Meade during one of his visits to the United States. Gus suggested to Miss Meade that her fiancé might get the job of painting murals for the Boston Public Library. Although working in pen and ink for years, Abbey had more or less recently branched out into oils, discovering a gift for color. Miss Meade was all for the idea of the Boston murals, although she and Saint-Gaudens realized that finesse would be necessary. The Library Committee was still complaining about costs. Gus was doing a medallion of Miss Meade to give to Abbey for a wedding present and they had time to discuss strategy. Gus wrote to Abbey as follows: "McKim, White, Sargent, thee and I dine at the Players, Wednesday night this week at 7:30 D.V., so help me. . . . McKim don't want any other fellows around, although I tried to [get] the whole crew together as we agreed. . . . If you can't come, let me know right away." Gus was not happy about his portrait of Miss Meade at this point, so he added, "The medallion looks like hell. I thought I had done a good thing, but it makes me sick."

McKim further developed the plot in an innocent-sounding letter to Samuel A. B. Abbott, member of the Massachusetts legislature and prime mover for McKim, Mead and White on the Boston Library Committee. McKim dated his letter May 9, 1890. "I received one morning a little over a week ago, an excited note from Saint-Gaudens, stating that Abbey had just returned from Boston and was at the moment dining with him. It appears that while there, Abbey had gone over to the library and was so impressed that he could talk of nothing else. This, at least, was the substance of Saint-Gaudens' note."

McKim told the story of the Players' Club dinner, making it sound as though everything had happened by chance — even to the point of finding a big piece of paper on the scene. "Abbey, with the spontaneity that characterizes him, could resist no longer and seizing his pencil, sketched out almost in a moment, upon a sheet of brown wrapping paper which happened to be at hand, two compositions for the Shakespeare Room. . . .

"It was impossible to restrain our admiration as he went from one thing to another, talking as he drew and it was good to observe the pride which Sargent evinced in the powers of his brother artist. . . ."

Abbey and Miss Meade were married very shortly[3] and Gus and Gussie invited the bride and groom to dinner. They also asked McKim who was astonished to learn that Abbey had already made an oil sketch to show to the Boston Committee. In his letter of May 9, McKim proposed that Abbey go down to Boston "next Wednesday" to talk the matter over with Mr. Abbott. "Abbey sails immediately for Capri, with his bride of two weeks. Saint-Gaudens and I are anxious that you should meet and know him, hence this sudden dispatch," McKim explained.

Abbott agreeably got the trustees together and McKim hired a private car to be coupled onto the Wednesday train for Boston to accommodate the architects, the artists Sargent and Abbey — and Saint-Gaudens. On arrival in Boston, they all went first to a baseball game.

It was the ballgame that Saint-Gaudens really enjoyed. In his boyhood, he had never had time even for sandlot baseball. What excited him now was not the score but the action of the players — the pitcher leaping to catch a ball seemed to Gus a most beautiful sight. He would have loved to put such a figure into bronze and the fact that a runner was out made no impression on him — save that he liked to watch runners, especially when they went into a slide for base.

As to the conference with the Boston Public Library trustees — Abbey eventually agreed to paint a frieze 180 feet by eight feet, for $15,000. "Second thought led him to illustrate the quest for the Holy Grail, rather than Shakespeare's plays — his first idea." "An understanding" was arrived at with Sargent.

In New York, in April, 1889, there was "little talk except about the Centennial" — at least for a few short weeks. The Washington Centennial was a three-day affair, in the course of which President Harrison was rowed down the Hudson from Elizabethtown in a decorated barge, to commemorate Washington's triumphant entry into New York at the end of the American Revolution. Stanford White designed an elaborate wooden arch which was built on Washington Square at the foot of Fifth Avenue; Whittier wrote an ode for the occasion — and Augustus Saint-Gaudens designed a commemorative medal.

The Saint-Gaudens medal was "magnificent," said Richard Watson Gilder. It was "the first medal of real artistic value made in this country. I hope that in an indirect way it will have an ultimate effect upon our coinage." Eventually, Saint-Gaudens would have not an indirect but a direct effect upon the coinage, when he designed gold pieces for Theodore Roosevelt.

There was a "terrible crush" to meet President Harrison — it had rained the day before and all the flags were wet and drooping, but Tuesday, April 30, was a fine day with masses of people out to see a parade more than five miles long. The papers said that there were more than a million strangers in town. It was rumored among the artists that "Stan White's wooden arch would be built in stone" and when, eight years later, this was accomplished as a result of much money-raising, the Saint-Gaudens medal was recast in silver as a gift to Richard Watson Gilder, prime mover in the project.

In May, 1889, Gussie wrote to her "Dearest Rose" Hawthorne Lathrop, complaining, as one woman will to another, of her husband's shortcomings. They were at 22 Washington Place and Rose had been visiting. "My dear, things are no more settled than they were when you were here," Gussie said. "My husband seemingly will not make up his mind and at a few hours notice I may go, but I think it is more probable that I shall not. . . ." She referred to a proposed trip to Paris — "our little spree," she called it. Of course she had talked to Dr. Polk about it, "and he urged it very strongly, saying it was by far the best thing I could do. When I said, 'Is it really necessary?' he said, 'Necessary things can be expressed in so many different ways but it's important for you to go to Europe again.'" It would almost seem as if that inspired listener, Dr. Polk, was the one who needed the vacation.

"Still, I do not feel that I can take the responsibility of going with Homer, without Augustus," Gussie went on, "so I am simply preparing to go to Windsor at the same time with a very unsettled feeling and leaving many purchases unmade that I must make before going to Windsor, such as carpets, curtains, mattresses, country wagon, etc. If I only knew — but now we do not even talk about the summer at all, only night before last Aug. [Augustus] said, 'I may decide to go next week! . . .' The worst is the moral responsibility of what to do with my servants in the event of my going. Well, a way will be pointed out I suppose, when the time comes. I have been so busy and altho' I am never wholly free from pain, I don't say anything about it. . . ."

The way was pointed out when Augusta's older sister, Lizzie Nichols, agreed to take the Cornish place, servants and all, during the summer of 1889. Lizzie and Dr. Nichols brought their children, Rose, Marian and Margaret, and they loved Cornish so much that during the following winter they bought the nearby Chester Pike farm. They called their place "Mastlands" because they were told that high trees on the property had once been cut and floated down the Connecticut

River for use in the Royal Navy before the American Revolution. After making improvements to the house, including fashionable "piazzas," the Nichols family moved into "Mastlands," which became their summer home for many years. Saint-Gaudens was never without a niece or two underfoot, whom he loved as much as he would have loved daughters of his own.

With Lizzie established in the Saint-Gaudens' Cornish house, the sculptor and his wife set out for Europe. Gus was eager to see another "Exposition" and renew old friendships; Gussie was hopeful as always that she would be able to gain health by drinking the evil-tasting water in some Swiss resort. Saint-Gaudens described his voyage and some of his impressions in letters to Mariana Griswold Van Rensselaer.

Mrs. Van Rensselaer had just completed *Henry Hobson Richardson and His Works* and Saint-Gaudens had just completed her portrait in bas-relief — excessively high collar, curled front hair, stiff backbone and all. Mrs. Van Renssalaer was an art critic whose books no American with any claim to culture would dare to miss — or dare to disagree with. Gus wrote to her in the seriocomic vein proper when addressing lady authors.

The impressions of his two-week trip abroad were Homeric Greek in character, Gus said. For the first time in his life he wasn't seasick but enjoyed the way the steamer first rose on the waves in the bright sun on leaving Sandy Hook. The Cornwall coast was glorious with the rising sun on it. For the first time he liked England — evidently because it wasn't raining; he felt the strength of London instead of its gloom. The extraordinary largeness of Paris surprised him and so did the wonderful fête success of the Exposition.

Augusta went off to Switzerland as planned and MacMonnies, now living in Paris, found a little box of a room in the Latin Quarter for Saint-Gaudens. Gus went around to Mac's studio where the *Nathan Hale* for City Hall Park was in process of completion. The figure tipped forward. Gus lifted it a little in front, under protest from his former pupil — so he called for a plumb line. Mac said he didn't bother with such things anymore, well aware that Saint-Gaudens always insisted that his pupils use a plumb line constantly. One was found for Saint-Gaudens and he was right — the statue had been decidedly out of line.

Saint-Gaudens wrote Mrs. Van Rensselaer about the incident. "But MacMonnies, in company with all the other Gauls . . . must have a

Portrait of Mrs. Mariana Griswold Van Rensselaer (The Metropolitan Museum of Art, gift of Mrs. Schuyler Van Rensselaer, 1917)

change and a figure that is simply and naturally standing on its feet according to the laws of gravity is everyday and commonplace. One that doesn't stand on its legs but stands on an ear or has a foot growing out of its biceps or behind its head, or out of its stomach, or one that has an arm which disappears mysteriously — 'Oh! Oh! *mon Dieu! quel audace! quel genie!*' Therefore Mac is crazy to get his *Hale* tumbling on its nose again."

On this visit to Paris, Gus did not actually feel as bright and gay as he wanted the brisk lady art critic to think he did. Looking out of his window into the courtyard in the cool gray of early morning, he saw an old chap emerge from a studio door across the way. The old boy had on a dressing gown and was peacefully smoking his pipe. "He trudged along, in among the paths over to one particular flower bed which was evidently his property, and with great care watered the flowers. Soon another old codger appeared from another door in trousers and slippers . . . and then a third came from the other end of the garden, wearing a scullcap. This one, with the greatest caution, mounted a little stepladder, tying here, cutting away there, among his plants. . . . These were the satanic comrades of my youth at the Beaux Arts, the devils who made me bawl the Marseillaise for months," Gus said. He was now forty-one, dashed up and down piles of boxes and high ladders, and sang at the top of his lungs when work went well. He had forgotten to grow old.

On the whole, both Gus and Gussie were glad to get back to the United States. There was still time for Cornish — time for Rose Hawthorne Lathrop to visit. After Rose went home, Gussie wrote to tell her what had been going on. "I think I have never been busier than the entire time since you left, nearly three weeks ago," Gussie wrote to Rose. "My husband, after planning a great deal of work to be done and, for lack of better, consigning it to inefficient people, left two days after you did; that is, you went Tuesday, my husband Thursday, the Dewings, Friday. On Friday the men began work at the studio and for three days there were six or seven men constantly at work with no better boss than I, who did not comprehend very well as each man had received separate and seemingly contradictory directions from my husband, each thought he knew, wasn't quite sure, and after long consultation would follow his own sweet will. I was off getting lumber, nails, irons etc. etc. till finally . . . I had to go to bed for nearly two days and in that time they managed to make a serious mistake. Smith had been so lazy and impertinent that, to have any self respect, I was forced to send him off and afterwards I found I had done it in the presence of his father who had that morning come to work and I didn't know his name. Such a nice old man!" Unfortunately, the formidable Mrs. Saint-Gaudens lacked the art of letting a nice old man know she liked him.

The work was done at last, and Gussie sent her father's sister, "Aunt Hannah," to New York with the servants while she set out for Roxbury "with Homer and the cat. . . ." But she was not happy. "Some day I hope Mother will sell this place and then I may enjoy visiting her where her surroundings are different," Gussie explained. "This morning in church when they sang 'Watchman What of the Night' I broke down entirely. It seems as if in nine years [since her father's death] the wound might heal — and it does excepting here."

In another letter to Rose, Augusta said she was back in New York, had been to see Dr. Polk and was "now to have a surgical operation on the left side and as soon as I am well enough, there has to be a second operation on the other side." Dr. Polk "says he cannot *advise* me to have it done, that it is always hard for a physician to do that and harder with me, as he does not feel towards me as towards an ordinary patient, but if I were his sister he should advise her doing it and that he would not let his wife suffer as I have been suffering for so long. . . . I look so well you would find it hard to believe me in trouble. He has told me the case as it seems to him, viz. that for years the right kidney has been coming down, keeping me under a perpetual harrow, that now the left kidney is doing the same thing and that it may be years in the process. This operation, he feels, will arrest the trouble and benefit me nervously and possibly help the noise in my head. . . ."

On November 9, 1889, Saint-Gaudens reported to Genie, "Gussie is really better and although it seems fabulous, the noise in her head, the terrible one, troubles her no more." And to Gussie's cousin Lizzie, he wrote, "It is all over and . . . was not so bad as Gussie dreaded, the ether caused her only a momentary suffocating feeling and she dreads it no more. . . . She is doing well . . . and everything runs smoothly in the house . . . Mother will stay here till Genie can come. . . ."

Genie soon arrived and a note from Gus at his studio was in his usual jocular mood. "I won't be home to supper but I think a man around where women are is a pleasant thing for the man. I think Mr. Brewster a man, and a good one, but not *too* good which makes him better, so a note to him at his room may land him at 22 Washington Place for dinner instead of at some restaurant where the food will be better but the company less attractive. . . ." Gus was always trying to find a beau for Genie, who was now thirty-five, still pretty, but more and more the family nurse, housekeeper and unpaid governess to nephews and nieces. Charles Brewster was impervious to her charms, but he was just the friend both Gus and Gussie needed, for he was a lawyer able to help them in their dealings with clients' contracts and unscrupulous art dealers who would have liked to steal copies of Saint-Gaudens medallions to sell for their own profit.

Sargent had come to Boston in December, 1889, bringing his sister Violet with him — a really beautiful girl. They were in New York by February, when Sargent gave a party for the popular music-hall entertainer, Carmencita, in the vain hope of selling a painting of the girl to Mrs. Jack Gardner. But Mrs. Jack had set her heart on the *Spanish Dancer;* a different and earlier dance scene. Saint-Gaudens apparently paid no attention to Carmencita, but one look at Violet Sargent's profile was enough to make him decide to do her portrait in bronze. She had an almost Grecian nose, the short upper lip Saint-Gaudens most admired, and a beautifully rounded chin. The two artists, who had known each other since Paris days, agreed to an exchange of work — Sargent to paint Gussie and Homer, Saint-Gaudens to model Violet.[4]

"I don't want to influence you in any way, in fact it is just because I feel that you will do just whatever strikes you as best, that I feel I can risk entering a suggestion which you will please chuck out if you don't like it," Sargent wrote to Gus (heading his letter "Wednesday").

"I have a sort of feeling that, given my sister's head, I should rather have a ron-bon — even ever so slight, than a bas relief. It seems to me owing to the shape of her face, cheeks, etc., it would be better. However, you know best and I am sure you will do something charming in any case and I will admire it tremendously.

"I don't even know if it will take you more time and work, in which case, don't think of it.

"At any rate, pardon my silly interference. I am surprised at myself behaving just like the worst bourgeois and you can have your revenge on me about your boy. I like his head very much by the way."

Of course Gus did exactly as he pleased. His portrait of Violet Sargent was not in particularly high relief, but it was full figure instead

Portrait of John Singer Sargent. Saint-Gaudens gave a replica of this medallion to Mrs. Jack Gardner and it is now at the Isabella Stewart Gardner Museum, Boston, Massachusetts (The Metropolitan Museum of Art, gift of Mrs. Edward Robinson, 1913)

of just the head. Violet, sitting on a classic bench such as White might have designed, was playing her guitar. The treatment was so light, so gay, that the plaque itself almost seemed to play guitar music. The handling of horizontal and diagonal lines in the wide, rectangular composition was new and refreshing. Surfaces were kept simple, directing attention to a lovely face; ornament was restrained, severely classic, with, in the upper right corner, just an ivy wreath and the name — "Violet Sargent."

Nothing Saint-Gaudens had done to date was more beautiful, but Royal Cortissoz, literary and art editor of the New York *Tribune,* called the "effect awkward and ugly" — and worse still, he called it "modern."

Sargent's painting of Gussie and Homer, meanwhile, was proceeding apace. There sat Homer, sidewise on a carved chair, dressed up in clothes any boy would hate, from flowing bow at his throat to patent-leather dancing pumps. He was a beautiful boy with a spoiled expression and in his eyes a look of dislike for the artist, which must have amused Sargent. Just behind him sat his mother, reading a story aloud to him. As usual, Sargent caught character in a pose, just as Saint-Gaudens did. Gussie looked handsome, as indeed she was, but also anxious, as she made herself a background for her adored offspring and worried lest the boy get completely out of hand. The picture, when completed, was exhibited at the Paris Salon and at the World's Columbian Exposition, entitled *Portrait of a Boy.*

On January 10, 1891, Saint-Gaudens replied to a letter written him by Charles C. Beaman five days earlier. "I agree to buy of you the house and buildings commonly known as Blowmeup with the land about as indicated in the plan I sent you last summer, for the sum of $2500.00 and as further compensation, I agree to make a medallion of you, either in the country or in New York. . . ."

Through the Cornish property a mountain stream came tearing and tumbling along, known from time immemorial as Blow-Me-Down Brook. It would suit the Saint-Gaudens humor to call his summer home "Blowmeup," but as soon as the place was really his, he named it "Aspet" in honor of his father's birthplace in the French Pyrenees — and also because the view from the Cornish hillside was beautiful. Nothing was said about the amount of land in this letter, but eventually Saint-Gaudens owned eighty-three acres. This official letter to Mr. Beaman was at the same time informal and friendly. "I will agree to a

Portrait of Miss Violet Sargent (Photo from Augustus Saint-Gaudens *by Royal Cortissoz, Boston, 1907, by courtesy of Houghton Mifflin Company, Boston)*

PORTRAIT OF A BOY *by John Singer Sargent. This painting of Augusta Saint-Gaudens and her son Homer was done in exchange for the Saint-Gaudens bronze bas-relief of Sargent's sister Violet (Collection of Museum of Art, Carnegie Institute, Pittsburgh, Patrons Art Fund)*

right of way but as to the location, I think it can only be determined on the spot," Gus said. "The path now existing nearest the house I want to have simply as a footpath, letting it become overgrown as it was before it was cut away." A right-of-way would have to be as near the eastern boundary of the land as possible and not through the middle of the property. There must be "no risk of having that path and surroundings constantly disfigured as last year when Johnson with his ox team came up that way and across the place continually on his way to and from Mr. Platt's."

The Saint-Gaudenses now had neighbors up the hill beyond them. Charles Adams Platt, architect, landscape architect, painter and native New Yorker, had been building a house for himself and his family. He had a studio on Washington Square North, not far from the Saint-Gaudens apartment on Washington Place; he and Saint-Gaudens were both members of the Players' Club on Gramercy Park. In 1890, the brilliant painter Dennis Miller Bunker, prime favorite among Mrs. Jack Gardner's young men, came to live in New York with his bride, Eleanor Hardy. Bunker's death from pneumonia followed within months of his marriage and three years later, Charles Platt, a widower, married the beautiful Eleanor. Portraits of her by Bunker, who had been Platt's friend since student days, hung on the walls of Charles Platt's house.

The Platts were a great addition to the Cornish art colony. Farmer Johnson's ox team was soon no longer needed for the Platts' construction work and the forest path with "a little footbridge" across the brook would be exactly what both families would like.

Mr. Beaman had proved a reluctant seller to the last. "I fully appreciate your desire to retain the piece of woodland," Saint-Gaudens told him, "and I thank you sincerely for your kindness and courtesy in agreeing to let me have it under any conditions. On the other hand, I think it but justice to myself to say that it is only my great desire to have some trees and water, that causes me to agree to the execution of the medallion as compensation for what you value so highly. My time is so occupied by my larger work that I [am] refusing to do medallions for a price that would more than pay for the entire property and I could not agree to execute for you in connection with this agreement, a portrait of any one but yourself. . . ."

Gus did a delightful portrait of Charles Coatsworth Beaman, a stoutish gentleman, one hand in his pocket, one hand somewhat tightly clenched, doubtless a characteristic gesture. He inscribed it, "By your friend, Augustus Saint-Gaudens," and dated it 1890.

In 1890 the building at 22 Washington Place was sold and Gus and Gussie had to move from the apartment where they had lived ever since Homer was born. At times Gus cursed the flights of stairs, when he came home leg-weary from climbing ladders to model huge figures. Gussie despaired of keeping out soot from factory chimneys, but fellow artists had studios on Washington Square, friends lived in apartments nearby. There was nothing to do but move out, however, and on May 1, Gus signed a contract with Mrs. Charlotte W. Throop of Albany, owner of a house and lot at 51 West Forty-fifth Street. The lease was for five years at $150 a month. Gus agreed not to keep boarders or lodgers and not to "use the premises for any purposes than that of a dwelling" for himself and his family.

Gus promised to put in one or more artistic wooden mantels, paint, paper and make other necessary repairs, he to spend $500, Mrs. Throop to put up $200.[5] By May 13, Gussie was telling Rose Hawthorne Lathrop all about it. She had been south for her health until "about two weeks ago," and had been "ever since in such dust and turmoil," she had no time to write. "Plumbers and masons are still in the house," she said, and she had "nothing to show for it but our old mantle pieces from 22 Washington Place instead of the hideous marble ones. The whole plumbing has been torn out, nearly, and new pipes put in; bathtub and washtub alone being left and those may leak at any time. . . .

"The painters and paperers come next and when it is done we shall be simply *clean*, not pretty. . . ." Augusta was very "nervous and so tired from the moving and turmoil."

Gussie complained so constantly of rising expenses at home and at the studio that it seems strange she should go away so often on journeys which must have cost a good deal of money. However, her mother had a life interest in her father's annuity from the Sidney Homer estate, so probably Mrs. Homer paid some of Gussie's bills at health resorts in all sorts of places.

Without realizing it, Gussie put her health and her child first in her mind, her husband coming in a poor third. "Mother and I sail for England on the 28th [of May] and then on to Italy and the latter part of June for Norway and the North Cape," Gussie wrote to Rose. The

Portrait medallion of Novy, given to Novy's mother, Davida
(Saint-Gaudens National Historic Site)

cook, Maggie, "will stay here all summer and look after my house and my husband."

Because of her health, Augusta visited her husband's studio less and less often. Perhaps for a while he tried to tell her about his work, but she was too deaf to hear. She was in Nova Scotia when the angels at the Morgan tomb were burned — so she may never have seen the model who posed for them, and for the angel commissioned by Mrs. Anna Maria Smith for a Newport, Rhode Island, cemetery. The model's name was Davida.

Changing and revising his design, not in the round now but in high relief, Augustus gave a similar figure lovely wings and had her hold a tablet over her head. It was again Davida who posed for this bronze, known as the *Angel with the Tablet*. Once more Gus revised and changed, his angel becoming still more beautiful as the famous *Amor Caritas*.

Davida was very young, her body slender like a child's just crossing the threshold of womanhood. Her expression was gentle and sweet, the eyes slightly pathetic because of shadows under the brows which trended downward at the outer edges. Something in the way Saint-Gaudens designed them made angel wings becoming to her. Davida was not only sweet; she was compliant.

If Augusta had visited the studio in 1892, she might have seen a new portrait medallion. It was circular and showed an appealing little boy, the inscription indicating that he was three years old and that his name was Novy. But Augusta never saw the portrait at this time, and it was not a commission from a wealthy patron. Saint-Gaudens gave it to Davida, the child's mother. The little boy was their son.[6]

No one in the New York art colony seems to have surmised that the lovely young model was Saint-Gaudens' mistress. It was an era of the double standard and those who knew of Gussie's difficult moods would never have blamed him. No one would have been surprised in any case, but almost all the other artists would have assumed that Gus would tire of the girl, pay her off and forget her. That was the way of the world, but it was something that Saint-Gaudens could not do.

18

THE NINETIES BEGIN TO BE GAY

EVERY schoolchild knew when "Columbus sailed the ocean blue," but it seems not to have occurred to their elders until 1890 that a chance for a big celebration was coming in just two years. Then suddenly everyone agreed that there should be a fair; something on the order of the Paris Exposition, only bigger and better. Every city of any importance wanted to be the site of the fair, but by the time Chicago had offered five million dollars and then won by doubling New York's matching offer, everyone also knew that the World's Columbian Exposition was going to be late.

New York celebrated on time. They had the usual parade, they changed the name of the Grand Circle to Columbus Circle and Stanford White designed a "trellis arch" to be put up temporarily at Fifth Avenue and Broadway. The trees on Madison Avenue were hung with lanterns, where a promised pageant turned out to be a bicycle race!

But in 1891, Saint-Gaudens was summoned to Chicago along with other leading architects, artists and sculptors. Late or not, the World's Columbian Exposition attracted the attention of the whole country from that time forth. Looking around at the crowd that assembled for the luncheon at Kinsley's restaurant, the Chicago counterpart of Delmonico's, Saint-Gaudens said that it was "the greatest meeting of artists since the fifteenth century." This much quoted comment pleased everyone and struck the keynote for the neo-Venetian–Graeco-Roman–Renaissance "White City" that was to rise in what was once a swamp, now drained by "lagoons" but still decidedly muddy at times.

The Chicago Fair Committee offered to pay Saint-Gaudens fifteen thousand dollars to "supervise the creation of sculptural projects." One was a seventy-five-foot figure called the *Republic*, by Daniel Chester French, to go at one end of the "Center Lagoon," and at the other end, there would be a huge fountain, representing the Ship of State, by MacMonnies. Overwhelmed by unfinished work in his own studio, Gus agreed to "indicate a general scheme" for three thousand dollars, and then let French and MacMonnies "proceed with their work entirely free" from supervision. The committee agreed to this and the sculptors were delighted.

Daniel Chester French went up to Cornish to work on the model for his seventy-five-foot *Republic.* He was born in 1850, in Exeter, New Hampshire, and his gift as a sculptor had been rather a shock to his father, Judge Henry Flagg French. However, the judge encouraged both Dan and an older boy, Will, in their efforts but made it clear that art was a hobby, not a serious life occupation. Daniel spent most of his early years in Concord, Massachusetts, where he said he learned about armatures and how to build a clay figure from Abby May Alcott, who gave him his first modeling tools.[1] Dan went to the Massachusetts Institute of Technology but stayed only a year, probably because he refused to study anything but drawing. He studied painting with William Morris Hunt, but his only formal instruction in sculpture consisted of one month in John Quincy Adams Ward's studio in New York. French was twenty-three when, with his famous *Minute Man,* he won the competition for a monument to commemorate the battle of Lexington.

Saint-Gaudens already knew young Mr. French. In fact, Mrs. Daniel Chester French declared that Saint-Gaudens was responsible for postponing her wedding date! She was to have married her cousin Dan in June, 1888, but "a few weeks before the date was set for the wedding" French wrote her, "What would you think if I told you that, even now at the last moment I must change my statue — and I am afraid it will put off our wedding for a month?" French was doing a figure of Gallaudet, teacher of the deaf, for the Deaf Mute College near Washington, D.C., and was working in his New York studio. "Saint-Gaudens has been in and says that the legs are too short," French explained. "Perhaps I should have known this without anyone telling me," he said, but he confessed that he had been "diverted by prospects of approaching matrimony." However, "when you can pin Saint-Gaudens down and get a real criticism from him, it is better than anybody's and so what can I do except give the Doctor an inch or two more of leg and meanwhile what kind of a lover will you think me, anyhow?" Mary Adams French was married to Daniel Chester French in July instead of June, and held no grudge against Saint-Gaudens but enjoyed knowing him. They lived in Cornish "during the summer before the World's Fair and the summer after it."

Mrs. French described the Saint-Gaudens house in Cornish as it looked to her in 1892. "There was an elaborate fence around the top of the bank with Greek heads at regular intervals and a big, elaborate porch at the front. . . ." On the "porch" the Saint-Gaudens family ate their meals, looking toward Ascutney, "just as in Sicily they look toward Etna and in Japan toward Fujiyama." Later, the Frenches built a summer home in Stockbridge, Massachusetts, a huge affair of many guest rooms, and nearby, a studio having a small pergola, almost a replica of the one in Cornish — facing an equally sacred view of the Berkshires.[2]

Mrs. French had never seen one of those sudden moods of mimicry that came upon Saint-Gaudens to his friends' delight. But one evening he remarked that he liked to jog along behind a slow horse, enjoying the countryside, and she said she liked a horse that could *go*. Gus pulled his knees high in front of him, snatched a round lamp mat from a table beside him and stuck it sidewise on his head. Then he leaned forward, gathered up imaginary reins, slapped an imaginary horse with them and began to jounce up and down and sway from side to side. "Here's how Mrs. French likes to drive," he said, and everyone could see him "tearing down the road like a disreputable jockey." Mrs. French said "it did look exactly like the picture" she had brought up — and she joined in the laughter.

The French statue symbolizing the Republic, for the Chicago Fair, was massive and serious. To balance and contrast with it, Saint-Gaudens wanted "a tremendous fountain, all movement, gaiety and exuberance." MacMonnies came over from Paris, got the fifty-thousand-dollar commission to do the fountain, "a great symbolic Ship of State." Then he went back to Paris to work on it, decidedly free of supervision. It was the sensation of the Fair. On a huge white ship, "loftily enthroned," sat Columbia — a buxom lady. On the prow of the ship was "a tall, exuberant figure of Fame." Maidens bent to oars as if rowing the Ship of State. There were twenty-seven figures in all, elaborate in every detail, and then there were cherubs, sea horses, dolphins, cornucopias spilling fruit, wreathes and festoons. Visitors to the Fair hired Venetian gondolas, poled by genuine gondoliers, to go out on the lagoon for a better look at MacMonnies's maidens, rowing hard, carrying the Ship of State into the gay nineties. The fountain brought instant fame to Mac, who collected commissions for still more exhuberant statuary — the "shifting tides of fashion" being blamed when his popularity waned.

Of course the Chicago Fair people very much wanted something by Saint-Gaudens and hoped that he would do the figure of Columbus for the entrance to the Administration Building. Gus had no time, however, so he got the job for a gifted young girl — the girl whom the sculptor Tonetti married when he came to the United States in search of a fortune. "My pupil, Miss Mary Lawrence, modeled and executed" *Columbus,* Gus wrote, "and to her goes all the credit of the virility and breadth of treatment which it revealed."

Saint-Gaudens consented to design a medal, however, to be presented to prizewinners at the Fair. On one side of the World's Columbian Exposition medal was a figure of Columbus taking his first brave stride upon the shores of the New World — on the other was a nude young boy, torch in hand and having also a shield where the name of the recipient could be engraved. The design was simple and quite charming. Saint-Gaudens sent the plaster model to the Philadelphia mint to be cast — the Chicago Fair having been voted a federal project receiving federal funds.

"Of course you have heard of the great medal controversy," Augusta wrote to her brother Tom, who was a lawyer. "It's amazing, the excitement about it. The house has been besieged with reporters, as well as the studio. One man came at two A.M. and was almost kicked out of the house by the irate sculptor, only as his [Saint-Gaudens'] feet were bare he thought it would hurt him more than the man."

The story was that the medal was to be kept a close secret, no one to see it until the awards were made in Chicago. But Senator Chandler of New Hampshire wrote a letter of introduction to the director of the mint for an employee of the Page Belting Company of Concord, New Hampshire. This man, claiming that he was interested in art, asked to see the medal.

"He carried off in his brain enough of the details" of the Saint-Gaudens medal to have drawings made which the Brooks Bank Note and Circular Engraving Company struck off as letterheads. These, the Page Belting Company published on their circulars, saying underneath that this was the medal they had won and that they were the only company authorized to use it. The whole thing, as Gussie put it, was "all a monstrous, infamous lie." Worse still, the pirated drawing of the nude boy was crude and ugly. Some of the newspapers called the design immoral — and the mint made Saint-Gaudens do the medal over, three times.

One paper made "a pretty bad man out of the sculptor," Gussie told her brother Tom and she wanted Tom's advice about bringing suit. Mr. Beaman thought that New Hampshire farmers would be the jury on a case against a New Hampshire firm and that they would be unlikely to see where Saint-Gaudens had been very much injured. Tom said that Gus had a good case but might not want to spare the time to testify.

Saint-Gaudens decided not to go to court, but he took the case to the public by way of letters to the New York *Tribune*. Only now it was not the Page Belting Company that enraged him — it was the Philadelphia mint. The people at the mint had combined the Columbus side of his medal with the work, on the other side, of a not particularly gifted mint employee. This they had done without permission. They "might have the legal right to do such a thing," Gus wrote, "but the raw shamelessness of such an offense will be appreciated by all my confreres at home and abroad and it is as much in their interest as my own . . . that I make this protest public." Letters poured in, supporting Saint-Gaudens.

This was not to be the last time that Saint-Gaudens would be attacked for trying to graft the Greek ideal onto American culture. In 1891, he designed a seal for the Boston Public Library, to be cut in stone and placed over the main entrance. Two young figures supported a shield and when sufficiently puritanical Bostonians had taken a good look at it, the "boys without pants" controversy got under way — then died under an assault of ridicule.

Saint-Gaudens was angry but by no means ready to haul down his flag. That same year, 1891, he decided to live up to Emerson's philosophy as quoted by Will Low to Stevenson. He modeled a goddess but did not "drape his goddess warm." She was *Diana*, a beautiful nude figure, designed for a weather vane to go on top of Stanford White's Madison Square Garden. The building was to be just as festive as the Chicago Fair buildings but of golden terra-cotta and brick rather than white plaster. Everyone supposed that it would be a permanent ornament to New York.

Stanford White had had the Garden project in mind ever since he put some of his money into the Madison Square Garden Company, formed by rich men such as J. Pierpont Morgan, Herman Oelrichs, Adrian Iselin and others. These men raised four hundred thousand dollars to buy "Gilmore's Garden" which belonged to the Vanderbilts. Saint-Gaudens remembered the days when it was a passenger station for the Hudson River Railroad, then a train shed and finally a place where people went to hear music or to watch John L. Sullivan fight.

The new company invited bids from architects, and McKim, Mead and White submitted a plan for a building that would house a concert hall, a theater, a roof garden, and at street level an arcade for shops. All plans from competing architectural firms were judged by Professor William R. Ware, of Columbia University, who gave the commission to McKim, Mead and White. And when anyone asked the partners who actually designed the building, the answer was "White."

The style was "adapted" Spanish Renaissance with a tower reminiscent of La Giralda in Seville. In Spain, the top of La Giralda had a small dome with, above it, a sixteenth-century female figure representing Faith — a *giraldillo,* or weather vane, which gave the tower its name. So White designed a small dome and Saint-Gaudens, as fired-up over this gaily arcaded amusement palace as White was, contributed a weather vane in the New York Renaissance spirit. His *Diana* was done in "beaten copper," gilded, resting lightly on one toe, her only garment a ribbon of copper, looped and seeming to float behind her.

Diana, when completed, was eighteen feet, six inches high. She weighed two thousand pounds, but it took only "the pressure of half a pound of wind to move her." She was in perfect balance, but her pose, standing on the toe of one foot, was so difficult for a mere mortal to hold that Saint-Gaudens' model could keep it for only a few minutes at a time.

Diana was hoisted to the top of the Madison Square Garden tower, three hundred feet above the sidewalk, and unveiled November 1, 1891. "Great lamps in and about the goddess were lighted for the first time," said the New York *Tribune.*[3] Wires had been strung "up into her head, around her shapely limbs and at the tip of her ever-poised arrow. About five o'clock a workman climbed to the top of her head. Her robes were fluttering in the wind as she veered about. . . . Hundreds in Broadway stopped to watch. The politicians gathered in front of the Fifth Avenue Hotel and the Hoffman House, their minds not on politics.

The Diana *in the studio, in both copper and plaster, with Saint-Gaudens in the background (Courtesy of the Board of Trustees of Dartmouth College)*

"A workman sitting astride *Diana's* shoulders removed the muslin from there and, as he came down, stripped the shoulders bare. . . . Then at five-fifteen the show continued as the big searchlight in the loggia was turned on the statue and then the lights around her head. The effect was beautiful. . . . The golden limbs and the golden bow of the goddess, set off by the dark background of the heavens . . . were more graceful, more charming than ever. . . . The people never seemed to tire of *Diana!*"

But when White and Saint-Gaudens saw *Diana* in place, they were dismayed. She was too big! They had arrived at her height together, but they both knew they had made a mistake. "Well, you've designed quite a pedestal for Saint-Gaudens, this time," Babb is supposed to have told White, jeeringly. Saint-Gaudens went to work to make another *Diana*, half as heavy and only thirteen feet high. As always, he welcomed the chance to make changes. The pose of the first *Diana* had been altered "by the metalworker," who drove a heavy rod through her foot so that she seemed to stand not on her toe but on her heel. The new *Diana* stood properly poised on her toe, and being lighter, she was "thus more reliable as a weather vane," the papers said.

But meanwhile a furor had arisen, not because a few architects thought *Diana* was out of scale but because, as someone wisecracked, here was this beautiful girl at the fashionable Madison Square Garden "with literally nothing to wear."

"During the past two weeks, there has been a marked change in the character of Madison Square," wrote a reporter, happy to grind out copy, even if he had to call upon his imagination. "Formerly this beautiful little park was the gathering place of children. Now all this is changed. Occasionally a stray child may still be seen, but more generally, what children come there are rushed through at breakneck speed in the tow of a nurse or some older person. In their place the Square is now thronged with clubmen, armed with field glasses. Where babyhood once disported itself, today elderly gentlemen, Delmonico elegants, casino Johnnies and every variety of local dude, linger in restless idleness. . . .

" 'It's all along of her,' " a policeman was supposed to have said, "pointing to the summit of the Garden tower, where *Diana*, adorned with only her beauty and a thin veneer of gilt, blazed in the sun. . . . 'People as has kids, says as how she's immoralizing and so they won't let them young ones come here no more. Not as I blames them. I don't think no such statue should be allowed myself, not in a public place.' "

The DIANA *atop Madison Square Garden, New York City*
(Courtesy of The New York Historical Society, New York City)

"And yet this brazen — or more properly, copper image has been praised by artists and art critics as one of the great productions of modern sculpture and acclaimed by connoisseurs as the only fit and appropriate crown to the work of the architect who gave us Madison Square Garden. . . ."

That his *Diana* was out of scale worried Saint-Gaudens far more than these remarks. In 1892, "Cholly Knickerbocker" said in the New York *Recorder*, "So our pretty *Diana*, the highest kicker of them all, is to be taken down and sent to aim her arrow through the murky atmosphere of Chicago. . . ." The first *Diana* was to go to the Columbia Exposition, to be set on top of the Agriculture Building. In the New York *Tribune* for August 1, 1892, the report was that "the Chicago Fair has offered $2500 for it."

Mrs. Potter Palmer, having understood that Chicago had refused *Diana*, offered to pay the expenses of having her mounted on the Women's Building at the Fair. The Chicago *Tribune* saw fit to be shocked. "When she [*Diana*] arrived, thousands (including some of the oldest inhabitants) blushed. . . . What! (with one voice, shouted the Windy City — or at any rate the better elements) a statue without a stitch of clothing on top of the Women's Building! The idea!"

But in New York, by 1893 the winds of opinion had changed. "Our new *Diana* . . . will rise at dawn today, weather permitting, to delight the eye with all her glistening beauty as well as tell New Yorkers which way the wind blows," announced the New York *Tribune* for November 18.

The two *Diana*s cost Saint-Gaudens time, trouble and money, but Tiffany agreed to sell a large reproduction for $200 and a smaller one for $175. Other Saint-Gaudens pieces were made and sold in replica so that, in 1899, "We advise some advertising to an amount not to exceed $200," Tiffany wrote, "and a sufficient number of pieces should be placed on sale to fill a table large enough to make an impression upon a visitor to the great bronze room." Copies of *Diana* were bought for a garden ornament but rarely, if ever, for a weather vane!

Diana was one of Saint-Gaudens' happiest achievements. People who remembered New York in the nineties said that the golden goddess typified the city at a joyous period when the future seemed bright, the gilded era never-ending. When Madison Square Garden was pulled down in 1925 and *Diana* disappeared, a light seemed to go out.

Diana went into a storage warehouse and in 1932 she was acquired by the Philadelphia Museum of Art. In 1967, Mayor John Lindsay of New York asked Mayor James H. J. Tate of Philadelphia to give *Diana* back. "When no one wanted this poor orphan girl, Philadelphia took her in," Mayor Tate replied. He said he "put the question up to *Diana* and she answered, 'New York is a great place to visit but I wouldn't want to live there.' "⁴

Diana typified the gilded era in New York, but the mood of cheerful optimism was not confined to the city. In Cornish, New Hampshire, at the Nichols summer home, "Mastlands," near "Aspet," one of Saint-Gaudens' nieces, Margaret Nichols, told all about it. "Cornish is very gay," she began on August 7, 1896. There was "a fine party at the Beamans' " — she met some boys, much to her satisfaction, for she was not quite seventeen, and it was all of twelve o'clock when the band struck up "Home Sweet Home" and she had to leave. At the Evarts house there were "flowers for favors and a german." Her cousin Homer was "very nice" and even danced with her "quite often."

Excitement at Uncle Augustus's house was provided by the swimming pool. Youngsters went into the ice cold water with nothing on but, as a rule, girls were not invited. A companion of Margaret's, Frances Arnold, lived nearby and she and Margaret "went in bathing twice at the pool." Frances Arnold "wore a simple black jersey, tight pair of pants and a tight waist." Margaret did not say what her bathing costume was like, but she thought it was fortunate that "no one appeared on the scene." Her friend's brother, Harry Arnold, "was very much shocked when he discovered his sister had been in but she didn't care."

The Arnold young people were great friends of Saint-Gaudens'. Their grandfather Benjamin Green Arnold's marble bust by Saint-Gaudens, elegant with "Horace Greeley whiskers," was a familiar sight of their childhood, but their aunts hated it, for it represented Mr. Arnold's brief enjoyment of these manly ornaments. He wore them only a year and then shaved them off, to the relief of the young ladies of the family.

In 1897, Saint-Gaudens at last completed his statue of Peter Cooper, not quite ten years after the "Citizens of New York" had agreed to pay him $25,000 for it. Gus said it gave him lots of trouble and it is easy to see why it might. Somehow, Cooper's huge beard looked as false as that of a department store Santa Claus, and White must still have been under the influence of the Columbian Exposition, for he designed such a grandiose pedestal and canopy that Cooper looked like a sixteenth-century Pope of Rome in a nineteenth-century frock coat and trousers. Gus could not overcome his gift for telling the truth in portraiture. As the old inventor, the builder of a fortune from a glue factory, sat there, he had what was almost a grin on his face, as though he were laughing at the whole ponderous affair.

The equestrian statue of General John A. Logan was more to Saint-Gaudens' liking. It was a spirited composition, a young man grasping and holding aloft a flag. Again, Saint-Gaudens had trouble with a statue, but this time it was the fault of Homer and his pet goat! The horse had been modeled in Cornish and was standing, pointed by hand and enlarged full-size, in the big studio. Saint-Gaudens had been working on other things in the small studio, recently built. But one morning he walked into the former hay barn with its big skylight let into the old roof, to have a look at the Logan horse. He saw instantly that something was radically wrong. The horse's hindquarters were askew! The assistant, who had been at work on the figure all summer, was summoned. Careful measurements were taken — the sculptor's eye had been only too accurate and the Logan horse had to be done over, beginning with a small figure in modeling wax. A summer's work on this commission had been lost.

Years later, Homer confessed. One noon hour, when the assistants were having lunch and the big studio was empty, he had gone in there with his goat.[5] This was the charming pet who had knocked down unwary guests, to Homer's glee, and now the goat "made his dive," hoping to butt Homer. But this was only part of the game. Homer dodged behind the modeling stand and the goat "drove his horns with a crash against the pedestal. For a second the horse rocked to and fro but it did not fall"—and Homer didn't tell. The assistant never noticed that part of the wax model had shifted slightly, but in the enlargement, the mistake was plain. Some years later, Saint-Gaudens was telling friends about the mysterious trouble with the Logan horse. "By that time I was too large to spank," Homer said, so he confessed to what had happened and "my father contented himself with a smile."

The Logan statue was finished only seven years after the signing of the fifty-thousand-dollar contract. This was a good record as works of Saint-Gaudens went. General Logan's son became impatient, but the treasurer of the committee appointed under the Illinois legislature was

Saint-Gaudens, Homer, and Homer's goat, "Seasick"
(Courtesy of the Board of Trustees of Dartmouth College)

positively insulting — implying that Saint-Gaudens had received in-
stallment payments without doing the work he claimed to have done.
To the general's son Gus explained his desire for perfection, but to the
committeeman he replied sharply, "You speak of other sculptors. You
may remember that I did not seek the commission and that the work
of other sculptors was submitted to you before I consented to accept
it. . . ."

Saint-Gaudens rarely had time for personal friendships, but acquaintance with Mrs. Jack Gardner, of Boston, seems to have begun
around 1892 when she invited Saint-Gaudens to dinner. She collected
artists as well as works of art. Gus however proved difficult. "Thank
you very much for the kind invitation to dinner but I am a fickle being
and I must not accept it as I am not certain of being in Boston at the
time of your musicale," he replied on February 14.

This must have surprised Mrs. Jack who was accustomed to have
artists at her beck and call. She proposed that Saint-Gaudens do a
medallion of Paderewski, she to pay for it.

"I hate to tell you what follows, but what must be done must be
done and that's all there is to it," Saint-Gaudens wrote her. "From two
thousand to four thousand would be the cost of the medallion — according to what I might do. If your project survives the above, I am
flattered, and in any event I shall feel highly complimented."

And, on March 3, "Although I feared it would be so, I am very
disappointed that the portrait of Paderewski is off — still, had I done
it, the bitterness of gall and wormwood would have been in the hearts
of some good people. That is avoided. In the next planet, he may have
more time, I may — and there will be no bitterness of heart. . . ."

Mrs. Jack was not used to artists who never called her "dear Lady"
and seemed actually pleased not to have her patronage. She per-
severed in her scheme but she was dealing with an equally independent musician. Five days later, Saint-Gaudens wrote, "Paderewski has
not appeared but should he come, I am prepared."

Paderewski never turned up at the Saint-Gaudens studio, but Gus's
acquaintance with Mrs. Jack progressed pleasantly. "I thank you sincerely for the ticket," he wrote her in June. I feared I would never hear
from you again. I shall certainly appear on Friday."[6]

In 1894, "Mrs. J. Gardner" made an appointment to call on Saint-
Gaudens at his studio in New York, bringing "Mr. and Mrs. Paul
Bourget," the latter a French novelist in search of local color for his

book on life in the United States. There were no further entries in the Saint-Gaudens engagement book concerning Mrs. Jack, but in 1902, when he was in Boston, he was invited to see Mrs. Gardner's palace. "The place is really wonderful," he told Gussie. "No matter what her defects, that woman has accomplished a big thing." Perhaps acquaintance changed to friendship at this point. Gus gave Mrs. Gardner a copy of his medallion of Sargent as a young man and wished the likeness were more worthy of the original. She placed it in a case in the Long Gallery at Fenway Court.

It was probably in 1897 or 1898 when Saint-Gaudens addressed a letter to someone who had approached him on the subject of a portrait medallion of Mrs. Jack. Gus replied most tactfully. "With regard to a medallion of Mrs. Gardner, my experience for the last 2 or 3 years is that I invariably pass a great deal more time on these serious portraits than I have contemplated and that, unless well paid, it is not worth while to undertake them. My interest increases and they always develop far beyond my original intention. That's the way I'm constructed.

"The head alone would not satisfy me and I should certainly branch off, a luxury I cannot afford at my time of life without sufficient remuneration, however great the temptation, and I should have to ask $10,000. Our good friend interests me greatly and surely something pretty fine could be made, with her remarkable personality. . . . If Mrs. Gardner could come here (to New York) as Mrs. Gray did last year, it is quite possible I could begin on it this summer." Mrs. Jack was usually thought of as a tremendous egotist, but she was not in a mood to spend ten thousand dollars on a bas-relief portrait of herself.

Saint-Gaudens had placed his price high, hoping for a refusal, perhaps partly because in 1897, the long-delayed *Shaw Memorial* had suddenly come to life in his mind. It had been almost ten years since the contract had been signed "at the suggestion of H. H. Richardson," and the work was supposed to be completed in two years. The Commonwealth of Massachusetts granted land in front of the Statehouse for the memorial. The grounds were already adorned with the Webster statue by Hiram Powers and the *Horace Mann* by Emma Stebbins. But perhaps the spot opposite the top of Park Street was reserved for a Shaw by Saint-Gaudens. It was not until 1903 that *General Hooker* by Daniel Chester French (the horse by E. C. Potter) filled this space.[7]

Saint-Gaudens' disappointment in being forbidden to do an equestrian may have contributed to his delay. He finished horse and rider long before tackling the really difficult part of his composition — that background of marching men. Well before the great bronze panel was completed, it was obvious that it would never fit into any remaining space on Statehouse grounds. "It was thought best to choose a site where the memorial should be on a terrace within the lines of Boston Common" was the official verdict.

Saint-Gaudens began to look for models for his soldiers. He wanted fine-looking Negroes, not all of them of the type considered "African," but representing the variations he saw about him, among Negro Americans. It ought to be easy to get the right models, he thought, and he wrote to his brother-in-law, Tom Homer, to negotiate for the services of two waiters, John and Riley Lee, whom he had seen at Young's Café in Boston. They were "so gorgeous that I wish to put 'em in the Shaw monument," he said. Tom Homer was to get permission for the men to go to New York, expenses paid, to work for Saint-Gaudens without loss of their permanent jobs — if they seemed right for the composition when he got them into the studio. Gus had talked to the headwaiter, "E. Mac Duffie, a most intelligent man," and apparently this plan worked well.

It was in New York where the trouble came. On seeing a young man just the right height, of fine physique and with a resolute look such as Shaw's soldiers must have had, Gus would approach him, saying he was an artist looking for models. This made them "suspicious," Gus said — and they wouldn't listen to further explanation. He tried just offering a job. A few went with him to the studio and posed "with guns over their shoulders and caps on their heads." But almost none of them had ever seen the inside of a sculptor's studio and one man, who got only as far as the studio door, peered inside and saw plaster casts of heads, bronze-colored and apparently cut off at the base of the neck. He ran for his life.

Finally, as Gus told it, "I found a colored man to whom I promised twenty-five cents for every Negro he would bring me that I could use. The following day the place was packed." Now Saint-Gaudens had trouble, not only in choosing the finest types, but in explaining to the others why there was no job, after all.

A technical difficulty was harder to overcome. This was the handling of perspective in showing a regiment, their ranks disappearing into the background. Saint-Gaudens remembered now how the troops had looked to him when he saw "the bayonets above the crowd" on the day when the Massachusetts Volunteers crossed New York. Behind Shaw's reined-in horse, Saint-Gaudens placed upraised gun barrels, but without bayonets. He remembered profile behind profile as the ranks went by and this he rendered eloquently with his Negro models. In the handling of legs and feet in increasingly low relief, the problem was to avoid confusion of line. Saint-Gaudens had collected photographs of works of art and the *Surrender of Breda* by Velasquez, in particular, was said to have been helpful.

Saint-Gaudens' passion for modeling something ideal or symbolic led him to place in low relief a floating figure of a sad lady above the troops. One of his closest friends, the artist Bion, to whom he sent sketches, said the figure was unnecessary, and that it would be just as sensible for Millet to have painted a figure in the sky representing Simplicity over his *Gleaners*. Bion was right. But Gus argued that the Greeks would have added allegory and Royal Cortissoz, the American art critic, echoed the opinion of most contemporaries when he admired the "melancholy beauty of the figure that floats above the young Shaw."

There was speculation as to the identity of the model for the symbolic figure. Homer Saint-Gaudens wrote, long after, that his father "tried first the beautiful head of Miss Annie Page" who often visited the Platts in Cornish. But this would have been "too personal" so that, in Homer's opinion, his father "relied wholly on his imagination to produce a result his friends and pupils have said somewhat recalled his mother, and somewhat a former model in Paris." As a matter of fact, the pathetic eyes, the gentle mouth, recall Davida, in his *Angel with the Tablet*.

19

THE *SHAW MEMORIAL*

EARLY in the morning, on May 31, 1897, Saint-Gaudens stood on Beacon Street, Boston, opposite the Statehouse. A light rain was falling, the streets were deserted. Then, "little by little, the streets awoke" — there was going to be an enormous crowd and people were already coming into Boston Common. Veteran of unveilings though he was by this time, Saint-Gaudens was anxious as he surveyed the flags and bunting that concealed the *Shaw Memorial*. Would they fall properly or would they catch and require some workman ignominiously to climb a ladder? He had long ladders concealed behind the great bronze panel — just in case. All too soon, it was time for him to join the military parade.

"I was assigned to a carriage with Mr. William James, the orator of the occasion and we followed slowly at the tail-end of a long line of regiments and societies," Gus said. He was very nervous because he hated to be stared at. "It soon dawned on me that to this great crowd, this monster that lined the streets, I was nothing more than the usual fellow or public official that one finds in carriages in processions. They generally appear very insignificant. Yet to see this line of faces on each side of the streets, continuing for miles and miles, and all the windows filled with persons gazing at you, is really a profound experience. . . ."

The long line of march was most gratifying to the citizens of Boston and the parade wound up at last at the Statehouse. Gus was back again in front of the *Shaw Memorial*. He was assigned a seat on the lowest platform, which was built over the steps leading to the State-house, a vantage point from which he watched veterans marching toward him up Beacon Hill. These were the officers and colored men of the Fifty-fourth Massachusetts Regiment, whom Shaw had led. "Many of them were bent and crippled, many with white heads, some with bouquets and . . . one with a carpet bag.

"The impression of those old soldiers passing the very spot where they left for the war so many years before, thrills me even as I write these words," Saint-Gaudens said. The Negro veterans faced the *Shaw Memorial*, as the flags dropped. And when this part of the ceremonies ended, they saluted the statue of their young leader while the regimental band played "John Brown's Body." The Negro veterans "seemed as if returning from the war, the troops of bronze marching in the opposite direction — the direction in which they left for the front, the young men in the bas-relief showing these veterans the hope and vigor of youth." Saint-Gaudens felt that "it was a consecration."

When the ceremonies in front of the *Shaw Memorial* were over, the parade got under way again. Gus breathed a sigh of relief — as he and William James got into their carriage. Everything had gone well. Then they were driven to the old Music Hall where the commemoration services took place, and Gus began to worry again. "Here, I so dreaded being seated in a conspicuous chair on the platform that I stole away and went in after I knew the others would be placed, when I hoped to find a corner in the back. This was not to be. I was recognized and brought forward to occupy the one vacant chair in the front row, conspicuous by its vacancy." Everybody else had been seated by this time and of course Gus attracted far more attention than he would have if he had not tried to hide in the crowd.

Booker T. Washington "created a great sensation" when he spoke and William James's address was "noble and poetic," according to the papers, but Gus heard scarcely a word. "Fright had taken possession of me, because I knew that sooner or later I would be called upon to say something or other," he wrote.

The time came. Saint Gaudens stood up. "It was an awful moment but it would be stupid to deny that at the same time it was thrilling to hear the great storm of applause and cheering that I faced," he admitted. Friends wrote him of that "tumultuous sea of applause and gratitude and admiration." It was one of Boston's "greatest ovations."

The newspapers were full of praise and in the Boston *Herald* next day Thomas Bailey Aldrich had "a poem of seventy lines or so, worthy of him and of the monument," Thomas Russell Sullivan commented in his diary.

Bishop Lawrence's lively young daughter, Marian, wrote a diary account that Saint-Gaudens himself would have liked if he could have seen it. On the day before the unveiling, "Boston is all excitement over the Shaw statue," she said. She, personally, was more excited over equestrian young friends in dress uniform than heroes in bronze. The New York Seventh Regiment "were all over town, walking five abreast down the Mall, and driving, riding and biking in the Park." She and her family drove in from Cambridge early next morning to see the procession.

"The Governor rode through the lines and after him came Battery A on the dead run. Then Jake Peabody and Charley Dabney on horseback. Others less fortunate were riding on the back of the heavy artillery wagons, clinging on for dear life and looking as if they were being shaken to a jelly. The N. Y. Seventh marched wonderfully and had a splendiferous band. Lorimer Worden towered above the crowd. The Veterans of the old 54th (Shaw's Regiment) came in for great applause, especially when the torn but still bright colors went by, held up by a lame old Negro. The Aides were very swell. Bob Wolcott was one and looked extremely well on horseback."[1]

Miss Marian Lawrence did not go to the Music Hall ceremonies, but her father, the bishop, was there and said it was a fine meeting. "Booker T. Washington made the best speech." The following day, "Amos came, in his swell turnout and drove me to Aunt Minnie's reception for St.-Gaudens who, of course, is being much feted," Miss Lawrence wrote. "The Governor and staff were there and many officers from the warships, several of whom were introduced to me."

The guest of honor, Mr. Saint-Gaudens, did not particularly impress Miss Lawrence — in comparison with young naval officers. He had "a rather shaggy appearance, not at all slicked up," she was later to remember.[2]

Early in May of this same year, 1897, Saint-Gaudens had modeled his charming double portrait of William Dean Howells and his daughter, Mildred. Both of them said that Saint-Gaudens looked like a lion, not just because of his thick, shaggy hair, but because his close-set eyes had such an intent look and he had a "noble, leonine nose."

But being lionized was something Gus could never get used to. He had been offered an honorary degree of L.H.D. from Princeton in 1896, the occasion of Princeton's one hundred and fiftieth anniversary. President Cleveland was to be honored on this same gala occasion and Gus, after writing to Gilder about what to wear and how to acquire academic robes, felt he had everything under control when he left Cornish, the day before the event. He spent the night in his West

The SHAW MEMORIAL *on Beacon Hill, opposite the Statehouse, Bosta*

OMNIA RELINQVIT
SERVARE·REMPVBLICAM

assachusetts (Courtesy of the Board of Trustees of Dartmouth College)

Forty-fifth Street house, rose early next morning and opened his bureau to take out a clean white shirt. There were no shirts! After he had ransacked other bureaus, his calmness left him and he bellowed for Margaret, the servant Gussie had left in New York, "to look after my husband," as she put it. Margaret said that Mr. Saint-Gaudens had not left any shirts in New York. Anguished swearing in French and English by her employer ensued.

Gus rushed out to buy a shirt, but the stores were not yet open. He dashed back again, put on the shirt he had worn the night before, wilted as to collar and gray with soot from the train. Then he put on the new frock coat and trousers and the top hat which Gilder said he must have, and made for the railroad station. He missed his train.

There was a second train to Princeton. Gus might barely have reached the open-air platform in time if he had known that the ceremonies would take place within walking distance of the station. But he took a cab and the cabdriver took the long way around. Gus heard the sound of distant hand-clapping. The giving of degrees was over.

Saint-Gaudens could do nothing but go to the president of Princeton and apologize. On looking around at the crowd, he observed that he was the only one wearing a top hat! For a person who hated to be conspicuous, this would have been a disaster — even if he had not arrived too late.

Princeton honored Saint-Gaudens in 1898. And when Harvard gave Saint-Gaudens the honorary degree of LL.D. that same year, he was careful to pack clean shirts but did not bring his top hat. He arrived with time to spare, but when he looked over the crowd in Harvard Yard, there were plenty of top hats. There were also derbies and straw hats, but only one fedora — his own!

Letters from old friends, new acquaintances and strangers poured in. This was fame such as Saint-Gaudens dreamed of as a boy, standing on the omnibus platform in New York and wondering if the men around him realized "how great a genius was rubbing shoulders with them." But Saint-Gaudens was nervously exhausted. The day after the Shaw unveiling, when he got up and stooped over the bowl to wash his face, he found he could not straighten up again. There was a pain like a sword thrust in his back. The diagnosis was sciatica and Gus was given a strong painkiller.

Suddenly it seemed to Gus that he must go back to Paris. The streets of New York, which he had once loved, now represented nothing but noise and confusion. The Thirty-sixth Street studio had become intolerable because the elevated railroad rumbled overhead so close to it, while trolley cars at street level banged along, their motormen constantly stamping on the button that operated a bell. Horse-drawn ambulances dashed by, drivers whanging on their gongs. And fire engines that had once thrilled Gus were now a torment, smoke, fire and cinders pouring from polished brass smokestacks, bells clanging — all hell let loose. Gus set the date for sailing — October, 1897.

There was one big unveiling, that of the equestrian *General John A. Logan,* in Grant Park, Chicago. Saint-Gaudens went to Cornish early in July and then Gussie, Homer and he set out together. "It is to be a great affair, the governors of thirty states, troops galore, much music and more champagne," Gus wrote to his sister-in-law Genie. But he told her he did not think anything could compare with the Shaw unveiling.

Genie was not going along — her address was now Hawaii. On February 13, 1896, Eugenie Homer had married Oliver Pomeroy Emerson, her faithful suitor for the last twenty-eight years, it was said. The Reverend Oliver was the son of the Reverend John, who had gone out as a missionary for the Congregational church to the Hawaiian Islands in 1831. Thirty years later, the Reverend John, on a visit to the United States, received an M.D. degree from Dartmouth and returned as a medical as well as theological missionary. Genie's husband, the Reverend Oliver Emerson, was born in Hawaii — the missionary couple's seventh child. Of course the Homer family were reluctant to lose Genie's services as ever obliging maiden aunt and they wondered if she were "wise." At forty-two, Genie was as wise as she ever would be and Gus, for one, was delighted to see her begin a life of her own.

Genie and the Reverend Oliver had enjoyed a long honeymoon, setting out for Hawaii by way of Granada and sending photographs to Gus from Athens.[3] On October 20, 1896, they were "on the Pacific." Genie's new home in Honolulu had been her husband's home for years and she was thrilled with it. Coconut palms grew in the front yard of "The Jungle," as their house was called. Genie wrote of romantic dinner parties by moonlight, the "ladies in light dresses, gentlemen in dinnercoats."

On Thanksgiving day, Genie said it was "confusing" to be wearing "my white P.K. dress and fanning myself to keep cool during courses."

She remembered crisp New England weather with hardly a touch of nostalgia, however, because she found she could grow orchids in her garden.

"Gussie works at the flowers with much effect," Gus told her, "but we must not talk of flowers, we New Englanders, to Hawaiians."

The Logan unveiling was as handsome an occasion as Gus supposed it would be. The days when the bronze founder rated higher than the sculptor were over, at least for Saint-Gaudens. "I was put in one of the Holy of Holies alongside Mrs. Logan, if you please, and the president of ceremonies," he wrote Genie. "At the right moment the complicated arrangement of flags dropped, the band played, Mrs. Logan wept and I posed for a thousand snap photographs."

There was one more equestrian statue being modeled in the Saint-Gaudens studio — the *General Sherman* for New York City. The contract was signed March 21, 1892, the date agreed upon for completion May 1, 1894, and the amount promised $45,000. It was already four years late and although Saint-Gaudens seemed outwardly unperturbed, the nagging of committeemen contributed to his nervous state of mind. He had a new horse for his model, a famous jumper named Ontario, past his competition days in the big horse shows but no less handsome an animal. Gus had him shipped to Cornish where models of him were well advanced, so far without help from Homer's goat.

In New York, Gus found a professional model of about General Sherman's build whom he posed astride a barrel which represented the horse. George Parsons Lathrop, dropping in at the studio, saw this model who took pride in being able to pose for long periods without moving a muscle. Assuming that it was a wax figure, Lathrop pinched the model's leg — just to make sure. The man's insulted yell of protest informed him! For the head of Sherman, Gus planned to use the bust he had modeled from life — when General Sherman was in New York in 1888.

Not content with his conception of a huge equestrian, Saint-Gaudens began to dream of a statuary group with more than one figure, designed to form a unit. He began to visualize a symbolic "peace with victory" — an "ideal" angelic form leading Sherman in the path of destiny. Always longing to do what he called the "ideal," he set to work. In 1897, the painter and etcher Anders Zorn was in the United States and called on Saint-Gaudens. He was fascinated by the sculptor's intense gaze and made two etchings with a studio background.

*This etching by Anders Zorn shows Saint-Gaudens in his New York studio
with a model on the stand behind him. In his biography of his father, Homer
Saint-Gaudens used a different Zorn etching, minus the model (New York
Public Library)*

Writing to his niece Rose Nichols, Saint-Gaudens said, on February 17,
1897, "At the Twenty-seventh Street studio . . . I had another day
with the model for Victory, last Sunday. . . . Zorn, the Swedish artist
was with me all day, making an etching of me while the model rested;
it is an admirable thing and I will send you a copy of it."[4]

With Stanford White to help him dream, Saint-Gaudens imagined a
colossal Sherman, all gleaming in gold leaf, with an angel to lead him,
reining in his horse in front of Grant's Tomb on Riverside Drive. In his
present state of nervous exhaustion, however, Gus could not make the
clay on his hands take the shape of his dream. This was a new and
frightening experience, but perhaps in Paris the *Sherman* would begin
to come out right.

Then there was the matter of expenses. As early as 1895, Saint-
Gaudens had four New York studios. Although the big white studio on
Thirty-sixth Street was still his official address, Gus was less and less
often to be found there. Now that fame had come upon him, floods of
callers filled his reception room. Most sculptors would have been
delighted. J. Q. A. Ward, for example, had a big room decorated in

the Pompeiian manner, which he would have loved to see filled with visitors — but his popularity was on the wane. Gus kept his small room and tried to hide from the callers, many of whom wanted a portrait bas-relief or a memorial tablet he had no time to work on. He would sooner or later be run to earth, of course, at the small studio on Twenty-seventh Street, or the almost-filled place on Twentieth Street or perhaps at Fifty-ninth Street where Ontario posed in winter. Each studio was staffed with assistants who must be paid.

Saint-Gaudens taught occasional day and evening classes at the Art Students' League, not for the small amount of money teaching would bring, but because he had not forgotten the years when he himself longed for help from an experienced sculptor. The gifted pupils gave him great pleasure, but when he discovered that they needed money (as they usually did), he hired them as assistants, paying them not necessarily what they were worth but what they needed to get along. Remembering personal hardships, he was generous to a fault.

All this would be changed if he could get to Paris, Saint-Gaudens felt sure. He would have just one studio and only one assistant. He would work in peace on one statue — the *Sherman*. And then after that he would do the groups for the Boston Public Library, now about five years late, with little done save preliminary sketches. Of course Gus would have to bring a few things with him to Paris. Plaster casts of Ontario must go, models of the rider and of Sherman's bust. Other casts must be cleared out of the New York studios and sent into storage or to Cornish. A sculptor's belongings became immensely cumbersome as time went by. Storage, crating, land and ocean freight were all expensive. He was "in a whirl of annoying things," Gus said. But if, in an effort to save money, he was spending a great deal, Gus always imagined that a completed commission with its final payment would leave him with money in his pocket. And then, of course, he could always sign a new commission with an advance payment that would set everything straight.

On October 20, 1897, the trustees of the "Lincoln Monument Fund," created under the will of John Crerar, agreed to pay Saint-Gaudens $100,000 for another heroic statue of Lincoln for Chicago. This was his largest commission and with a substantial advance, he set out for Paris. He did not say whether Gussie went with him or whether she stayed behind to attend to the endless details of closing the Cornish house and of emptying the West Forty-fifth Street house and trying to sublet it until the lease ran out. She went to Paris eventually, only to return to see about Homer's schooling, then to go to Paris again.

Nothing was said about the whereabouts of Louis Saint-Gaudens, either. He had completed in 1894 the great golden lions, carved from Siena marble, for the staircase in the Boston Public Library and when Gus saw them finished and oiled, he said they had "a very swell look." Louis had become impatient with working for his brother and wanted to strike out on his own. Gus gave him every encouragement, but it was never possible for Louis to stand on his own feet. Eventually, he too was in Paris, but whether he was there already or still to come is not clear. But in writing of his voyage, Gus spoke as though he were not alone.

The boat train for London was waiting at the dockside in Liverpool when Gus arrived. Spending only one night in London, he set out for Paris next day. The French countryside looked good to him from the train windows. It was the sort of landscape Millet liked to paint — peaceful and dreamlike under the clear sky. A plowman and a boy alone on a distant hillside followed the horses and plow as long straight furrows unrolled behind them. There were no fences and only a small clump of trees. After the noise and confusion of New York, the scene was "all so orderly and grand," Gus said.[5]

Once in Paris, this fleeting sense of peace vanished and Saint-Gaudens plunged into an exasperating, nerve-wearing search for a studio. In a fever of impatience, he dashed back and forth across Paris. At last he found a place in the Passage de Bagneaux,[6] a little byway, having the address Number 3 Rue de Bagneaux. "A garden-like place," he called it, and it was not far from the Luxembourg Gardens. His former studio on the Rue Notre-Dame-des-Champs which he had left to go back to New York, was nearby and he felt he might really recapture some of the old joie de vivre which he remembered as being so much a part of life in Paris.

But the sun refused to shine, skies were gray and winds were raw. Like most sensitive people, Saint-Gaudens had always been depressed by bad weather and a prey to alternating moods of elation and despair. But now, for the first time, he was completely overwhelmed by despair, his mood of depression lasting not just for a few days at a time but for six months or more. He was frightened and went to a doctor who said he had "neuresthemia." Gus confessed that he had thought such illness imaginary. Now he realized that there was something very real the matter with him.

He took out the drawings for the Boston Public Library groups, but all his ideas seemed cold and dead. He could not seem to care whether Force was on the right or the left of Law, and although he was certain that Art belonged in the same group with Labor, art itself was nothing but labor because his love for his work had left him.

Gus wrote to McKim in December, 1897, to say, among other things, that he was homesick, that Paris was a disappointment and that he wished he were back in New York. McKim tried to write a cheering reply. "*Shaw* is a constant joy in Boston . . ." and McKim's "only fear is that your homesickness will pass away too soon and that, once established, we shall find it hard to get you back."

Things were not going too well in New York, McKim said. "As for competitions, I never want to go into one again. We lost the New York Public Library to Hastings; and Babb the National Academy of Design to the same gentleman. I feel sore, not in the least over Hastings' victory but over the folly of having gone into such a contest. Babb feels sore because he considers that he had the best design. . . . I hope Tommy Hastings' double triumph will not turn his head." Thomas Hastings, thirty-eight-year-old partner of Hastings and Carrere, was a good friend to Saint-Gaudens. He reserved two big niches, one at each side of the main entrance to the New York Public Library, for Saint-Gaudens to fill with anything he pleased. But Gus wasn't interested and MacMonnies filled the niches with "fountain figures" minus the water.

The doctor suggested a change of scene for Saint-Gaudens, and he agreed to take a trip. His father was no longer living,[7] but Gus remembered the plans to send the old man back to Aspet, his native town which he had so much wanted to see again. Well — the plan fell through and now it was too late. Then there had been the matter of the louis d'or, the gold pieces given to Gus to pay for a trip to Aspet — but this money had slipped through his uncle's fingers. Gus now looked up his old friend Garnier and invited him to take a trip to Italy with him — by way of Aspet and the Pyrenees — all expenses paid.

Garnier, his hair and beard now white, demurred, saying he had neither time nor money. But Gus argued that the money Garnier could help him save, by traveling third class instead of first, and at hotels, by defending him against those thieves, the hotel managers, would pay Garnier's way and show a profit.

"Oh, I saw at once that it was his generous heart that was saying to him, 'If I don't take Garnier to Italy, he'll never find a way to get there. I'm going to make him believe he's obliging me — that will decide him.' Oh I saw the dodge, but it tempted me and I said yes," Garnier confessed.

The trip to Saint-Gaudens country came first, Salies-du-Salat their first stop. "It is impossible for me to describe my emotions on arriving at the village," Gus said. "I had heard my father speak of it so frequently." He saw his name over a door at the head of a narrow street and it excited him far more than the sight of his name in the papers at home. "A cousin lived there who was in the shoe-making business and also sold wine." He saw the ancient ruins of a thirteenth-century castle and the moat where his father played — "for father passed his childhood in this town," Gus said. Next day, a cousin drove Gus and Garnier up to Aspet, about three hundred feet above the plateau.

"We got there in the evening — to Aspet — in a cart along an endless road which climbed and climbed, winding all the way. It was beautiful country with small towns along the road where everyone is polite and pleasant. We stopped at an old hotel, well-known in the district, kept by two ancient maiden ladies, sisters, who were . . . elegant-mannered and at the same time humble." These were Garnier's impressions.[8] Gus was decidedly more lyrical about the long road.

"It is beautiful country I come from, my boy," Bernard Saint-Gaudens had said, but Gus had hardly believed it. Now he saw that it was true. The "scenery of the Pyrenees" was "gorgeous. . . . You come upon the village of Aspet suddenly" and "enter the principal street and directly at the head of it . . . is the snow-capped Pic du Cahire of which I had heard my father speak so often." Again there was a discovery of cousins and a family welcome for Saint-Gaudens. They asked about his wife and he promised to bring her to meet them.

Gus and Garnier left early next morning, "to the clink of the village blacksmith" — a sound Gus knew his father must have heard. They set out on foot, walked down into the valley of the Garonne, crossed the river and climbed a gentle slope to the town of Saint-Gaudens. Here they rested awhile at a little café where tables were set out of doors in the village square in full view of a range of snow-capped Pyrenees. Gus thought that the location of the square, facing such a fine view, showed the townspeople's love of beauty, but he wished he could say as much for their love of cleanliness.

After exploring the village of Saint-Gaudens for two or three hours, Gus and Garnier took the train for Toulouse and "our beloved Italy," as Gus said in a letter to Gussie. He told her that the town of Saint-Gaudens was "a pink place and brown velvet" — and that Aspet "was wonderfully romantic."

There was one drawback on this journey for old comrades. Garnier now snored like a whole army of Rip Van Winkles. In Nice they found an old-fashioned hotel and were shown to a room with high ceilings and tall windows, "everything on a scale which made us feel lost in space," Gus said. Here he was really first aware of Garnier's snoring. He thought someone was moving furniture in the next room — perhaps wild men or lunatics. Then "the rhythmic character of the noise revealed the extraordinary snore of my friend." Gus shouted "Garnier!" again and again, to no avail.

By this time it was nearly dawn and from a belfry across the square, chimes began to ring. "I realized why we had been given such a beautiful room for so small a price. Moreover, it was Christmas morning." Gus and Garnier had lost track of the date!

The bells pealed, but Garnier's snore was louder. The bells continued, "broken only by my shouting and Garnier's trumpeting." Gus finally seized Garnier by the feet and woke him by dragging him out of bed. "Snore?" said Garnier. "Why, I never snore." Gus was reminded of his father and Dr. McCosh.

The two friends took to the road again just as they had done in student days — this time walking along the coast from Nice to Ventimiglia. At Ventimiglia they took the train for Rome, arriving at one A.M.

Gus "insisted upon our sallying forth from the hotel immediately, to go to the Café Greco and climb the Spanish Steps," said Garnier, who really would have preferred to resume snoring. At the Café Greco, Gus found the same waiter who had brought him coffee in the days when the *Hiawatha* was being cut in marble and the beautiful Angelina had posed for the *Silence*. The waiter was now very old but insisted that he remembered Mr. Saint-Gaudens. Gus did not ask about Angelina.

Back to the hotel went the friends at last and Garnier was not too exhausted to remember the walk "along streets where there was no one" — but everywhere "great fountains and a splashing sound of water in the night."

Next day they looked up their old comrade Defelice, who had been such a good friend to Saint-Gaudens when creditors hounded him. "He and *Auguste* walked me everywhere," Garnier said a trifle wearily. "Defelice came with us into the Campagna — we were still there after nightfall, which was most beautiful."

By now, it was January, 1898. Fortunately for Gus, the weather in Rome was still cold enough to discourage mosquitoes, but he urged Defelice to go on to Naples with them, their next port of call — but Defelice resisted all temptation. "Finally, we went off alone," Garnier said, "but on the morning when we had to take an early train and it was not yet daylight, here came Defelice. . . . What joy to find, after thirty years, the three of us together!"

He found it "impossible to describe" his feelings about Pompeii, Garnier declared. "It was *Auguste* who was happy in showing me everything. The next day we went, all three of us, to Paestum. I don't know what adjectives to use. I stop. Overcome."

Alfred Garnier did not actually stop telling the story of renewing his youth, however. Defelice returned to Rome and the other two walked from Salerno to Amalfi "on a day and a moonlit evening which were beautiful beyond belief." Then, taking a carriage, they drove to Castellammare where they found they had missed the train for Naples. A cabdriver was hanging around the railroad station just in the hope that someone would come by too late for the train, and he tried to force Gus and Garnier to get into his carriage and drive the seventeen and a half miles to Naples — for a fancy price.

"*Auguste* was angry and this cabman pursued us, putting his carriage right across the street. There was no use getting mad," the calm Garnier wrote. "But *Auguste,* perfectly furious, leaped at the driver, cane lifted. When I saw that I said to myself, 'If he hits him there's going to be a scandal — we'll be arrested. Saint-Gaudens arrested! What a thing! And for fighting a cabman.'

"Then I said to myself, 'If that happens to me it wouldn't make any difference' and I jumped in front and then I don't remember any more of what happened or what I said to the driver but all of a sudden he cleared out." Gus and the much agitated Garnier "were both so mad," they had to take a walk along the quay "to get calmed down."

Pretty soon they remembered that they hadn't had any breakfast, so they went into a harborside eating place where they saw "a beautiful girl surrounded by three or four bold fellows who seemed to be bothering her." A few remarks from Gus and Garnier, the old boys in search of their youth, and the "bold fellows" decamped — "all four of them." (Now Garnier was sure there were four rather than "three or four.")

Gus gave their order and they sat down at a table with a bench in front of it. The girl came over and sat down too and a big cat got up on the bench beside her. "What's the cat's name?" Gus asked in Italian.

"Ask her if she'll have breakfast with us," Garnier suggested.

"Oh, si, signore, si!" the girl said and Garnier noticed that she was "pretty good with the fork when the food came." She said she was a contralto singer in a stock company, and although Garnier seemed to doubt this, he said she had a nice speaking voice.

After giving the girl a big meal, Gus and Garnier got up and shook hands with her, "like good comrades," and said goodbye. The girl was "astonished." She hadn't realized that "we were giving her a meal and that was the end of it" — no further services required of her beyond her pleasant company.

"I remember all, I see all again as if I were there," Garnier wrote. They went next to "wonderful Florence" and Gus proposed Venice, but Garnier thought Gus "didn't seem very well and I decided that we would go back to Paris right away," he said.

Gus told it differently. "By this time, although it was only ten days since our departure from Paris, Garnier had grown homesick for his sacred city habits. . . ." Garnier was older than Gus, who was now fifty, and as a matter of fact both gentlemen were tired out, trying to be young art students again.

It was a good sort of physical exhaustion, however, and when Saint-Gaudens went back to his studio, "I felt more cheerful than I had for many months," he said.

Augusta was visiting her mother in Boston about this time. She was worrying about Homer's lack of prowess at boarding school, about money and the complaints of the committee for the Sherman statue. Then there was the matter of her getting to Paris. She didn't feel "strong enough" to travel alone with Homer. Genie, safe in Hawaii, was no longer available as nurse-companion. Her mother was growing old.

These details bothered Gus less than they had before. On February 26, 1898 (for once dating a letter), "Dear Gussie," he wrote, "Just a line to say I received your third letter this morning. You must hunt up Mrs. Alexander who is coming to Paris about the same time you do.

"I am feeling very well now and the *Sherman* is progressing very well. I am sure the committee will forget the delay when the work is done. I am working at nothing else and in about a week I will have the model entirely finished, Victory and all. Lovingly, Gus, for I love you more than you think, or I ever express."

20

RUE DES BAGNEAUX STUDIO

D R. HENRY SHIFF had a luxurious apartment on the slopes of Montmartre overlooking the city of Paris. He joyfully welcomed Saint-Gaudens but was distressed by the sculptor's mood of depression. The genial doctor set to work to cheer him, seeing to it that Gus combined work with more pleasure than had been his habit. Dr. Shiff had the enthusiastic cooperation of two American girls in this endeavor. They were Helen and Mary Mears, of Oshkosh, Wisconsin.

Mary Mears planned to become a writer and had sold stories to American magazines. Her sister Helen, now only twenty-six, was already an accomplished sculptress.[1] Her father, who had studied medicine, had taught her what an artist needs to know about anatomy when her talent for modeling was discovered. As a little girl of nine, she exhibited her first sculpture, a head of Apollo in clay which she baked in her mother's oven and sent to the county fair. At twenty-one, after a few weeks of study with Lorado Taft in Chicago, she won a commission to do a nine-foot statue called the *Genius of Wisconsin* for the Columbian Exposition. Later, this was put into marble, set up in the rotunda of the State Capitol at Madison, Wisconsin, and Helen won a prize of five hundred dollars from the Milwaukee Women's Club. She used this money to come to New York to study at the Art Students' League but counted on getting part-time work of some sort to keep her going. Helen Mears was one of those gifted students Saint-Gaudens helped with employment in his studios.

The Mears girls had been traveling in Europe, their expenses paid by an anonymous wealthy woman. They were on their way home when Helen got a letter from Saint-Gaudens, offering her a job in his Rue des Bagneaux studio. The sisters promptly turned in their return steamer tickets and took rooms in Paris. Gus introduced them to Dr. Shiff who found them naive and all agog about the city of their dreams. He and Gus set to work to show them sights not listed in their guidebook. Mary began a novel about student life in Paris while Helen worked on the Brimmer bust for Saint-Gaudens. At night Mary, Helen, Gus and Dr. Shiff helped Mary collect material for her novel.

Their favorite restaurant was on the "Boule Mich" where they sat at tables out on the sidewalk with the "daughters of joy." (Gus said this was Stevenson's translation from the French for harlot.) When they finished their apéritif they went inside and found the restaurant "simply packed with medical, legal and School of Mines students — a very few with their mistresses." Gus studied the crowd with an artist's eye and saw "an unusually good lot of faces."

Then there was the brasserie on Montmartre where Shiff was in the habit of meeting the mistress of one of his friends, "a charming woman and a young and ardent socialist who earned a living doing massage." They went to a workman's ball in rooms over the Collège de France and to a "strictly workman's café" which Gus described as "a char-mante place over in the Quartier St. Antoine." But their favorite was always the Café de la Paix where the "Hungarians swung their waltzes" and the waiter, an old man, circulated among the patrons, carrying a coffeepot.

Mary, practicing for her novel, described the scene at the Café de la Paix, "the lights, the clouds of smoke and people's faces seen through smoke . . . the music, shaken out, drummed out and wooed out by different instruments of the orchestra. . . . The rifts of smoke seemed to sever the heads from the bodies and they floated on it, as on a stream . . . most of the faces smiling and reckless." It looked to Mary like a poster, "beautiful but horrible" and perhaps she met Toulouse-Lautrec who was then at work — saying the same thing with paint and brush.

When Augusta arrived in Paris she found the Brimmer bust being completed in the Rue des Bagneaux studio, although her husband had said he would do no more work of this kind. It was a memorial to Martin Brimmer, first President of the Boston Museum of Fine Arts. He had died in 1895, a much loved Bostonian, patron of the museum and amateur of the arts, with good taste and discrimination. Saint-Gaudens had seen him but never really knew him. He sent for photographs as usual, but when Mrs. Brimmer came to see the portrait in October, 1898, she was not sure that Saint-Gaudens had quite done justice to her late husband's "beautiful, delicate nose." When the bust was done she was in ecstasy over it and ordered a copy in bronze for herself. Writing from Boston after the bust had been put in place, she quoted the opinions of her friends, one of whom said he could see "the social expression and the Harvard Corporation look both strongly portrayed." There had been plenty of routine work, such as the finishing of the costume, that Miss Mears could do. Gussie said she supposed the Brimmer bust would "help boil the pot."

Augusta went out with Gus, Dr. Shiff and the Mears girls a few times. She could surely hear the Hungarian waltz music that they liked so much — but it drowned out voices. As they sat around a little table together, everyone was gay except Gussie, who couldn't hear a word they said. It didn't help matters when they spoke French or, worse still, a combination of French and English. "How different my life would have been if I could hear," she said.

Homer had come to Paris with his mother. He had been in boarding school, had taken entrance examinations for Harvard, passing four subjects and failing four. They told him he could try again in September. A school was found for him in Paris, which he didn't like, but he liked the Mears girls and he liked going to cafés, imagining that the French he picked up would help him in a Harvard exam.

Augusta had a great capacity for work but almost no aptitude for play. She answered her husband's neglected correspondence, especially in connection with money owed to Saint-Gaudens. But her efforts at recreation were a disaster. Bicycling was the rage in Paris, so she took it up and a letter from Dr. Polk in answer to hers of June 3 tells a sad story. "Of course the shock of being knocked down by a cyclist would, in a measure, account for the increased racket in your head. I do not think the condition of the kidney is now responsible. As you have found in the past, any nervous strain or nervous shock increases ailments that are dependent on the nervous system." He approved of her plan to go to Aix-les-Bains.

Homer stayed behind in Paris and Gus was happy to have a chance to get acquainted with his boy. "We both enjoy knocking about Paris and I'm getting to know him and he me during these last few days than during years beforehand," he wrote Augusta.

Gus took his son to visit the field of Waterloo, observing with amusement that the boy was not impressed. When they went to Rouen the Mears girls were along and this made it more fun for Homer. On a Sunday in June they went out to Fountainbleu to have dinner with the

George de Forest Brushes and supper with Proctor, a young sculptor who had recently won the Rinehart Scholarship for study in Paris. "We took a walk with Brush and Proctor and two of Brush's lovely children — the two oldest," Gus wrote. "Brush has just started another swell picture, all the family this time. He is a remarkable feller. But Proctor is doing nothing."

At about this time Augusta's niece, Marian Nichols, wrote that while she was in London, "each day we expected that Uncle Augustus might turn up but finally we had a telegram telling us that his visit to England and Scotland had been postponed. It was a great pleasure and surprise, a few days later in Amsterdam, first to hear that he was coming with Homer to Holland and then to have them really appear one evening at our hotel."

After listening to his brother-in-law's descriptions, Gus had concluded that Dutch cities were dull. "It was Kermess season in many places," however, according to Marian, and Gus was delighted to find "the whole population walking up and down the streets till late at night." Dr. Nichols did manage to show Saint-Gaudens two "quaint, quiet towns," but after that Saint-Gaudens and Homer went back to Paris.[2]

Gus was afraid that he himself, like Proctor, might be said to be doing nothing this summer. His health improved only slowly if at all, however. The Sherman horse had been enlarged, but in the process, some of the accidents to it would have been funny if they had not been so costly in time and money. Gus decided not to trust the new French pointing machine but to have the horse pointed by hand. The pointers made a mistake and one of the legs was too short so that when it was cast, it cracked. Workmen plugged up the crack without telling what had happened, but Saint-Gaudens saw what was wrong, measured and found the leg short by all of four inches! He sent a man back to New York to get a cast from among those left there in storage — and the man came back with the wrong hind leg!

It was a good idea to leave the studio and go to Boulogne with Homer in August. The George de Forest Brushes were there, living in an apartment over a candy store. A religious festival was going on and Gus joined them to watch the procession from their window overlooking a public square. They heard music and out of a dark, narrow street, a column of priests and laymen emerged. A golden figure stepped into the sun. She had great gilded wings made of real feathers, long curling golden hair and gold robes. Little Nancy Brush thought she was seeing a real angel just down from heaven. She looked up at Mr. Saint-Gaudens who was standing just behind her and he had tears running down his face. Nancy did not know that grown-ups sometimes cried for joy and she thought he didn't like the angel.[3]

Three days later, Gus wrote to Gussie from Paris. "The weather is very fine and I have gotten to work again with great freshness."

But Augusta soon found that Aix-les-Bains didn't suit her. The water, famous for curing all sorts of ills since Roman days, had a high sulphur content and the taste of it was horrible. She went to Vichy, where the chief chemical ingredient of the water supposed to work miracles was bicarbonate of soda — according to Gussie's Baedeker's guide. The taste was reasonably pleasant and different springs were supposed to be specific for different ailments, so she could try one after the other for entertainment. Nothing helped her hearing; the inner noise continued, outer sounds blocked. But in Vichy she found her cousin Sidney Homer and his wife, Louise, so that at least she was less lonely.

Neither Louise nor Sidney took the waters, however. At this time, Vichy was not only a health resort but a music center, and Louise Homer's Paris agent had arranged an engagement for her in an opera company. This was an important step forward in her carefully planned campaign to win a role in grand opera. She was younger than any other star in the cast at Vichy, a newcomer whom the opera habitués were prepared to treat coldly. But her first appearance was a sensation. When Gussie wrote that Louise was "a tremendous success," she was not overstating the case.

Members of the Homer family, Gussie' sister Lizzie for example, had been inclined to be patronizing toward Louise. They said she was just a stenographer whom Cousin Sidney had fallen in love with when she was his pupil in harmony. She also took singing lessons, it seemed. In 1895, when Gussie went to Philadelphia with Gus for the unveiling of his *Garfield Memorial,* Cousin Sidney had called at their hotel. Gus got tickets for Sidney and Louise to see the unveiling and the illumination afterwards. President Garfield's son was coming to the Saint-Gaudens' hotel rooms and Gussie asked Cousin Louise to come and bring some music. She would please sing — with Cousin Sidney at the piano. Louise Homer obliged — she was always generous. She had a thrilling contralto voice which poor Augusta could never hear properly.

Louise Homer was the daughter of Dr. William Trimble Beatty,

Augusta Saint-Gaudens in early middle life (Courtesy of the Board of Trustees of Dartmouth College)

Louise and Sidney Homer (Courtesy of their son, Sidney Homer)

founder of the Pennsylvania College for Women as well as a clergy-man. Louise grew up in Westchester, Pennsylvania, where her widowed mother had sisters who had also married clergymen. Her father, who died when she was still very young, had eight children, five of whom became musicians. It was true that she was a stenog-rapher, for she learned this skill in order to earn money to cultivate her voice.

Sidney Homer had indeed been her harmony teacher; he was also a composer, and together they developed the career of one of the greatest contraltos ever to enchant an audience. Sidney benefited, just as Augusta Saint-Gaudens did, under the will of the famous "Uncle Sidney."

During the winter of 1898–1899 the Sidney Homers were in Paris, preparing for Louise's debut at Covent Garden, London, her next important step. They had to arrange a loan to pay for costumes for Louise, for "we had almost no money," Sidney Homer said – the annuity from Uncle Sidney being but a drop in the bucket in compari-son with the cost of launching an opera star. Sidney Homer remem-bered borrowing "twenty-five dollars from Augustus Saint-Gaudens." This was something Gus never mentioned, but he remarked that "Sid-ney Homer is a swell feller."

When Augusta came back to Paris from Vichy, the question of her son's further education had to be settled. Homer was for going back and giving the Harvard entrance exams another whirl. His father said he hadn't a chance and favored "the Dresden plan and the discipline and firm hand" Homer would get in "Mr. Hallam's school." So Gussie took Homer to Germany. She arranged for him to live with a German family where he could learn the language, had his bicycle sent to him from Paris and told him he could join the fencing club. In due course Mr. Hallam reported that Homer was bright enough but didn't care to work and refused to speak German.

Returning to Paris, Gussie spoke sadly of having "about decided to stay" there for the winter. "Our rooms are west and will have no sun," she said. "But there is little sun in Paris in winter anyway. I get frightfully homesick for my New York friends but my husband likes Paris more and more."

Now that the Brimmer bust was done, the Mears girls had gone back to Oshkosh and it was Mary who described how it felt. "Poor old Oshkosh is so white and still. . . . It might be a cemetery and its houses tomb stones. It might be anything but the home of Nellie and me — which it can never be again. We love the poplars always reaching but never touching the sky and we love the maple trees in our yard. They are like hands spread lovingly which try to hem us in as they did in our childhood. But they cannot hold us now. We shall say goodbye to them some day and perhaps we shall find happiness. Or perhaps our hearts will break."

And on the next to the last day of December, 1898, Saint-Gaudens wrote to Mary and Helen Mears. "It has been snowing all day and I have appropriately been putting a new cloak on General Sherman. . . . I'm as pleased with the new cloak as I am with the Victory — so pleased that I fear it can't be good."

Early in November, Gussie had reported that Gus was doing the Sherman cloak all over again and she was "making lots of little cloaks" for him to put on small experimental models, arranging the folds differently on each. When he finally found the right effect, no one would ever dream that such simple lines could have cost him so much time and trouble to achieve.

The *Victory,* that symbolic figure leading Sherman, had been modeled and remodeled. She now looked like the golden angel in the procession at Boulogne except that she had the free forward-swinging step of a young American. Her features were soft and sweet, like the face of the *Angel with the Tablet* — about to be renamed.

Saint-Gaudens seems now to have been working on a new version of his earlier bas-relief and wrote to his niece Rose Nichols about an inscription to go on the tablet which the angel held upraised.[4] "The figure means so much that a wide range is possible," he said. He proposed "To know is to forgive." He also thought of "Peace on Earth" and "God is Love" — but finally chose *Amor Caritas.* When the Luxembourg Museum asked for a copy of this beautiful bronze bas-relief, he sent them the angel with these words on the tablet.

Gus took Gussie to the Café de la Paix on New Year's Eve. She did not like it. And then it was 1899. On the 7th of January, Gus was in Edinburgh for a consultation with a committee about a Robert Louis Stevenson Memorial for Saint Giles's Cathedral. He had stopped over in London to see Sargent who had gotten up a luncheon for him, studded with celebrities. Sargent was experimenting with low relief as a part of mural decoration and Saint-Gaudens had been helping him to get a bronze crucifix cast and colored in Paris. This interested him, as did

Davida posed for the AMOR CARITAS, a plaque shown in Paris and requested as an acquisition for the Luxembourg Museum. It was developed from designs made for the Morgan tomb in Hartford, Connecticut, and reproduced with variations later. This photograph shows the gilded bronze plaque made especially for the Metropolitan Museum of Art (The Metropolitan Museum of Art, Rogers Fund, 1918)

the new work Sargent was designing for the Boston Public Library —
a mass of symbolic figures with colors in close harmony. But for Saint-
Gaudens the social luncheon was an ordeal and London seemed a
depressing city where poverty and hopelessness prevailed. In New
York, Gus had known poverty, but, as he remembered it, there was
always hope of some kind for hard-working people like his parents and
their friends. Gus took the train for Scotland without regret.

"Here I am at the house of a Scotch solicitor, Mr. Bell. Tomorrow I
go to St. Giles at ten to meet the vestrymen, then at eleven thirty or
thereabouts I take the train, thank God," Gus wrote. It was agreed that
the *Stevenson Memorial* should be based on the original Stevenson
portrait bas-relief. Saint-Gaudens was to redesign it in rectangular
form to fit the space he saw in Saint Giles's Cathedral; the purely
personal lines by Stevenson to Will Low he would change, using a
prayer by Stevenson, and he would substitute a quill pen for the
cigarette in Stevenson's hand. "They have only 5000 dollars" to pay
for this plaque, Augusta said, feeling that it was not worthwhile. But
Saint-Gaudens had loved Stevenson and would have given his services
if he could. "The people have been exceedingly kind," he told Gussie,
"and I find that all the nobility of England are connected with the
Memorial, beginning with Lord Roseberry who is the originator of the
scheme and the chairman."

But in Edinburgh, low-lying clouds obscured the castle on its great
rock. There were no flowers blooming along Princes Street and no
bagpipes playing in the castle courtyard. Saint-Gaudens saw ragged
children begging along "The High" — the principal street in the old
part of the town. "The weather has been dismal beyond expression and
I have been so depressed that I have felt only once before such a
complete absence of ambition, a carelessness about all I have cared so
much about and a desire to be ended with life. This feeling is uncon-
trollably strong," he told Gussie, "and I sympathize with you when you
have had that terrible depression that makes you want to cry. . . .
There is too much misery and unfairness in the world and all this
struggle for beauty seems in vain and hopeless."

This was about as sad a conclusion as an artist could come to. It was
also a confession to Augusta that her husband had not always understood her and it was a plea for understanding on her part now. For too
long a time, Homer had come first in her mind, but now she explained
to the boy that she was going to look after his father. "When you and I

have been sick we have had nothing to do but to take a rest and change while he has his work and the stopping of supplies to think of . . . ," she told Homer. She and Gus were going to take a trip to Aspet and then on to Spain, just the two of them — but not until after the Paris exhibition.

21

THE SALON

IT was to see the annual art show known as the Paris Salon that Saint-Gaudens made his first trip abroad. Full of boyish ambition, he must have imagined a work of his own someday standing in a place of honor in the hall of sculpture. When his *Farragut,* placed low and hidden under a balcony, won only an "honorable," he was heart-broken.

In 1898, Saint-Gaudens was acclaimed in the United States as the leading sculptor of his time and was overwhelmed with offers of work he could not possibly accept. But he still wanted to win recognition at the Paris Salon and it was MacMonnies who won prizes. This year, the Salon was held in "Machinery Hall," a dreary building of glass and iron near the Champs Elysées.[1] Roland Strong, art critic for the New York *Times,* said that it would please Americans to know that the most striking exhibit in sculpture was a colossal bronze group by Mac-Monnies, "a triumphant figure standing on a chariot and driving a team of most spirited steeds." Again, Saint-Gaudens was disappointed.

There were four horses in the MacMonnies sculpture, only two of them attached to a chariot. The other two were being led along by winged females who seemed to have brought spares in case the other horses went lame. The group actually looked well when placed high in the air on top of the Soldiers and Sailors Memorial Arch in Grand Army Plaza, Brooklyn. However, after the *Times* critic looked at them again at the Salon, several weeks later, he decided that the general effect was one of enormous weight and that he would hardly like to say that MacMonnies had produced a work of genius. The huge sculpture "seemed to crush everything anywhere near it." Saint-Gaudens would not have been human if he had not envied the success of his former pupil. At the same time, he could not possibly admire Mac's work.

A year later, in 1899, the rage was for statues made from different-colored marble. *Nature Unveiling Herself* was the popular favorite; a large female raising a yellow marble veil, wearing robes of violet and pink, caught at the waist with a cord of blue marble! Her arms were flesh-colored, her eyes described as "delicate blue" and her hair auburn. This time, the Paris correspondent informed New York *Times* readers that *Nature Unveiling Herself* was "truthfully artistic."

"I have been much torn in my mind about exhibiting the *Sherman* at all," Saint-Gaudens said and if he visited contemporary studios where polychrome marble figures were being produced, it is easy to see what he meant. Even if MacMonnies had no "team of horses" this year, what chance had a one-horse statue? He had not planned to show the *Sherman* with the figure of Victory, anyway.

But somehow, Saint-Gaudens could not quite give up. Baumgartner, his master caster, said he couldn't get the *Sherman* into plaster in time, but Gus found other casters at the last moment. He had eleven men in the studio, some of them working all night, and he described himself as their "boss lunatic," laughing, shouting, tearing his hair — rushing out into the street for air. Then the big plaster cast was done. The specialist in packing and transportation arrived and (according to his bill) carried the *Sherman* to the door of the Salon, then took the rider down from the horse, trundling the two pieces separately as far as the entrance to the main gallery on a handcart. There the gallery workmen took charge, waited for the decision of the judges, then set up the *Sherman* in the place of honor.

Gus said he had a swelled head for the first time in his life. The equestrian "really looked bully and was smashingly fine."

The New York *Times* critic agreed. The "so-called place of honor" had gone to Saint-Gaudens this time, and the "colossal statue" had "the same sweeping impetuosity which characterizes the *Shaw Memorial* in Boston."

"At last I am free. I have just left the Salon and have come back to the studio where I am alone," Gus wrote. "I have sent the men off for a holiday which they well deserve after the rush of the last fortnight. . . . On all sides I am grasped by the hand and as for the Americans I meet, they want to hug me. I see it in women's eyes and some of them I visit would put the thought into action and the tones of the men's voices show it too."

Gus said he felt like dancing a jig but that there was always the "triste undertone" in his heart that came from his Irish mother. The sad undertone became an overtone very shortly in a reaction from his peak of elation. With Dr. Shiff as her ally, Augusta succeeded in getting her husband to take a vacation. On the 25th of May, 1899, "I believe we are really to start for the Pyrenees tomorrow," she wrote to Homer. "I hope your father will get rested rapidly when once we get away from the turmoil of Paris and the studio. We are heading for a place where they play golf but who knows — we may get into Spain."

This idea of golf, or as Gus spelled it, "golph," was another scheme of Dr. Shiff's. Scottish though the game was, Gus saw nothing of it in Scotland but began to play it on this vacation. He bought a set of "golph sticks" which he said were very large and much admired in Paris, where he later found a place to use them, in one of the parks.

True to his promise to relatives, Gus brought his wife to Aspet in the French Pyrenees. Augusta brought her sketchpad and pencils, doing a very creditable street scene in the old town. But golf was not sufficiently exciting for Gus who always flung himself into recreation as intensely as he concentrated on work. He attempted to climb an almost perpendicular peak, nine thousand feet high, but at eight thousand feet he got dizzy and had to come down — angry with himself for this defeat. To restore his pride he organized a trip to Spain over a brigand's pass. Gussie said she felt like making her last will and testament the night before they left — but she went along just the same.

It was Augusta who wrote the account of adventures, from San Sebastián, Spain, on June 11.[2] "We were the first to cross the pass [so early in the year] except mountaineers on foot. The donkey with her pack rolled off a piece of road that gave way. We crawled along dizzy precipices in the snow and altogether had a rough time of it. On the Spanish side, we encountered smugglers and had an armed escort from the frontier cabins to the first village. We ate at a place like a pigsty and slept in what was once a mansion of a Marquis which was all tumbling to pieces. The Marquis himself was getting in hay and the Marquise, in a patched petticoat, cooked wild boar."

Sargent, already in love with Spain, wrote to Gus to be sure not to miss Burgos, so this was the first stop. Gus also promptly fell in love with Spain when he walked into the sculptured magnificence of Burgos Cathedral. On leaving the city, they were robbed of one of their pieces of luggage, but Gus "appealed to a fine-looking man who turned out to be the Station Master" and just before their train left, their missing "shawl strap" with some of Gus's clothes and a pair of shoes wrapped up in a steamer rug "reappeared" — with no questions asked.

In Toledo, Gus and Gussie felt that they had discovered "the real Spain," as they wandered around the town, untouched since the Middle Ages. Like dutiful tourists, they left Madrid for a trip to the Escorial, the palace and burial place of Spanish kings, but Saint-Gaudens found it so cold and silent that he became depressed. Gussie was upset to discover that there was no diligence to take them away from there before nightfall.

Returning to Paris, Augusta set out for the United States, feeling that Gus was well, but worried about her other responsibilities. Homer was "allowed into Harvard" with conditions and she wasn't sure that he had worthy companions at his boardinghouse in Cambridge. Gus told her that if Homer wanted to work, it didn't matter what his housemates did. In September, Homer forgot to register at Harvard on time and by November, he had flunked French, to his surprise, Gussie said — and math, which hadn't surprised him. His mother hurried out to Cambridge to see about a tutor. Dean Briggs agreed to tutoring for Homer but suggested that it would be better if Homer applied himself to his work.

Augusta's mother was ill. "I often think of her kind heart as one remembers a sunshiny day," Saint-Gaudens wrote, but no affectionate messages could reach her. She hardly recognized Augusta. Mrs. Thomas J. Homer had sold the big house and had been living first with Lizzie and then visiting Gussie. This was her last illness, which ended in her death in August, 1899.

Gus had written to his wife in a cheerful vein in July. He was homesick for Cornish, he said, and he complained humorously because Gussie wrote him no news of what interested him "more than anything else on earth, wife, child, God, the angel Gabriel, everything, i.e. the POOL back of the studio and the water works pertaining to it." He wanted a letter about nothing else but the *pool* if he were to continue to bear with life.

Funds were beginning to accumulate, Gus said. He had sold a large replica of his Madison Square *Diana* for $1200. In ten days he would send a bill to the Brimmer people and ask them to put $1000 in Gussie's account in their New York bank. Then she could "pay the dam taxes" in Cornish, but he wondered what they had done to the place to make the tax bill go up so much. "What does Platt pay?" Gus wanted to know — thinking of the architect's house on the hill. But high taxes or no, Gussie was to get Homer a saddle horse if he wanted one.

In Paris, it was "hotter than 40 hells" during July. Henry Adams came to the studio and took Gus to walk in the Bois de Boulogne and afterwards to dinner at what Gus described as his "splendid apartment right near the Bois, itself." Gus might have regarded with mixed feelings what Adams was writing about him in his diary, after their various meetings together.

The Salon had closed in June, but while the exhibition was going on, Adams "stopped almost every day before the St. Gaudens's *Sherman,* which had been given the central post of honor. St. Gaudens himself was in Paris, putting on the work his usual interminable last touches and listening to the usual contradictory suggestions of brother sculptors. Of all the American artists who gave American art whatever life it breathed . . . St. Gaudens was perhaps the most sympathetic, but certainly the most inarticulate. . . . All the others, — the Hunts, Richardson, John La Farge, Stanford White, were exuberant; only St. Gaudens could never discuss or dilate on an emotion or suggest artistic arguments for giving to his work the forms that he felt. He never laid down the law or affected the despot. . . . He required no incense; he was no egotist; his simplicity of thought was excessive; he could not imitate, or give any form but his own to the creations of his hand. No one felt more strongly than he the strength of other men, but the idea that they could affect him, never stirred an image in his mind."

Adams said that Saint-Gaudens' spirits were low and, since he was just as depressed himself, it was a risk to go to see him. However, Saint-Gaudens "sometimes let Adams go about in his company," and they went together to Amiens to look at the cathedral "with a party of Frenchmen."[3]

"Not until they found themselves actually standing before the west portal, did it dawn on Adams' mind that, for his purposes, St. Gaudens on that spot had more interest for him than the cathedral itself."

It surprised Adams to find that Saint-Gaudens liked "the stately monument much more than he liked Gibbon or Ruskin." Adams seems to have been pouring quotations from both these authors into Gus's ears while Gus tried to concentrate on the effect of light and shade achieved so simply and effectively in the fourteenth-century stone figures he had come to see.

Adams said that Saint-Gaudens "loved their dignity; their scale;

their lines." So it seems that Gus could not have been completely "inarticulate," since he managed to explain this much. But Adams had a theme he was riding hard these days: that the Virgin was "a channel of force," creating the art that they saw before them. Saint-Gaudens could be forgiven if he had no idea what Adams was talking about.

"Yet in mind and person, St. Gaudens was a survival of 1500; he bore the stamp of the Renaissance and should have carried an image of the Virgin round his neck, or stuck in his hat like Louis XI . . . ," Adams insisted. "St. Gaudens was a child of Benvenuto Cellini smothered in an American cradle." And finally exasperated because he could not make Gus echo his own ideas, Adams decided that "For a symbol of power, St. Gaudens instinctively preferred the horse." To Adams, the Virgin "became more than ever a channel of force; to St. Gaudens she remained as before, a channel of taste."

Saint-Gaudens and Henry Adams were not often together, which perhaps was fortunate for both of them. In September, Gus went back to Boulogne where he saw again the religious procession, and it was just as beautiful as before, he said. He went swimming and passed days on the cliff in the wind and sun. He was offered a chance to do figures for the Capitol of Maryland for $24,000 but refused with regret. It made him still more unhappy to refuse to do a Lafayette, to be presented to France,[4] but when he went back to Paris he went to work instead on the long-delayed figures for the Boston Public Library.

There was a medium called "plastoline" in which he roughed out the Boston figures. It was as easy to handle as clay and was said to be much less liable to injury from drying, freezing or cracking. About ten days after getting started, Gus wrote to McKim that he was "getting excited about the second group" and felt he had "some good ideas. . . . I am banging away, full of good health and good spirits," he said, ". . . blues and hell generally vanished like morning mists."

Louis Saint-Gaudens had been in Paris, back in New York and then in Paris again, his whereabouts often unknown. Gussie had now gone back to the United States and Gus told her what had recently happened to Louis. There was a girl named Annetta Johnson, from Ohio, who had come to Paris to study sculpture. She had previously sent Saint-Gaudens a photograph of some of her work in terra-cotta. He had been kind but not overenthusiastic about her talent. In Paris, she came to his studio often, however, perhaps hoping to be taken on as an assistant. This Saint-Gaudens could never do because she just wasn't good enough, but she studied hard and her work improved. Later, he compared her favorably with other young American students.

To Saint-Gaudens' astonishment, both Baumgartner, his master molder of casts, and his brother Louis fell in love with Nettie, as she called herself. Or, as Gus put it, "It was Miss Johnson who captured Louis, fell in love with him and would have him, regardless of everything." Louis had "contended with Baumgartner" for her affections for over a year. Annetta chose Louis, "although he told her frankly that he was a drunkard, that his wife told him to go away and take another woman."

Louis's marriage, apparently his second and presumably to a French woman, was news to Nettie. But "she decided then, to go off with Louis and live with him as man and wife. That's all right," Gus said. "Perhaps it is his saving for she is a good girl of sound, healthy stock." Nettie and Louis had gone to Nettie's home and Gus was pleased about this because "evidently he can get no alcohol in Ohio." He wrote to Nettie to thank her and tell her that Louis was really a fine man and that she was giving him a chance to begin a new life.

After Louis left Paris, Saint-Gaudens mentioned something in letters to him that he and Nettie knew about. Davida was in Paris. Saint-Gaudens did not say when she arrived and it is useless to speculate as to whether he tried to break off relations with her when he left New York or whether she went with him in the first place. His remodeling of the *Victory* suggests that he might have sent for her when his work went badly, without her. In any case, he told Louis that their boy Novy was growing big and strong but that Davida had decided that she didn't like France and wanted to go home. "Gussie don't like it and comes over on the *St. Louis,* November first and so the funny world goes round," Gus wrote.

Augusta stopped over in London, which she liked much better than Paris. She found what she said was an uncomfortable room at the Hotel des Saints Pères in Paris and began visiting bronze founders who were casting Saint-Gaudens reproductions. These must be shipped either to Tiffany's or to Doll and Richards in Boston in time for the Christmas trade, and time was running out. Gussie plunged into business with all the enthusiasm of a true Homer merchant.

Gus hated London, loved Paris, and made a few more attempts to show Gussie how to have a good time. He took her to an amusement park and she reported on her reactions. "Last night we loafed around that place in Clichy till I was nearly frozen. It's quite impossible to imagine what fun there can be in riding around on wooden rabbits!"

Then there was the little circus on Montmartre where Gus liked to go and laugh at the same jokes and silly farces he had laughed at twenty years before. It was an old-fashioned one-ring show. People sat close to the ring and Gus admired at close range "the beauty in tights and spangles on the white horse." He said he remembered how, as a boy, he used to wonder "if I loved such a goddess would she ever love me." But Gussie on her part had never been in the least enamoured of a mustachioed ringmaster and would have none of this childish nonsense.

Business was not going well, but Gussie wrote cheerfully about it. "I have been attending to getting off some bronzes but the South African war has interfered terribly with that. Now why the Boers and *Diana of the Tower* should have differences is hard to understand, but *Diana* wants to go to Boston and three different steamers on which she was invoiced to sail have been immediately taken by the English to carry their troops to Africa. The *Cephalonia, Canada* and *Victoria* have all been confiscated and now the poor belated *Dianas* have to go by the *Bostonian* and the Saint-Gaudens family won't have any money for Christmas presents which is a great *Boer.*"

Of course Augusta kept books on bronze-replica transactions, but many of her records were destroyed by fire. From accounts that survived, however, it is possible to take a look at Gussie's bronze business. A *Diana of the Tower* which she listed as "large" brought in $160 after she had deducted the twenty percent commission charged by Tiffany or Doll and Richards. This *Diana* cost $60 at the foundry, $10 for freight, and Gussie put down $90 in her profit column. She received $140 for a "small *Diana,*" costing only $36 to produce, the freight also being $10 and the net profit $94.

All replicas were carefully copyrighted and Augusta watched like a hawk for possible infringement. She kept a Tiffany price list and prices varied from time to time, but the surviving record seems to cover 1901 and 1902. *Diana* came in at least three sizes, one of them only seven and a half inches high, one "on half-sphere or ball with marble base," one listed as "life-sized." The least expensive cost $60 at Tiffany or Doll and Richards while a *Diana* forty-one and a half inches high was priced at $500.

Replicas of the much loved Stevenson bas-relief were the most profitable. A circular *Stevenson,* three feet in diameter with the owner's name cast in bronze, the medallion framed in carved wood, was priced at $1500. Augusta received, after commission, $68 for a small circular *Stevenson* which cost only seven dollars to reproduce and five dollars for freight.

Among higher-priced items, a bronze replica three feet high of the "Standing *Lincoln,*" including chair, cost the customer $2000. By the time the Sherman equestrian reached its pinnacle of fame, a Victory from the group, three feet high, mounted on a marble base, was priced at $3000.

When Gussie first got back to Paris, she found Gus still working on the *Victory,* which she supposed had been finished long since. But the new *Victory* was "very stunning," Gussie had to admit. She was glad to see that Gus was working on the library groups which were coming along well. Then, as time went by, Gussie's nervous energy seemed to increase while her husband's drained away. She made three trips to bronze founders in four days while Gus was just "poking along on the *Victory*" and only occasionally "making a dig at the Boston library figures. . . ."

There was no good news at all until the 1st of December. Then Saint-Gaudens was notified that he had been made a member of the Institut de France — the overall organization which included the five French Academies. It had been "a beautiful election — by a vote of 120 to 89," one of the members told Gus. The Institut ranked higher than the Legion of Honor, but "there is no red ribbon attached to it, so all the world won't know. . . . Only two other Americans have ever had it; Motley the historian, and William M. Hunt, the great painter." It was Gussie who explained all this to Homer. "Your father is very well again, so he says," she went on, "only his nervousness is abnormal and a minute of daylight lost is an affliction."

Plans for an International Exposition, to take place in Paris, were under way early in January, 1900. While Saint-Gaudens rejoiced in being a member of the Institut de France, he discovered once more, as back in New York, that duties and obligations go with fame. John B. Cauldwell, United States Commissioner General of the International Exposition, wrote, assuming that Saint-Gaudens would put on a big show of his work, with a cast of the *Shaw Memorial* among many other items — Saint-Gaudens to pay all costs of course. Cauldwell wanted to know how much the Shaw cast would weigh and just what were its exact dimensions. He took it for granted that the *Sherman,* not just the equestrian but complete with the *Victory,* would be shown.

It was generally assumed that Saint-Gaudens had plenty of money these days. No one had any idea of the cost of producing a colossal equestrian statue, while stories of high commissions paid to Saint-Gaudens were current gossip. As a matter of fact, he had received $4000 by the end of 1899 from the Boston Public Library Committee and that money was long gone. There was $6000 due on the *Sherman* but not until it should be unveiled in New York. Saint-Gaudens had been proud and happy to have the Luxembourg Museum ask for ten of his medallions and to receive a similar request from Berlin. Gus would have donated them except, according to the rules, the museums must pay. Payment was nominal and Gus could not keep from reworking a detail or two.

There was also the "wear and tear," as Gus put it, of having casters in the studio. He had made so many changes in the *Sherman* that the 1899 cast was out of date by 1900. "Your letter," he wrote to Mr. Cauldwell, "brings me to the point where I must say definitely what I will do about exhibiting at the coming World's Fair. The whole subject has troubled me very much and has hindered my work to an unusual degree. . . . I beg of you, not to try to persuade me to exhibit, for it will only tend to renew my indecision. . . ." Then, feeling guilty about letting Cauldwell down, Gus offered his services on any committee where the Commissioner General might need help.

John B. Cauldwell promptly disregarded Saint-Gaudens' plea to be let alone. The American exhibit simply could not get along without him. As to help — certainly Cauldwell needed plenty. He put Gus on the jury to choose those works by American sculptors to be accepted and shown at the Paris Exposition.

Gus wrote to Helen Mears, telling of "forward and incompetent young women" who immediately began to pester him. He said that their lack of talent seemed to be "in inverse ratio to their activity." He was glad that Nellie Mears was not sending anything and he told her that it was better for her to devote all her energy to making one beautiful work rather than to be like a certain "Miss Yandell" who was making "an awful fountain for Providence." Nellie must not get herself "put down as an incompetent in bronze in the public streets."

There was to be a statue of Emma Willard in Washington, D.C., with both Enid Yandell[5] and Helen Mears competing for the commission along with many others. Helen asked for advice. Gus told her to work out her small model very carefully, leaving only a few changes to be made when it was enlarged. This was his own system. And as to costume, "I don't think I would put a shawl on Miss Willard unless she actually wore one," he said.

Miss Yandell asked for no advice, but she required services. Not only did she want to exhibit a great deal of her work in Paris but she wanted Saint-Gaudens to write a letter of recommendation for her to the Willard Committee. She said she already had one from Daniel Chester French. "I told her I could not, that I had written one for you," Saint-Gaudens wrote Nellie Mears, "and I gave her to understand that even if I had not, there were three or four others I should prefer to recommend." Nettie Johnson, now in America with Louis, was one of these and Elsie Ward — later to be a Saint-Gaudens assistant — was another.

Enid Yandell was not in the least discouraged. She went right on making the kind of statues Saint-Gaudens deplored; she started a summer art school in Edgartown — and her *Emma Willard Memorial* went to Albany, New York. But it was Helen Mears who won the Washington, D.C., commission.

The woman sculptor whose work Saint-Gaudens most admired was Mary Lawrence. Her first recognition had come at the Chicago Exposition with her *Columbus*. Saint-Gaudens was disappointed when she had nothing to show in Paris, but she had married and given up her career. "Mary Lawrence is going to marry Tonetti, the half Italian, half French Faun who was Mac's assistant for a great many years," was the way Gus told the story. "He is a regular picnic feller and as she is a regular picnic girl there'll be lots of festive children, I suppose."

As a matter of fact, they had five children and Mary said she gave up sculpture without regret. They bought a church on Fortieth Street in New York, converted it into studio and living quarters with space to rent as well. Some people were shocked at the use to which they put the former church — for the parties they gave were the most fun of anything going on in town.[6] Tonetti did some of the huge figures to go on top of the New York Customs House.

The Paris Exposition would open on April 15, 1900, and Augusta wrote that the city was getting ready for it with a vengeance. In March, the new bridge over the Seine was almost ready for traffic, with high pedestals at each end, on top of which were "gilded Pegasuses" rearing and prancing among human males and females, "legs and wings and arms flying in every direction." New buildings along the river were "an architect's nightmare, leaving nothing new under the sun to be thought of."

The long dreary Paris winter ended suddenly in early March. Gus wrote that "male dogs in hordes pursue female dogs all over Paris and general joy is the rule." The streets were all torn up just the way they always were in New York, but "Paris in spring is not to be compared with spring anywhere else." Dr. Shiff, "in this his 68th year, has fallen violently in love with a blond-headed concert singer." Gus said he supposed that "old age rid one of that," but he was "evidently very much mistaken."

Gus himself said he had been acting like the red-headed monkey that he was, jumping from branch to branch apropos of nothing, hanging on by his tail and throwing coconuts at the other apes in his efforts to get ready for the Exposition.[7] Having yielded to Cauldwell's entreaties, he had installed his own exhibit, the *Sherman, Shaw, Puritan, Angel* and fourteen medallions. This had cost him two thousand dollars.

Augusta returned to the United States and Gus took a quick trip to Spain toward the end of May. "Bull fights, dancing gypsy girls, sunshine, orange groves and so on for eleven days," was the way he described it to McKim. He had returned to Paris to work on the Boston Library groups. "That work is now en train," he said, "and nothing in the way now until its completion."

At the Paris Exposition of 1900, the Grand Prize was awarded to Augustus Saint-Gaudens. In September, André Saglio, French member of the Ministry of Fine Arts and Art Commissioner for Expositions at Home and Abroad,[8] wrote to Gus. "Three weeks from now at the latest, one of your friends (me perhaps) will telegraph you of your nomination as Officer of the Legion of Honor. The thing has been done, I may say, and the official publication is only delayed by the procrastination of foreign chancelleries. . . ." But by September, 1900, Saint-Gaudens was no longer in Paris to wear the red ribbon in the city where everyone who saw it would know what it meant.

22

CORNISH ATELIER

SAINT-GAUDENS had learned to come to terms with nervous exhaustion. Pain was another matter. Sciatica or dyspepsia yielded to the strong sedatives his doctors prescribed so freely, but early in July, 1900, he saw three leading Paris physicians, all of whom said that he had an intestinal tumor. It surprised them, perhaps, that Saint-Gaudens, who sometimes seemed so French, should take immediate passage for New York.

Augusta met her husband in New York on the 23rd of July and sent for Dr. Polk, "who will not arrive until tomorrow," she wrote.[1] She supposed that Gus would "continue in this state of mind, thinking he has something dreadful the matter with him," until Dr. Polk got there. Two days later, she was staying with her sister Lizzie Nichols on Mt. Vernon Street, Boston, and her husband was in the Massachusetts General Hospital.

By August 4th the operation was over and pronounced successful, but Augusta was now terrified lest someone should tell her husband that the tumor had been malignant. She talked to the surgeon who was not optimistic. Discovery had come late and he could not say how long it would be — perhaps five to seven years — before another operation might be necessary. "We must take the greatest pains not to worry or excite him in any way," Augusta told Louis. Homer was sent for but warned to say nothing about certain disastrous marks at Harvard.

Saint-Gaudens was in pain, but he complained only of weariness, Augusta said. He finally left the hospital and was in Cornish by the middle of October. The tone of Saint-Gaudens' letters suggests that he knew the nature of his illness but was determinedly cheerful, packing all the pleasure he could into days of hard work. A minor operation must be attended to in November, he said; then "I shall return here for the winter. Think of that!" Babb, the architect, and Finn, architect and painter of portraits, were visiting and they painted the studio walls white as usual, so that "it seems like old times," Gus told his brother. He began to hope that Louis and Annetta and their small son Paul might like to live in Cornish.

On December 15, the second operation was over. Augusta said privately that it was not a success, but Gus again wrote cheerfully. He was back at "Aspet," enjoying fourteen-below-zero weather and sleigh rides every day. An invitation to do a statue of Parnell for Dublin, Ireland, had reached him while he was still in Paris and now he resolved to go to work on it at once. It would be a satisfaction to him to have a statue of his in the city of his birth. Moreover, this was a forty-thousand-dollar contract with a payment of fifteen hundred dollars on signing and five thousand at the end of a year's work.

Gus was not homesick for the Café de la Paix at New Year's, 1901. At "Aspet," he slept with his window wide open when the temperature was twenty below and declared that it wasn't half as cold as "slushy Paris or torn-up New York." An official letter arrived from Paris and Gus told his brother about it in an exuberant and, at the same time, sardonic mood.

"An Officier de la Legion d'honneur, by God! All I'm living for now is to get back to Paris to paralyze the S.O.B.s of waiters in some of the swell restaurants and invite Frederick William MacMonnies, simple Chevalier, to come and dine with me on the occasion. I'm wicked enough to wish to make him feel uncomfortable. It's impossible to make him feel small. . . ."[2]

By March, Gus had what he called "a big gang up here" — a corps of assistants such as filled the ateliers of artists during the Italian Renaissance. He named them off: Hering, Miss Ward, Fraser, Wells (an Englishman), Antonio — a boy whom native Cornishmen called "Eyetalian" but who was from Paris — another studio boy named Harold, and Charley Bryant, described as the man about the house. As a rule, assistants lived outside the house in boarding places nearby where they added materially to the income of neighboring farmers.

Long before winter sports were so much as heard of in the area, Saint-Gaudens introduced them. He and his assistants built a huge toboggan slide, taking off from the roof of the studio. Gus said that he "skated like a ten year old, tobogganed and sleighed from sunrise to sunset." Village young people and children from Windsor were invited over to join the sport and remembered all their lives how the sculptor welcomed them and saw to it that they had fun.[3]

Gus was unprepared for mud time in snow country, however. As soon as the snow began to melt, the hill road became a river of mud. Farmers changed over from runners to wheels, but wheels bogged down almost hub-deep. One day the Plainfield stage got stuck on the river road for two and a half hours. The mud was "hellish after a glorious winter," Gus said as he departed for New York and Washington, D.C. Augusta had long since left for some southern health resort.

In New York, Gus visited McKim, arriving at exactly the moment when plans were being set in motion to rebuild and beautify the city of Washington. The original idea had been to improve Washington in time to celebrate the one hundredth anniversary of the establishment of Congress there, instead of in Philadelphia. That was in 1800 and the centenary passed while planners quarreled. Now a Senate Park Commission had been created to "recover as much as possible of the sadly mutilated L'Enfant plan." Daniel H. Burnham was the architect in charge, La Farge and McKim were deep in the project, and McKim never missed a chance to involve Saint-Gaudens in any scheme where Gus might gain glory and cash. Congress had voted funds an architect could gloat over.

Daniel H. Burnham was already a good friend. Gus had known him in Chicago, where Burnham had been chief architect of the Columbian Exposition, his fame already made with a Chicago office building, said to be the first ever called a "skyscraper." Burnham now had drawings in his office for the Flatiron Building in New York, to be built in 1902 and to be acclaimed as the world's tallest building. McKim sat down to write to Burnham in behalf of Saint-Gaudens.[4]

"We have reminisced as much as you might expect from two old fellows of questionable health, past fifty, and have gone over the last twenty-five years since I met him [Saint-Gaudens] an obscure would-be sculptor with his first commission." After the sort of preamble that led Gus to call McKim "Blarney Charles," the architect came to the point. "I would suggest that Saint-Gaudens be made a full member of the Commission." This was promptly attended to and Gus made trips to Washington as a consultant in sculpture, his time and expenses paid. Of course the planners wanted a Saint-Gaudens statue for Washington, but Gus had neither time nor strength, so he recommended sculptors whose work he admired. Daniel Chester French's

Lincoln was decidedly Saint-Gaudens-inspired. Louis Saint-Gaudens eventually produced some handsome figures for the Union Station — a building which was part of the scheme for improving the city. For some reason, President Charles W. Eliot of Harvard was asked to choose the subjects for Louis — "Fire," "Electricity," "Constructive Imagination" and so on! Whether at the suggestion of the President of Harvard or not, Louis made three nine-foot models of Roman soldiers, representing the states of the Union, to go inside the railroad station. Louis was a good sculptor and his figures were judged to have power and dignity.

Gus turned down a government offer to do a bust of Theodore Roosevelt for $5000, but John Hay willingly paid $10,000 for a bust and agreed to come to Cornish for sittings. Distinguished sitters were often guests at "Aspet," writing lyric bread-and-butter letters when they returned home. Hay spoke of the "beautiful exotic house which combines the attractiveness of the Mediterranean shores with the New England hills." Saglio, the French art commissioner (as a friend but not a sitter), recalled "the green and velvet lawns where runs the robin" and spoke with enthusiasm of the "robust grace of the Irish servant-girl."[5]

Stories of the delights of Cornish spread among the distinguished and wealthy people who visited Saint-Gaudens. This was at least one reason why people of wealth began to buy up land and build big country houses. They followed the artists in the hope of enjoying the simplicity that artists found there and sharing the fun that artists created.

Prices rose with the influx of wealthy summer residents who never counted pennies. Not that Augusta ever gave up the fight — she audited all Cornish bills. For example, there was the matter of tolls across the covered bridge to Windsor. An annual bill of six dollars was sent, from which Gussie deducted three dollars on the ground that no one from "Aspet" used the bridge during certain winter months. After considerable correspondence, the toll collector agreed, "as you say you will not pay," but he was still "hoping you will look at the matter in a different light."

The artists retaliated against the invasion of their paradise by calling those who were not artists, musicians or writers, "Philistines." It became philistine to keep a horse. Everyone rode bicycles, pushing them up the steep hills, slithering and bouncing downhill, not breaking their necks because God looks after fools and children, the natives must have said. Mrs. Dewing demonstrated how to ride a bicycle while wearing an evening dress with a train. She "looped the skirt over the handle bar." On leaving a dinner party, just as she started downhill, she was thrown over the handlebars but wasn't hurt. She got up, brushed her gown and "proceeded without loss of dignity," as she had done after falling seven times on her way over to the party in the first place.

Various people, non-philistines, of course, described Cornish. The beautiful Maud Howe, now Mrs. John Elliott and a successful writer, lived there in 1903. Maud told how her husband "painted endlessly in Cornish. The velvet pastures inspired him, the bubbling spring and above all Ascutney in the distance towering against the sky." He was especially fond of painting the silver birch, his favorite tree.

Being every inch a Bostonian, it amused but also slightly annoyed Mrs. Elliott to be called a "New Yorker" by native Cornishmen. But it was their name for all outsiders.

Unknowingly, the John Elliotts risked being called philistine because Jack drove a handsome bay mare called Gypsy, which he hitched to a gay little yellow cart. But they were forgiven because they both loved children, and children "played an important role in the life of the colony," being almost always included in all festivities. Maud remembered an evening picnic "on a high hilltop" where people assembled to watch the sunset and stayed till moonrise. "The children made garlands to wear and danced against the purple background of the mountain." Someone had brought a guitar, someone else a flute — everyone sang.[6]

Tableaux were the indoor sport for artists. A large picture frame was set up at the end of a room, then covered with gauze, tightly stretched. Lighting, not too bright, was carefully studied. Sometimes subjects were original, sometimes the idea was to reproduce famous paintings. The artists had collections of costumes, while those who posed were chosen for their resemblance to figures by the old masters. Charades, gotten up on the spur of the moment, were equally popular. The unrehearsed dialogue was full of humorous allusions to members of the audience, with Fred (Maxfield) Parrish and Charles Platt considered the wittiest.

An admiring member of the audience was Frances Grimes. She was born in Braceville, Ohio, studied at Pratt Institute in Brooklyn and her first job was with her teacher in sculpture, Herbert Adams, at his summer place in Cornish. Frances Grimes was thirty-two when she went to work for Saint-Gaudens in 1901. His assistants were always free to do work of their own in their spare time, which he was glad to criticize, and Miss Grimes was one of his most gifted assistants, accomplishing a good deal of original sculpture in later years.[7]

"Cornish was then a place where artists worked summers or prepared studies for work in winter," Miss Grimes observed.[8] "It was the rule that no one ever paid a visit in the morning or before four o'clock in the afternoon. This rule was broken when an artist was invited to see another's work for criticism or consultation; these were weighty visits, visits of state."

Augusta must have broken the rule when she drove her horse and buggy up the excessively steep road to Cox's studio to take her Aunt Hannah to see him. The drive came out right in front of the privy, Gussie reported — the Coxes evidently having no indoor plumbing. "Cox was pretty sour at first but got warmed up and finally said" that Saint-Gaudens "for a long time had done everything with great charm but that in recent years had done them with great force." Gussie was so pleased that she shook hands "ardently" with Cox and then almost backed her horse over a precipice.

Miss Grimes said, "Dinners given by the artists were supposed to reflect their student days in Paris and food had to have 'charm.'" Picnics were best of all and "rain did not keep us in." Frances remembered walking in the pine woods with rain coming down, water pouring off the brim of her hat while she marveled at "the mystery" of all she saw.

It was her first Cornish employer, the sculptor Herbert Adams, who said that women should be careful what they wore on picnics because "it made such a difference. They should wear white or bright colors." After this, Miss Grimes always wore white.

Frances Grimes was not beautiful — a Saint-Gaudens cartoon shows her overanxious, long-necked and goggle-eyed. But people who knew her thought of her as pretty and having the kind of beauty that comes from within. She was thoughtful of the sort of person usually overlooked and she remembered to thank those whose services others took for granted. She herself said that she always wore white because "the pictorial sense is so important."

Pictorially, Frances was not always successful. One evening at a Saint-Gaudens party she wore "a sort of fillet of small leaves bound around her head" and in the eyes of the young Nichols nieces this Greek fillet "looked exactly like a row of curl papers." At a party at "Mastlands" she wore a thin gold chain as a fillet and "acknowledged that she sometimes smoked a cigarette," but Marian Nichols "would not have suspected it." Frances would have liked to be called by the romantic name of Francesca but knew that the name the young men with whom she worked in the Saint-Gaudens studio always called her would have to do. "I suppose 'Grimesey' is best," she said.

Her admiration for others was untinged with envy and Cornish was a place of beautiful women, according to Miss Grimes. She wrote of her first impression of Eleanor Platt, Charles Platt's wife, "sitting very erect in a buckboard." Frances felt a thrill at seeing anyone "so proud and beautiful as she looked that day." Many famous painters had asked her to sit to them, but Miss Grimes said that in Cornish, "it was looked upon as getting an unfair advantage to have Mrs. Platt pose for you; the proportions of her shoulders, neck and head conveyed an impression of nobility which somehow got into your picture if you copied her."

George de Forest Brush had brought his family to Cornish, hiring an almost empty but handsome old house which he never bothered to furnish. They cooked and slept out of doors, taking cover only when it rained, with fireplaces to cook over and floors to sleep on. Outsiders found it strange, when they called, to find nothing in the big drawing room but an easel and a chair for the model. Even Miss Grimes thought that Mrs. Brush might not strike one as beautiful at first, but when one had seen her husband's paintings of her, "they clarified the mystery of her face into beauty."

Frances Grimes described Mrs. Saint-Gaudens as "unassimilated," explaining that with "her extreme deafness, her barbaric manners and temper, she was too difficult to get on with, so she was called on, and returned the calls, asked to dinner and had people for dinner, but all quite on the outside."

The house was "usually guarded by Mrs. Saint-Gaudens," and Miss Grimes thought that "the square pool at the back of Mr. Saint-Gaudens' studio and a feature of it, was so placed in order that no one could enter the back door unannounced."

The Saint-Gaudens nieces had described Frances Grimes, never suspecting that she had observed and would describe them in turn.[9] Rose, Marian and Margaret Nichols were "large, handsome young women well-dressed and impressive. They wore long, brilliantly colored scarves which floated from the carriage as they drove by."

During the summer of 1901, Louise and Sidney Homer came to Cornish. "We rented a farmhouse next to our cousins," Sidney Homer said. It was a "funny old place" with ceilings too low for singing, so they fixed up a corncrib, with open sides to be sure, but with a high roof. Louise practiced in the corncrib and "her tones used to float down the road and through the trees" to the Saint-Gaudens studio.[10] Their first child, "Baby Louise," loved Cornish, after her two or three summers spent at European resorts where her mother had engagements to sing and where the best she could hope for was a walk in the park.

Augusta's cousin Sidney was not the sort of musician to shudder at a less than perfect piano and refuse to touch it. He made Augusta's upright sound a great deal better than it was and encouraged Gus to get out his flute. Augusta's brother Joe was visiting at the Nichols' Cornish home and Louise soon discovered that Joe's wife, the former Constance Smith, had a well-trained and beautiful soprano voice. She came to "Aspet" on many a summer evening to delight Saint-Gaudens as she sang duets with Madam Louise Homer.

One day, Madam Homer heard singing, coming from one of the Saint-Gaudens studios. She went down the hill to investigate, following the sound of the voice — and found that it was Gus, singing as loud as he could, the way he always did when work went well. She told him that she thought Plançon, a famous basso profundo from the Paris opera, must be there and asked him where he had studied. Gus told her that he had never had a singing lesson in his life but that he had always wanted to study music. In Boston and New York Madam Homer gave choice opera tickets to the whole family and received them with open arms when they came backstage to see her.

But Saint-Gaudens actually had little time for music. Early in April, 1901, William A. Coffin, Director of the Fine Arts Division of the Pan-American Exposition to be held in Buffalo, New York, began a series of almost daily letters to Saint-Gaudens, hounding him about an exhibition of his work. Coffin had been in Paris where he had arranged to have the cast of the *Shaw Memorial* sent to Buffalo, along with several other examples of Saint-Gaudens' work. But the cast of the equestrian *Sherman* had been sent from Paris to Cornish and the *Sherman* was what Coffin wanted most of all.

The GENERAL SHERMAN *in plaster in Saint-Gaudens' studio, with James Earle Frazer (second from left), Saint-Gaudens (third from left), Henry Hering (fifth from left), Antonio the studio boy (seventh from left), and Elsie Ward (right) (Courtesy of the Board of Trustees of Dartmouth College)*

The *Sherman* had arrived from Paris in a battered condition. Since extensive repairs would be needed, it naturally occurred to Saint-Gaudens that here was a chance to make a few changes and improvements. He was not satisfied with the symbolic winged figure and of course he could not rest until he felt he had it right. The Sherman Monument Committee in New York would just have to wait and William A. Coffin might as well forget about the *Sherman.*

Saint-Gaudens had seen a new model he wanted for his *Victory.* She was a young girl named Alice Butler, living with her parents on the main street in the village of Windsor, Vermont. Although not mentioned in Miss Grimes's list of beautiful women, she was so handsome that even the neighbors who had always known her turned to look at her in the streets. She was tall, dark, had a classic nose and a short, curving upper lip such as Gus had never seen except on a Greek coin. Her chin was too heavy, but Saint-Gaudens could model that to suit himself, so he asked her to pose for him. Alice was puritanical and also shy — there had been talk in the town of models who wore no clothes. But Miss Butler posed in pieces of cambric, draped and then sewed together here and there by Miss Grimes to represent a Greek classic dress. It was said that only her head was used for the *Victory.* Her face was not an angelic one but strong and much better suited to the *Sherman*'s restudied, simplified lines.[11]

The work went well; William A. Coffin continued to demand the *Sherman,* so the all-too-familiar bedlam of casting in plaster took place once more. Soon, in the field beside the old brick house with its Italian gardens, there stood a great white horse and rider. New Hampshire horses, clip-clopping by, paid no attention because this horse smelled of plaster. But riders and drivers turned to stare. It was a handsome sight and after they got used to it, Cornish people liked it. Of course they hadn't supposed that Alice Butler was quite as beautiful as that angel with the big wings.

Mr. Coffin had been insisting that Saint-Gaudens come to Buffalo with the *Sherman.* There couldn't have been a better drawing card for the show. But Gus, although he never mentioned his illness, was subject to attacks of pain, and also exhausted by his efforts to finish the commissions in his studios. He sent Henry Hering,[12] a gifted young sculptor and his chief assistant, to set up the whole Saint-Gaudens exhibit, mending broken casts which came from Paris, painting the Shaw plaster the color of bronze. Hering received three dollars a day while traveling and five dollars a day while at work, which was apparently regarded as high pay. Before the Exposition, Mr. Coffin made no objection to Hering's wages — Saint-Gaudens was just to send in his bills for all expenses.

The *Sherman* was to stand out of doors in front of the Fine Arts Building at the Pan-American Exposition. There would be no other work nearby to detract from it, Mr. Coffin promised — or would Saint-Gaudens rather have the statue inside? They would put it in the center of the gallery. Saint-Gaudens chose the outdoor location, of course — since the statue was designed for open air, all the fine shadows depending on light from the sky. But Coffin insisted that the statue should face the Fine Arts Building.

Yielding to the temptation to see his work handsomely displayed, Saint-Gaudens made a brief trip to Buffalo. He walked all around the *Sherman* and finally decided that the equestrian looked well, but he still felt that the horse seemed to be trotting into a barn instead of bravely setting forth as it was supposed to do.

At the Pan-American Exposition, the Saint-Gaudens sculptures received an award described as "above and beyond all other awards." A diploma was engrossed and a special gold medal struck. "You will be the Great Laureate of the entire Pan-American," William A. Coffin wrote in an official letter announcing these honors. At the bottom in his own hand he added, "Old man, I almost have tears in my eyes as I sign this."

Mr. Coffin managed to dry his tears rather quickly however. The Exposition was over and, as always in such affairs, funds were gone and there was a deficit. Coffin had promised to pay expenses, but now there was no longer any need to hold out inducements to exhibitors and Mr. Coffin thought that Saint-Gaudens would find it embarrassing, after receiving that gold medal, to ask the Pan-American Exposition to pay bills, as promised. Probably Augusta handled the correspondence at this point because Mr. Coffin found that he could sell the big Shaw Memorial cast, plus sundry smaller casts, to the Albright Museum for $2000, turning the money over to Saint-Gaudens.

An offer was made for the *Sherman*, but Saint-Gaudens wanted it back, along with a cast of "Deacon Chapin" which he said was the only one he had. "We applied for a car to ship the *Sherman* on and the cases will be trucked over when we get it," Mr. Coffin wrote. The story on the *Puritan* was not as reassuring. Mr. Coffin thought it was in a safe place, although he didn't seem to know just where it was. Vandals had smashed the cast of the MacMonnies *Bacchante* after the Exposition closed. Mr. Coffin had his troubles in returning work to artists all over the world, as he pointed out. But nothing was as much fun after the Exposition as before it. He finally found the *Puritan,* but he sounded rather like a small boy who didn't want to pick up his toys.

Saint-Gaudens began to experiment with gold leaf. In October, 1902, a gold horse and rider stood in the field on the Cornish hillside. It was something a real horse might shy at, except that by now Cornish horses were used to almost anything.

Meanwhile, the journey of the plastoline models for the Boston Public Library groups from Paris to Cornish had been disastrous. They had been badly packed in hay and arrived crushed past recognition. To Augusta they represented four thousand dollars cash, paid in advance and now gone. To Saint-Gaudens the whole library project must have become a nightmare.

At the time of Saint-Gaudens' operation, Augusta had admonished everyone not to excite or worry him. This rule she herself could not keep. All was not well between them, their quarrels so spectacular as to be commented upon by outsiders. Financial pressures could have been the cause. There could have been another reason for bitterness on Augusta's part. It seems to have been at about this time that she learned of the liaison between her husband and the model Davida.

Certainly Augusta found out about Davida during one of her many absences from home. She wrote a letter to her husband, but what bitter words she put down seem mercifully not to have been kept. The undated letter her husband wrote to her, she saved.

"Dear Gussie," the letter began, "Sweetness and kindness in a woman is what appeals mostly to men and a blessed charity for human failings makes one beloved.

"The quiet dignity of Mrs. MacMonnies and Mrs. White toward the gross actions of their husbands is far finer and commands a deeper respect than any other attitude they could possibly have taken and way down deep in their hearts their husbands respect them all the more. Although my action is a mere peccadillo in comparison to them, it has caused me a misery of mind you do not dream of.

"You are a noble woman, Gussie, and I love and admire and respect you more than you have any conception of. We are both sick and for a mutual peace of mind on this earth I beg of you not to come down from the high place you hold in my heart."[13]

Estrangement was inevitable, at least for a time. Homer knew about the affair and perhaps both parents told him. It was a shock to him of course. He must have had angry words with his father because his father took down the bas-relief of Homer as a baby and put up the one of Novy instead. Guests, or perhaps servants, told the story that sometimes, after a dinner party, when Saint-Gaudens was talking about the plaster casts that hung on the walls, his wife would pause before the bas-relief of Novy and say sarcastically, "Now tell us all about this one." Then there would be silence. If true, this was a piece of cruelty, both on Gussie's part and on the part of her husband who had banished the portrait of their child. It might also be an example of what Miss Grimes called Mrs. Saint-Gaudens' "barbaric manners." From Saint-Gaudens' point of view, Homer was a boy who had been given everything and never thanked anybody for anything. Novy, on the other hand, never had a break, yet he may have been as gentle as his mother looked.

Perhaps it was a sort of olive branch when Saint-Gaudens changed his Sherman angel and modeled a very different girl. He also modeled a separate head of *Victory* in bronze, crowned with olive instead of laurel — the face that of Alice Butler. It became a most popular piece, selling at Tiffany for ninety dollars. The new *Victory* was photographed in the studio and went to Buffalo. But when the *Sherman* finally went to the bronze foundry, some people said that the new head of *Victory* was not used. Whether this is true or not, the new *Victory* was less soft and sweet but more like a girl from Windsor, Vermont, wings added.

23

FIRE ON THE HILLSIDE

THE Sherman equestrian statue was begun in New York City sometime in 1892. It was finished and exhibited in plaster at the Salon
in Paris, changed and shown at the Pan-American Exposition in
Buffalo. In 1903, it was cast in bronze and gilded, and lay in the snow
at Windsor, Vermont, waiting for a freight train to take it to New York.

Flatcars were finally shunted onto the Windsor siding. But when the
bronze reached New York, it was not carried in triumph to a waiting
pedestal, but hauled off to a city-owned shack somewhere in the vicinity of the present Metropolitan Museum of Art. The hassle over where
in New York the *Sherman* was to be set up had been going on for
several years and there seemed no hope that it would soon be settled.
Gus told the committee that his part of the bargain had been kept, the
delay was no fault of his and therefore a final settlement was due. The
committee thought not.

McKim's idea of having the *Sherman* on Riverside Drive in front of
Grant's Tomb had always appealed to Saint-Gaudens. It was the
dream of the best New York architects to make Riverside Drive one of
the most beautiful streets in the nation. There was the lordly Hudson
on one side, fine houses and apartments would soon be built on the
other and McKim was particularly interested in making Columbia
University a culminating triumph. He had been building Morningside
Heights higher, instead of leveling it down — to everybody's amaze-
ment.

But the Grant family put an end to the idea of the Grant's Tomb site
for the *Sherman*. They would have no rivals to dim Grant's glory.

William C. Coffin felt proprietary toward the *Sherman* ever since he
had helped to get a gold medal for it at the Pan-American Exposition.
He had ideas about a site for it and favored "the upper end of Longacre Square with the wide stretch of Broadway curving left and

Seventh Avenue reaching northward." The place he was talking about was actually Times Square! Few people besides Coffin had called it Longacre Square since 1872, when it was so named because it was supposed to resemble London's Longacre and was the center of New York's carriage-building business. A fine view of "the illuminations of Broadway" could be obtained from here, said a local guidebook.[1] Mr. Coffin urged Gus to put his statue "between two great currents of traffic, among men and buildings, not among trees. . . ."

Frederick Law Olmstead, Jr., had wanted the *Sherman* among trees. He had been very much occupied with designing parks for Washington, D.C., being on the same committee with McKim and Saint-Gaudens, but he was still interested in Central Park, New York, and he favored the center of the Mall for the *Sherman*. Everyone was pleased with this idea except the sculptors whose statues were already in the park. The golden equestrian would overshadow them all, so at last the city fathers decided not to let the *Sherman* through the gate.

The spot finally chosen, with Olmstead's cooperation, was just outside the Fifty-ninth Street entrance to the park. As one New Yorker, Nathalie Smith, young daughter of an Episcopal minister, described it, "Clicking hoofs and the gentle clash of polished chains came from the high-steppers who pulled the victorias in which sat ladies handsomely attired for their afternoon drive. . . . Dowagers were enclosed in one-horse broughams and young men drove blooded roadsters harnessed to light buggies . . ." and they all crowded their way into the park at the Fifty-ninth Street entrance.[2]

McKim, rather than White, designed the pedestal for the *Sherman* and, with the help of Frederick Law Olmstead, Jr.,[3] laid out an oval around the statue. There was a group of five young elms at this spot and two, which obscured the statue, were ordered cut down. Immediately, there was an outcry with letters to the papers on the theme of "Woodman, spare that tree." All was forgiven, however, once the *Sherman* was unveiled, for it was a handsome sight and most New Yorkers loved it.

The unveiling date was May 30, 1903. Saint-Gaudens had been at the site the day before, as usual, and reporters spotted him. They said he "expressed himself as well pleased with all the arrangements . . . ," but next day he succeeded in hiding himself in some inconspicuous corner. Unlike Bostonians, New Yorkers did not rout him out and make him ride in the parade with the mayor, aldermen, committeemen and Elihu Root, the speaker. But if the mayor and his cohorts expected to monopolize the center of the stage, they were disappointed. Miss Alice Roosevelt stole the show. She "displayed special interest in certain detachments of Negro veterans and once or twice showed amusement at certain bizarre figures, most notably, the matronly vivandière who strode in front of the Lafayette Guards."

There was the usual long procession, the marchers, the mounted men. But something new had been added. Automobiles enlivened the parade, one of them by quitting and having to be pushed to the curb by cheerful, jeering onlookers; others by backfiring so that horses reared and plunged, some riders displaying horsemanship, others their lack of it.

The great Saint-Gaudens equestrian stepped bravely into a new world. The horse-drawn era was coming to an end, and the gilded era also, but three layers of solid gold leaf would last the war-horse and rider well. The *General Sherman* by Saint-Gaudens was to be counted among the world's greatest equestrians.

There was a minority opinion, of course. Southerners had no reason whatever to admire General Sherman, and as for his memorial with its winged figure of Victory, it was "just like a Northerner to send a woman ahead of him — so nobody could shoot," went the comment. And "Who but a Northerner would let a woman walk while the man rides!"[4] If Saint-Gaudens ever heard these comments, it seems likely that he would have laughed.

As the horse-drawn era ended and daring young people "averaged up to 22 miles an hour" in their Rocket-Schneiders and Pierce-Arrows,[5] the attitude toward heroes and statues thereof changed drastically. Among the many irreverent verses set to the tune of "Humoresque" was one that went:

> *In the evening after dark,*
> *We goosed the statues in the park,*
> *If Sherman's horse can take it*
> *So can you.*[6]

Nevertheless, the *Sherman* was and is a much loved statue. It was a present-day taxi driver who very recently pointed out the Sherman equestrian. "That's by Augustus Saint-Gaudens," he said, "and a very fine thing it is, too." Gus would have liked that.

The GENERAL SHERMAN, *at the entrance to Central Park, Fifth Avenue and* Central Park South, New York City (*Courtesy of the Board of Trustees of* Dartmouth College)

Gus told McKim that he took a three-month vacation after the Sherman unveiling. It was true that on November 8, 1902, he was in Hot Springs, Virginia, for he wrote to Gaetan Ardison,[7] whom he had left in charge of the Cornish studios, to send him "the golf balls that are on top of the wardrobe with the mirror on it in my room." But in 1903, after the unveiling, Gus was supervising his assistants in the New Hampshire atelier. He took time every day to try to play golf on his own meadows and pastures, and he decided to organize a Cornish golf club. A house and farm of 185 acres, with fine views, was for sale near "Aspet" for three thousand dollars. Saint-Gaudens proposed that he and his neighbors take shares at a hundred dollars a share, buy the place and turn the fields and pastures into a golf course for their own pleasure and to preserve open land. The Platts agreed to take five shares "if the thing goes through," and Winston Churchill, the novelist, made the same contingent offer, as did Norman Hapgood, editor of *Collier's Weekly*. Maxfield Parrish, who was in Italy, wrote that he couldn't afford to join. He was flat broke, he said, but he didn't want it known. Arthur Nichols, Augusta's brother-in-law, said the whole scheme was impractical. Unfortunately, he was right.

The idea had to be given up and Gus was obliged to content himself with knocking a ball around his own pastureland, a few acres of which he cleared for the purpose. The golf-club idea, however, must have been the basis for the myth which circulated to the effect that Saint-Gaudens was so rich he owned a private golf course.

Augusta's frequent consultations with doctors gradually helped her to achieve peace of mind. She still needed Dr. Polk's great gift of listening to her troubles and as usual he prescribed a journey. Gus had already told her that they got along better by correspondence than face to face. Now that the story of Davida and the child had been told, Gussie faced the facts and realized that her only course was to forgive and try to forget.

Writing from Spain in November, 1903, "I know the ordinary letter does not interest you," Gussie began. She cut down on her customary travelogue. Her symptoms she also described much less at length, but merely referred humorously to being almost eaten alive by mosquitoes in Seville. She looked as though she had smallpox and said, "I'm glad you cannot see me." She signed her letter "lovingly, Gussie," which was something she had not done for some time. "If you think this is worth reading, forward it to Homer, please," Gussie suggested.

Gussie longed for letters from Gus and told him that she felt at the ends of the earth. When letters came from her husband, the tone of affection that she wanted to hear was in them, along with humor, which meant that they were friends again.

"Dear Gussie, I write with pencil because I have just emptied the inkstand on the floor and I'm too lazy to get up and get the ink where I think it is hid — behind the books on your dresser," Gus began. Did the ink go on the rug? Did he or did he not mop it up properly? Poor Gussie would worry about that and he knew it.

Rose, the cook, kept a dirtier kitchen than ever, Gus told Gussie. But what an artist she was at the stove — what a Thanksgiving dinner she had prepared! "The house runs along all right, of course, but not so orderly as when the Mistress is here."

By the end of November, 1903, Gus described himself as "in a fever of work on the *Brooks*." He would try to be careful of his health but he really wanted to complete the *Phillips Brooks Memorial*, and "the trouble now is for me not to be in the studio too much." It was a letter which would make Gussie happy, for he said, "Life seems strange here, without you and I miss you very much, Gussie, — but I'm getting on all right." And now, instead of his customarily abbreviated "Affy," Gus also signed his letters "lovingly."

On her way home, Augusta stopped over in Paris to attend to Saint-Gaudens replicas for Tiffany in New York and for Doll and Richards in Boston. All reproductions in any form Gussie carefully copyrighted in her husband's name, even before they were finished.

But the first thing Gussie did in Paris was to go to the Luxembourg Museum to see her husband's medallions. "I simply had the creeps all up and down my spinal column, the thing does look so beautifully. The patina and light are wonderful. Of course you know I mean the *Amor Caritas*," she wrote to Gus. "The bas-reliefs are also well placed and seen to great advantage . . . but I will tell you all about it."

Her husband's two dearest friends, Dr. Shiff and Garnier, came to call on Gussie at her Paris hotel. With a touch of her natural-born tactlessness, she told Gus they were both "quite freakish-looking." She mentioned Garnier's long-pointed white beard. But she "enjoyed them immensely" even if she thought the hotel porter would wonder what kind of people she entertained.

The Stevenson memorial plaque had arrived in Edinburgh. Begun in Paris, it was finished in the United States and dated 1902. From Paris,

A studio scene showing a variation of the AMOR CARITAS *and in the background the* PHILLIPS BROOKS MEMORIAL, *with a pointing machine used to enlarge a sculptor's work (Courtesy of the Board of Trustees of Dartmouth College)*

Augusta wrote, and then telegraphed to Edinburgh, hoping to be able to attend the unveiling ceremonies. In December, 1903, ceremonies were put off and so she put off her sailing date. Then there were more delays, so finally she gave up and came home.

But before leaving Paris, Gussie had a confession to make to Gus. "The cold weather and sunshine came together one morning, and so intoxicated me that I lost my head altogether and without intending to do so at all, went into Sandler's and ordered a long red cloak all lined with fur and with a big high collar, to be ready for sleighing. . . . Will you give it to me for Christmas?" Gus would indeed. Nothing could please him better because Gussie was more like the girl he married than he supposed she ever could be again. She returned to Cornish in plenty of time to wear the new red cloak.

Gus not only gave Gussie the fur-lined cloak but paid for her trip to Europe, which surprised and pleased her. Together, they bought more land in Cornish, including a choice piece to give to Homer. Gussie wrote sharply to him because he thanked her but failed to thank his father for it. They both hoped that when Homer married he would build a house on this land.

Homer, having been to Lawrenceville, to school in Paris and Dresden and to Brown and Nichols tutoring school, finally graduated from Harvard in 1903. He consulted his father about his career because he was undecided whether to choose architecture or literature. His father told him that architecture would be likely to provide a living, although he refused to "bulldoze" his son into anything but would be equally happy to see him a "literary feller." Homer's first job was on the New York *Evening Sun* as "real estate editor." While still in college, he had met the girl he wanted to marry.

Carlota Dolley, daughter of a Philadelphia doctor, spent summers at Chesham Lake near Keene, New Hampshire.[8] She was handsome, had beautiful blond hair and was extremely popular with the young men at the lake. Barry Faulkner, a classmate of Homer's at Harvard and later an assistant to Saint-Gaudens, was said to be the one who brought Homer to the lake. Homer promptly acquired a sailboat and laid siege to the heart of Carlota.

Barry, who afterwards became a mural painter of considerable note, painted a picture of Homer and Carlota — who, if his accuracy could be relied on, was a rather buxom girl. The sketch showed a calm Carlota at the tiller of Homer's boat with Homer, dark and handsome,

standing in a heroic pose on a perilously canted deck. Sails seemed to
be in irons, set broadside to the spectator and surely not responsible
for the indicated speed of the boat. It was an amusing decorative
picture, even if it was astounding from a sailor's point of view. Barry
was red-faced and countrified, according to one of the other girls who
came to the lake. Homer was handsome and sophisticated. Friends
laughed when they saw the picture, and said that Barry had painted
Homer "going off with Carlota."

Those who said that Barry Faulkner was in love with her had it
wrong, according to Barry's much younger and observant cousin. It
was Nancy Brush whom Barry loved and certainly it was true that he
made an exquisite pencil drawing of this beautiful, gentle-faced young
girl. Her heart was elsewhere, however. She failed to notice his devotion and Barry never married. He came to Cornish to gild and tint in
watercolor some small reproductions of the head of the Sherman *Victory* and was nice to the somewhat older Frances Grimes, who thought
the world of him. Francesca, he called her, when he discovered how
much she loved the name.

When Augusta went abroad in 1903, the house in Cornish was still
unpainted. When she came home, it was pure white like the pillars,
pergolas and ornamental fences already surrounding it. "The house
looks very well," Gussie conceded. Although she still preferred the old
brick and had held out for it, the house was "by no means spoiled."
What she said when she found that her husband had also covered her
ancestral four-poster beds with white paint seems not to be on record.
But she probably made no great objection because the time had yet to
come when antiques would be prized for their beauty and crafts-
manship.

Homer was now definitely engaged to Carlota Dolley and Carlota
was a constant visitor at Cornish. In 1902, she came to spend Christmas and stayed well into January. Already a good artist in oils, she
pleased Saint-Gaudens by asking to study modeling and he set her up
in the small studio.

"I'm copying a bas-relief of a Greek Nike and have got the head
nearly done," Carlota wrote to her family back in Philadelphia.[9] "They
tell me that while I am studying I should finish everything I do to the
bitter end, so I am trying to make an exact copy of this cast. I enjoy so
working out there. It is quiet and warm."[10]

Invariably, Saint-Gaudens modeled his figures first in the nude, then

"Aspet," the home of Saint-Gaudens in Cornish, New Hampshire: (above) at the time when he first saw the house and (below) as transformed by Saint-Gaudens (Courtesy of the Board of Trustees of Dartmouth College)

Saint-Gaudens in his garden at "Aspet" (Courtesy of the Board of Trustees of Dartmouth College)

draped them.[11] "Phillips Brooks with nothing on but an open coat stands above me with outstretched arms and the big *Stevenson* stands beside," Carlotta said. "There is a great big mirror on casters which reflects the whole room and all the figures and casts and myself standing on a box at my easel. . . . The skylight is so soft and clear!"[11] She asked if she could have a skylight put in her painting room at home.

Charles McKim had been visiting. Carlota described Mr. McKim as "a little fat man from New York, an artist or architect or something." McKim had a well-developed ego and this would not have pleased him even though Carlota added that he was "lots of fun."

Saint-Gaudens went to New York, returning January 7, 1903, and Carlota had "all the fires crackling brightly for him. He is much better for the change. You know, he has to have the doctor every night and day," she said.

Barry Faulkner was also visiting and painting "cartoons and wall decorations" at Homer's "little house." Carlota thought the murals were "very nice." There was "only one, though, of the boat with Homer and me in it."

Carlota drove Mr. Saint-Gaudens over to Windsor, Vermont, in the little red sleigh. He got out on Main Street to do an errand and told her to drive on until she found a good place to turn around and come back for him. She "turned ever so slowly on an almost level place but over went the sleigh and away went the horse." Carlota "hung on to the reins and was dragged almost two blocks." Fur rugs and parcels were strewn all over the street. Someone caught the horse, but he had cut his leg on a sleigh bell and had to be taken to the veterinary. The dog was thrown out and was lame next day, but Carlota was all right!

In June, Carlota came back for a long visit. They had suppers "on the porch looking out at Ascutney" and then, "after the table was cleared," they sat in silence, listening to the hermit thrushes. After the thrushes also fell silent one night, "Mr. Saint-Gaudens got to talking about a horse in New York that he wants to buy," Carlota wrote. "Finally he suggested that Homer go down on the mid-night train and look at it and try it in the Park, buy it if he liked it and come back on the noon train next day." Carlota marveled at the way Homer "just stepped over to New York" the way she would go downtown in Philadelphia.

Carlota ate breakfast alone about eight next morning, "for Mr. Saint-

Gaudens does not eat breakfast," she explained. "Then I went down where he was with the men who were chopping and clearing for the golf course. The fields extend in front of the house and back of the house and stables and he has eleven men working at the foot of the slope in front of the house and has cleared about two acres, I guess, of scrub pine and brush and it is all as smooth as the rest of the fields — all in a week. . . . It seems like magic."

Carlota thought the tall pines at the edge of the clearing looked "very Japanese and with the grass growing right up to them and the blue mountain behind, it looks like tapestry scenes all around. . . . And then there is a little boy and a wooly dog who drive forty sheep over the place. . . ."

In July, 1903, "I rode Mr. Saint-Gaudens' new four-hundred-dollar horse. He is a stunner. Homer took my picture," Carlota said.

And on August 2, "Homer has given me the engagement ring. It is a most wonderful diamond. I feel very queer wearing it." She was nineteen years old.

It was in April, 1904, when Augusta and Augustus Saint-Gaudens conveyed 4.76 acres of land in Cornish, New Hampshire, to Louis Saint-Gaudens in consideration of one dollar. Gus, in a long letter in French to his old friend Garnier, described what Louis and Annetta did with their land, which was "somewhat higher up the hill" than "Aspet." Annetta had bought "a house which used to be a sort of Protestant temple of a sect called Shakers. Their religion was no love and no children." Two aged Shaker survivors sold the building which was located about twenty-five miles from Cornish. "It's made of wood, they took it off its foundation and put it on the [freight] train and set this hundred-year-old up again, here. Mine is a hundred also but it's brick and was formerly a *maison de joie*. You see funny things in life!"

In 1904 a Sherman payment was made. Somehow the city fathers contrived to deduct $7000 from the $23,500 that was nearly a year overdue, but a member of the committee made up the difference. The Parnell statue for Dublin, Ireland, was almost done and a $1300 advance had been paid on it. Henry Hering enlarged the "Seated *Lincoln*," photographs were sent to Chicago and $15,000 on account was paid by the Crerar Fund. A statue of Marcus Daly, Irish-born miner who became a millionaire operator of mines, was practically ready to go to Butte, Montana.

All these commissions had passed the small-model stage and were being worked on in the big studio — once the old barn. When the $15,000 payment on the "Seated *Lincoln*" came in, Gus took out a $20,000 fire-insurance policy in favor of the Crerar Fund — but he said it was hardly necessary. This handsome statue was going to the bronze founders very shortly.

After a successful summer's work, Saint-Gaudens went to his favorite club, the Players', on Gramercy Park, New York. He often invited Homer to go to the theater with him, after dinner at the Club, and on the night of October 7, Gus was at a play. So, also, and at the same play, was Henry Hering — in New York without his employer's knowledge or consent.

Augusta was in Cornish. She had a dinner engagement for the night of October 7, so she put on her black dress and had the handyman drive her to the house of friends, some miles away over the hills. As soon as her back was turned the servants slipped out on dates of their own.[12]

At the Westgate farm, about a mile from "Aspet," three Saint-Gaudens assistants, Frances Grimes, Elsie Ward and Barry Faulkner, had just finished their supper. Frances stepped out the door and came back to say that she saw something that looked like a big fire in the direction of Aspet.

Barry Faulkner "pelted down the road." Mr. Westgate hitched up his horse and followed with the girls. The fire was not just "in the direction of Aspet" — it was in the big studio. When they got there "no one was on the place and the fire was burning fiercely."

Part of the studio building was still used as a barn, with hay for the horses stored there. Henhouses and sheds were attached and it was already too late to save the livestock. Just as Barry Faulkner arrived, the roof of the storehouse fell in and the fire "was eating into the east wall of the studio."

Barry rushed in "and carried out a small, low-relief portrait by Frances Grimes, her first original work, and hid it in the ravine." He said he knew that Mrs. Saint-Gaudens would be annoyed if she found out what he had done.

"And now the girls and Mr. Westgate, as well as Michael Stillman, Rose and Marian Nichols arrived. We carried to safety the heavy bas-relief portraits but the two nearly completed statues of Parnell and Marcus Daly on their pedestals, we could not budge," Barry said.

Hering had blocked the wheels of these stands with lumps of clay to keep them from rolling accidentally. He could have knocked off the clay, but no one else knew it was there — and he was away without leave.

Elsie Ward dashed up a ladder and saved the portrait heads of both Parnell and Daly. They were "detachable," Barry said. The *Parnell* was in plasteline and she put it in a sandbox on the golf course. Considering what headway the fire had made, even before it was discovered, it was remarkable how much was saved — modeling tools, big and little turntables, photographs. But as always, something of comparatively little value was rescued at considerable hazard. In this case, Mr. Westgate "sprained his back carrying out a cast-iron stove."

Rose Nichols frantically begged everyone to get out of the burning studio. She was the Saint-Gaudens niece who had said she wanted to see bullfights and wished she could play "the blood-thirsty game of football." Her sister Marian, a quiet, more feminine type of girl, rushed in and out of the studio, carrying anything she could get her hands on and yelling at all the rest to help her. Everyone got out "just as the studio's great north light crashed to the floor."

Sparks spread to the low roof of a horse stable near the house. Barry climbed up on this roof and covered it with wet blankets which people handed up to him. Bells in Windsor had been ringing. Horses dashed up the hill, bringing fire fighters from the town. People brought buckets, but there was almost no water and little anyone could do now except watch the studio burn.

Word reached Augusta, who drove back at top speed across the hills. Barry Faulkner saw her and said, "Mrs. Saint-Gaudens stood upon a rise of ground, black, silent and motionless."

24

THE MASQUE

THE first snow of winter fell at Cornish on October 8, 1904. Ascutney was white. At "Aspet," the ruins of the studio stood out, black as a funeral pyre against the pure whiteness all around it. There was a clean fresh smell of pine woods in the air, except at the site of the disaster where the smell of smoke would linger for a long time. Barry Faulkner arrived, early in the morning, full of sympathy, asking what he could do to help.

Barry was looking at the ruins when "Mrs. Saint-Gaudens met me there and without a word of thanks for efforts of the night before, dismissed me from the place. She said there was nothing more for me to do. She was right but I resented her ungraciousness." Barry went back to the Westgates', packed up his things and went home, not to return for several years. He had not noticed, as he approached the scene of the fire, how trampled the snow was getting to be — evidence that sensation-seekers had already come and gone.

Brought up in the New England spartan tradition, taught from childhood the axiom "Never wear your heart on your sleeve," Augusta stood tall, her naturally sculpturesque features as motionless as marble. If she had been weeping bitterly, her neighbors would have loved her, although they themselves would have tried to practice stoicism under similar circumstances.

Saint-Gaudens, in a letter to Homer written at about this time, explained Augusta, proving once and for all that he loved her. "Poor woman, she means so well and has this infernal hardness of manner! Her mother, who was one of the sweetest people in the world, also had it."

When Saint-Gaudens came back to Cornish, "the sense of his loss came over him on his way from the station" and he wept, openly and unashamed. After all, he was half French and half Irish and emotion

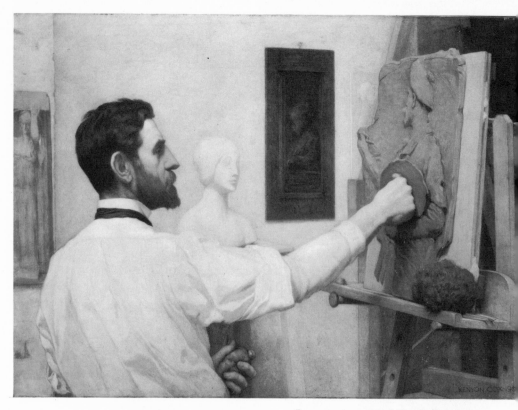

Portrait in oil of Saint-Gaudens at work, by Kenyon Cox (The Metropolitan Museum of Art, gift of Friends of the Scupltor, 1908)

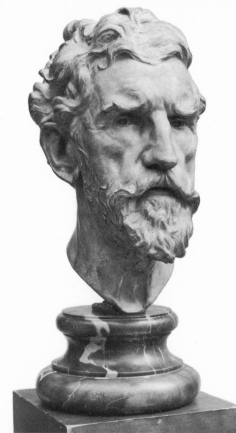

Bust in bronze of Saint-Gaudens by John Flanagan, begun in 1905 and completed in 1924 (The Metropolitan Museum of Art, Francis Lathrop Fund, 1933)

always moved him to tears, which no one in his family ever thought unmanly or told him to suppress.

Frances Grimes wrote to Barry Faulkner a few days after the return of "the Saint," as everyone now called him. "Happily, he is intent on building a new studio which is to occupy the same place as the old. The things he grieves most for are the drawings he made of his mother, long ago — the portraits of him by Lepage and Cox and the letters from Stevenson and Sargent, all stored in that awful barn." Bastien-Lepage had died in 1884 at the age of thirty-six — a young painter of great promise. He had been fond of Saint-Gaudens, writing in naive delight when Saint-Gaudens helped to persuade the Metropolitan Museum of Art in New York to buy his painting *Saint Jeanne d'Arc Listening to Voices*. He had painted a portrait of Gus in exchange for his portrait medallion by Saint-Gaudens which the Luxembourg acquired. There was now nothing left of the Lepage portrait except the record that it once existed.

Kenyon Cox had sketches and his own memory to rely on. He recreated his portrait of Saint-Gaudens at work on a bas-relief of William Chase, painter and friend of both of them. One sketch, perhaps not the best, of Saint-Gaudens' mother remained, and the Stevenson letters survived in print, probably because copies had been sent to Stevenson's biographer and published — with variations.

By October 19, the work of reproducing the lost statues was being organized. Saint-Gaudens wrote to the committee on the *Parnell,* in Dublin. The portfolio of documents and photographs of the *Parnell* had been saved as well as pen sketches and architectural drawings for the base. "It is a serious loss," Gus said, "as there was no insurance and there is nothing to do but face it and begin again. I have already done so. With the intimate knowledge I have of every fold and line of work, the new model will progress rapidly. . . ."

As to the "Seated *Lincoln,*" "I had refrained from proceeding with the casting," Gus told the Crerar Fund Committee, "as there was ample time and I kept it in the studio in order to make further improvements. . . . I made considerable and important changes before casting it in plaster. Of the figure in this final condition there is no replica or record, other than some photographs; with these however and a few parts of extra casts that were saved, I can begin again. . . ."

Saint-Gaudens had all the courage of youth, but in his search for good health he tried doctor after doctor. A man who wrote and sold

The "Seated Lincoln," Chicago. This statue was studied by Daniel Chester French in preparation for his Lincoln in Washington, D.C. (Courtesy of Chicago Historical Society)

books for self-cure sold Saint-Gaudens one entitled *The No-Breakfast Plan and the Fasting Cure*. Gus wanted so much to be well that he was sure that this helped him, although he became alarmingly thin. A lady of his acquaintance urged him to see a man who had cured her of her fear of horses! There were many suggestions, many letters from all sorts of people. One theme was common to all of them, however. Even the obvious charlatans wanted Saint-Gaudens to get well. Correspondence might begin on a purely commercial note, but it rapidly changed in tone to one of personal affection and friendship.

Writing to John Hay on October 13, 1904, "You have no doubt seen in the papers about the burning of the big studio," Gus said. "It's a devil of a thing and I would like to get my hands on the throat of the loafer who smoked in the stable." This seems to be the only mention of the probable cause of the fire. "The new studio, where you sat is all right," Gus assured Mr. Hay. "One model of your bust is there and two were in New York, one at the bronze founder's and the other at the marble man's." And in answer to anxious queries from the Hay family, "I am being X-rayed for my pain and I have had in consequence the first relief in months. That counter-balances things."

A check for $1500 arrived very shortly, in payment for copies of the Hay portrait. The Dublin committee sent $1550, but all the insurance money on the "Seated *Lincoln*" went direct to the Crerar Fund, since the policies were made out to them. An insurance company that had issued a $9000 policy on the burned building paid only $463, contending that the loss of livestock, carts and farm implements was all that they covered. The Daly Committee had $5000 worth of insurance they might be persuaded to part with, to help Saint-Gaudens start over again on the Marcus Daly statue. Naturally, it was Augusta who did all this figuring.

Gussie blamed herself bitterly. She was under nervous tension and needed a rest but she said, "If I left Cornish I would see a great conflagration every time I tried to sleep." "Last year I went away with the result that they added a $3000 addition to the studio and there was no additional insurance on that or anything else but the horses."

Studio space was a problem. It was decided that Saint-Gaudens would stay at the Players' Club in New York, borrow space in Tonetti's studio to re-create small models, attend to portrait commissions — and come to Cornish now and then to supervise the work of assistants. Henry Hering was going to enlarge the *Parnell* in Louis's studio, higher up the hill — Miss Grimes could use the small studio where the Hay bust had been modeled.

Augusta wanted to stay in Cornish to keep the house open for her husband's visits. "If I go these servants will go," she said. They were already complaining of being lonely in the country now that all the big summer homes were closed. "Miss Grimes is all broken up and may stop and go away any time." Otherwise, Miss Grimes could act as housekeeper. Then there was the business of building the new studio, involving "no end of details that need a head."

Homer required a few words of advice from his mother. "I have never talked to your father about your getting married, for with all his pain and trouble, it seemed as if he had all he could manage." Evidently, Homer wanted financial help. "You know very well your father has tried all his life to meet your wishes and your happiness is our first aim. If you have any plan to propose, talk to him." But if money was what Homer wanted, he had better postpone an interview.

The Louisiana Purchase Exposition was just about to close in St. Louis, when Gussie consented to take a short trip and see sculpture exhibits on her way to New Mexico. She observed and reported to Gus. Daniel Chester French "dominates the sculpture" with figures "so big that your *Puritan* is a jewel and never looked better. Louis' *Art* is far ahead of French's figure but it was too cold and windy to stand outside and study it. Miss Mears's fountain is finely placed but does not shine. I wish it hadn't been so cold and everything so dirty and strewn with dead leaves and picnic papers but it was the end and everybody was tired and it wasn't worth while not to be frowzy. . . ."

Augusta had written many travel letters home to her husband, but now she spoke for the first time of their going on a trip together. She really hoped she could get him to finish the work in hand quickly, take on nothing too big and get away for a rest. "The Indians are superb," she told Gus, trying to tempt him with the idea of seeing them. "There are many of them about and I wish I had someone to go to the Reservation with me. Won't you get well and take a journey with *me* sometime when we can stop and see the people who really live in these mud huts." She wanted to ride with her husband "over these boundless prairies." And looking at a church which dominated a cluster of houses, "It would be great to be a good Catholic and why can't I be one? I suppose it's because some of that striding old Puritan is in me. . . ."

At Christmas, Gus sent Gussie two necklaces from Tiffany, "to be worn together," he told her. He had selected them himself, which particularly pleased her. She said she loved them, and she longed to come home. By the end of January, she was on her way and wrote of a wonderful eighteen-mile stage ride over a pass "where the Spaniards tried to ambush General Freemont," according to her stage driver. At a water tank on the railroad, she ate her lunch out of a brown bag while waiting for a freight train to come along. "After taking up a carload of hogs, they hoisted me into the cupolo of the train hands' car." She asked the brakeman if he knew Marcus Daly.

"Yes, I knew him well," the brakeman said. "Once he got on my train and I asked him to come up in the cupolo and see the country and he said 'Young man, I've been all over it with my blanket. I know it well.'"

Gussie showed her ticket, good on the "Limited," one of those splendid trains with parlor cars and diners of which the railroad was proud. It was not a ticket often used on a freight, Gussie surmised, and the crew in the caboose gathered around. Like a passport, the ticket described Gussie, "tall, slim, dark hair, blue eyes, middle-aged." One of the trainmen gallantly said that he was middle-aged too. She told Gus that she wished she were as young as the railroader. Gussie was fifty-five and at long last she seemed to have found out how to have a good time. She said she would have liked to ride the freights all the way home.

While Gussie was away, Gus wrote to her more at length than usual, his letters calculated to keep her from worrying. "Here I am at the studio, writing without pain. In fact, most of the time I forget I have anything the matter with me. What pain I have is very slight and is purely rheumatic. I think it foolish that I should not stay and settle down to work but everyone, as well as the doctor, thinks it wise that I should keep up the treatments at least three weeks longer." This was the X-ray treatment, referred to in his letter to John Hay.

"The Daly pointing is finished very satisfactorily. Miss Ward comes in a few days a week . . . Ardisson [who was making plaster casts] drags to fussy, slow lengths along. Louis is getting on admirably with his Brearley medallion."

There was one bit of news that Gussie would not find reassuring. "I don't know about Michael," Gus told her. "Sometimes I think he is a treasure and is making me all sorts of economies and then I think he is a wild harum-scarum who is leading me into all sorts of expenses. . . ."

Michael Stillman, also called "Long Mike" because he was six feet, five and a half inches, was in charge of rebuilding the studio. He was extremely handsome, the son of the beautiful daughter of a Greek banker of London, and William Stillman, Rome correspondent of the *Times* of London. One of his first appearances at the Saint-Gaudens studio was on the night of the fire, when he arrived with the John Elliotts. He dashed into the burning building, wrenched off the head of the enlarged statue of Bishop Brooks and carried it to safety. It was Maud Howe Elliott who described Long Mike's act of heroism and also Mike's mother, who was "the loveliest of Victorian women and the last of the Pre-Raphaelite painters."

The John Elliotts were living in the Palazzo Rusticucci in Rome when they met Mike's parents. Mike had been in the United States for some time and was looking for a job when the Elliotts bought a Cornish cottage, and they had him help with alterations. As to his qualifications as an architect — Mrs. Elliott liked the kitchen he designed for her and on this recommendation, plus his lovely Italian manners, he got a job at "Aspet." The Nichols nieces already knew him and they said he "looked funny" dressed for tennis in a sailor suit. He was not a good player, according to Margaret, herself a champion who twice defeated Eleanora Sears in doubles.[1]

On the 4th of January, 1905, Saint-Gaudens addressed a letter to Michael Stillman. There was "almost unanimous complaint" and "for the smooth running of things" the young man was to correct his "intolerant and impatient attitude" toward the artists who were Saint-Gaudens' assistants.

There had also been an accident. "You agree with everyone indirectly, that driving is not your forte and will understand therefore my desire that someone shall accompany you when you drive," Saint-Gaudens wrote. "You will avoid as much as possible making trips that could be accomplished by telephone" — there must be no "necessity for constant teams." No more galivanting for Long Mike. And his employer had further requests to make. "If possible, regularity at meals will contribute to the smooth running of the house" and the young man was informed that there was "a difficulty in keeping help in the country."

Stillman was to remember, also, that the local carpenters were "good men who do their work well in their own sphere. I know them," Gus said, "their qualities and defects, and know that with a little tact much can be accomplished." The Italian-bred young aristocrat had evidently been treating the neighbors as though they were peasantry and this would have to stop or "it would mean war."

There were two more points. Stillman was not to take the whole work force down the hill and over to Windsor to a fire; he must never leave the place unprotected but must keep a ladder "lying on top of the west porch, in case of fire, as well as on the terrace on the north side of the house."

Saint-Gaudens saved a special admonition for last. "Another matter that is important and that we of the Colony are particularly *cranky* about, i.e. that there shall be no shooting. First, it is a bad example and attracts hoodlums who argue that if shooting is going on, why shouldn't they." Then there was "the increased danger of fire" plus the noise, which bothered everyone, and the fact that "all the colony" was unanimous in wanting to protect wildlife. *"Please,* no shooting while you are in my employ," Saint-Gaudens wrote.

"You ask me if Stillman is in trouble," Frances Grimes wrote to Barry Faulkner. "Heaven yes — he is having a horrible time. Mr. Saint-Gaudens does not like him — Mrs. Saint-Gaudens cannot wholly resist his manners but she hates what he represents — an expensive new studio. . . ." Frances admitted that she could not help sympathizing with him and that he was "trying not to look too lonely" now that pretty Elsie Ward was away. She thought Stillman's girl in London "must be having nightmares."

Gus tried to leave his troubles with building a studio behind him in Cornish when he went to New York. But "I don't seem to be able to get to work here," he confessed to Gussie. "I don't want to work in Tonetti's studio, his stuff is so awful to look at and he, although the cheerfulest and best of fellers, makes speeches about art that make me sick at the stomach."

Parties at the Tonetti's ex-church, now studio and home, were all right however. Mary Lawrence Tonetti was considered original when she used a new-fangled invention called a chafing dish, with its alcohol flame to cook at table. There were tableaux like those at Cornish, one of their most notable being "Salome" with Kenyon Cox posing as John the Baptist, all of him hidden except his head which seemed to be severed as it lay on a platter.

While in New York, Saint-Gaudens received a letter dated December 5, 1904, telling him that he had been elected a member of the National Academy of Arts and Letters, "chosen one of the first seven members" of the newly formed American group. The others were William Dean Howells, Edmund C. Stedman, John La Farge, Samuel L. Clemens, John Hay and Edward A. MacDowell. Gus was delighted to be an "Academician" both in France and America, and as soon as he had a chance he proposed the name of Winslow Homer, a painter he greatly admired — a cousin of Augusta's. Winslow Homer was duly elected but refused the honor. He said he was in his seventieth year, "unloading and shaking many responsibilities . . ." and "securing" himself "a peaceful old age." He added unsolicited advice. "Do you not wish you could control your ambition and have the same?"

But Saint-Gaudens was just fifty-six and not thinking of a peaceful old age. He lunched with Edith Wharton and Henry James and dined one night at the Gilders' "to meet some nice fat people from Buffalo and her Excellencée Mrs. Cleveland." On a Sunday he "lunched alone with Dana Gibson and his wife who is more beautiful than ever."

The big event of January, 1905, was the dinner in Washington given by the American Institute of Architects. Saint-Gaudens sat on the right of Secretary of State John Hay; La Farge on the left of Elihu Root, ex-Secretary of War. To Saint-Gaudens' dismay, he had to make a speech — "ten lines of oratorical idiocy," he called it.

"Well, Gussie, the dinner is over at 1:30 this morning," Gus wrote on January 12. "Henry James, La Farge, Owoki, La Farge's Jap valet, and I got into a cab built for two and came home to bed. The dinner was a great success, from the President of the A.I.A. who presided and was toastmaster and was drunk, down to my speech which was decidedly the best because it was the briefest. . . ."

Justice Harlan said "in *his* speech that he could not refuse to come to a dinner at which would be the President of the United States — the Ambassador to the French Nation — the Cardinal of the Roman Catholic Church, Gibbon, the great Secretary of State Hay, the great ex-Secretary of War, Root, the Attorney General of the United States — and last but not least, Saint-Gaudens."

Gus said he appeared very calm but was "frightened stiff." He understood now how ministers become actors and how much of an actor any public speaker ought to be, and he told Gussie, "I am convinced that I would be a great actor . . . I would be a great speaker, I am sure. . . . The trouble with me is however a fundamental one. I have nothing to say!"

Gus continued his letter from the office of the American Institute of

Architects where he had been chatting with Henry Adams, "who is always delightful to me in Washington and I feel at home here," he said. Henry James had not put in an appearance. "He is writing, Adams says. La Farge is dressing, which he can do in five minutes or twenty-four hours according to the state of his mind. Mrs. Roosevelt has sent word that she is coming to lunch and there will be other ladies. At four I see Taft about the Von Steuben monument that I have abandoned."

Back in New York again, Saint-Gaudens received an official letter from the Inaugural Committee, asking him to design a gold medal, "about one and three-quarters inches in diameter" with a portrait of Theodore Roosevelt on one side of it and on the other "such artistic work as your wonderful genius can suggest."

A few days later another official letter arrived from Washington. "The Treasury Department is considering the advisability of making some changes in the designs of our American coinage with a view of improving the artistic effect. . . ." This letter was from George E. Roberts, Director of the Mint, who went on at length. "No designs have been prepared and nothing definite is in mind. The department is not even ready to give a commission but the counsel of such artists as yourself is desired. The Secretary of the Treasury would be pleased to hear from you with any suggestions that you might feel disposed to make, or if you chance to be in this city, would be pleased to have an interview with you." This letter, which was supposed to put Saint-Gaudens in his place, actually contained no news for him. It was the Director of the Mint who was going to get news which he was not going to like.

Before the letter arrived, "I had an interesting time with Roosevelt," Saint-Gaudens wrote to Augusta. He and Theodore Roosevelt had decided to redesign the currency together! The bureaucrats at the mint would fight them every step of the way and they would both enjoy the battle.

Augusta was back in Cornish in time for her husband's birthday on the 1st of March. "I cannot believe I am fifty-seven," Gus said. "I feel as if I were twenty-five or thirty and it's incredible that I am so far along in life. I'm feeling better and celebrated my birthday by working all day for the first time in a year."

In April, Gus sat down to write to Henry Adams. He had made a cartoon of Adams, showing a bald head with wings above it and porcupine quills below. It was lettered with some of his favorite neo-Latin, as follows: "Porcupinus Angelicus Henricus Adamso," and Saint-Gaudens now addressed his "dear old Porcupinus Poeticus" to thank him for a book, *Mont-Saint-Michel and Chartres* which Adams at first published privately and gave to friends. Adding another salutation under the first one, "You dear old Poeticus under a Bushelibus," Gus went on, "I thought I liked you pretty well but I like you more for the book you sent me the other day. Whether I like you more because you have revealed to me the wonders of the 12th Century in a way that never entered my head, or whether it is because of the general guts and enthusiasm of the work, puzzles what courtesy calls my brains.

"You know, damn you, that I never read, but last night I got as far in your book as the Virgin, Eve and the Bees and I cannot wait to acknowledge it till I'm through.

> *Thank you, dear old stick in the mud,*
> *The cocks are crowin'*
> *The buds are growin'*
> *And poets are on fire,*
> > *But*
> *Why in Hell*
> *I like you well*
> *I cannot tell*
> *But that I do, tru lu, lu lu*
> *I do, I do, I do, I do*
> *I do, I do, I do, I do*
> > *Your brother in idiocy*

Gus signed this with his cartoon profile.

Spring came early to Cornish in 1905, according to Miss Grimes, and Gus seemed to be in a springtime mood with his lines to Adams. Gussie said he seemed to be "in a perpetual rage, the new studio goes so slowly," but he had improved the Brooks statue and was now at work on a second figure. In his original plan, an angel representing Divine Inspiration, perhaps, was to stand behind the famous preacher. Now he had decided on a figure of Christ. He wrote to artist friends who had been in the Holy Land and who described costumes. "Mr. Saint-Gaudens is changing the drapery, opening the eyes a little — I am trying to get his point of view by reading the New Testament in

French," Miss Grimes wrote. In the end, the figure was remarkably similar in feeling to the carving at Amiens, called *le Beau Dieu,* which Saint-Gaudens had seen when he visited the cathedral with Henry Adams.

On June 5, 1905, Homer Saint-Gaudens was married to Carlota Dolley in Philadelphia. The bride was "blond as wheat, blond, blond," said the groom's father. The groom's mother wore a white dress with a Venetian lace collar, a costume so important to her that she kept it for the rest of her life and left it to Carlota in her will!

Miss Grimes felt sorry for Homer and Carlota because she thought Gussie planned their wedding trip for them without letting them have any say in the matter. The bride and groom found a New York apartment, the small size of the rooms being a shock to Carlota, but she loved New York and hated to leave when Homer decided to live the year round in Cornish on the land his parents gave him.

Homer's "little house" a remodeled cottage, would do for summers for a while. It was fashionable to use animal skins as decoration, so Carlota had some, only hers were different — instead of the popular bear or tiger skins, hers were small animals: fox, raccoon and squirrel, dressed with the tails left on them. She used them as chair seats — the tails hanging down. Frances Arnold, pleased to have a young neighbor, came by to see her one afternoon, observed the tails and said, "Carlota — that looks awfully funny."[2]

"If you think it looks funny now, you should see how it looks when a man sits in one of the chairs," Carlota told her. It was a joke her father-in-law would have appreciated, if not her mother-in-law.

Augusta wore the dress she had had made for Homer and Carlota's wedding to grace another occasion scheduled to take place the 20th of June, 1905. Invitations to a "Fête at Cornish" read as follows: "You are invited to witness the performance of a Masque at 'Aspet' Cornish, New Hampshire . . . in celebration of the Twentieth Anniversary of the founding of the Cornish Colony by Augustus and Augusta Saint-Gaudens. . . ." The card was signed by the committee, Beaman, Cox, Charles Platt — nine in all. Down in the corner in small print were the words, "Please bring your own hitching-rope."

"Great and secret doings are going on all over my field," Saint-Gaudens told John Hay. He was "being kept in ignorance," but invited Mr. and Mrs. Hay to come to the celebration.

The 20th of June had been chosen, the hour, six o'clock. The Saint-

Gaudens field, the track for toboggans in winter, was a green fairway in summer forming a natural amphitheater. Huge pines edged the field with a screen of green leaves behind them where hardwood grew low, along the banks of a ravine. The westering sun gave a perfect light upon this living backdrop.

The river road was full of rolling carriages as soon as the four o'clock train came in. Before the play began, "some hundreds of guests" had assembled to see *The Masque of the Hours*. Surprise and delight came within moments because Arthur Whiting, who grew up in Cornish and was now a noted composer and concert director, had brought members of the Boston Symphony Orchestra to play the music he had composed for the occasion. The musicians were "hidden," but there was no hiding the quality of the music.

After the overture, Iris appeared, dressed in flowing robes of "muted rainbow shades." She carried a staff made from Iris flowers from one of the famous Cornish gardens and she said that Jove had summoned her. She proceeded with lines written by Percy MacKaye.

Next came an unveiling. Green curtains parted to disclose a Roman altar within columns supporting a roof. It was designed by Henry Hering with advice of the architect, Charles A. Platt, and executed in wood painted white to represent marble. Festoons of laurel and flowers swung from column to Ionic column under the entablature.

Miss Grimes said that Louis Shipman, playwright, told her that the colors for the masque would be "white and poypul," but the artists prevailed with a full palette. Pluto and his court wore black, purple and gold; Neptune with "flocks of Nereids" were all in sea-green and blue; Venus and her bodyguards dressed in "tender rose." Maud Howe Elliott was Pomona, goddess of fruit trees.

There was one comic figure — the Centaur. He was Maxfield Parrish, prancing along, the wonderful hind legs which he had contrived in his own workshop working beautifully. He was followed by "a rout of children." A plot of sorts held the masque together. Jupiter told the assembled gods and goddesses that he was going to abdicate. Pluto and Neptune contended for Jupiter's place until Minerva was called by Fame to choose a new ruler for Olympus.

Minerva struck the altar with her spear, whereupon smoke and colored fire burst forth. A sybil arose, "holding aloft a golden bowl." (She was Alice Kennedy, a tall handsome girl from Windsor.) Minerva took the bowl and drew out a name. The name was Saint-Gaudens.

Percy Mackay as Hermes

Mrs. Percy Mackay as Juno

Miss Hazel Mackay as a nymph

(Saint-Gaudens National Historic Site)

Now a white Roman chariot was drawn out "from concealing pine boughs." Saint-Gaudens was crowned with laurels, told to get into the chariot along with Augusta and they were drawn in triumph up across the meadow, to the house — the whole cast having harnessed themselves to the chariot.[3]

Augusta, shouting without realizing it because of her deafness, warned her husband about the chariot. "Be careful, Gus. The paint is still wet!" she said. No one in Cornish ever forgot this unexpected curtain line.

25

GOLD EAGLE

"THE older I grow the more things I see to enjoy and the more my youth seems good to remember," Saint-Gaudens wrote to his friend Alfred Garnier. "But I don't regret the march of years . . . and I have found new strength in the air at daybreak."

Gus was at work on a plaque commemorating the Cornish fête. Two feet high, in low relief, it was one of the prettiest things he had ever done. He used Hering's temple for the center of the design, beside it a young god, naked, with handsome feathered wings and classic lyre. This time, no one was going to object to an undraped figure. Flames curled up from the altar which bore the words "Amor Vincit." Pine trees, two masks and stylized folds to represent a stage curtain framed the rectangular design. Above and at the base, lettering formed part of the design. The plaque carried the names of all who took part in the masque, beginning with Carolyn Cox and Mabel Churchill and ending with Arthur Whiting. Across the base in larger letters ran the words, "In affectionate remembrance . . . Augusta and Augustus Saint-Gaudens." Reduced to three inches in height, a copy of this plaque went to everyone whose name was on it — to become a cherished heirloom in all the families of the Cornish colony.

After this plaque was finished, Gus began sketching eagles with a sharp pointed instrument on circular tablets of clay. Then he summoned friends for one of those typical conferences among Cornish artists, lined up all his sketches and this informal jury decided which sketch was best; whereupon he changed all the sketches and chose his own favorite. Communications from the White House appeared with regularity in the Windsor post office. Theodore Roosevelt was becoming more and more interested in a Saint-Gaudens coinage.

On November 11, 1905, Gus replied to the President. You have hit the nail on the head . . . of course the great coins (you might almost

say the only coins) are the Greek. . . . Nothing would please me
more than to make an attempt in the direction of the heads of Alexander but the authorities on modern monetary requirements would, I
fear, throw fits. . . .

"Up to the present I have done no work on the actual models for the
coins but have made sketches and the matter is constantly in my mind.
I have about determined on the composition of one side which would
contain an eagle very much like the one I placed on your medal. . . .
On the other side some kind of (possibly winged) figure of Liberty,
striding energetically forward as if on a mountain top, holding aloft on
one arm a shield bearing the stars and stripes with the word Liberty
marked across the field; in the other hand perhaps a flaming torch, the
drapery would be flowing in the breeze. My idea is to make it a living
thing and typical of progress."

Saint-Gaudens discovered soon that there were a series of singularly
frustrating laws concerning what might and might not appear on
United States coinage. "I remember you spoke of the head of an
Indian," he reminded Theodore Roosevelt. "Of course that is always a
superb thing to do, but would it be a sufficiently clear emblem of
Liberty as required by law?"

On November 22, Gus told President Roosevelt that he had been at
work on the coins and was "feeling enthusiastic. . . . I can perfectly
well use the Indian head-dress on the figure of Liberty. It should be
very handsome," he said in reply to the President's most recent letter.

Gus knew just the genuine Indian warbonnet that he wanted for a
model. It had been used by Adolph Weinman, a former pupil, so he
wrote, asking to borrow it. Weinman said that Solon Borglum actually
owned the chief's headdress and was delighted to have Weinman send
it to Cornish — and how about "other parts of the Indian costume?"
But Gus and Theodore Roosevelt had decided that Liberty was going
to wear her Greek dress with that Indian warbonnet. Weinman also
sent photographs of eagles.

During the previous two or three years, Saint-Gaudens had made
frequent trips to Washington, D.C., and according to his brother
Louis, "he enjoys the youthful enthusiasm his wife shows for the gay
life he has introduced her to in Washington where she goes to great
dinners and balls every night." This was decidedly an exaggeration as
to their going out every night, but Gussie had an "old rose satin dress"
made to "wear at the White House" and a "black lace over white" to

wear at "a White House garden party." It was still hard for her not to be self-conscious because she was deaf, but it helped to have handsome clothes and to see the approval in her husband's eyes.

Saint-Gaudens was constantly besieged by people wanting him to accept commissions these days. He refused most of them, but when McKim asked him to help raise money for the American Academy in Rome, he wrote begging letters, much as he hated the chore. Mrs. Jack Gardner, who was on his list in 1905, replied, referring to a recent hassle of hers with customs officials. "I paid duty on every work of art except 27. . . . Then suddenly the U.S. Government — *suddenly* last Autumn, demanded $200,000 duty on those 27 consignments. I did not have the money so I had to borrow, to mortgage my Beacon Street house. . . .

"Because I could not afford to pay the interest on the mortgage on my house I had to sell the house at the worst time for selling! I have done, at great sacrifice and cost and single-handed for America what no school in Rome could ever do. I am quite happy to have done it. But please realize that I haven't as much as the income from $100,000 to live on. It does seem funny to be spoken of on the same list as Morgan and Vanderbilt whose daily income is much more than my capital. A joke isn't it.

"When you pass through Boston please stop here. If my pictures could bring you, that would be another reason for their existence."

It was a far longer letter than Mrs. Gardner usually wrote and her last paragraph was more gracious than many that other people had received. But after the letter was mailed, Mrs. Jack might have thought she had been a little harsh toward a friend whom she had known for more than ten years. She must have heard that Saint-Gaudens' temper, when aroused, could be as formidable as her own. His answer surprised her and she wrote, "I care so much for you, dear Mr. Saint-Gaudens, that I want to thank you for your kind, triste note received just now. The other one, the one about the Roman School, didn't annoy me in the least — it only seemed very funny — for me to be asked for money.

"Shall I ever see you again?"

Of course Gus saw Mrs. Jack again, but he had much better luck with what McKim called his "hundred thousand dollar letter" to Henry Clay Frick, who made a hundred-thousand-dollar reply, thereby becoming a founder of the American Academy in Rome.

Saint-Gaudens was completing sketches for the memorial to James McNeill Whistler which Charles Freer of Detroit was giving to West Point. It was Whistler who awakened Mr. Freer's interest in Oriental art, of which he was now a collector, and Gus and Freer had become good friends in Paris. "I have made some quite elaborate designs, but finally reduced it down to the simplest form possible . . . ," Gus told Mr. Freer. "I want to get it as chaste and distinguished . . . and as much like what Mr. Whistler himself would have liked."

It was during his last visit to Paris that Gus found out what Whistler liked. "At dusk, on his way home from work, Whistler would come to my studio," Gus said. "And in my studio he would sit and chat in his extraordinary, witty fashion. . . . At times, he, MacMonnies and I . . . dined at Foyot's, opposite the Luxembourg. . . . We formed a strange, lantern-jawed trio . . . he dark, MacMonnies blond and curly and I red, where time had left the original color." Whistler had a studio "at the top of a long flight of stairs," was reluctant to show his paintings which "were piled in stacks against the wall."

The *Whistler Memorial* went well — Stanford White was designing the architectural mounting for it. Gus wrote cheerful letters to friends and only Augusta's anxious notes to Homer spoke of what Gus called "pull-backs" — periods when he suffered intense pain. Gussie saw a doctor in New York to whom she described her husband's symptoms. "Any return of the old trouble for which Dr. Harrington operated seems unlikely," this doctor wrote — without seeing the patient.

And then on the 7th of March, 1906, Augusta wrote to Homer. "We are to leave, D.V. at 3:00 P.M. today and tomorrow I suppose your father will go to Corey Hill Hospital in Brookline. . . . He has had no fever for three days but great pain again last night so that he had to have morphine as well as codeine." On March 13, the second operation for cancer was over. It had been drastic, and Dr. Richardson said the tumor would return in five or six years while Dr. Harrington said it would return "much sooner." Both doctors agreed that further surgery would be useless.

"I am now getting my courage together to tell your father, on every occasion and looking as happy as possible, that they found no return of the tumor and to lie about it with an honest face and to live up to that lie," Augusta wrote. Touchingly she added, "He wants to hold my hand!"

About three weeks after the operation, "Your father wandered about

the halls on his own feet yesterday, disdaining the wheelchair . . . ,"
Augusta said. "This afternoon a stenographer is coming and he is
going to start on his autobiography." As he had said to Garnier, Saint-
Gaudens found his youth good to remember. He told of his boyhood
in New York with humor, remembering the small-town atmosphere
long since swallowed up in big-city life. It never occurred to him to
feel sorry for himself because of his brief schooling and family's lack of
means.

By April 10, Saint-Gaudens was back in Cornish, "doing a lot of
dictating to the talking machine but so far it hasn't the good style of
his dictation to his stenographer," Gussie thought. "Austen finds he can
typewrite from the machine." The end of the month saw Saint-Gaudens in his studio again, writing his usual optimistic letters to clients.

The largest contract was with J. J. Albright of Buffalo, who wanted a
Porch of the Maidens in Saint-Gaudens style for the Albright Gallery
that he was building in his hometown. The total sum due to be paid
was $84,000. There were to be eight caryatids, two of them "original
models," for each of which Mr. Albright would pay $25,000. The other
six maidens were to "contain modifications in some detail of dress or
accessories" and would be worth $3000 each. Material was to be "Ver-
mont, Italian or Tennessee marble." The cost of cutting the marble for
the eight pieces would be whatever the marble cutters should charge,
but it was estimated at $2000 for each piece.[1]

"I have been back about four weeks from an ugly time at the hos-
pital and am beginning to work, thank Heaven; also to play golf, thank
Heaven again," Saint-Gaudens wrote Mr. Albright. He suggested that
Albright come to Cornish for a consultation, "the sooner the better."
But Albright went fishing.

In May, 1906, Stanford White proposed coming to Cornish with
McKim. "As to your visit here — for God's sake, I have been trying to
get you up here for twenty years and no sign of you and Charles," Gus
wrote. "And now that we are having the worst spring that ever occurred (the roads are in awful condition) you want to come up in five
minutes. Now you hold off for a little while and I will let you know,
perhaps in a couple of weeks from now. But, come to think of it, our
friend Ethel Barrymore is coming up here.[2] Perhaps that's the reason
you old suckers want to come up now. . . ."

To which White replied, "Beloved!! Why do you explode so at the
idea . . . if you think our desire came from any wish to see any

damned fine spring or fine roads, you are not only mistaken but one of the most modest and unassuming men with so 'beetly' a brow and so large a nose, 'wot is.' We are coming up to bow down before the sage and seer we admire and venerate so. Weather be damned and roads too! If you have a side show anything like Ethel Barrymore, that will be sweet incense at the altar and we will bow down all the more. . . ."

The two old friends never made their visit. In June, Saint-Gaudens had another attack of pain and went to New York for a course of X-ray treatments to continue for several weeks. He stayed at the Players' Club as usual and fellow members saw that he had been severely ill and had not really recovered. On the morning of June 26, 1906, people at the Players' would have given anything to be able to keep Saint-Gaudens from seeing the newspapers.

He had to know, of course. Newsboys were shouting at street corners. "Stanford White murdered! Read all about it!"

Mrs. White had been at their summer home on Long Island. Their son, Larry, and a friend of his from Harvard were in New York and White took them to dinner at the Café Martin. After dinner they drove to the Amsterdam Theater where the boys got out. There was a new show opening that Monday night at the Madison Square Garden roof, called *Mamzelle Champagne*. White got there at 10:55, just after intermission, and took a table down front at the left. The Garden caterer came by to talk with him, then left. White was alone.

This was one of the things that must have shocked Saint-Gaudens. White, the exuberant, the man always surrounded by a crowd of friends, was alone when Harry K. Thaw walked up behind him and fired three shots at close range.

The newspapers reveled in the story. Harry K. Thaw, member of a well-known and wealthy Pittsburgh family, was the outraged husband whose wife had been seduced, was the way they told it at first. They also said that Florence Evelyn Nesbit had lived with Thaw for a year before she and Thaw were married, but she was twenty-one and beautiful. White was fifty-two. He had helped Evelyn get into the Flora Dora dancing sextette and the papers assumed that White had exacted payment both before and after her marriage — no one bothered to bring up the point that Evelyn might have been extremely generous by nature.[3]

Richard Harding Davis, in an article for *Collier's* for August, made a fine statement in defense of White. "One who is permitted to write a few true words about a man who never spoke an unkind one, resents the fact that before he can tell what Stanford White was, he must first tell what Stanford White was not but, owing to the manner of his death and the conduct of certain newspapers, a preface is necessary. To the truth, which was sad enough, the untrue has been added. Within three days the awful charges fell to pieces of their own rotten- ness. . . . Why — if these charges were true, — were they made only after White's murder? Fortunately, testimony to their falseness comes not only from those who knew and liked White, but also from the witnesses called against him, by the yellow press and by the creature who murdered him. The private detectives who for two years were hired to spy upon his every movement were unable to obtain one item of evidence against him. . . ."

It was hard for Saint-Gaudens to imagine life without Stanford White. They had been associated since the days of the *Farragut* and before. His drawings for the *Whistler Memorial* made his loss the more poignant and for a while Gus could not bring himself to complete the bas-relief or work with any other architect. He wrote to Garnier, who had known White in Paris, referring to Thaw as "an idiot who has shot a man of great genius for a woman with the face of an angel and the heart of a snake."

Saint-Gaudens was still in New York on June 28 when he replied to a letter from Theodore Roosevelt, asking about the coinage. The beautiful Alice Butler had been summoned from across the Connecti- cut at Windsor. Hers was the head of Liberty in profile, wearing the Indian warbonnet. "The eagle side of the gold piece is finished and is undergoing innumerable experiments with reduction. . . .

"Now I am attacking the cent. It may interest you to know that on the 'Liberty' side of the cent I am using a flying eagle; a modification of the device which was used on the cent of 1857. I had not seen that coin for many years and was so impressed by it that I thought if carried out with some modifications, nothing better could be done. It is by all odds the best design on any American coin." Saint-Gaudens had dies made in Paris that would reproduce a coin as clearly modeled as a portrait bas-relief, and sent them to Washington.

"These models are simply immense — if such a slang way of talking is permissible in reference to giving a modern nation one coinage at least which shall be as good as that of the ancient Greeks," President Roosevelt wrote. "I have instructed the Director of the Mint that these

The head of Liberty, posed for by Miss Alice Butler (Saint-Gaudens National Historic Site)

dies are to be reproduced just as quickly as possible and just as they are. It is simply splendid. I suppose I shall be impeached for it in Congress but I shall regard that as a very cheap payment."

Of course the matter did not proceed as promptly as Theodore Roosevelt assumed it would. The people at the mint said that the Paris-made dies would not strike a coin with one blow but required two blows. Moreover, the relief was too high — the coins would not stack properly. Roosevelt asked Saint-Gaudens to come to Washington for a conference.

"Evidently it is not a trifling matter to make Greek Art conform with modern numismatics," Gus replied. It would not be too difficult, however, to lower the handsome high relief and still have a beautiful coin, and another die could be made. The President had chosen the full figure of Liberty carrying an olive branch for the twenty-dollar gold piece with, on the other side, an eagle flying.

But as to going to Washington, "I am extremely sorry that it will be wholly impossible for me to leave Windsor at present," Saint-Gaudens wrote. He did not mention that attacks of severe pain had returned and that his strength was ebbing. But in May, when Augusta took a short trip to Richmond, Virginia, for a rest, she summoned Barry Faulkner to come to stay with her husband because Gus could not stay alone.[4] She was unaware that she had offended Barry, and he was the sort of person to forgive willingly.

When he was well enough, they carried Saint-Gaudens out to the studio nearest the house where he lay on a couch on the terrace — the leaves of the wild grapevine overhead not yet big enough for shade. He had had a plaster cast of the Parthenon frieze set into the outside wall of the studio, which he wanted Barry to paint in colors. Archeological discoveries in Athens had revealed that much of the Greek sculpture had been painted and Gus enjoyed watching Barry Faulkner's efforts up on top of a stepladder. They tried blue for a background. "It was rather gay and pretty," Barry said. "The Saint liked bright colors, blazing colors."[5]

Barry told how Augusta had made a place for her husband to lie in the sun on the porch roof when he felt too weak to go any farther and how his room on the northwest corner of the house was the best room in the house — connecting with hers, with a bath between. While Barry was at "Aspet" they had music in the evening, Miss Grimes at the piano.

After her short vacation, Augusta rarely left her husband for more than a night at a time. She went to New York or to Boston for two purposes — first, to interview some new doctor in the hope of finding a miraculous cure for cancer, and second, to try to raise money.

A letter to Charles Freer[6] tells the story of both problems facing Gussie. "Mr. Saint-Gaudens will not be able to see you or anyone for some time to come," she wrote. "I am going to tell you the situation as I think, on account of your friendship for my husband, you may be able to help in this emergency. . . ." Augusta spoke of the cancer operation of "more than six years ago." Mr. Freer would know what fine work Saint-Gaudens had produced "in the interval and in spite of acute pain." Then Augusta confided the hope that was in her heart. "Three months ago, the surgeons told me there was a recurrence of the trouble. . . . As a last resort, the Trypsin cure of Dr. Beard of Edinboro was suggested. We had a physician come to be here constantly. . . . Apparently a miracle has happened for the tumor has nearly disappeared. What remains is presumably dead and it looks as if he were on the road to recovery but his nervous system is a wreck and can only be saved by the greatest care. . . ."

It was essential to keep Saint-Gaudens free from financial anxiety, Augusta explained. "Meanwhile, I cannot stop the studio expenses which amount to about $1000 a week. . . . The statues in various stages" could not be completed without a corps of assistants.

"I find myself confronted with an almost overwhelming financial problem. . . ." Saint-Gaudens had "put by only a few thousand dollars which will last but a short time." So Gussie had borrowed money "of the Fifth Avenue Bank at 6% interest," but "before long I shall not have the proper security to give them. As a friend and a business man, you can advise me what to do.

"This place with two studios and stables is willed to me," Augusta continued. She could offer them as security but could not get a mortgage on them without her husband's knowledge — "and he must know nothing of the present financial situation; must know nothing of studio affairs and yet, should he be well enough to get to the studio he must find people and things going on as usual. . . .

"Dear Mr. Freer, I cannot tell you why, but I feel that if we can bridge over the next six months or a year . . . and when he is able . . . to go to some place where the change is great so that he can perhaps forget for a time the agony he has undergone . . . ," the new treatment would bring about a cure. Gussie could not cease to believe that her husband could come back to finish the work he longed to do.

"But that interval will be expensive and yet *he* must not know it and I must ask you to realize how entirely confidential this whole letter is. I do not know you well. . . . It is useless to apologize for what I have done, for I have done it. I hope you will understand why and for whom I have been so bold."

Freer arranged for Gussie to draw funds on a Detroit bank up to $32,000. With this money, Augusta could borrow day-to-day cash for the studio expenses. Louis Saint-Gaudens, working elsewhere on commissions his brother had gotten for him, wrote, "I have slathers of money and would like to pay that note of mine of August 15, 1905, for fifteen hundred dollars which Gus lent me. Do you think you could get it for me without speaking to Gus about it? I would rather you didn't mention it to him and I would feel proud to pay some of my indebtedness."

Photographs of the small clay version of "the McMillan Monument" which Mr. Freer had commissioned were sent to him. He was planning a long trip to Egypt, Java and Ceylon, but before leaving he posted forty bonds of the New York Central and Hudson River Railroad Company, par value, forty thousand dollars, for Augusta to draw on. Freer kept an option to buy the bonds back from the bank at their purchase price plus five percent interest, within twelve months.

"I shall of course avail myself as little as possible of your generosity," Augusta told Mr. Freer. She said she thought she could see her way clear "at least until the middle of November."

Alice Butler posed for the Boston Public Library figures, drapery intended to be Greek slipping off one of her handsome shoulders. The "new" Boston Public Library was already twelve years old.

Louis Saint-Gaudens, after quarreling with the Library Committee and threatening to tear up his contract, had long since finished the two huge marble lions for the foot of the grand staircase. They were the most noble, most benign of beasts. McKim had haunted Corlears Hook, where the marble from Italy was brought in for ballast and landed. He was looking for a certain golden-yellow stone called Monte Riete, or Convent Siena, from a quarry owned by a religious order who only had a block or two taken out by primitive methods when the convent needed money. McKim got hold of all the Convent Sienna

Miss Alice Butler posing as Art (Saint-Gaudens National Historic Site)

that was brought into New York during the building of the library, arranged the slabs so that the darkest in color were set at the bottom of the staircase, the color gradually lighter in tone as the walls rose. In all, four hundred tons of marble were required. The effect would have satisfied a prince of the Renaissance, but McKim's job was over and he had been glad to turn to projects in Washington, D.C. — and to white marble mined in Vermont. Saint-Gaudens worked on the clay models of the library groups whenever he had strength — which was not often.

Henry Hering had been to Washington and settled the matter of the coinage. During the summer of 1906 he was not in Cornish, but he returned during the winter of 1906–1907. He wrote to Barry Faulkner, to tell him how things were going.[7]

"When I was here in the winter, the Saint so shocked me the first time I saw him that I'm afraid he noticed. But I saw him every day and grew used to his gaunt face . . . and his look of being hunted by death and knowing it, but turning at bay with sheer will and self-creation. When they could carry him out to the studios and place him in front of his work, the dejection, the grim unhappy will, the constant looking over his shoulder so to speak, as if death were there, would vanish in an illumination of beauty; his eyes would burn again in the moment's victory. . . ."

There had been "progress in the studio" when Hering first returned. "The *Lincoln* and the *Hanna* had been sent away; the *Phillips Brooks* practically completed." There was "a change in Christ's face from the dead but risen Presence, to a helpful, human, loving presence – no longer the divinely dead God, but a humanly live man, an altering attributive I think, to the sculptor's losing his hold on outside help of any kind. . . ." Hering much preferred the "divinely dead presence," and the statue itself suggests that this first model may have been used instead of Saint-Gaudens' second one.

"The Caryatids for the Albright Gallery in Buffalo" were being enlarged as Saint-Gaudens conceived them, "great noble creatures bearing a sense of the calm of the Arts in their superiority to life," according to Henry Hering.

"But in spite of all this evidence of accomplishment," Hering said that when he returned to Cornish in the late autumn he found Saint-Gaudens "with a look in his face that told me at once of his being near death.

Formal photograph of Saint-Gaudens by DeWitt C. Ward, 1905 (Courtesy of the Board of Trustees of Dartmouth College)

"From the first week that I was here, I had supper with him every night. Strange meals they were — Mrs. St.G. (whose devotion has been very true and beautiful), the nurse and I! He wanted us to talk and let him listen; now and then he would ask that we talk louder so that Mrs. [Saint-Gaudens] might hear, though it was harder than usual with her; for, poor lady, she said almost nothing, sitting there with the love of her youth."

Saint-Gaudens modeled his last portrait bas-relief. It was Augusta, holding in one hand the "golden bowl" presented by the Cornish colony. She had the faint trace of a smile, a suggestion of the dimple which had so pleased Augustus when he first saw her. Her lips were closed with all the firmness of her character, however. She looked like the perfect housewife, carrying flowers she had just arranged to place them just so in the exact spot of her choice. It was a lovable face, nonetheless. There had been storms enough to shipwreck an ordinary marriage, but Gus and Gussie had come through and this was a portrait of a woman made by a man who loved her.

On July 28, Saint-Gaudens lay on a couch on the terrace at "Aspet," watching the sunset with Henry Hering. There was a "great stormy surge of clouds over Ascutney that gave way at their base to a low level of orange light — chaos pacified," Hering wrote. Saint-Gaudens spoke of wanting to go away to a remote place.

Four days later, Saint-Gaudens sank into a coma. He died on Saturday, August 3, 1907, at ten minutes of seven in the evening.

26

AUGUSTA

AUGUSTA, whose health had always been considered precarious, had nineteen more years to live after the death of her husband. To a great extent, she devoted these years to his memory.

The first problem confronting her was the completion of unfinished work so that she could pay her debts. Charles Brewster, her friend as well as her lawyer, coached her in his letters, regarding patience and tact. He also made suggestions concerning her own letter-writing. "It would be a help in filing your business letters if each refers to one subject," he remarked a trifle plaintively, " — or at least put a catch word at the beginning of a paragraph referring to a new subject." This, poor Gussie could never do and besides, separate letters would have required extra two-cent stamps.

Augusta's letter to the Phillips Brooks Memorial Committee "probably has driven them almost to veronal to quiet their minds," Brewster told Augusta and she wisely left negotiations concerning the Boston Public Library groups entirely to her lawyer. The contract between the city of Boston and Augustus Saint-Gaudens had been dated November 30, 1892; the "two groups of statuary" on "two large pedestals on the platform in front of the Copley Square entrance" to be completed within two years. Fifteen years had gone by.

In 1905, the trustees had threatened to cancel the library contract, but Saint-Gaudens talked them out of it. During that year and the next, he pushed the groups forward to the point where models were "completed in clay" and (according to the contract) could be finished "by such persons as shall be designated by McKim, Mead and White," should the sculptor "die or be incapacitated." Not being able to take out additional life insurance, as the city of Boston required, Saint-Gaudens put up two shares of Calumet and Hecla stock to cover advance payments.

One of the groups, "Science, Labor and Music," was developed in clay in half-size during February and August of 1907 — the other had already reached this stage. Augusta now wanted Henry Hering to finish the groups, but he asked more for the job than Brewster said she could afford. Mr. Mead, of McKim, Mead and White, appointed Louis Saint-Gaudens to supervise the finishing of the project.

But now the Boston committee began to delay decisions and to withhold payments. They had to "lay the whole matter before the entire committee" and one member was abroad. Gradually, Augusta began to realize that the city of Boston had no intention of accepting the Saint-Gaudens groups. They took the ground that Saint-Gaudens himself had not actually finished them.

Charles Brewster presented an excellent case to the effect that the contract would be fulfilled. He came up against a stone wall and the reason may have been that the Saint-Gaudens groups were partially undraped. Certainly one undraped statue had already been taken out of the library.

In 1890, Charles McKim had presented the Boston Public Library with a gay fountain figure by MacMonnies.[1] It had been shown at the Paris Salon and a copy of it bought by the Luxembourg Museum. Set up in Boston in the inner courtyard of the library in 1896, the fountain figure was that of a young girl holding aloft a bunch of grapes and carrying a child on her arm. Surely it was harmless enough. The fountain would spout water, not wine, and children were allowed to eat grapes. But there were two things wrong. The girl hadn't any clothes on and the name of the statue was *Bacchante*.

Artistic Boston, represented by Edward Robinson, Director of the Museum of Fine Arts, for example, liked the fountain and found it in keeping with the Renaissance style of the building. The City Art Commission accepted it. Then came public protest, with Charles W. Eliot among the leaders of the opposition. "Considering what might stand in the courtyard, a Pallas, for example, or a Juno or a Mercury or a Nike — the setting up there of a naked woman, presumably engaged in a drunken revel, seems to me distinctly impudent . . . ," he wrote.

Newspapers, seeing a chance for copy, sent writers to the dictionaries; "Bacchante . . . a woman addicted to intemperance and riotous revelry," they quoted. A committee of clergymen said they were not opposed "to the nude in art" but that the MacMonnies fountain was "in effect a glorification of the sensual," making "lewdness beautiful."

The controversy raged until McKim withdrew his gift which he had intended as a memorial to his late wife! Always magnanimous, McKim said that Boston was not to blame for rejecting the fountain — only a bunch of "long-haired men and short-haired women."[2]

The Saint-Gaudens figures were anything but "sensual" or "lewd" — they were serious. Labor was "represented by a stalwart rugged male figure . . . a modern Vulcan." But he was nude under his leather apron. Art was a "thoughtful, graceful, reposeful yet quietly awake female figure," but her "long and loosely draped robe" did not entirely cover her. Justice was a thoroughly clothed female, but it would seem that Music and Art were just too incompletely draped for the library committee to take a chance on — after the Bacchante scandal.

Charles Brewster succeeded in convincing the lawyer for the city of Boston that Mrs. Saint-Gaudens was fully entitled to all the money her husband had been paid and that the city had no claim against her. Bela Pratt produced two heroic-sized female figures for that "platform" in front of the library. They were heavily draped from head to foot, as though sheltering themselves from an east wind.

Charles Freer paid $20,000 for the Saint-Gaudens Boston Library Groups in advanced sketch form, rendered in bronze. He had acquired a collector's item for his art gallery in Washington, D.C.

The Brooks statue had been "completed in clay" and was now to be enlarged, Augusta told her lawyer in 1907. The figure of Christ, in the early French Gothic manner, was strangely out of key with the very human portrait of Bishop Brooks, but the *Christ* is reminiscent of the *Adams Memorial* in that it means different things to different people. To some, the austere figure seems to judge and admonish an over-worldly prelate. One old woman, however, after studying the statue for a long time, spoke to a kindly-looking gentleman who was also looking at it.

"Who is that man behind our good Bishop?" the woman asked.

"That is the figure of Christ," she was told.

"*Well!*" she exclaimed indignantly — "It don't look like him!"[3]

In a letter to Charles Brewster, Augusta listed eight works as in process of completion within a few weeks of her husband's death. Next to the Boston Library Groups, the Albright caryatids would be the most difficult for her to negotiate. "Three principal models" were "finished in plaster, two more well along and only one more to do." Albright paid money due to "Mrs. Augusta Saint-Gaudens, Executrix," (as Brewster instructed Gussie to sign her letters,) and he finally agreed to let Miss Grimes finish the maidens with help from James Earle Fraser.

Miss Grimes remained in the studio at "Aspet" for some time. "My affairs hang in the balance," she wrote Barry Faulkner. "I am bound by Mrs. Saint-Gaudens not to talk about plans as yet," and Frances told what it was like to work in the studio without "the Saint."

"I have returned to the Caryatids — no prisoner with a chain attached to his leg would go to his work with so tired a spirit. I want to feel nobly about them and remember that I am finishing them for Mr. Saint-Gaudens — but I am so mortally tired of them and that studio of his has become most horrible to me. I have never felt so about a place. No matter with what courage I start in the morning, just a step inside the door, and it is gone and I am cold inside and out.

"Mr. Saint-Gaudens is so entirely gone. The little physical tokens of his interests and likes are gone. Mrs. Saint-Gaudens rules all — Homer is less and less in power each day. We all bow before her, she controls every nook and cranny — the whole place is like her house — clean, orderly and desolate. She suffers most but does not know why."

At first, Augusta had hoped that Homer could run the bronze-replica business and attend to financial affairs for her. But she was forced to conclude that the Homer family's business acumen had not been handed down to her son. He had jobs with newspapers and magazines, had written short stories and attempted a play. For fourteen seasons (except for the interval of the First World War) he would be with Maude Adams as assistant stage manager. To put it in his own words, he was "a very poor actor" and "producer of her final play." Homer also said that he "had the handling of the practical side" of his father's studio in Cornish, but here he was borrowing his mother's laurels, at least during her lifetime. In 1923 he became Director of the Fine Arts Department at Carnegie Institute, Pittsburgh.[4]

As soon as the enlarging, casting and delivering of work by Saint-Gaudens was done, Augusta turned to the project close to her heart — that of seeing her husband's work properly displayed and appreciated. She had always reproached him for being too modest. The thing to do now was to have a memorial exhibition in the Metropolitan Museum of Art in New York — that city he had claimed as his own.

Miss Grimes told about it. "You would be interested to see what a personage Mrs. Saint-Gaudens has become — a large, somber figure —

she looms up in front of the artistic world of this country like some already historic woman — black-clad and potent.

"There is to be a huge exhibition of Mr. Saint-Gaudens' work . . . there are to be casts of the *Lincoln,* the *Adams Monument* — perhaps the Caryatids — the *Farragut* and many others. She is saying what they can have and in what form. She is like some Fate Mr. Saint-Gaudens himself might have set in motion, striding along, carrying his laurels."

The exhibition was opened on the last day of February, 1908, with a memorial service for Saint-Gaudens at Mendelssohn Hall. The mayor of New York spoke in praise of the sculptor instead of in praise of himself and donors. There was music, but not by brass bands. A quartet played music most often chosen by Saint-Gaudens for his studio concerts — the Schubert Quartet in D minor; Bach's Air from the Suite in D and Beethoven's Quartet in F major, opus 59. Artists were there, the famous and the unknown, friends who were celebrities came, and people to whom Saint-Gaudens had been generous in their time of need. Reporters filled columns; art critics prepared books — and Augusta guarded her husband's laurels.

Augusta instructed Charles Brewster to buy Saint-Gaudens gold coins for her. Very shortly, however, he could find "but three more" twenty-dollar gold pieces and warned her that there was "a premium of $10 on the double eagle." This time Augusta was not asking for advice; she told him to buy all he could, especially the high-relief examples. In 1968 the extra high-relief double eagle would probably sell for about $20,000 and the $10 wire edge[5] with periods before and after the legends for about $2000. Augusta gave her coins to members of her family, most probably sold some as the price increased — and saved one for display at "Aspet."

The idea of "Aspet" as a permanent memorial to Saint-Gaudens was uppermost in Augusta's mind as the years went by. She and her husband had once visualized years of living there together surrounded by young people; their son and his family; Louis, Nettie and their boy. But the plans of parents have a poor chance of pleasing succeeding generations. Homer and Carlota did not like the country and Louis could stand Augusta's rule for only a short time before heading west and then far west. The thing to do, Augusta realized, would be to establish a fund with trustees to administer it and hold the Cornish property.

Homer and Carlota were allowed to take certain items from the house as keepsakes or family heirlooms, but Augusta told them not to take too much. Homer therefore chose Sargent's portrait of himself and his mother, taking it down from the wall over the dining-room fireplace and substituting one of the copies of the *Beatrice Cenci* which his mother had painted in Rome. Neither Homer nor Carlota cared anything about the paintings Augusta had made of the Paris apartment where she had been happy as a bride, so these remained to prove that she could paint — in a style well liked by her generation. Homer liked tapestries and carried off two but had little use for American antique furniture so that a handsome highboy remained in the front hall.

Augusta tried to make the Saint-Gaudens studio attractive to visitors by having Frances Grimes at work there, modeling something. This, however, Miss Grimes would not stand for. She was perhaps the only assistant who even dimly understood Augusta, but she was not going to be a sideshow. She went to Buffalo to work on the Albright caryatids, but seven years went by before she got the three thousand dollars she was promised by the Albright people and then this included "Mr. Fraser's compensation" which she had to pay. Eventually, she had her own studio in New York, designed an overmantel for the Washington Irving High School in New York City and received various prizes in sculpture.

Fraser modeled the buffalo nickel for the mint and did the equestrian statue of Theodore Roosevelt to stand in front of the Museum of Natural History in New York. Henry Hering had a New York studio in which he successfully modeled portraits. He married Elsie Ward, who gave up her art, but some of her sculptures were better than his.

There was one more project on Augusta's mind, after the studios were emptied of work and workmen. She had the beautiful little temple made at the time of the masque reproduced in Vermont marble to become a Saint-Gaudens funeral monument. Her husband had been buried in Ascutney Cemetery, Windsor, but she brought his ashes here, arranged for her own to be placed beside his — and carefully mentioned in her will exactly which members of the family would eventually be entitled to rest there and have their names inscribed on the base of the altar.

And as soon as she felt safe financially, Augusta bought herself a black Pierce-Arrow limousine. It was driven by Donovan, her

Augusta Saint-Gaudens in her Pierce-Arrow
(Courtesy of the Board of Trustees of Dartmouth College)

Augusta Saint-Gaudens in her Florida home after her husband's death
(Courtesy of the Board of Trustees of Dartmouth College)

chauffeur, with whom she communicated by a speaking-tube from the back seat behind glass. When she invited her Cornish friends to ride with her, she was apt to suggest that they walk partway to meet her — in case their own driveway should be too rough for the car. She never drove for mere pleasure but always on an errand of some sort as an excuse for causing wear and tear on this impressive vehicle. Some of her guests found this unflattering.

Augusta built a house in or near Cocoanut Grove, Florida, in which to spend her winters. It was well designed for both sun and shade, with deep verandas and wide windows to catch a breeze; rattan furniture looked cool and appropriate. A channel along the property provided anchorage for small boats belonging to Homer. It also provided a source of argument between Gussie and her neighbors as to charges for dredging.

During her later years, Augusta wrote and rewrote her will, adding codicils, then revoking them, but all to the effect that after Homer had had everything he wanted, there still must be "the Saint-Gaudens Memorial . . . incorporated by an act of Congress of the General Court of New Hampshire, approved by the Governor on February 26, 1919." She gave to the corporation of this Memorial, five thousand dollars for upkeep and repair. A "direct descendent of Augustus Saint-Gaudens" must always be one of the trustees — and should always have the right to use and occupy the homestead, the vegetable garden and flower garden and the service buildings. It was like Gussie not to forget the vegetable garden.

Perhaps, however, she recalled the behavior of some descendant, because the trustees could call a meeting and ask any descendant "selected for occupancy" to leave if "found unfit" or careless in "preservation" of house and contents, garden or grounds. A substitute descendant could be chosen or, if none were deemed "fit," a caretaker could be "designated." Gussie did not say anything about pay. But someone must have proposed an idea that seemed horrible to her, for she expressly decreed that the residence must never under any circumstances "be used as a school or a dormitory."

Through Homer, with Louis as intermediary, Augusta sent money to her husband's son by Davida. She could never bring herself to deal directly. The boy became a farmer in California, had a son whom Nettie met and she wrote of him that "he looked at me with his grandfather's eyes."

The Saint-Gaudens family Memorial at "Aspet" (Courtesy of the Board of Trustees of Dartmouth College)

To her grandson, Augustus Saint-Gaudens, Augusta bequeathed "his paternal grandfather's watch and chain." She also gave him "one embroidered table cloth which I made myself" and it is to be hoped that he appreciated it!

In one of the codicils to her will, Augusta withdrew from the Saint-Gaudens Memorial her gift of "the Marie Stuart cameo" which Gus had made for her in Rome and also "the cross of the Legion of Honor, the Gold Medal from the Pan-American Exposition, the Gold Medal from the American Society of Arts and Letters and the first strike of the Double Eagle." Homer wanted these things. This codicil was dated August 2, 1920.

Augusta was usually in Cornish every summer, keeping a stern eye on the Memorial. A woman from Windsor came over every day to work and was exasperated to find Mrs. Saint-Gaudens waiting for her — ready to remind her that she was late as usual. Admission to the Memorial was free for Cornish people, although everyone else had to pay a fee.

And now, as the years went by and Augusta finished her work in her husband's memory, her health began to fail. Augusta Homer Saint-Gaudens died at "Aspet" in 1926.

In 1965 the Saint-Gaudens Memorial became a National Historic Site. It is administered by the National Park Service in cooperation with the trustees of the Memorial — this last exactly as Augusta decreed. She would be delighted with the pride and affection the men of the Park Service bestow upon it — although of course if she were living she would never show appreciation lest it go to their heads. "Aspet" is open from May through October and it more than repays a long, thoughtful visit. There are concerts and exhibitions of contemporary art from time to time.

Such an extensive collection of the work of Augustus Saint-Gaudens can be seen nowhere else, but there is something that transcends bronze or marble. It is a sense of peace in a troubled world, a happy atmosphere of sun and shadow which is the sculptor's legacy.

ACKNOWLEDGMENTS

I WANT to express my gratitude to so many people in Cornish, New York and Boston that it is hard to know where to begin. Mr. John Dryfhout, Curator of what is now the Saint-Gaudens National Historic Site, has been of immense help in the research, and in his interest and enthusiasm for my project. He has an inquiring mind, boundless energy and the knack of digging out little-known facts which he made available to me. His associates, especially park historians Hugh Gurney and Ted McBurnett, were very helpful.

On my first visit to "Aspet," I was so much interested in the Saint-Gaudens house, studios and gardens that I asked if there were papers concerning the sculptor that I might see. I was told that everything of this sort had been given to the archives at Baker Library, Dartmouth College. My husband and I drove to Hanover, New Hampshire, only eighteen miles north of Cornish. Mr. Kenneth C. Cramer, Archivist of the Dartmouth College libraries, told me that the Saint-Gaudens papers had only recently been received and were not yet arranged and catalogued, although work was in progress. I want to express my deepest appreciation not only for permission to use these papers immediately, but for the extraordinary kindness of Mr. Cramer in finding temporary research facilities for us in the office of a professor on leave, and having box after box of material taken to this office. Mr. Edward Connery Lathem, Associate Librarian, Dartmouth College libraries, added his cordial permission and encouragement. Miss Dorothy Beck, Mr. Cramer's assistant, was unfailingly patient and helpful during the many weeks when I was working at Dartmouth. It was a pleasure to meet again Mrs. Charles Hazard, of the library staff, who had previously been so helpful in the matter of Henry James letters, and who again gave assistance. Photographs, snapshots and film were to be found among the mass of Saint-Gaudens material, and I want to thank

Mr. Adrian Bouchard, of the Dartmouth College Photographic Bureau, for taking such pains with what was often poor material. He performed miracles in providing photographs for my use and study as well as for illustrations.

Comprehensive though the Saint-Gaudens papers are, it would have been impossible for me to write this biography without the help of Mr. and Mrs. William Platt. Even before serious research began, my husband and I were invited to visit at the Platts' house, on the hillside above "Aspet," built in Saint-Gaudens' time by Charles Adams Platt, eminent artist and architect. Here we met Mr. and Mrs. William Platt, Mr. and Mrs. Charles A. Platt and Mrs. Philip Littell, Mrs. William Platt's mother. We spent an unforgettable afternoon while members of the Cornish colony came to share the hospitality of "High Court" and to talk of Saint-Gaudens. I saw one of the medallions in commemoration of the masque given by the colony to honor Saint-Gaudens, and many of the names on the plaque were those of guests — descendants of the original group.

I want to express especial gratitude to Miss Frances Arnold, to whom I am indebted for lively stories of Cornish young people. My husband and I were made to feel like old friends of hers. Mrs. Archibald Cox remembered Mrs. Saint-Gaudens, impressive in black, at Beaman dinner parties. Her home is in Windsor and she recalled seeing my friend Miss Alice Butler on the village street. Mrs. G. D'Arcy Edmondson found time to talk to us at her home, giving us insight into the Cornish colony days.

Mrs. Richard Crocker, a daughter of Joseph Homer, spoke a good word for her cousin, Homer Saint-Gaudens, a playmate older than she whom she admired. Mr. Richard Crocker told of early visits to the area and of his amusement when Windsor people talked of the artists "on the hill." I want to thank Mrs. Buckner Hollingsworth for giving me many interesting and important items out of her personal knowledge of "Aspet" and also as a result of her study for her book, *Augustus Saint-Gaudens,* in the "American Sculptors Series."

I deeply regret that my proposed call on Mr. Barry Faulkner of Keene, New Hampshire, came too late. He had been in good health and would have been happy to see me, Mr. Francis Faulkner told me — after his uncle's sudden death. Mr. Francis Faulkner himself was extremely helpful, showing me copies of some of his uncle's letters, the originals of which are now in Washington, D.C. He suggested that I call on his cousin, Miss Ellen Faulkner, who was most kind, talking of Chesham Lake days when Homer Saint-Gaudens came to see Carlota Dolley, his future wife. At Miss Faulkner's house I saw sketches by Barry Faulkner.

At station WKNE, Keene, New Hampshire, Mr. Joseph Close was most helpful in locating printed material and the Barry Faulkner tape recording concerning Saint-Gaudens.

Mrs. Harold Bowditch, the former Nancy Brush, most kindly gave me reminiscences of her childhood when her father, George de Forest Brush, and Saint-Gaudens were together in France and in Cornish. The late Dr. Harold Bowditch has long been of the utmost help to me in previous biographies. From his papers, Mrs. Bowditch sent me valuable material concerning the building of the Boston Public Library.

One of my own early memories is that of being taken by my father to see the Saint-Gaudens statue, known in Springfield, Massachusetts, as "Deacon Chapin." I want to thank Miss Catharine Chapin who talked with me about this "ninth great grandfather" of hers. Miss Chapin told me that the family was originally French Huguenot so that Chester W. Chapin, Saint-Gaudens' friend and early patron, had a French heritage in common with the sculptor. At the Springfield Public Library, Mrs. Dorothy Mozley assembled genealogies and firsthand accounts of the Deacon Chapin unveiling, so that the limited time at my disposal could be used to best advantage. This kind of help is rare and is something I greatly appreciate. At the Museum of Fine Arts in Springfield, Mrs. Sarah Morris kindly showed me records of work by Saint-Gaudens formerly at the museum. Mrs. Frank B. Gifford, of the Connecticut Valley Historical Museum, located photographs of a Chapin bust in plaster by Saint-Gaudens, formerly owned by this museum but destroyed by fire.

I would never have been able to write a true and sympathetic account of Augusta Homer Saint-Gaudens without the help of Mr. and Mrs. Sidney Homer. Mr. Homer's genealogical chart proved indispensable. Sisters, brothers and distant cousins all mentioned in Mrs. Saint-Gaudens' letters were to be found on the chart, their relationships made clear. He also gave me copies of highly useful documents and he lent me *My Wife and I*, the story of Madam Louise Homer and her composer husband — Mr. Homer's father. This was of especial value because of many references to Saint-Gaudens. Mr. Homer wrote to other members of the family in my behalf and Mrs. Homer sent me articles on Gramercy Park, containing references to the Saint-Gaudens shoemaker's shop. Still further illuminating the story of the Bostonian Augusta Saint-Gaudens, Mrs. Franz J. Inglefinger showed me family pictures and gave me the important information that manuscripts concerning the Homer family had recently been given to Radcliffe College.

Mr. and Mrs. Thomas J. Homer showed us examples of Saint-Gaudens' work in their home and found photographs for us of Augusta Saint-Gaudens' mother and of the house in Roxbury, thereby authenticating our picture, found at Dartmouth.

Saint-Gaudens was first of all a New Yorker. I want to thank Miss Rosamond Gilder, daughter of Richard Watson Gilder, not only for the use of letters but for help in re-creating the New York scene of Saint-Gaudens' day. Mrs. John D. Gordan assembled New York friends, among them Mrs. Peter Borie (a Beaman granddaughter), Mrs. William M. Evarts, Jr., Miss Louise Watson (also connected with the Evarts family), and Mrs. Walter W. Palmer, sister of Miss Gilder. I learned much concerning Charles C. Beaman and William M. Evarts, both early patrons of Saint-Gaudens'. I also want to thank Mr. Lately Thomas for his generous sharing of notes he collected concerning Madison Square and the *Diana*.

I am much indebted to the Rosary Hill Home, Hawthorne, New York, for the use of letters by Augusta Saint-Gaudens to the founder of Rosary Hill and her close friend, Rose Hawthorne Lathrop, and to Mrs. Frank Hawkins, great-granddaughter of Nathaniel Hawthorne.

Contacts with New York City art museums and libraries were many. Mrs. Henry W. Howell, Jr., made my work a pleasure, as always, at the Frick Art Reference Library. I was fortunate in finding work of Saint-Gaudens in a special exhibit at the Metropolitan Museum of Art, and Miss Rebecca Sielenitz, of the Catalogue Room, and Miss Nada Saporiti, of the photograph library, were especially cooperative. At the Whitney Museum, I was pleased to see a very large Saint-Gaudens *Diana* at a special exhibition. Miss Alice G. Melrose, of the National Academy of Design, was able to locate useful material and, as on many past occasions, the staff at the New York Genealogical and Biographical Society was most helpful.

The staff at the New York Public Library, Main Branch, was extremely useful, as always. I want especially to thank Mr. Timothy Beard, of the Genealogical and Local History Room, for help in finding early Saint-Gaudens addresses in New York City. In the Print Room, Mr. David Johnson and Miss Elizabeth E. Roth were of great assistance in discovering a copy of a rare Zorn portrait of Saint-Gaudens.

At the Princeton University Library I was given the most cordial assistance by Mr. Paul Wagner, of Rare Books, and Mr. M. Halsey Thomas, of the Princeton University Archives.

I am indebted to the Sterling Library, Yale University, for use of newspaper microfilm and for locating the Saint-Gaudens bust of former President Theodore Dwight Woolsey. My friend Mrs. Kenneth Hoffman, herself a sculptress, helped me to understand some of the mysteries of that form of art.

Boston, Massachusetts, affords many opportunities for the study of Saint-Gaudens. I want to thank Mr. Walter Muir Whitehill, Director of the Boston Athenaeum, for coming to my assistance in the matter of statues already in Boston at the time of the Shaw Memorial unveiling. At the Isabella Stewart Gardner Museum, Mr. William N. Mason once more helped me, this time in locating the Saint-Gaudens medallion of John Singer Sargent and Saint-Gaudens' correspondence with Mrs. Gardner. Mrs. Davis Maraston, assistant to Mrs. Ropes Cabot at the Bostonian Society, found addresses and contemporary photographs. My friend Mrs. Richard Lee sent me her study of the Copley Square area. I want especially to thank Mrs. Harold Peabody for writing me of Saint-Gaudens as she saw him during the Shaw celebrations.

Saint-Gaudens correspondence was most kindly shown to me at the Houghton Library, Harvard University, where Miss Carolyn Jakeman was, as always, exceptionally helpful. I am particularly grateful to Mrs. Robert Knell, of the Arthur and Elizabeth Schlesinger Library, Radcliffe College, for permission to use material concerning the Homer family, as yet uncatalogued because so recently acquired. The staff at Radcliffe also sent me a copy of an article from the *Radcliffe Quarterly* on Eugenie Homer, sister of Mrs. Saint-Gaudens.

Many museums kindly supplied photographs of work by Saint-Gaudens or other material. Among these were the Boston Museum of Fine Arts; the Carnegie Institute, Museum of Art; the Los Angeles County Museum of Art; the Illinois State Historical Library; the Houston Museum of Fine Arts; the Chicago Historical Society; the Freer Gallery of Art, Smithsonian Institution, and the American Numismatic Society. Miss Elizabeth M. Smith, Director of Social Service at

Sailors' Snug Harbor, Staten Island, New York, went to a great deal of trouble to supply a photograph of the Saint-Gaudens statue of Robert Richard Randall.

It was not always necessary to travel far afield. I want to thank Miss Grace Walmsley, of the Reference Room, Ferguson Library, Stamford, Connecticut, particularly in the matter of suggesting old New York guidebooks as a means of re-creating the Saint-Gaudens period. The staff of the Darien Free Library, Darien, Connecticut, was extremely helpful, as always.

CHAPTER NOTES

1: HORSE-DRAWN NEW YORK

1. The unswept condition of Broome Street was mentioned in a letter from Saint-Gaudens to his wife after he had revisited some of the scenes of his boyhood during the summer of 1884.
2. Augusta Homer described Saint-Gaudens as American-born, in a letter to her parents, Feb. 8, 1874: Saint-Gaudens papers, Archives Department, Baker Memorial Library, Dartmouth College, Hanover, N.H.; hereinafter referred to as Dartmouth.
3. The work of Mary Saint-Gaudens was described in the *Gramercy Graphic*. The photocopy of an excerpt from this paper was very kindly sent me by Mrs. Sidney Homer.
4. New York City birth records, in which the name of Andrew Saint-Gaudens would have appeared, were destroyed by fire, so that the exact date remains a mystery. Louis Saint-Gaudens was born in New York City in 1854 and died in Cornish, N.H., in 1913.
5. These early childhood memories were written by Saint-Gaudens for his four-year-old son Homer and enclosed in letters to Mrs. Saint-Gaudens.
6. Events of early youth were recalled by Saint-Gaudens during his convalescence in March, 1906, at the Corey Hill Hospital, Brookline, Mass. His son Homer had been urging him to write his reminiscences, but he felt it was "an awfully egotistical thing to do," according to a letter from Mrs. Saint-Gaudens to Homer. But one morning in March, she found her husband "quite himself" and "dictating to the nurse or whoever happened to be on hand." Saint-Gaudens entitled his narrative "Tales of an Idiot."

   On returning to "Aspet," his home in Cornish, N.H., Saint-Gaudens continued his story, now dictating it to a phonograph. The typewritten sheets have survived, at least in part, and are now at Dartmouth. After the death of Saint-Gaudens, they were worked over and revised to become a part of the two-volume *Reminiscences of Augustus Saint-Gaudens*, edited and amplified by Homer Saint-Gaudens and published by the Century Company, 1913, now a part of Meredith Press.

   Fortunately, both Homer Saint-Gaudens and his mother had an aversion to throwing anything away. The original Saint-Gaudens first draft can often be identified by the humor and simplicity of the artist. This I have used wherever possible, in preference to the printed source with its literary embellishments, deletions of proper names and other mannerisms of the period between Saint-Gaudens' death, in 1907, and 1913, when it was published. The printed text, when quoted, will be referred to hereinafter as *Rem.*
7. For Daniel Edgar Sickles, see the *Dictionary of American Biography*, hereinafter referred to as *DAB*.
8. New York City directories give the various Saint-Gaudens addresses.

9. Mary Saint-Gaudens' part in her husband's business is from the *Gramercy Graphic*.
10. The description of paintings in oyster cellars is from "New York in Slices," a pamphlet issued in 1849, selling for 37½ cents.
11. A photograph of the home of A. T. Stewart appears in the *Columbia Historical Portrait of New York*, by John A. Kouwenhoven, Doubleday, 1953.
12. *Manna-Haten: The Story of New York*, written anonymously and published by the Manhattan Company of New York (successor: the Chase Manhattan Bank), has the story of "Tri-Insula."

2: THE CAMEO CUTTER

1. *The Diary of George Templeton Strong*, edited by Allan Nevins and Milton Halsey Thomas, Vol. III, Macmillan, 1952, gives one of the best descriptions of the draft riots. "Colored Half Orphans" is Strong's phrase.
2. The description of Saint-Gaudens' singing voice is by Madam Louise Homer, in *My Wife and I*, by Sidney Homer, Macmillan, 1939. She was Louise Homer, the famous contralto with the Metropolitan Opera Company. Her husband Sidney was Augusta Saint-Gaudens' first cousin.
3. For Peter Cooper, see *DAB*.
4. Information concerning the National Academy of Design is from *The Memorial History of the City of New York*, edited by James Grant Wilson, New York History Company, 1893.
5. According to Saint-Gaudens, he went to work when he was just thirteen. This would be March or April, 1861. He said he worked for Avet for three and a half years, or until about October, 1864. Lincoln was shot April 14, 1865. I feel therefore that *Rem* and *DAB* are in error when they say that Saint-Gaudens was working for Avet at the time of Lincoln's assassination. Of course, Saint-Gaudens may have forgotten exactly how long he worked for Avet, but he was allowed time off to watch the cortege and to join the line at Lincoln's bier. It was more in character for Le Breton than for Avet to allow him this liberty.
6. The story of Capitaine is from a letter from Saint-Gaudens to a friend addressed as "Borse," undated but written at the time of the fencing master's death.
7. Louis Saint-Gaudens wrote of their French relatives for his nephew Homer. He said that his uncle Bertrand, the former shoemaker, also became a contractor and that Uncle François became a hanger-on in politics and never had any business or trade that he knew of. He had a country house in Lieusaint, but Louis never knew where Uncle François got the money to keep it.
8. John Dryfhout, Curator of the Saint-Gaudens National Historic Site, has compiled a list of the Saint-Gaudens cameos from museum memorial exhibition catalogues and other sources. It includes three topaz cameos, set in a pendant, with the head of a child on each; an onyx brooch, with the head of the Roman goddess Flora; an onyx brooch and earrings with the heads of Ceres, Hermes and Apollo; an onyx brooch with the head and shoulders of Mary, Queen of Scots, and a brooch with the figure of a flying eagle.

3: STUDENT DAYS

1. "It was Hell generally"; Saint-Gaudens to Augusta, Nov. 3, 1899: Dartmouth.
2. After the death of Saint-Gaudens, Alfred Garnier wrote long letters in French to Homer Saint-Gaudens for his use. These were translated by Louis Saint-Gaudens in an adequate but somewhat stilted style. Fortunately, the originals

are at Dartmouth, where I photocopied them to take home and translate at my leisure. Garnier wrote a reasonably legible hand and I have enjoyed making my own rather more colloquial translation.

3. Early editions of Baedeker's guides provide information as to the streets and environs of Lieusaint.

4. Garnier kept the letters Saint-Gaudens wrote to him, and sent them to Homer Saint-Gaudens. I have retranslated the original French, the text differing from that in *Rem*.

4: ROME

1. Harriet Hosmer's *Letters and Memories,* Moffat, Yard and Company, 1912; hereinafter called Hosmer.

2. The story of Eva Rohr is from the Ardisson scrapbook, Dartmouth, and an article entitled "Saint-Gaudens' Early Art Is Found," by Malcolm Vaughn, in the Magazine Section of the New York *Herald Tribune,* Mar. 24, 1929.

3. Robert Jenkins Nevin was born in Allegheny, Pa., Nov. 24, 1839. This and other details are from Appleton's *Cyclopaedia.* The spelling of this name in *Rem* is in error.

    Under the dateline of February, 1881, Lillie de Hagermann-Lindencrone, in *The Sunny Side of Diplomatic Life,* described "Dr. Nevin our pastoral shepherd" and said that he had "really done a lot for the American Church here and ought to have a vote of thanks." There was no "better match for the wily dealers than the reverend gentleman and the pert little cabmen don't dare to try any of their tricks on him."

    In *To Be Young Was Very Heaven,* by Marian Lawrence Peabody, Houghton Mifflin, 1967, Mrs. Peabody quotes from her diary, Mar. 8, 1901: "Mamma, Papa and I, dressed in our best to dine with the Rev. Dr. Nevin. He is rector of the American Church and quite a swell; has a fascinating house full of rare and beautiful things."

4. This complicated correspondence between Saint-Gaudens and Gibbs is at Dartmouth. The letters written by Saint-Gaudens were evidently drafts in many cases, the handwriting most difficult to read. Mr. Gibbs, on the other hand, is clear and meticulous. Of course, much that is repetitious has been omitted.

5: ENTER MISS HOMER

1. I have not attempted to mention all the works of Saint-Gaudens. A careful study is in process, conducted by John Dryfhout, Curator of the Saint-Gaudens National Historic Site in Cornish, N.H., with a fine collection of photographs almost completed. Of course, the largest single collection of Saint-Gaudens' works is in Cornish. For the student of American art history, the originals, replicas and photographs will be invaluable. I have chosen for discussion and description only such work as I found typical of a period in Saint-Gaudens' career, or of human interest as to sitter and sculptor, or of national importance and easily visited.

2. The *Silence* in 1967 was in the Masonic Home, Utica, N.Y.

3. Changes in New York are from *Manna-Haten.*

4. Now and for many years to come, Saint-Gaudens found Tiffany a good firm to deal with. Young Louis Comfort Tiffany, son of the founder of the company, was born in the same year as Saint-Gaudens. His family allowed him to study art, and in 1871, just before Saint-Gaudens returned to New York, Louis Tiffany had been accepted as an associate of the National Academy of Design.

Mr. John Dryfhout, Curator of the Saint-Gaudens National Historic Site, has supplied information on the silver candelabra. It may be that Bennett won it himself.

5. Hosmer.

6. Saint-Gaudens to Gibbs, July 8, 1872: Dartmouth.

7. Florence Gibbs to Saint-Gaudens: Dartmouth.

8. Much of the information for these months in Rome comes from letters or rough drafts of letters from Saint-Gaudens to Willard, in explanation of lack of progress on the *Silence*. Dartmouth.

9. Louis to Homer Saint-Gaudens: Dartmouth.

10. Augusta Homer kept a brief diary in Rome and wrote voluminous letters home to her parents. Now and then the diary reveals an item not suitable for parents. These papers are at Dartmouth and, with the information so generously supplied by Mr. Sidney Homer, have helped to bring to light the young Augusta, unknown to those who met her only in her later years.

6: MAY I BE ENGAGED?

1. Homer family letters are in the Arthur and Elizabeth Schlesinger Library, Radcliffe College, hereinafter referred to as Radcliffe archives. A few business letters to Thomas J. Homer from employees in St. Louis in 1849 tell of disasters — the cholera epidemic, with "5 to 800 dead in a week," and the "awful conflagration of Thursday night" when employees tried to save some of the stock in the store by carrying packs of merchandise on their backs. "Many of our goods were stolen and many destroyed in the streets," Mr. Homer's associate wrote him, telling of fruitless efforts to save their building, of explosions "from alcohol in nearby warehouses." Somehow the firm survived, but in 1866 an assignee, the son of Mr. Homer's lawyer, was appointed for the firm of Homer, Rex and Tracy, wholesale drygoods, 75 Main Street, St. Louis. It would appear that bales of cotton, contracted and paid for early in the season, had not been delivered, but sold to someone else at a much higher price.

   Thomas J. Homer seems to have given his brother Sidney custody of certain securities. On Mar. 18, 1867, Mr. T. J. Homer wrote to his brother from St. Louis, "Your long silence on the subject of the securities I sent you is causing me much uneasiness . . . hints in one or two of your letters . . . make me afraid you might insist upon holding on to them, this I'm sure you would not do but from the kindest intentions, and yet such an act would place me in a much more disagreeable position than any I have yet been in, in fact it would disgrace me in a community where, though I have been unfortunate, I have been considered, and justly so, an honorable man."

2. Sidney Homer's will provided that all annuities would cease on Jan. 1, 1920, on which date Augusta's brothers Tom and Joe, and Louise Homer's husband Sidney, would each receive $50,000, if still living. The remainder of the estate would be divided among "the heirs at law." This opened the door to extensive family litigation, and apparently the lawyers had a field day, so that Augusta and her sisters eventually found themselves among seventeen defendants.

3. William Gedney Bunce (1840–1916) was born in Hartford, Conn. According to *DAB*, he went to Europe in 1867 to become an "artist resident of Paris. His studio there joined that of the famous sculptor Saint-Gaudens." According to Saint-Gaudens' own account, however, he and Bunce met for the first time in Rome in 1870. Bunce was suffering from "a stroke of paralysis" and expected to die. Saint-Gaudens was sent around to see him with the idea of renting his studio.

4. Augusta Homer's Rome diary tells that "Gus gave me my ring."

7: "YOUNG LION"

1. Annie Bunker Homer (1843–1924) was the daughter of Peter Homer, one of Augusta's uncles. Cousin Annie lived in Paris most of her life.
2. The correspondence between Low and Saint-Gaudens is at Dartmouth. There are many letters concerning this complicated affair.
3. The panic of 1873 is from *A Century of Banking in New York,* by Henry Wysham Lanier, Gillis Press, 1922.
4. Mrs. Saint-Gaudens told her son she thought Richardson wore a yellow tie — not a yellow waistcoat!
5. Eugenie Homer wrote of Saint-Gaudens in Boston for her nephew Homer: Dartmouth. "I understand that Uncle Joe has the head of the Sumner figure," she said.
6. Humorless explanations have been made concerning the inscription on the Shiff medallion. I think Dr. Shiff and Saint-Gaudens understood it as a sort of pun in Italian, as I have indicated in my retranslation.
7. The German Savings Bank Building was one of the first office buildings to use cast-iron elements. It was built in 1870–1872 on the southeast corner of Fourteenth Street and Fourth Avenue. See *Lost New York,* by Nathan Silver, Houghton Mifflin, 1967. The iron staircase was one of its wonderful modern features.
8. There are various versions of the first meeting of Saint-Gaudens and Stanford White. *Stanford White,* by Charles C. Baldwin, Dodd, Mead, 1931, is a useful source.
9. The *Hiawatha* by Augustus Saint-Gaudens was last seen on the Henry Hilton estate in Saratoga Springs, N.Y. A missing-statue search has been going on, conducted by the U.S. Department of the Interior, National Park Service, and Mr. John Dryfhout, Curator, has sent me a report.

   The story begins in Rome, of course, where the *Hiawatha* was completed in 1872, the marble purchased by ex-Governor Edwin D. Morgan. It was exhibited at the National Academy of Design in New York in 1875, at the Philadelphia Centennial the following year and at the Metropolitan Museum of Art, New York City, "before 1886." The *Hiawatha* reposed in the entrance hall of Morgan's house in New York in the interval. After Morgan's death, the *Hiawatha* was bought at a sale for the benefit of Morgan's heirs by Henry Hilton, one of the benefactors of the Metropolitan Museum. He wanted the statue for himself, however, and had it set up on his estate, "Hilton Park," Saratoga Springs. The *Hiawatha* was last seen there. Mr. Hilton's art collections were sold at the American and the Anderson art galleries between February 13, 1900, and January 7, 1914. The *Hiawatha* was next put up for sale at auction at the Concord Art Galleries, Inc., New York City, a photograph, *Hiawatha by Augustus Saint-Gaudens,* advertising the sale in the New York *Sun* for December 8, 1939 — the auction to take place January 8, 9, 10, 1940. The Concord Galleries have since disappeared from New York directories so that Mr. Dryfhout was unable to ask about the purchaser of the marble. So *Hiawatha* is lost — perhaps to be found at last, even though he has broken his trail as a proper Indian should.

8: PARIS APARTMENT

1. The story of Augusta's voyage is from letters to her mother, Mrs. Thomas J. Homer; Saint-Gaudens papers: Dartmouth.
2. According to *DAB* William H. Rinehart was born Sept. 13, 1825, and died Oct. 28, 1874, of Roman fever. In a letter to Florence Gibbs, Oct. 25, 1874 (Dartmouth), Saint-Gaudens wrote as follows: "Mr. Rinehart has been back

in Rome for more than a week and he will not live more than two months, the doctors say. Poor fellow, he is greatly changed. It's the consumption he has." Saint-Gaudens was with him the night he died.

3. Young Sidney Homer's bet is from _My Wife and I_.

4. The description of the Paris apartment is from a letter from Augusta to her parents, Oct. 12, 1872: Dartmouth.

5. _A Chronicle of Friendships,_ by Will Low, Scribner's, 1908, contains good material about Saint-Gaudens, including the scene when the Saint Thomas reredos was candle-lighted in Paris.

6. The story of Saint-Gaudens' first call on Gilder is from the _Letters of Richard Watson Gilder,_ edited by his daughter, Rosamond Gilder, Houghton Mifflin, 1916.

9: ROME AND RETURN

1. Correspondence from Stanford White is in the Saint-Gaudens papers, Dartmouth.

2. _The Life and Times of Charles Follen McKim,_ by Charles Moore, Houghton Mifflin, 1929, hereinafter called _McKim,_ provides information concerning McKim. There is also correspondence at Dartmouth.

3. The trip to Southern France is in part from _Stanford White,_ by Charles C. Baldwin, and in part from the Saint-Gaudens papers, Dartmouth.

4. Eugenie Homer wrote to family and friends about her adventures in Paris. These letters are at Dartmouth. She was Mrs. Oliver Pomeroy Emerson, the wife of a clergyman and onetime missionary to Hawaii, at the time her nephew Homer Saint-Gaudens asked for her memories of Paris days. Her account, also at Dartmouth, was most circumspect, as was the carefully edited passage in _Rem._ The original letters are quoted here.

5. An article entitled "In Memoriam," by Marian Clarke Nichols, Radcliffe '99, in the _Radcliffe Quarterly,_ gives this story.

10: THE _FARRAGUT_

1. In 1882, Henry Villard commissioned McKim, Mead and White to build him a house, later numbered 451 Madison Avenue. Later a connecting center building and a matching northern wing were built and occupied by various other owners or tenants. The block of brownstone mansions faced a court which opened through iron gates on the east side of Madison Avenue. Reading in the New York _Times,_ Sept. 29, 1968, that these houses may be doomed to demolition, my husband and I went to see them before it was too late. The original Villard house, owned by the Archdiocese of New York, seems to be the only one where carvings and mosaics have been respected and preserved. In the center section and in the north wing all decoration has been destroyed. The receptionist at the Administrative Office of the Catholic Archdiocese of New York was most kind, supplying my husband and me with an excellent historical pamphlet, handsomely illustrated, and giving us leave to look around the building. Henry Villard, who changed his name from Hilgard after leaving Bav iria, spared no expense. Stanford White made the preliminary designs in 1882. Then he was "out of the office for some time," according to the account. He was, I think, on his honeymoon. Joseph Wells took over the interior design, first announcing that he would change whatever he pleased. It was at about this time that Wells and Saint-Gaudens collaborated on the concerts at the Saint-Gaudens studio. The mosaics and carved mantels in the Villard house are very similar to photographs of those in the Vanderbilt mansion — and more beautiful than I had imagined. There is Tiffany glass, a Tiffany-designed clock and a staircase such as McKim was to design on a

much larger scale for the Boston Public Library. And on one mantel were bas-relief lions, possible precursors of Louis Saint-Gaudens' magnificent Boston Library lions in the round. But artisans did not expect to sign their work and serious sculptors often neglected to sign potboilers. Mr. Villard lived in his American Renaissance palace only a year, having lost the fortune he was celebrating when he built it.

2. The Saint-Gaudens papers, Dartmouth, furnish all the direct quotations in letters from White to Saint-Gaudens concerning the Farragut pedestal, the McKim, Mead and White partnership and other matters. See also, "The Intimate Letters of Stanford White," Architectual Record, vol. xxx, 1911. Augusta's letters to her family give the feminine side of the story.

3. Frederick Law Olmstead was ousted as landscape architect of Central Park in 1878 by political opponents. This left him free to design Prospect Park in Brooklyn, the Capitol grounds in Washington, D.C., the Arnold Arboretum and other Boston parks, among many commissions.

4. The description of Madame Sarah Bernhardt is from *Background with Figures*, by Cecilia Beaux, Houghton Mifflin, 1930.

5. *Sculpture Inside and Out*, by Malvina Hoffman, W. W. Norton, 1939 (copyright renewed, 1964, by Charles Hoffman) gives descriptions of the bronze-casting process.

11: NEW YORK STUDIOS

1. Correspondence, Saint-Gaudens papers: Dartmouth, tells of this wild-goose chase to Albany.

2. Perhaps at one time William Gedney Bunce had a studio that "joined that of the famous sculptor," according to *DAB*, but he shared the Saint-Gaudens studio on the Rue Notre-Dame-des-Champs while White was there.

3. The first high-wheeled bicycle appeared in New York in 1877. The elevated railroad system was completed to the Harlem River in 1880, according to *Manna-Haten*.

4. The party in celebration is from a letter to Augusta Saint-Gaudens: Dartmouth.

5. Augusta would have to wait until 1886 before the Pasteur Institute could begin its work of reducing infant mortality.

6. William Webster Ellsworth wrote an account of seeing the senior Saint-Gaudens in front of the *Farragut*, for Homer Saint-Gaudens. Ellsworth became Secretary of the Century Company in 1881.

12: SUMMER IN NEW YORK

1. Material about the *Randall* is from correspondence: Dartmouth. Other expanded versions seem apocryphal in detail without adding much in the way of fact.

2. In a letter to Rose Hawthorne Lathrop, Augusta Saint-Gaudens tells of her apartment "seven flights up." Actually, it was on the fourth floor, so Augusta must have been counting flights between landings.

Rose Hawthorne Lathrop, the daughter of Nathaniel Hawthorne, was in all probability Augusta's most intimate friend. Letters to Rose, afterwards Mother Alphonsa, founder of the Order of the Servants of Relief for Incurable Cancer, are at Rosary Hill, Hawthorne, N.Y. Letters from Mother Alphonsa to Mrs. Saint-Gaudens are at Dartmouth. Through the kindness of the late Beatrix Hawthorne Smyth, granddaughter of Nathaniel Hawthorne, I was able to visit Rosary Hill and use the letters in connection with my book *The Peabody Sisters of Salem*, Little, Brown, 1950. It was with surprise and pleasure, therefore, that I discovered this friendship between Rose and

Augusta and used the letters from Mrs. Saint-Gaudens, thus completing the correspondence and gaining much information.

3. In 1883, Rose Nichols, niece of Augusta Saint-Gaudens, visited the Saint-Gaudens home and expressed a child's point of view: "Aunt Gussie has a very funny kind of pretty apartment but very small . . . New York isn't anywhere near as nice as Boston. . . ." Radcliffe archives.

4. Francis Lathrop was the brother of George Parsons Lathrop, who married Rose Hawthorne.

5. These letters from Saint-Gaudens on his western trip seem to have been enlarged upon in *Rem*, but I used the original version: Dartmouth.

13: THE MORGAN TOMB DISASTER

1. White's "Settled by God" letter: Dartmouth.

2. The buying spree is itemized in *Stanford White*, by Charles C. Baldwin.

3. Some Saint-Gaudens portrait medallions were rendered in marble, with copies in bronze.

4. A letter to Rose Hawthorne Lathrop tells of Anne's pilfering. Rosary Hill.

5. This mantelpiece was given to the Metropolitan Museum of Art in 1926. "Mrs. Vanderbilt's gift is a generous and welcome one," the *Bulletin* of the Metropolitan Museum announced. "The caryatids are perhaps Saint-Gaudens' finest draped female figures. Their attitude is one of reposeful strength and dignity. . . ." But in due course, tastes change, and later the Metropolitan Museum tactfully suggested that the Vanderbilt family might like to take back their fireplace.

6. One of the most attractive of the plaster casts of medallions to be seen at "Aspet" is that of Gertrude Vanderbilt Whitney as a child.

7. Information on MacMonnies and de Quélin is from "Early Days with Mac-Monnies in St. Gaudens' Studio, a Personal Reminiscence," by René de Quélin, *Arts and Decoration*, Apr. 1922.

8. This unpublished letter to Richard Watson Gilder, concerning MacMonnies, I quote through the kindness of Miss Rosamond Gilder.

9. My husband and I visited the Cedar Hill Cemetery, Hartford, Conn., where the custodian was most helpful in directing us to the Morgan tomb, by Richardson. It is indeed far from the entrance gates, the scene from the hilltop still suggesting the place where an arsonist might have found concealment.

14: COUNTRY OF LINCOLN-SHAPED MEN

1. A portrait bust of "old Mr. Chapin" was given to the Connecticut Valley Historical Museum, Springfield, Mass. It was kept in a basement room, along with another unsigned but similar bust, and both were destroyed by fire in 1954. A photograph remains, but, probably for the purposes of the photographer, it was lighted from below, and all shadows especially around the eyes, are lost. This picture is hideous. Light plays tricks with sculpture, so that the anxious letters Saint-Gaudens wrote to his sitters concerning the display of his work are easily understandable.

2. There are various versions of the story of the meeting between Saint-Gaudens and Charles Dana Gibson. Perhaps the best is to be found in *Portrait of an Era as Drawn by C. D. Gibson*, by Fairfax Downey, Scribner's, 1936.

3. I have used the date on the contract in the Saint-Gaudens papers: Dartmouth.

4. The original Volk life mask was presented to the National Museum in Washington. See *Letters of Richard Watson Gilder*.

5. The modern visitor to "Aspet," the Saint-Gaudens home, studios and gardens in Cornish, N. H., would be unlikely to take a train! A chain of highways

supersedes the railroad. Route 91 moves along the Connecticut River valley, bypassing cities and cutting through hills across Massachusetts and Vermont until Ascutney appears in views Saint-Gaudens never saw. However, at Windsor, Vt., the traveler leaves the highway. For the present, at least, the old covered bridge still crosses the Connecticut River; the road to the left, over the bridge, passes the well-marked hill road to the museum on the right. Tall trees still line this steep road, but blacktop has overcome the mud that Saint-Gaudens so much disliked. His house, no longer gaunt and forbidding, is on the left.

6. Saint-Gaudens' account of his first sight of the old house in Cornish is from *Rem* I. In an article in *Western New England Magazine,* 1913, Brewer Corcoran says that the old house was first known as Higgins Folly. It was more commonly called "Huggins Folly."

15: THE "STANDING *LINCOLN*"

1. For Dr. Polk, see *Who's Who in America,* 1903–1905.
2. These comments on "Aspet" in process of alteration are often quoted with variations — for example, in the article, "Saint-Gaudens Forever," by Lawrence F. Willard, in *Yankee,* Nov., 1965.
3. It has been stated that George de Forest Brush was in Cornish with his wife and family during the first summer. If the "first summer" was 1885, as Saint-Gaudens said (see *Rem* I, 311), George de Forest Brush, born in Shelbyville, Tenn., Sept. 28, 1855, was just under thirty and as yet unmarried. On Jan. 13, 1887, he married Mary — always called "Mittie" — Taylor Whelpley. Their first child, Alfred, was born in 1887 and died that same year. Gerome was born March 11, 1888, in New York City, and Nancy Douglas Brush, in Paris, July 4, 1890. There was a total of eight children, but it is Nancy to whom I owe much information concerning the Cornish and the Dublin art colonies. Herself a painter, she married one of her father's most brilliant young pupils, William Robert Pearmain, was early widowed and married the late Dr. Harold Bowditch. He was long my friend and advisor concerning the Boston background for many of my biographies.

I have placed the teepee incidents in the period of the Henry George political campaigns, as this seems the most probable date. Later, the George de Forest Brush family did have a tent (larger than the teepee) and they camped on Saint-Gaudens' grounds, as Mrs. Bowditch remembers. She also recalls that they rented a house in Cornish before making Dublin their home.

4. Mr. John Dryfhout, Curator of the Saint-Gaudens National Historic Site, has recently seen the Dewing portrait and says that it is not black but that Mrs. Saint-Gaudens is "quite pretty."
5. I am indebted to the Sterling Library, Yale University, for the use of their fine collection of newspaper microfilms.
6. Thomas Russell Sullivan was one of Mrs. Jack Gardner's many young admirers.
7. In *This Was My Newport,* by Maud Howe Elliott, The Mythology Company, 1944, she writes that Stevenson was visiting the Charles Fairchild family, who lived in a house called "Bel' Napoli," standing along the water's edge. Mrs. Fairchild was "a poet, Stevenson's friend and correspondent."
8. In some editions of Stevenson's letters, this revised opinion of the appearance of Saint-Gaudens is omitted.

16: THE "GOD-LIKE SCULPTOR"

1. This General Sherman and Mrs. Stevenson story was written by Mr. Philip Littell in a letter to his wife. Mrs. Littell very kindly allowed me to make a copy of the letter.

2. Will Low writes in *A Chronicle of Friendships* about the stay in New Jersey.
3. While Stevenson was at Saranac, it is said, Saint-Gaudens modeled Augusta's hands for the Stevenson medallion, because they were similar in type. He made changes when Stevenson was again available for a sitting.
4. Saint-Gaudens said that he lost all his letters from Stevenson in the studio fire in 1904. After Stevenson's death in 1894, however, Sidney Colvin, his friend, published various editions of his letters, and Saint-Gaudens must have sent copies of his Stevenson letters to be included. The letter to Homer was published by Sidney Colvin, as were the others quoted here.
5. *The Letters of Mrs. Henry Adams,* edited by Ward Thoron, Little, Brown, 1936: postscript.
6. Mrs. Barrett Wendell's diaries are in the Houghton Library, Harvard.
7. The letters between MacVeagh and Saint-Gaudens are at Dartmouth.
8. The Beckwith diaries are at the National Academy of Design.
9. The McCosh statue was burned when the chapel at Princeton University was destroyed by fire, May 14, 1920. Almost miraculously, however, the original plaster remained, from which another casting was made in a beautiful golden bronze.
   The original head was found in the chapel ruins by R. Tait McKenzie and Louis Milione, who had it mounted for the Princeton University Library. It is an interesting but sad relic. My husband and I saw it first and then crossed over to the chapel to find the re-created *Dr. McCosh,* looking down with a gentle, benign expression upon a service in progress below him. This was a rewarding experience.
10. The conversation between the father of Augustus Saint-Gaudens and Dr. McCosh is from *Rem* I and from the first draft of *Rem.*

17: DAVIDA

1. *McKim* quotes Saint-Gaudens' letters about the Boston Public Library and tells of the plot to get a commission for Abbey.
2. Sargent's *Frieze of the Prophets* was installed in 1895 — $15,000 subscribed for it. See *Sargent's Boston,* by David McKibbin, Museum of Fine Arts, Boston, 1956.
3. Sargent was a member of Abbey's wedding party in April 1890. See *Sargent's Boston.*
4. Violet Sargent went to Cornish to visit the Saint-Gaudens family, perhaps to sit for her bas-relief portrait. Augusta and Homer sat to Sargent in New York. See *Sargent's Boston.*
5. Lease agreement: Dartmouth.
6. The story of Novy, understandably suppressed by Homer Saint-Gaudens, comes from letters from Louis Saint-Gaudens to Annetta Johnson and from Annetta to Homer Saint-Gaudens. These letters came to light when a house formerly occupied by Louis Saint-Gaudens was sold. I am indebted to John Dryfhout for their use.

18: THE NINETIES BEGIN TO BE GAY

1. In *DAB,* French is said to have learned the rudiments of sculpture from Louisa May Alcott. It was the writer's sister, Abby May, who was the artist, however. Mrs. Daniel Chester French is correct in her *Memories of a Sculptor's Wife,* Houghton Mifflin, 1928. Mrs. French refers to Miss Alcott simply as May, which is the name by which Abby May was known.
2. "Chesterwood," the studio of Daniel Chester French in Stockbridge, Mass., is well worth a visit and contains work by Margaret French Cresson as well as work by her father.

3. In the course of collecting material for his book *Delmonico's,* Houghton Mifflin, 1967, Lately Thomas made copies of entries concerning Madison Square and the *Diana* from the files of the New York *Herald* and the *Herald Tribune.* These he most generously made available to me.
4. The New York *Times, Time* magazine and others carried articles concerning *Diana's* 1967 reentry into public notice.
5. The name of Homer's goat was "Seasick," according to letters at Dartmouth. Nobody bothered to explain!
6. Saint-Gaudens' correspondence with Mrs. Jack Gardner is from the Isabella Stewart Gardner Museum.
7. For the location of statues in Boston, I am indebted to "Boston and the Civil War," by Walter Muir Whitehill, Boston Athenaeum, 1963. I asked Mr. Whitehill many questions that troubled me, and as always, he had the answers — this time, in this most attractive pamphlet.

19: THE *SHAW MEMORIAL*

1. There are many accounts of this famous unveiling. Direct quotations from Saint-Gaudens are from *Rem II.* Comments by Miss Marian Lawrence are from *To Be Young Was Very Heaven,* by Marian Lawrence Peabody.
2. The description of Saint-Gaudens was given me by Marian Lawrence Peabody.
3. Eugenie Homer Emerson and her husband went to Hawaii by way of Europe. Genie wrote letters to her mother telling of the strange Hawaiian customs and of wearing "light dresses" at Thanksgiving time. Her experiences were happy and she and her husband left Hawaii with regret. Mr. Emerson took a church in East Providence, R.I. See *The Haverhill Emersons,* by Charles Henry Pope, vol. II, 1916.
4. With the help of David Johnson and Miss Elizabeth E. Roth, of the Print Room, New York Public Library, a copy of Zorn's *Saint-Gaudens and His Model* was found.
5. The description of the French countryside is from Saint-Gaudens' recollections, *Rem* II.
6. The Passage de Bagneaux can be found in early editions of Baedeker's *Paris* but not on all modern maps.
7. In spite of my efforts and those of Mr. Beard, of the Local History and Genealogy Room at the New York Public Library, the date of Saint-Gaudens' father's death has not come to light. An entry in a Saint-Gaudens checkbook in Augusta's hand is marked "Funeral," $148.00, the check drawn June 2, 1893. This is by no means conclusive, but it seems possible that Bernard Saint-Gaudens died at this time. His name disappeared from New York directories in 1892.
8. Garnier to Homer Saint-Gaudens; retranslated from manuscript: Dartmouth. Direct Saint-Gaudens quotations are from the early draft of *Rem.*

20: RUE DES BAGNEAUX STUDIO

1. Helen Farnsworth Mears was born in Oshkosh, Wis., in 1876 and died in New York in 1916, according to the *Catalogue of American Sculpture,* published by the Metropolitan Museum of Art, New York. She won a silver medal for a bas-relief, the *Fountain of Life,* at the Louisiana Purchase Exposition in St. Louis in 1904. Her bas-relief of Edward Alexander MacDowell, musician and composer, is owned by the Metropolitan Museum of Art.
2. Saint-Gaudens' trip to Holland is told by Marian Nichols in a letter to her mother: Radcliffe archives.
3. Mrs. Harold Bowditch remembers this golden angel and told me of it.

4. A photostat of a letter of Saint-Gaudens to his niece, Rose Nichols, telling of the success of the *Sherman* in Paris, was kindly supplied by Mr. Sidney Homer.

21: THE SALON

1. For accounts of the Paris Salons, see newspaper microfilms: Sterling Library, Yale University.
2. Augusta told of the trip to Spain in letters to Homer: Dartmouth.
3. *The Education of Henry Adams: An Autobiography,* Houghton Mifflin, 1918, tells of the trip to Amiens.
4. When first offered a commission for the *Lafayette,* in 1898, Saint-Gaudens was sure he could do a statue in time for the Salon of 1900. He wrote to the Rev. Winchester Donald, rector of Trinity Church, to ask him to appeal to the committee for the Bishop Brooks statue, to grant a delay. The *Brooks* was supposed to have been finished in 1896, according to a 1893 letter from Saint-Gaudens to Donald: Dartmouth.
5. Enid Yandell was born in Louisville, Ky., in 1870. She graduated from the Cincinnati Art School, was a pupil of Philip Martiny in New York and of MacMonnies and Rodin in Paris. Her medals were many. *Who's Who in America,* 1912–1913.
6. *Young in New York: A Memoir of a Victorian Girlhood,* by Nathalie Smith Dana, Doubleday, 1962, gives a fine picture, not only of the times but of the artists of the period.
7. Saint-Gaudens' description of himself as a "red-headed monkey" is from a letter to his brother Louis: Dartmouth.
8. André Saglio was a member of the Ministry of Public Education and Fine Arts, and the Art Commissioner for Expositions at Home and Abroad.

22: CORNISH ATELIER

1. A mass of correspondence to and from doctors was gathered together in the desk on the stair landing at "Aspet." This was Augusta's desk and it might seem that she, alone, was trying to keep her husband alive and in ignorance of his illness. Now that all the correspondence can be read together, it seems clear that Saint-Gaudens knew he had cancer, and fought hard to keep alive and finish his work.
2. John Gunther, in an article entitled, "What Is Happening in Paris," *Reader's Digest,* Mar., 1968, describes the importance of being an Academician. "A member of the Academie Française is seated higher than anybody else" at a social affair. After him come "ambassadors and holders of the Grand Cross of the Legion of Honor. . . ."
3. Mrs. Archibald Cox, of Windsor, Vt., told of childhood memories of festivities at "Aspet" and Saint-Gaudens' pleasure in welcoming children.
4. The account of McKim's efforts in behalf of Saint-Gaudens is from *McKim,* and from letters to Saint-Gaudens: Dartmouth.
5. Letters from Hay and Saglio: Dartmouth.
6. *John Elliott: The Story of an Artist,* by Maud Howe Elliott, Houghton Mifflin, 1930.
7. *Girl by a Pool,* in marble, by Frances Grimes, is at Brookgreen Gardens, Murrells Inlet, S.C. The outdoor museum at the Gardens was founded by Anna Hyatt Huntington, well-known sculptress. *Brookgreen Gardens,* by Beatrice Gilman Proske (Brookgreen catalogue), gives a brief biography of Miss Grimes.
8. Frances Grimes wrote down her reminiscences of the Cornish colony, a type-

script of which is at Dartmouth. John Dryfhout called my attention to the newly acquired letters from Miss Grimes to Barry Faulkner. Miss Frances Arnold gave me firsthand impressions of Miss Grimes, who was her close friend.

9. The comments of the young Nichols nieces are from the Radcliffe archives.

10. The corncrib music room is from *My Wife and I,* by Sidney Homer. Mrs. Richard Crocker, daughter of Joseph and Constance Homer, told of her mother's duets with Louise Homer and of going backstage to a joyful welcome, when she was a child, after being required to sit painfully still during a long opera.

11. When I was a student at the School of Fine Arts in Boston, I lived at the "Students' House" on the Fenway, a girls' dormitory sponsored by Emmanuel Church and headed at that time by Miss Mary E. Libbey, a deaconess. Assisting Miss Libbey was Miss Alice Butler. Miss Butler's profile was so very beautiful that I finally plucked up courage to ask her if I might attempt a sketch. She was very nice about it, told me to go ahead, and in the course of conversation, said that she sat to Augustus Saint-Gaudens and that hers was the head on the ten-dollar gold piece. She said she had seen a bust that Saint-Gaudens made of her, for sale in an art store. She wanted to buy it for her mother, but it cost ninety dollars, which was more than she could afford.

Of course, when I began research on Saint-Gaudens, I tried to get in touch with her but found that she was no longer living. I was surprised to learn that Miss Butler was originally from Windsor, Vt. Mrs. Archibald Cox, who spent many summers there, recalled Miss Butler and remembered what a delight she was to look at as she walked along the village street.

Mr. John Dryfhout has been successfully engaged in collecting photographs for the Saint-Gaudens National Historic Site. He recently showed me two pictures, both of the same model, posing for a symbolic figure of Art, perhaps the one commissioned by Charles Lang Freer, donor of the Freer Gallery of Art in Washington, D.C., or for the Boston Public Library group. The model is Alice Butler, although at that time her face was more full than it was in 1917–1918 when I knew her.

After the *Sherman* became famous and after replicas of the small bust sometimes called the Nike-Eirene became popular, there was speculation in the papers as to the identity of the model. Like a novelist, an artist combines certain traits to produce an imaginary figure, but the "Victory head in bronze, second study made for the Sherman group," the Saint-Gaudens ten-dollar gold piece and the Nike-Eirene are all of them Alice Butler. Of course, my great regret is that I did not ask her more about Saint-Gaudens when I knew her.

12. Henry Hering was born in 1874, studied four years at the Art Students' League in New York and two years at the École des Beaux-Arts in Paris. He studied under Martiny and in 1900 became a pupil, then assistant, in the Saint-Gaudens studios.

13. It has been difficult to assign a period for this undated letter, but there is a reference to the Hay bust, and the Nichols nieces speak of Augusta as being in an almost irrational state of mind at this time. The word quoted as "peccadillo" is almost unreadable, but it comes very close to what may have been a Saint-Gaudens spelling in French or Italian.

There is a story that Saint-Gaudens, on his way to or from Cornish, would "stop off in Darien" to see Davida. In the horse-drawn era, many a gay young blood tooled his coach to Darien, Connecticut. New Yorkers drove out in carriages, but it was certainly not a stopover on the railroad between Cornish and New York. Darien has been my home for more than thirty years, and an elderly resident, no longer living, told me of one prominent New Yorker who was said to have bought a house here for his mistress. However, it was not Saint-Gaudens. According to the few contemporary documents I have found, Davida seems to have lived in New York, in Paris, and after Paris to have gone west.

23: FIRE ON THE HILLSIDE

1. *Rider's Guide to New York City* supplies details about Times Square.
2. *Young in New York,* by Nathalie Smith Dana.
3. Frederick Law Olmstead died Aug. 28, 1903, three months after the *Sherman* was unveiled. His sons, Frederick Law Olmstead, Jr., and John Olmstead, had been carrying on his work for some time, but the senior Olmstead never lost interest in Saint-Gaudens.
4. I am indebted to Patricia Schartle for these Southern comments.
5. The speed of cars and their makes is from *To Be Young Was Very Heaven,* by Marian Lawrence Peabody.
6. My husband, Carey E. Tharp, has supplied me with this deathless verse.
7. Ardisson is so spelled in letters by Saint-Gaudens in the "Ardison Papers" recently acquired by Dartmouth.
8. Chesham Lake was originally Breed's Pond and is now Silver Lake. When Carlota died, Homer Saint-Gaudens gave the cottage which she had inherited to Barry Faulkner. Miss Ellen Faulkner told me of good times at the lake where Carlota, she said, was beautiful and popular.
9. The Dolley papers, Dartmouth, contain letters from Carlota to her family. Carlota said that "Homer dances beautifully" and that they went down the ski slope "over and over again, two on one pair of skees."
10. During one of her visits to Cornish, Carlota painted a miniature of Saint-Gaudens, recently presented to the Saint-Gaudens Museum.
11. Saint-Gaudens described his method of draping clay models to Abbot Thayer, the painter, who was a member of the Dublin art colony. "After many trials, I found my first and simplest way the best. Most of the muslin, calicoes etc. that you would very likely try for your purpose have very little starch in them. I have found that after wetting and laying over the model, they remain very well, if I pin them here and there. Of course this cannot be done with silk or things of that kind but by selecting the material that is only slightly starched you will get what I have obtained. That is the way the drapery on the Sherman *Victory* is done. After it is dry, in order to make assurance doubly sure, I go over it all (with the greatest care) with shellac with a very delicate brush piece by piece, doing first the hollows to strengthen the rest as you proceed. Another good way is to dip the cloth in a mixture of clay and water of about the consistency of a very watery mush. That holds pretty well when dry and on this, if you wish, use shellac as explained above."
12. According to *Rem* II, the servants were there, but not according to Miss Grimes.

24: THE MASQUE

1. For Margaret Nichols as tennis champion, see *Lively Days: Some Memoirs of Margaret Homer Shurcliff,* Literature House Ltd., Taipei, 1965.
2. Miss Frances Arnold also said that when Carlota first visited at "Aspet," she and her friends were amused because Homer's fiancée was called "Miss Dolly," as though she were a doll.

    Miss Arnold was asked by Saint-Gaudens to criticize the Hay bust after having lunched with John Hay and his wife at "Aspet." She was not herself an artist but eventually was the much loved headmistress of the Brearley School in New York City. On this occasion she was terrified and had no idea what to say, except that she thought the bust was a wonderful likeness. Later, she realized that Saint-Gaudens really wanted a young person's non-professional opinion.

3. Different people remember the masque differently. Some say that Augusta was not in the chariot.

25: GOLD EAGLE

1. The Albright contract is at Dartmouth.
2. In *Memories,* by Ethel Barrymore, Harper and Brothers, 1955, Miss Barrymore writes of taking a cottage in Cornish, N.H., "a place of beautiful gardens where many artists and authors lived. To me the most exciting of all was Saint-Gaudens. He was then doing his wonderful *Lincoln* and he used to let me watch him work. The head was finished and I never could look at at it without wanting to cry."
3. On Jan. 19, 1967, the New York *Times* reported the death of Evelyn Nesbit. She was eighty-two years old and died in a convalescent home in Santa Monica, Calif., Jan. 18. After the murder she was divorced from Thaw. She tried to go back into show business but failed, and wrote "countless articles on the event" of the murder.
4. Shortly before his death, Barry Faulkner went to "Aspet" where he reviewed old times, talking into a tape recorder. An unfortunately defective record of the interview, conducted in behalf of the National Park Service, is at "Aspet." However, some parts of it can be understood.

   "Well, I'll talk as long as *you* don't talk," said Mr. Faulkner at one point.

   It was Mrs. Saint-Gaudens herself who had said, "*I* want you here," Mr. Faulkner recalled. He lived at "Aspet a year."

   "The Old Man didn't realize that it was sort of tough for the young men to go up there to work. There was nothing for them to do. Mrs. Saint-Gaudens was away a lot and then they had fun. Mickey Finn, a great friend, a jolly Irishman, came up once or twice. He came up one Christmas and brought a couple of girls with him."
5. In the interview, Mr. Faulkner took a dim view of later efforts to color the Parthenon frieze on the studio wall. He referred to a Miss Beckington.

   "I gave it a blue background. She painted out my blue. . . . *She* put colors into the figures. Isn't that blue? What the hell is it?"

   In a strictly formal interview, Barry Faulkner talked of Saint-Gaudens for Station WKNE in Keene, N.H. An excellent tape recording of this is available at Dartmouth. In it, Mr. Faulkner describes Saint-Gaudens as being "of medium height, sanguine in color with majestic features, a fine mane of coarse hair and a red beard. We used to think he looked like the Zeus on a Greek coin."

   James Earle Fraser, recalling the same period, said that Saint-Gaudens' "eyes were blue, gay and candid. Black, wavy hair, barely touched with gray, was in striking contrast to the red-gold of his beard, so streaked with silver that it was tawny." Fraser was told, while at work on his bust of Saint-Gaudens, that the sculptor himself saw "a marked difference between the two sides of his face. 'One side was French,' Saint-Gaudens thought, 'the other side Irish.'"
6. Charles L. Freer was born in Kingston, N.Y. He was eight years younger than Saint-Gaudens and, like the sculptor, claimed French descent. He left school at the age of sixteen and went to work as a clerk in a general store in Kingston. The offices of the New York, Kingston and Syracuse Railroad were in the same building, so a year later he stepped up to the job of paymaster of the railroad, and he was on his way. After working as accountant and then treasurer of the Eel River Railroad in Logansport, Ind., he decided that the manufacture of railway cars would be a good business to get into. Freer had

a genius for organization, eventually forming the American Car and Foundry Company, now ACF Industries. Inc. By the time Freer was fifty, he could easily afford to become an art collector and connoisseur. In 1906, he gave his entire collection to the nation and began plans for building the Freer Gallery — where he hoped Saint-Gaudens would be represented by especially designed sculpture. Freer was unusually generous to living artists, his purchase for $63,000 of the famous "Peacock Room" helping his friend James McNeill Whistler out of financial difficulties. He was a scholarly-looking gentleman with eyeglasses, a high forehead running into baldness.

7. Henry Hering did all he could to redeem himself after being away at the time of the studio fire. "He has been sympathetic, modest and kind — I wish to say it very loud," Frances Grimes wrote to Barry Faulkner. This account of Saint-Gaudens' last days is from a letter from Hering to Barry. Among several accounts it seems the most perceptive.

26: AUGUSTA

1. From *McKim* comes the explanation of why he owned the *Bacchante*. "MacMonnies, in recognition of these associations (with McKim and White) gave to McKim the original bronze of the *Bacchante* group. . . . McKim (with the approval of the sculptor) decided to add this group to his own gift of a basin and fountain in the Library court. . . . The MacMonnies group was offered to the Metropolitan Museum of New York where it was gratefully received."

2. Later, the Boston Museum of Fine Arts acquired a replica. According to *American Sculpture*, a catalogue published by the Metropolitan Museum of Art, "A small bronze replica formerly decorated the newel post of the main stairway of Richard Canfield's New York gambling house." This famous house gave the name "Canfield" to a game of solitaire.

3. It was my father, the Rev. Dr. Newton Marshall Hall, of Springfield, Mass., to whom the woman put her question in front of the Brooks statue.

4. From the Fiftieth Anniversary Report of the Harvard Class of 1903 come details of Homer Saint-Gaudens' career. He was "an Officer of the Legion of Honor, an Officer of the Crown of Italy, Chevalier of the Order of Leopold, Commander of the Hungarian Order of Merit, and the recipient of the Bronze Star, Purple Heart, Legion of Merit, Croix de Guerre with Palm, Victory Medal (six stars), American Defense Medal (one star) American Theatre Medal (five stars) and the Meritorious Medal of the State of Pennsylvania."

   In his autobiographical notes for this report, Homer Saint-Gaudens wrote with a pleasant touch of humor. He said that his chief love was the army, that he served through two world wars and "moved from a squads right enthusiast on Governor's Island to an over-aged suitably-festooned full colonel. . . ." His "unsought mission . . . was camouflage. . . ."

   In 1922, Homer Saint-Gaudens became Assistant Director at the Carnegie Institute in Pittsburgh and a year later, became Director of the Institute's Department of Fine Arts. He died in Florida in 1958.

   Carlota Dolley Saint-Gaudens died in 1927. She had three children, Augustus, Harold and Carlota. Harold died at "Aspet" in 1910 at the age of three, having found some medicine (on his grandmother's bureau, it was said) which he swallowed while "playing doctor." Homer Saint-Gaudens was remarried in 1929 to Mary Louise McBride.

5. In answer to my query, Henry Grunthal, of the American Numismatic Society, gave me this information. The double eagle of 1907 retails for about $100, whereas the high relief variety fetches approximately $800.

INDEX